The Journals of
Yaacov Zipper, 1950–1982

The Journals of
Yaacov Zipper, 1950–1982
The Struggle for Yiddishkeit

Translated from the Yiddish and edited
by Mervin Butovsky and Ode Garfinkle

McGill-Queen's University Press
Montreal & Kingston · London · Ithaca

© McGill-Queen's University Press 2004

ISBN 0-7735-2627-7

Legal deposit second quarter 2004
Bibliothèque nationale du Québec

Printed in Canada on acid-free paper that is 100% ancient forest free (100% post-consumer recycled), processd chlorine free.

Photographs are reproduced by permission of the Canadian Jewish Congress Archives (CJCA), the Jewish Public Library Archive (JPLA), and private collections (PC).

McGill-Queen's University Press acknowledges the financial support of the Canada Council for the Arts for our publishing program. We also acknowledge the financial support of the Government of Canada through the Book Publishing Industry Development Program (BPIDP) for our publishing activities.

National Library of Canada Cataloguing in Publication

Ziper, Yankev, 1900–1983 [Yaacov Zipper]
The journals of Yaacov Zipper, 1950–1982 : the struggle for Yiddishkeit / translated from the Yiddish and edited by Mervin Butovsky and Ode Garfinkle.

Includes bibliographical references and index.
ISBN 0-7735-2627-7

1. Ziper, Yankev, [Yaacov Zipper] 1900–1983–Diaries. 2. Jews–Quebec (Province)–Montréal–Social life and customs–20th century.
3. Jews–Quebec (Province)–Montréal–Diaries. 4. Montréal (Quebec)–Biography. I. Butovsky, Mervin II. Garfinkle, Ode III. Title

FC2947.26Z56A3 2004
971.4'28004924'0092
C2003-903148-9

This book was designed and typeset by David LeBlanc in Montreal, and was set in 10.5/13 Times New Roman

In memory of Avriel Butovsky

and Motty Garfinkle

To Rivka, for everything

Contents

Preface	ix
Acknowledgments	xi
Introduction	xiii
Illustrations	xxvii
Family Tree	xlii

The Journals

1950–1959	3
1960–1969	83
1970–1979	207
1980–1982	329

Epilogue: The Final Journey	337
Appendix	343
Glossary	345
Index	365

PREFACE

The author of these journals is not known to English language readers. Yaacov Zipper's reputation was based solely on his professional pursuits as an educator and writer in the Yiddish language, the mother tongue of the Jews in Eastern Europe and the vernacular for the transplanted immigrant Jewish communities across North America. With the steady and irreversible decline of Yiddish among post-immigrant Jews in recent decades – the 1996 Canadian census informs us that only eight per cent of Canadian Jews cite Yiddish as their mother tongue – even the number of potential Yiddish readers of his work in the original would be minuscule. It was this threat of imminent language loss that prompted us to undertake the translation of his journals and to make them available to a larger reading public. We consider the journals to be an invaluable eye-witness account of an era in the history of Montreal's Jewish community extending from 1950 to 1982 – an era that saw the community transformed from a raw Yiddish-speaking immigrant population clustered in the working-class neighbourhoods along "the Main" – St Lawrence Boulevard – to a largely English-speaking society residing in the new middle-class districts in the western reaches of the city. This demographic change amounted to a profound alteration in the cultural and social character of the community, and it was a major theme of Zipper's observations in his journal entries.

Yaacov Zipper's Yiddish conformed to the conventions of the spoken and written vernacular of Eastern European Jewry, including the pronunciation of Hebrew. In general, our translation methodology is based on the guidelines of YIVO, the Institute for Jewish Research, as outlined by Uriel Weinreich in his *Modern English-Yiddish/Yiddish-English Dictionary* and in the Index of the *Encyclopaedia Judaica.* Accordingly, Zipper's Hebrew terms were retained: Succoth is rendered as Succos, Brith as Bris, and Aleph-Bet as Aleph-Beis. In certain cases Hebrew and Yiddish words are left untranslated and appear in italics because an English word for them would have been too alien in the context. These include words like *chaver* and *chaverim*, as well as names of the months, holydays, and ritual objects, which are defined in the glossary at the back of the book.

Degrees of difficulty in translation usually relate to the formal proximity between the languages involved. Translations of French or Spanish to English, for instance, are relatively straightforward, given the common cultural and structural links these languages share, including a common Christian heritage. Yiddish, which itself consists of diverse elements – the Hebrew alphabet; medieval German diction, grammar, and syntax; Biblical Hebrew; Talmudic Aramaic – incorporates a vastly different set of cultural associations that would not likely be grasped by someone unfamiliar with the tradition. Since our aim was to produce a clear, readable narrative in English we tried to transmit the meaning of the Yiddish words while shaping the syntax in conformity with English norms. As mentioned earlier, when encountering a Yiddish term that bore untranslatable cultural connotations, we often retained the Yiddish word in italics and defined it in the glossary. This compromise seemed to us a better solution than imposing a too literal and imprecise meaning to a culturally charged term. We also felt that the presence of Yiddish or Hebrew words amid the English prose might offer the reader a taste of Zipper's language, a flavour of its "foreign-ness" without loss of comprehension.

Zipper's Yiddish was the language of a modern intellectual at ease in dealing with the terminology of Western thought in such areas as education, art and literature, history, and philosophy. His ability to address these subjects rested on a deep multilingual and multicultural foundation, his legacy of East European Jewish lore and sacred Judaic literature. The Yiddish spoken by Zipper and his educated peers incorporated Biblical Hebrew and Talmudic Aramaic as inseparable, organic components, so that Zipper's prose is studded with Biblical and post-Biblical references, most characteristically employed to summarize or validate an argument. These languages are not translated into Yiddish, but, retained in their original form, they become historic elements in a seamless linguistic mode that recalls ancient sources as it addresses modern experience.

Acknowledgments

The project of editing and translating Yaacov Zipper's journals extended over many years, during which time we incurred debts to friends and colleagues who gave of their time and expertise with patience and encouragement. None that we turned to ever refused our requests for assistance. We are grateful for the contributions of Ron Finegold and Eiran Harris of the Jewish Public Library; professors Esther Frank, Gershon Hundert, and Eugene Orenstein of McGill University; Janice Rosen, archivist, and Hélène Vallée, her assistant, at the Canadian Jewish Congress Archives. To Chana Shapiro for her constant help and advice. For their steadfast support: Chaim Spilberg and Manny Weiner. Daniel Bernard and Stuart O'Driscoll for their helpful computer and photocopy expertise. A very special thanks to Ira Robinson of Concordia University for his invaluable aid in locating and identifying the myriad Hebrew and Aramaic citations Zipper drew from the Hebrew Bible, the Talmud, and Rabbinic literature, and to Betty and Bert Fishman, generous friends and supporters of Jewish culture and education, who retained fond memories of Zipper and unhesitatingly gave their wholehearted support to the project. For her patient editorial guidance, our gratitude to Joan McGilvray of McGill-Queen's University Press.

For financial grants that helped meet the costs of our extended project we are pleased to publicly acknowledge with deep appreciation the Fishman Family Foundation, California, USA; the Institute for Canadian Jewish Studies, Concordia University; the Jewish Community Foundation of Montreal; the Secretary of State, Multiculturalism Canada.

Introduction

Yaacov Zipper, the noted Montreal Yiddish author and principal of the Jewish Peretz Schools for over forty years, began a journal in late June 1950. From that date, with the exception of a three-year lapse in the mid-fifties, he continued to write down his private thoughts for more than three decades, until 1982, some six months before his death. The language of his notes was Yiddish, penned in neat, minute, cursive handwriting and entered in small, lined student notebooks measuring 7" × 8" and consisting of twenty-eight pages each. Some thirty-one such notebooks and five larger ones measuring 8" × 11" were found among his papers, comprising 1,214 pages of Yiddish manuscript.

These journals only came to light after Zipper's death. During his lifetime he had never mentioned them to his family, and only when his will was read did the family learn of their existence. This would suggest that they were intended as a private account of his inner life, a narrative that, for reasons we can only guess at, he could not bring himself to share with others. Still, the very fact that he chose not to destroy the notebooks but retained them among his well-organized files may imply his desire to have them discovered and ultimately read by others. This view is also supported by internal evidence: Zipper provides explanations and elaborations about people and places that appear in the journals, data that would have been redundant were he writing only for himself. Such factors justified the publication of these private papers and helped overcome our reservations concerning issues of privacy and confidentiality.

The journals seem to have served multiple purposes. Primarily, they functioned as Zipper's repository for noting events and experiences that signalled the rapidly changing contours of his familiar world. The journal entries were his occasion for contemplating the meaning of these events and for assessing their relative importance to his scheme of things. His attitude to these changes was as an embattled individual, a maverick who often found himself at odds with community leadership on issues of education and social policy. The notebooks often expressed an anger or frustration with majority opinion on contentious matters that his sense of decorum or the requirements of community unity inhibited him from stating publicly.

At the same time the journals functioned as a writer's workshop, where Zipper could exercise his imagination in literary compositions depicting landscapes, character studies, and elaborate reconstructions of vivid, troubling dreams. These literary exercises underscore his identity as an author, and his frequent complaints that his roles as school principal and community activist were robbing him of the peace and quiet required for creative writing attest to a ceaseless inner conflict that would never be resolved.

Yaacov Zipper was born in 1900 and thus came to identify himself as a child of the century. In his personal life-story, and to some extent in the lives of his siblings, he saw a compelling account of some of the momentous events of modern Jewish history, and in his own family he saw enacted the drama of disruptive change that transformed traditional Jewish life in Eastern Europe. For instance, the range of ideologies adopted by his brothers and sisters included Labour Zionism, Communism, orthodox Judaism, secular universalism, and Jewish mysticism; each creed was a response to the turbulence that resulted from the decline of orthodoxy and the break up of the Czarist empire. Though Zipper enthusiastically embraced the new ideological concepts that helped subvert the beliefs and customs of the old world, his version of Jewish secularism remained rooted in the residual pieties of his remembered childhood.

His birthplace was the Polish town of Shebreshin (Szczebrzeszyn), and he was raised and educated in Tishevitz (Tyszowce). His father, Rabbi Avrom Shtern, author of commentaries on the Talmud, rabbinic responsa, and Chasidic hagiographies, served as a ritual slaughterer and mentor to followers of his Chasidic instruction. Zipper, the family's eldest, received a traditional education that equipped him with Yiddish and Hebrew and provided him with an indelible store of textual materials including the Bible, Talmud, and Chasidic lore and legend, which he drew upon for the images and metaphors in all his future writings.

The world of Zipper's origins was the pre-modern *shtetl* society created by East European Jewry over the course of a millennium and conforming, in Zipper's particular case, to the ethos of Chasidic myth and mysticism. *Shtetl* life was relatively self-contained, practically isolated from surrounding religions and cultures. It was a society organized to fulfill the intense religious strivings of the pious, who conceived of worldly history as merely a transient moment anticipating the desperately awaited Messianic deliverance. Their desperation aptly reflected the powerless political and economic condition of *shtetl* Jews who, in their long history, had suffered the recurrent outrages visited upon them by the majority peoples with whom they lived and consequently came to regard themselves as selected for a spiritually powerful role in divine history.

By the late nineteenth century, however, the winds of social and political change had penetrated even the most remote Jewish towns and villages in the Pale of Settlement, the area of Czarist Russia where Jews were permitted permanent residence. The ideas of the Enlightenment – rationalism, secularism, individualism – were introduced there many years after their revolutionary effect in western Europe. Yaacov Zipper was deeply influenced by these concepts and underwent a transvaluation of self and belief. While he had been raised in a traditional home and imbued with a pious attitude toward the ancient traditions, he early enlisted in the modern struggle for the internal reorganization of Jewish life. His personal rebellion against the intellectual restrictions of orthodox belief was expressed in his role as teacher, not in the religious schools or rabbinical colleges, but in the recently established secular mode that sought to give students an awareness of the political and scientific world that lay beyond the confines of a religious education, and to instill in them a sense of national dignity and personal assertiveness embodied in the potent ideology of socialist-Zionism.

In Zipper's view, the traditional Jewish world he had experienced in his formative years was being torn apart in the clash of conflicting religious and social beliefs. These conflicts often forced the young to choose between loyalty to the archaic, integral past or to a future that would join Jewish fate to the rigorous history of modern Europe. In seeking to extend the boundaries of Jewish awareness beyond self-enclosed traditionalism, Zipper was formulating a response to the stultifying social and economic conditions of the *shtetl*. His deepest commitment was to the ineradicable, humane spirit of his remembered European world, but, perceiving it weakened and enervated, he sought to strengthen it by fusion with the tougher modern notions of politics, science, and cultural nationalism. Increasingly, the moral vitality of *shtetl* existence came to embody his ideal of exemplary conduct. In its simple piety, unworldliness, and concentration on study and learning, he saw certain of his desired secular ideals made manifest. Ironically, the further removed he was in time and place from his native scenes, the more was he drawn to them. In later life he came to acknowledge that his quest for principles of individual and national fulfillment had been immanent in the lost mystical-religious stirrings of his childhood.

Zipper's youthful rebellion against the restrictions of traditional society brought him to the Hechalutz movement, a Labour Zionist youth organization committed to the renewal of Jewish national life in its ancient homeland. In the cultural and social program of the movement Zipper found a vital replacement for the rejected religious culture of his home. His transformation retained the devotional and spiritual energy of the traditional belief system while expressing itself in the bracing radical vocabulary of Jewish cultural nationalism and democratic socialism. Paradoxically, his attitude encompassed both a conscious revolt against what he considered to be the decadence of *shtetl* life and an intuitive desire to rescue from oblivion the precious spiritual features of the millennial-old culture. This attempt at reconciling the conflict between traditional religious life and the modernist secular ethos of socialist-Zionism articulated the most characteristic quality of Zipper's self-consciousness: he saw himself as a man of two worlds. By birthright he felt himself heir to his father's realm of sacred history, but at the same time he realized that his modern outlook had, in the words of the Talmudic parable, "banished him from his father's table." His lifelong struggle to achieve a viable synthesis of these two contending elements of his being was a source of intellectual and emotional tension and, as such, served as the richest, most powerful wellspring of his creativity and the recurring theme of all his imaginative fiction.

If this sketch of the journal's author describes his early years and certain aspects of the inner tension that marked his private life, what of the public world he encountered when he emigrated to Canada in 1925? The Jewish community that Zipper joined in Montreal numbered approximately 48,000 and represented over six per cent of the total metropolitan population, the highest proportion it would ever reach, making it the third largest ethnic group in the city after the French and English. Certainly it was the largest concentration of Jews in Canada, accounting for over sixty per cent of the total.

Most of the community was composed of recent immigrants, who in large measure came from East European countries such as Russia, Ukraine, Poland, Lithuania, and Romania. The greatest influx of Jewish immigrants to Montreal occurred between 1901 to 1931, when the population expanded from 6,975 to 58,032, so that Zipper's arrival coincided with this period of rapid growth of the community, which consisted mainly of Yiddish-speaking newcomers and their first-generation children. In fact, 94.4 per cent of the Jewish population of Montreal gave Yiddish as their mother tongue, and in two electoral districts, St Louis and Laurier, Jews comprised more than half the population, 54.8 per cent and 50.9 per cent respectively.

In the years between the end of World War I and Zipper's emigration to Canada he served as an itinerant organizer and instructor of adult education courses in the impoverished, war-torn Jewish villages and began to contribute articles to radical periodicals. This brought him to the attention of the Polish authorities. At one point he was arrested but managed to escape. In order to evade recapture he changed his name from Yaacov Shtern to Yaacov Zipper, adopting the maiden name of one of the parents whose children he taught. She, Gittel Zipper Pofelis, was to become his mother-in-law and in gratitude to her he retained that name for the rest of his life.

As a committed Labour Zionist Zipper had intended to settle in Palestine. However, unable to obtain the entry visa from the mandatory government, he appealed to an uncle and aunt who had settled in Montreal. They succeeded in furnishing him with the necessary documents. Before leaving Poland for Canada he married a former student, Sorke. One year after his arrival he managed to bring her, her twin brother, Berl, and her widowed mother to join him in the New World.

Within a year of his arrival in Montreal, Zipper found employment as a teacher in the Jewish Peretz School. Like all other Jewish secular schools of that period, the Peretz School functioned on a part-time basis, offering classes in the afternoon between 4:00 and 7:00 p.m. and on Sunday mornings to students after they had completed their full day in the Protestant school system. Originally named the National Radical School, organized in May 1913, its main support came from the Labour Zionist movement together with elements from a broad spectrum of left-wing ideologies including trade unionists, socialists, and anarchists. In 1914 a faction broke away to become the Folk Shule – the People's School – which placed Hebrew, rather than Yiddish, at the centre of its curriculum. In 1919 the Radical School changed its name to the Jewish Peretz School in homage to the memory of Isaac Leib Peretz (1852–1915), the foremost Yiddish author of his day and the most influential mentor to a generation seeking to direct Jewish life toward a secular world view.

A glimpse into Zipper's personal finances and a measure of his commitment to the teaching profession is revealed in a letter he wrote in 1925 to his young wife who was still in Poland: "So far I work three hours a day and earn six dollars a week. And the four dollars from the newspaper brings us up to ten dollars. One of these days I'll know if I have the job at the Peretz Shule and that will total seventeen dollars. In addition, with my earnings for the summer we will exceed twenty dollars – so we'll manage quite well." Even taking into account the purchasing value of the dollar in 1925, these were near subsistent wages.

As we know, Zipper did find employment at the Peretz Shule and in a few short years, in 1928, was appointed principal, a position he held until his retirement in 1971. An interruption occurred from 1930 to 1934, when Zipper and the family moved to Winnipeg, where he served as principal of their day school; Winnipeg had organized the first Yiddish secular day school in Canada, many years before full-time Jewish education was introduced in Montreal and Toronto. The presence of a day school attracted him to Winnipeg but after four years he felt constrained by the provincialism of the smaller community and returned to Montreal, resuming the principalship of the Peretz Shule.

By the late 1920s and the early years of the 1930s, the school was successful in drawing significant enrolment from the immigrant community.

By 1928 the student population numbered approximately five hundred, and three branches were required to accommodate the students. The branches were in rented quarters located on Waverley Street and de Bullion Street East and the main branch, which they had purchased, was at a double premise on 834 and 836 Cadieux. These remained in operation until the Depression, when shortages of funds necessitated the selling of the Cadieux branch. Despite the financial shortages a day school was opened in 1941 and one year later the Shule moved into its first independently owned building on 120 Duluth Street East.

The curriculum of the Peretz Shule had two formats, one for the day school and the other for the afternoon school. The day school classes extended for a full day and provided students with general studies, in keeping with the standards of the Protestant School Board. In addition it gave a full program of Jewish studies, which included classes in Jewish history and literature, Bible studies, and the Yiddish and Hebrew languages.

Afternoon school was designed for students who were enrolled in the neighborhood Protestant school. After a full day of general studies they attended the Peretz Shule for a two-hour program in Jewish studies. This provided minimal exposure to Jewish studies but was regarded as a stop-gap measure for students who otherwise would receive no Jewish education.

Because many of the school's working-class clientele could not afford the full tuition and needed financial assistance, the school was always in financial difficulty and, as the journals amply testify, the financial burden fell heavily on the underpaid teachers. For most of Zipper's years as principal, salaries, including his own, were in arrears, often two or three months behind schedule. This brought him into direct conflict with the community funding agencies, the Allied Jewish Community Services and the Canadian Jewish Congress. Zipper insisted that Jewish education had to become a "community responsibility," rather than the obligation of each school. His most agonizing duty was dealing with the teachers' justified salary demands and he struggled to maintain their morale under trying conditions. It should be remembered that until the 1970s, Jewish schools did not receive subventions from the provincial government, nor was there any established system of subsidies for Jewish education from the organized Jewish community. Financial needs were met by student tuition and annual fund-raising campaigns among the parents and Labour Zionist supporters. In both cases the sums raised were insufficient for a balanced budget and much of Zipper's time was spent trying to raise enough money to pay off loans to banks and individual lenders.

Within a year of his arrival in Montreal Zipper managed to save the funds to bring his wife and her family to Canada. But a daunting challenge still confronted him: the need to rescue his entire family in Poland from the increasing threats to Jewish existence in Eastern Europe. He applied all his energies to the task and at a time when Jewish immigration to Canada was severely curtailed by both the King government and senior immigration bureaucrats, between 1930 to 1939 he was able to pay the passage for his entire family, consisting of his three brothers – Yechiel and his family, Sholem, and Yisroel – and two sisters, Henneh and Shifra, and Shifra's husband. Miraculously, he finally obtained travel documents for his aged parents, Reb Avrom Shtern and his wife, Gittel, who arrived safely on Canadian shores a mere four months before the outbreak of World War II.

At first the parents lived with their daughter on Clark Street while the Zipper household lived on Esplanade Avenue. Despite wide differences of religious and political views between Zipper and his siblings, as well as the gulf that separated his secularism from his father's religiosity, the family always gathered together in the celebration of the Jewish holidays and festivals and listened respectfully to their father's explications of mystical Chasidic tales.

Meanwhile, in 1943, Sorke began to teach at the Peretz Shule, and continued until her retirement in 1972. While she was employed at a full-time job, the household, which included two daughters, Ode and Chana, was cared for by Sorke's mother. Gittel prepared the meals, chaperoned the children, and worried, with Sorke, over Yaakov's health and well-being. She was an invaluable presence, relieving Yaakov and Sorke of much parental responsibility to devote themselves to their professional duties.

By the mid-1920s the new immigrant community had formed a closely woven network of social, political, educational, and welfare agencies to care for its needs. Aside from the particular function of each institution, their combined presence provided a collective coherence to recent immigrants as they struggled to achieve some balance between the world they had left and the often confusing society that surrounded them. Since their common language was Yiddish, it predominated in the home as in the market-place, the school, playground, workplace, and political meeting, offering the first generation, at least, an effective buffer against the inroads of foreign tongues and alien cultures. In these circumstances Yiddish served not only as the Jewish quarter's vernacular but also as a political statement. Those who, like Zipper, were committed to preserving linguistic continuity as the bulwark against the inevitable cultural erosions, relied on language as their chief means of defence. From his earliest years in Montreal, Zipper aligned himself with a select band of individuals who dedicated themselves to the task of preserving *Yiddishkeit* – Yiddish culture – in the new and challenging environment. These devoted individuals were drawn from the ranks of diverse professions and occupations: school-teachers and educational administrators, editors and publishers, bakers and seamstresses, poets and novelists, manufacturers and businessmen, religious leaders and lawyers. What these activists had in common was the fierce desire to conserve and reconstruct the essential elements of Yiddish culture as their means for resisting the siren-song of cultural assimilation in the engulfing homogeneity of North America.

For over forty years, Zipper devoted himself to the promotion and preservation of the Yiddish language, as the necessary means to a richly anticipated end. Yiddish was the expressive embodiment of the Folk – the People – and as such was the most immediate conduit to the inner soul of the Jewish masses. The language gave access to the human qualities that Zipper held most dear: compassion, tolerance, and moral sensitivity. These ideals derived from the ancient texts of Israel, particularly the prophetic writings on social justice and the visions of a sanctified community dedicated to their realization. For Zipper, the pre-modern *shtetl* society, despite his criticism of many of its practices, had actualized these precepts, created institutions for the maintenance of its spiritual life, and elevated men of learning to the highest social rank.

In Canada, Zipper wanted to transplant that ideal of community through the teaching of the Yiddish language and literature. He hoped to imbue his students with a sense of shared fate and communal belonging to the peoplehood of Israel that would offset the New World drive to acquisitive individualism. His educational goal was to produce a generation of youth which would identify with his ideals of Jewish cultural nationalism and find in the moral structure of their Yiddish and Hebrew heritage a sustaining source for conduct and conviction, once provided by the synagogue and religious authorities.

Zipper's quest, and the quest that animated his generation of secular Jews, was to find an alternate doctrine for conceiving Israel as a chosen people. Since they questioned divine providence as the basis for Israel's role in the world, they had to discover in ethical imperatives a secular source for the special characteristics they assigned to Jews. Ultimately, they resorted to the idea of an ethical culture as the redemptive foundation of morality and faith, often locating such precepts in secular literature, alongside select portions of sacred writ. But the twentieth century was hardly a propitious time for locating faith in universal ethicism. The betrayal of the Soviet Revolution, the unleashed destructiveness of Nazism, the world's indifference to the murder of Europe's Jews, all served to undermine the Jewish intellectual's faith in tolerance and learning, values that Zipper thought could resist the approaching darkness. Under the duress of modern history he did not abandon these ethical precepts but rather reabsorbed them into the primary values of *Yiddishkeit*, the single term that for Zipper denoted the humane features of a morally sensitive Jewish conduct.

Upon arriving in Montreal, Zipper gravitated almost immediately to the secular Labour Zionist movement, the Poalei Zion; his earlier membership in Hechalutz, the pioneering wing of the movement, had prepared him for a lifelong commitment to the adult organization that had taken root in Montreal. In his journal entry for 21 November 1954, Zipper proclaims on the displacement of traditional belief by the movement's social-democratic ideology, stating: "Our movement is the new House of Prayer." From its founding at the end of the nineteenth century, the Labour Zionist movement was not merely a political party. Particularly in North America, it also organized the lives of its members in a network of interrelated agencies. These provided immigrant families with schools for the children, medical and life insurance policies, free-loan societies for financial aid, *landsmanshaften* (societies of immigrants who came from the same European regions), burial plots, and a host of cultural activities including Yiddish theatre productions, lecture series on literature, debates on public issues, and sponsorship of the publications by local authors. These efforts helped foster a vibrant Yiddish-speaking community for years to come.

The movement founded and provided the leadership, and often the financial backing for those institutions deemed essential in the struggles to maintain the Yiddish language and culture. And it was to these educational and cultural activities that Zipper dedicated himself with unsurpassed zeal for over four decades. Among the most significant cultural agents in the modern secular community were the school systems that gave instruction in Yiddish and Hebrew at the elementary and secondary levels; the daily newspaper the *Keneder Odler* (while the newspaper was a privately owned commercial enterprise, its editors and staff were largely drawn from the ranks of the secularists); the Jewish Public Library and People's University, which offered adult education courses as well as a forum for literary debates and book launches; theatre groups performing works from the modern Yiddish repetoire; and summer camps for children and adults. These and other cultural bodies associated with the Yiddish secular movement were mainstays in the lives of its members. The cultural events attracted large audiences and earned for Montreal the reputation of being, aside from New York, the North American city with the highest quality of Jewish life.

That special prominence resulted from the efforts of those who were steadfast in their resolve to preserve *Yiddishkeit*, often in opposition to what they considered to be the assimilationist policies taken by the official leadership of the Jewish community. All shared the desire to resist the forces that would diminish their cultural endowments, in particular, the Yiddish language.

For a short time it seemed as if their labours would bear fruit, that the vigour of Yiddish literary creativity gave promise of cultural vitality and futurity. In the poetry of J.I. Segal, Ida Maze, M. Shaffir, A.S. Shkolnikoff, Sholem Shtern – later to be augmented with the arrival of the wartime and post-war immigrants, including the renowned Melech Ravitch, Rochl Korn, amd Mordecai Husid – Yiddish readers had access to authentic twentieth-century Jewish imaginative writing whose primary theme was exile from home, from faith, from belonging.

The theme of exile also dominated among the novelists and short fiction writers. Most commonly, their fiction concentrated on the early formative stages of personal growth in pre-industrial Europe than the actualities of their renewed lives in Canada. It was the "old country" that was usually foregrounded, the memorialized world of custom and tradition, a lost paradise gone forever. In Zipper's fictionalized autobiographies and in the fictive memoirs of Yehuda Elberg and Chava Rosenfarb, the tension between memory and history is sharply enacted. Only occasionally does the writer attend to the experiences of the New World and disengage from the shadows of the old. To the end of his life – as the journals iterate – Zipper lamented the fact that he never had available the conditions for writing the compelling story of his immigrant generation, to capture the drama of their lives in Canada.

When he resumed his journal entries in 1950, Zipper was fifty years old and recognized as a leading figure in the social and cultural life of Jewish Montreal. He had been principal of the Jewish Peretz School since 1928 and was an active member of the Poalei Zion and the Farband – he never abandoned the custom of referring to fellow-members as *chaverim*. He participated in the cultural activities of the Canadian Jewish Congress and served in many leadership capacities at the Jewish Public Library. In addition, he was a regular contributor to the *Keneder Odler*, where he published numerous articles and literary essays.

Widely known for his involvement in Jewish education and as a writer of Yiddish fiction and literary criticism and a tireless activist in a whole range of Jewish causes, what even his family, close friends, and colleagues could not have known was that the persona of the dynamic and energetic public figure was a projection of only one aspect of his complex character. His daytime face to the world masked another emotional reality that was expressed only in the confines of his private journals.

Here Zipper noted his thoughts and feelings on public and personal matters of concern. In the public realm his chief preoccupation was the financial viability of his school. As described earlier, the school lurched from crisis to crisis, constantly in arrears, with teachers' salaries unpaid for months at a time. This precarious condition was due to fact that in the post-war period the school enrolled many pupils – especially the children of Holocaust survivors, who had come to Montreal in significant numbers – whose parents could not afford the school's tuition. Zipper was determined to accept such students despite the financial burden this imposed on the school. As well as battling the Canadian Jewish Congress and the United Jewish Appeal for funds, Zipper was also angered and disappointed by the lack of support from the Labour Zionist movement, which seemed to turn a deaf ear to his many appeals. In addition to educational issues, in his journals he comments on current political events such as the rise of Quebec nationalism and the sense of trepidation registered by the Jewish community in the face of that sentiment. And much attention is paid to the developments in the new State of Israel, including the many crises and wars that threatened the newborn nation and aroused anxiety about the welfare of Zipper's many friends who had settled there.

In the personal sphere he notes the onset of the aging process in himself and his family and records the various illnesses that afflict him and impede his activities. Associated with aging disabilities are thoughts of mortality, and Zipper notes the many funerals he attends and the eulogies he gives. These deaths are not only sad for the loss of individual friends and colleagues but also painful because they signify the inescapable cultural loss of the diminishing Yiddish society – a loss that would never be replenished.

Many journal entries comment on Zipper's conflicted relationship with Shloime Wiseman, the principal of the Folk Shule, and this raises questions about the cause of the tension that existed between these educators and whether their personal attitudes toward one another determined the competitive relationship between the two schools these men had built. The passage of time has not made it easier to determine the cause of the friction and mistrust that characterized their relationship. On the surface they had a great deal in common. Both were dedicated educators whose schools were associated with the Poalei Zion and both educated their young in accordance with the social democratic ideological principles espoused by the Movement.

In some respects the conflict between the institutions was predicated on the role of Hebrew and Yiddish in the curriculum and was evident from the early history of the schools. Folk Shule's breakaway from the Peretz Shule in 1914 was a breach that never healed and the reverberations of that split could still be felt during the lifetimes of Wiseman and Zipper. The departure of Folk Shule adherents represented a political assertion for the strengthening of Hebrew and their insistence that it be taught at all grade levels.

Zipper's version of the unresolved quarrel seems to centre on the class distinction between parents and supporters of each school. In his view, Folk Shule's lay leadership included many who had become financially successful and had gained entry into the middle class. As a new bourgeoisie they came to see Yiddish as archaic, an impediment to their goal of rapid assimilation into Canadian society. By contrast, the Peretz Shule's supporters were mainly drawn from the working class and from recent immigrants from post-war Europe. They remained close to their cultural roots in the

Yiddish language and insisted on a Yiddish education for their children. These and other long forgotten factors may have contributed to their strained relationship.

Yet in retrospect the issues may be less political/cultural than temperamental. Both Wiseman and Zipper were strong-willed personalities, authoritative leaders with a firm sense of purpose and an unshakeable faith in the efficacy of education. So it seems a pity that over the years they could not see their way to the unification of their schools, which might have brought certain benefits to both institutions. But that was not to be. Only when the two men were overtaken by age and illness did the prospect of amalgamation become feasible. Only when their leadership positions were weakened and assaulted by the omnipresent financial difficulties was amalgamation insisted upon by the community agencies and the lay leadership of both schools. The merger of the two schools took place in 1970–71 and was followed by the founding of the Bialik High School in 1972.

In his journals Zipper also frequently voices the continual conflict between the demands of his communal responsibilities and his unsatisfied craving for the leisure and privacy required for his creative writing. But overshadowing everything in his personal notations is the growing tragic recognition that all his efforts to assure a secular Yiddish culture in the Diaspora would never be realized, that his relentless struggle to preserve the Yiddish tongue as a living language was in the end utopian. His bleak frame of mind during this period is constantly re-echoed in the two words most repeated in the journals: the Yiddish *shvair* – meaning hard, harsh, difficult – and the word *bitter* – which needs no translation. The present-day reader of these despairing sentiments, aware that Yiddish as a Jewish vernacular did not survive the immigrant generation, will understand why Zipper – the lifelong defender of Yiddish – could not deceive himself about the realistic possibilities for the language's survival in the face of North American assimilation.

Yet despite such dire misgivings, Zipper never wavered from his lifetime dedication to Jewish education and Yiddish culture. He continued to derive a measure of deep pride and satisfaction from his encounters with former students who gave evidence, in their knowledge and use of Yiddish and their identification with "*Folk Yisroel*," that his convictions indeed had taken root. His feelings of pessimism and personal despair were relegated to his private notebooks; in public he somehow summoned the energy and confidence to promote *Yiddishkeit* in the face of indifference and unavoidable acculturation, and for many years to offer vital leadership in the cause of Jewish education. Due to his tireless commitment – and the devotion of his "utopian" colleagues – Montreal's Jewish day school system is the most comprehensive in North America. And Yiddish, now taught at the university level, has, surprisingly, regained a degree of vitality through adult education instruction, Klezmer camps, and literary and theatrical societies. Understandably, all of these belated efforts will not bring Yiddish back to its former status as a folk language. Yet, in a small but meaningful way, they offer some resistance to the disappearance of the mother tongue.

Looking back to the East European immigrant epoch of Montreal Jewry it seems certain that in their incessant struggle to define the cultural identity of their society, Yaacov Zipper and his devoted contemporaries will come to be seen as an heroic element in modern Jewish history. By their personal sacrifices, determination, and unyielding convictions, they left a precious legacy that still resonates within the life of the community.

Family portrait prior to Zipper's migration to Canada (circa 1923). Sorke and Yaacov Zipper standing second and third from left. (PC)

Zipper (seated second from left) with his Zionist group in Ludmir, Poland. (PC)

Sorke and Yaacov Zipper on holiday in the Laurentians, Quebec circa 1927. (PC)

Israel Rabinovitch, editor of the *Keneder Odler*; J.I. Segal, renowned Yiddish poet; with Zipper circa 1927. (PC)

Shimshon Dunsky and Zipper share a light moment during a reception. (JPLA)

Yiddish poets on Esplanade Avenue: J.I. Segal, Kadia Molodowsky, Ida Maze, and Rochl Korn. (JPLA)

Jewish Peretz School, Duluth Street, 1942. (JPLA)

Ground-breaking ceremony for an extension to the Jewish Peretz School. (JPLA)

Students and teachers of the Jewish Peretz School celebrates Israel's first anniversary, 1949. (CJCA)

Yiddish leaflet for the Jewish Peretz School's fundraising campaign, 1952. (CJCA)

Students of the Jewish Teachers' Seminary with their teachers: Yaacov Zipper (far right) and his brother Yechiel Shtern (far left). (JPLA)

Family gathering: Yaacov and Sorke Zipper (centre), 1950. (PC)

Zipper addressing delegates at a conference in support of Yiddish culture. (CJCA)

Zipper at his life's work: instruction in Hebrew and Yiddish. (JPLA)

Community leaders Saul Hayes, Samuel Bronfman, and Michael Garber at a Canadian Jewish Congress regional conference, 1971. (CJCA)

Above: Reception marking the thirty-sixth year of Zipper's principalship of the Jewish Peretz School. (PC)

Left: Shloime Wiseman and Zipper exchanging toasts at a reception honouring their contribution to Jewish education, 1978. (JPLA)

Zipper at eighty. (PC)

Yaacov Zipper's
Family Tree

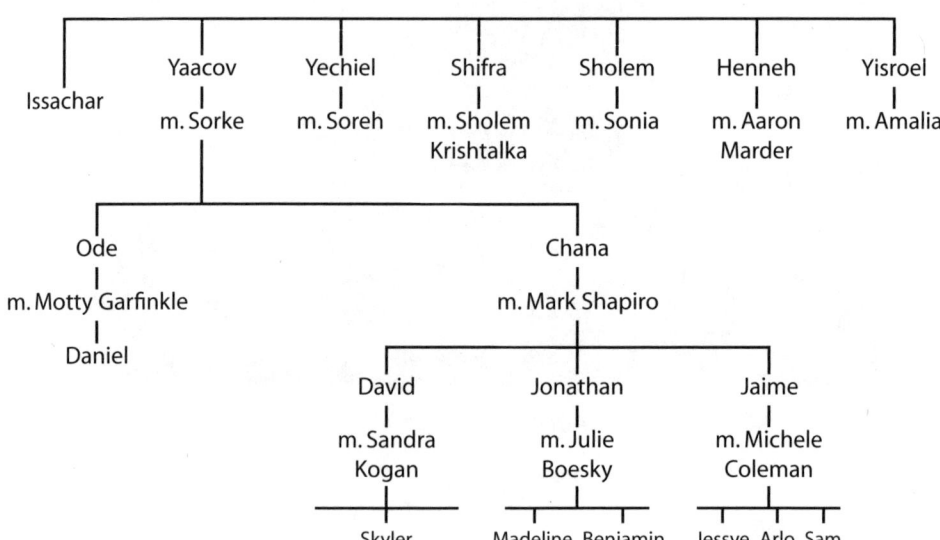

1950–1959

JUNE, 1950

I am approaching the end of my fifth decade. Without my willing it, something of a self-accounting begins to unfold. It appears to be very dark. So many dreams have remained unrealized. However, I still feel that something important can occur, although not as vital and sharp as it once was. I am no longer surprised by human pettiness, and in those cases where I might have expected a measure of greatness I now accept this with a grain of salt – could this be because of my profound disappointments? Or because my senses are beginning to grow duller?

Many years ago in the very early years of my youth I used to jot down thoughts and events. At that time it meant that I would later use these notes in life, in writing. Now I don't know why I want to begin writing these notes once again. There is great desire to speak to oneself without disguise – if that is even possible. Perhaps it is just a game, a kind of "hobby," or an attempt to regain the habit of writing, which has been seriously weakened in the last few years. I've almost lost the writer's impulse – to what end, to what purpose? Who needs it? Possibly, in writing for oneself, something might surface that would be of value to others. Many of my unfinished literary projects await a spiritual revival. My faith in mankind, and even in those close to me, falters. I have neither the desire to moralize nor entertain. But sometimes there is the desire to recall what has gone before. Days of my early youth often stand before me and beg: Tell our story, reveal us once more, relive our lives once again before we disappear forever. Everyone of our generation is actually the last exemplar of a world that is no more and that will never return. Does that signify the onset of age? The personal accounting begins to unfold, coming into being by bits and pieces. It is worthwhile to recognize and verbalize these thoughts, so I'll return to the form of fragmentary notes as they strike me, without embellishment.

I have experienced two world wars and a third is at the door. I have participated in the movement toward the secularization of Jewish life, lent a hand in the creation of a new type of Jew; was a part of the most beautiful things created by our generation: the *chalutz* in Israel and the cultural activists here in these regions where Jews are dispersed and wilting in the Diasporas. Lived through the greatest destruction and lived to see the redemption – the State of Israel: who could have imagined that this would be attained? Days of horror and exultation. Considerable hunger, and barely managed to subsist in my Canadian home. I was humiliated and diminished more than once during my almost thirty years of teaching. These were years of great pathos and belief and days of decline and small-mindedness. In practical terms, nothing accumulated and nothing stored up for my old age. If I lost my ability to work, I would be out on the street begging for bread. Has there been a spiritual gain, something accumulated? I would think so. It's to be found in the souls of hundreds of children; at least that's what I'd like to believe. I'm almost sure of that, but the fact that I am now bothered by the practical uncertainties with the future is probably not a good sign.

I wanted to build a new world, but in the meantime all I witnessed was the catastrophe. Yechiel, it would appear, looked upon it and retreated, and now wants to surpass even our pious father. He doesn't see even the smallest blemish on the traditional past and drives himself back into the generation-old faith and doesn't feel that we can be saved by postponing the end of days. He sees the messianic redemption before his eyes. I cannot accept this. The power and value of illusion is too clear to me to allow myself to be deluded into thinking that change of the real can be effected through illusion. This reality, it would seem, has never occupied a large part of my understanding of the world. It has always been easy for me to do without the many things that people seek in this reality, so I have no illusion that my return to putting on *tefillin* would result in the salvation of myself and traditional Israel. The play of symbols is too clear to allow myself to be captivated into following the everyday religious practices, even though they are necessary for sustaining *Yiddishkeit* – including the type of *Yiddishkeit* I want to see sustained. I myself feel this conundrum and can't seem to bring a thought to its conclusion.

I hardly write anything. I've lost the thread in the drama of the "simple folk." I can't read a book through to the end.

Important things like finishing my Biblical narratives, in which I think I have made innovations, are postponed until after my trip to Israel – I mean to Canaan. I can't begin to write the second volume of *Oif Yenner Zeit Bug*; all the heroes lie in Pitidin near the narrow bridge on the way to Ludmir. I can no longer struggle with them, just as their loves, conflicts, and, most of all, their dreams have come to nothing. Only a memory of green grass that shimmered and is no longer here. Often complete visions appear in my dreams and I see people actually complaining and beseeching: Why are you also aiding in the process of our being totally forgotten? I determine to begin writing, but can't bring forth anything. I know that the end to which I must lead is where they were led, and this is so futile, so improper, that I am helpless. It is as if I had brought them on and on and must now remain at the mountain with a single peak from which one cannot climb further – either ascent or descent – a sheer wall to the bottomless pit. Was this the purpose of a thousand years of Yiddish life in Eastern Europe? Will this be its moral meaning? Where in the past was there an intimation of this? Is it a leap that must be taken everywhere from time to time? Whose handiwork was it? What kind of Satan directs the world in this way?

Can another conclusion be drawn from all this? And how does one render this artistically? And how does one take this coolly and philosophically? I actually hear now the birds chirping in Pitidin, just as in those days in the early '20s when we were celebrating the new *Yiddishkeit*, the new secularism. The glowing evenings and the crisp dawns amid the poplars. I see the deep red moon between the branches and the magical silver of early spring. The scent of the fields intoxicates me even now, but I cannot see the connection, the sense and rationale of the end. Here they are all cloaked with the same magic of my imagination – but don't the shrieks of their final moments enter into this at all?

I lose all my desire to touch the subject.

JULY, 1950. IN THE COUNTRY

Within me, once more, there begin to rise images of my home. Tishevitz as it once was, thirty – odd years ago. Until now, I would always envision Ustilla, Shebreshin, Ludmir – with Tishevitz left to one side. Only sometimes, in a story, would she come forth. Now I see things differently. I have begun to write again according to the topographical traits that feature the bridges that lead to the town. Each bridge another chunk of life, intertwined with a particular neighbourhood and its life. This will lead to streets, and with the streets significant houses and people. The town looks fragmented but its wholeness will be expressed through its traditional way of life in those years. And to what extent the earlier generations were absorbed into the later times and people. I've already completed the story of six bridges and the beginning of one street. I'm drawn to writing and often it's difficult to tear myself away. But I'm doubtful whether it will be possible to extend the storyline in this manner without a central hero or major idea. It might be necessary to restructure totally, but in the meantime one must grasp as much as one can and record it on paper. I'm also working a little on a translation of *Oif Yenner Zeit Bug*. The summer vanishes and soon I'll have to reharness myself and I won't be able do any writing. So one must seize the opportunity now.

THE END OF JULY

Suffered two weeks with an earache and lost the habit of working again. Now I have to travel to a conference of the [Labour Zionist] Movement, so the remaining time will be wasted. It has been a long time since I've attended an education conference. It might be possible to effect some change there and, once again, I'll be able to familiarize the leadership with our financial troubles. Maybe they will provide us with a bit of deliverance. The financial situation of the school is so perilous that I'm terribly afraid that the approaching year might see the entire building threatened.

The financial crisis arises from the fact that the majority of children come from poverty and that the building has not been paid for. In addition there are the refugee children, each one of whom is a whole world of subjective and emotional hardships. This has led to continual deficits that jeopardize the entire school. We will have to become smaller in order to survive, and who knows whether it is already too late. And because of the financial crisis we don't even attend to the spiritual crisis, which is even more severe than the financial one.

It seems to me that the support group for a school such as ours has all but evaporated. The secularists have lost their power and the common people don't know what they want. They swim with the current, the newest fashion, and with anything that promises continuity and survival. They want a Bar Mitzvah but really desire the banquet that follows. Strive to join a synagogue, but are intent on mere belonging. They want to adopt Sephardic pronunciation and increase the Hebrew in order to identify with Israel, but are fearful of *chalutziut*. We have been left in a vacuum. Yiddish and East European life no longer have many supporters. Suddenly we are looked upon as odd. No one is prepared to sacrifice himself for this cause.

To this must be added the dispersion from the districts where our schools are located. The Talmud Torah will be unaffected. In the new districts they are building synagogues and alongside every synagogue a Talmud Torah. But we have to build independent institutions and there is no one to carry that out. An internal weakness is felt and only inertia keeps some of us going. The Movement is cool to its schools and we feel lost. It is impossible to discuss this with even my closest colleagues. It might be possible to raise these issues at the conference. Maybe. Knowing the "movers and shakers" of the school as I do, one can expect very little from them, nor that they might be able to elevate themselves to consider new policies.

MID-AUGUST, 1950

Returned from the conference exhausted and depressed, still somewhat renewed. Grew more intimate with some, amongst them the Auerbachs and Bialystotskys. Breathed in some literary atmosphere, so I felt better, but the issue of the school conference added to my depression. It is a lot worse than

I had imagined. The Movement, so far as it is concerned with this issue at all, is divided and in disarray. The younger faction, represented by a group of intellectuals who never aligned themselves with the Poalei Zion philosophy and refuse to accept it, see the remedy in a little Hebrew and preach a sweetened form of Zionism. Oddly, the Pioneer Women want a party - line school, and our commitment to the education of a culturally creative Jew would, according to them, be fulfilled by Israel. Here in the Diaspora, mere recitation will suffice, decorated with a bit of Hebrew. All else is overblown rhetoric and the pinching of cheeks to raise the colour. The old guard, with Entin at the head, is still somewhere thirty years behind, saying the same things but more nationalistically and holding forth about lofty issues when the minimum has yet to be attained. Teachers struggle with empty classrooms and deserted assembly halls. Cynicism devours them all and they argue over every word in a resolution. It makes a grievous impression, mere trickery. They resolved to call another conference, selected a program committee and left for home. Fine speeches were delivered, some were enthusiastic, even honest; however, behind the scene, no one believes even the clearest and most truthful words. I did my best to argue my case. They let me speak and wanted to hear more of what I had to say. I spoke unequivocally but only a small number heeded and regretfully acknowledged that something ought to be done. The rest of them, with Entin at their head, rebuked me: You shouldn't speak so openly. One shouldn't reveal the doubts, Entin argued. He holds the old-fashioned rhetoric close to his heart.

Our "leaders," except for [Louis] Segal, even refused to meet me and hear about the school's plight. The Farband pledged a thousand dollars. The ladies from Pioneer Women sent me off to a third-rung official and I spent an evening at her home. Good discussion, a fine woman this Levitt, her husband a staunch Poale Zionist and Hebraist, admittedly an intelligent person, but there was nothing beyond mere words. Not even a promise of anything. There is no money – the constant excuse. But the truth is there is no understanding of the entire matter, no desire to do anything. Their president didn't even respond to the telegram I sent her requesting an appointment. The Movement itself is like a beggar at the gate before those who control the treasury. No one cares and there is no vision. It would appear that our whole constituency is off the rails. Even the Farband leadership, which still clings to power, does so by virtue of being surrounded by a number of vulgarians for whom a Yiddish-speaking leader is excessive. A painful episode.

BEGINNING OF SEPTEMBER

Opened the school in a discouraged mood. Who knows how we'll be able to work this year. The neighbourhood is rapidly diminishing. Fewer children enrolled. Evening school suffered most – barely one class of grade 1. The community is moving out to the new districts and they are asking to open a school there, but where does one get the land or the money that would be necessary.

Under these conditions there will be less income from school fees. The situation is catastrophic. I called a meeting of the representatives of the local Movement. Only a few attended. The only ones who came with something concrete were the Pioneer Women, who pledged a thousand dollars, but no help from anyone in the campaign. We are surrounded by coldness. Our only resort is to petition once again the [Canadian Jewish] Congress and the Combined Jewish Appeal. Whether we'll be able to gain their support, God only knows. They would like to rid themselves of this matter. But perhaps I'm too pessimistic? I feel that the entire structure is collapsing and not everyone realizes it. One no longer believes that there is anyone who really wants us.

We have hired several male and female teachers. All of us still feel like strangers. But it looks as if they will adjust to the school's atmosphere. We survive on loans – for how long? The Jewish Teacher's Seminary is also in difficulty. Only one class. The director has no influence on the Board or the students. I foresee a bleak year. My own doubts about the developments in our work up to now increase. Will we find the strength to endure?

MAY 8, 1951

An unbearable meeting of the budget and finance committee took place. All the *chaverim* felt hopeless. The special committee of the Congress had informed us that there were no prospects for raising the sum of $31,000. The national executive had rejected the request for a special subsidy for the refugee children. The shadow of school-closing appeared before everyone's eyes. Even Zuker, who is always the optimist, always enthusiastic and full of plans, was in despair.

The decision to embark on a public struggle was the only one that could have been undertaken. It was also decided to convene the entire school body on the 14th of May and propose this plan. At the same time a letter should be sent to the Congress rejecting the argument that this issue is merely local. And plan to see Hayes again.

MAY 9, 1951

Didn't sleep the whole night, it was like a strange nightmare. It is difficult for me to face the teachers. Even the chidren, it seems to me, sense that something critical is in the offing. Miss Dansky asked me today whether she has a moral right to borrow money from friends on the assurance that she could repay them. Miss Freedman, stammering helplessly, came to tell me that she could wait no longer, she must have some funds. Others remain silent, but I feel it in everyone's glance. Miss Dansky, her usual lively and cheerful self, came to excuse herself for causing my distress, and I understand that she means well; she simply needs funds for her forthcoming trip to New York.

A teacher who had applied for a position for the coming year telephoned to say that, although she would have preferred working for us, she is withdrawing her application. She has accepted a position at the Folk Shule. She will be receiving a salary according to the new scale, and she understands that we're not able to meet those terms.

MAY 10, 1951

Chaver Zuker reported that Hayes had phoned him to say that the inner executive of Congress had once more discussed the question and decided to approach the Combined Jewish Appeal for permission to allow the Congress to include in its budget a sum of $5,000 over a period of four years in order to provide the full sum they had promised. Once more he requested the budgets of the last two years. And he also requested that their accountant have the right to examine our books for this year. One senses an injured tone on their part; they don't trust our figures. We have no choice. The figures and new budget were forwarded. Their accountant came and according to what he said, I could discern that he thought it was a poor business venture – always subsidizing losses. Too many poor children.

Because of the new situation it was decided at a special lunch meeting to postpone the assembly of the entire school body. I have to prepare a special letter to the school committees as well as a statement to the Jewish community about our circumstances. It was suggested that we make a financial appeal to the public. The question is: will the public respond?

I can't relax and simply do nothing. I must express my own deepest feelings. So I write letters in the name of parents and others, and try to empathize with their feelings, how they would feel and react if they were aware of our situation. Every morning when the mothers are waiting for the kindergarten children, I feel that they are looking at me with pity and reproach: Why don't you storm the walls? Just writing letters is not enough, someone must read them. Who – the general public, the Congress officials, and other prominent businessmen? How would it be if Sam Bronfman himself received a letter from a refugee with a tattooed number. In our school there are dozens of such families. Let the father tell about himself, about his child whom he has brought here safely. Let him describe how we treated him, how much effort and toil we have invested. Let Bronfman be reminded that wealthy Jews once supported Rabbinical schools and were immortalized as a result. They are celebrating his anniversary now. What does a few thousand dollars mean to him? I pour out my heart but don't feel better. Is it moral? Maybe I myself should cry out. What would be the better way? It is so quiet around us. Even close *chaverim* no longer ask how things are going. Only the inner circle continues to ponder and phone each other all day long.

MAY 11, 1951

Met with [Israel] Rabinovitch. I go over the whole situation. He hears me out in his unemotional way. He is busy correcting his book, which is being translated by A.M. Klein. He proposes: "You should issue a declaration, then I'll be able to react. Give me the figures and perhaps I will write a column immediately." Figures once more, and an editorial. On his desk lies "Interoffice Information," the bulletin from Congress. He leafs through it and sees that they have plans, that they intend to do something, etc. So perhaps we should delay. He hasn't oriented himself clearly about the whole issue. I try to make it clear to him: It is your affair as much as it is ours. All the delays and opposition to support us are due to the fact that ours is a school where Yiddish is taught in the proper manner and where the school has not made peace with denying its roots in folk culture. There is a silent boycott by those Jews who have no attachment to the poor. We are constantly underfoot. Therefore they profess one thing and do something else or nothing at all. Maybe we will become sick and tired of it all and close down. It is the wealthy classes' disdain for the ordinary man and especially for the new immigrants. What do they need a day-school education for, they complain, they should Canadianize themselves as quickly as possible.

He asks questions about the budget and salaries. He begins to gain interest when he learns about the fact that our salaries are so low in comparison with other institutions similar to our own that our Yiddish teachers, the best, receive barely enough for sustenance, and even this has not been paid for nearly three months.

It seems to me that his fingers itch to take up the pen. He plays with his pen and then inks in numbers. "So what are you waiting for?" he says, almost angry with me. "Why are you silent? I want to write and sound the alarm. Certainly this is our cause," he says thoughtfully. "But are there any from our side who would respond?"

I found myself feeling pity both for him and myself. The truth is that up to now even our own Movement has done nothing – except for the Pioneer Women with their campaign contribution of $1,000 and the Farband with $500. They didn't lift a finger. It's even likely that several of our *chaverim* through their sly remarks actually helped harden the hearts of the wealthy.

"Why is the Folk Shule silent, don't they realize that they are implicated in this as well" – he asks without answering and we both fall silent. I really have no need to speculate about their behaviour. They have never acted in any other way. The parvenu thinks that in this manner his status and glory are elevated.

Encountered Rabinovitch once again at the funeral of Rabbi Wachtfogel. We were repelled by the hypocrisy and deceit that was reflected in all the eulogies. From Rabbi Denberg's opening Yiddish address – he will be Wachtfogel's replacement – to the unctuous but coarse speech of the "genius" of the Adath Yeshurun Synagogue – it was almost as if they had planned to say nothing nor arouse a drop of grief from the assembly. The assembled believed neither the deceased nor them. I am left with a sense of strange emptiness and bitter feelings of humiliation that nauseate me. Despite all this, the old man was the last of the old-time Rabbis, who with all his weaknesses and pettiness represented the old-world rabbinate, although not of its finest quality. Nevertheless it was an integral world, and who are his heirs? And the whole community listens and doesn't shed a tear. Rabinovitch and I exchanged glances and something passed through my mind as if he were saying to me: The two of us will probably be given similar accountings as one generation succeeds another.

I decided to write and to declare: no eulogies to be said over me – not until I turn 120 years. Silence would be preferable. The deceased should be permitted to go to their eternal home without being talked about.

"A frightening emptiness," Rabinovitch says, drawing me into his boss's car. "Come, I have something to show you." We drive to the editorial offices. He shows me a letter that he received from the father of a pupil. It will appear in Sunday's edition. "People are responding," he reports with satisfaction. "As long the ordinary Jew reacts, there is no need to despair." It appears that the letter has been lying around the office for a few days and was held up by the typesetter. The father of a child who attends the school calls for the community to prevent its closing. These are parents whose only hope was to struggle to come to a Jewish community where they could live as Jews. Will the community leaders respond?

MAY 12, 1951

Zuker tells me that Dickstein, the head of the Movement and a cynic through and through, who believes that the entire leadership is in his pocket and that the wealthy community shivers in his presence, said to him: "You are using pressure. Our *chaverim* received letters telling them that they would be called up on the carpet. They are very angry." And he smiles slyly. His time will come – he too will face an accounting.

Spent a whole day working on the new budget. This is the most difficult of all the tasks I've ever had to perform as principal. The finance committee had arrived at the sum of $66,000, which according to them is the maximum we can expect for the coming year. The evening school continues to diminish, the neighbourhood grows emptier. Therefore the income shrinks, which means a cut of $13,000. This can only be achieved by reducing teaching hours, combining and eliminating classes, which results in firing teachers and cutting the salaries of the remaining staff. This decision had been taken several weeks ago but I couldn't bring myself to confront it. I had the feeling that with my own hands I was cutting into a living being. I have to squeeze a large body into a child's bed and who knows if this body will be able to continue to grow? Yet it must be done and no one else but myself can do it. The surgery must be performed. The usual fever that afflicts me at this time of year bothers me worse this year and I can hardly do anything. Have totally lost my appetite and the ability to relax either sitting or lying down. But it must be done.

Spent a couple of hours with Zuker. He looks sick and I'm alarmed. He says he can't sleep. His plan: to partially close the day school. To me this means closing the school by ourselves. I felt that he was pleased by my strong opposition to his plan. In case we are refused, he feels that we will have to sell the building to pay back the teachers. We must not default on the teachers, he maintains, and his face is grey and ashen. His dishevelled clothes hang on him as on a mourner – heaven forbid. Thirty-eight years of his life lie here, and I have difficulty looking into his eyes. I show him my plan and he calms down somewhat but not entirely. We agree that the teachers must be told the plain truth of the situation. The majority of the Yiddish teachers will undoubtedly accept the plan. Of the English sector teachers – not all. How will we survive? It might be that the operation was successful but the patient succumbed.

It could be that I am merely imagining this but at home they seem to be anxious about me. They glance at me sideways and tiptoe around me as if I were ill. They don't allow me much introspection. I myself sense that I don't meet their eyes either, as if I had been caught in a guilty act. I'll have to be more guarded in displaying my true feelings to them.

I try to make an accounting for myself but can't seem to accomplish that. Was it really wrong to absorb all the poor and the refugee children into the *Shule*? Maybe we should have accepted only the prosperous ones. Did I have right to endanger the entire building? And what's to happen to the teachers? And as for myself – without a penny saved and in debt as well. Did I have the right to take the risk? All these years I certainly knew that with the increasing number of indigent children the school was jeopardized, but could I turn away these children just for a few dollars? Has my trust in the community been undermined? Should I squander it all? But perhaps I am misinterpreting things. Even now I can't conceive of doing it otherwise. The registration for the kindergarten next year has increased, mostly refugees who have been here for two or three years. They can't afford to pay more than the minimum. Who knows whether this budget cut will help matters? How could one turn away a child born in Feldafing, the displaced persons camp, or Bergen-Belsen concentration camp?

I received an invitation to attend next week's meeting of the Dominion Council of the Canadian Jewish Congress. I'll pose this question to them. Maybe that will help.

SUNDAY, MAY 13, 1951

Attended the cornerstone ceremony for the Adath Israel school building. It will be a high school. A huge building at the cost of half a million. Only a small audience. Just an ordinary ceremony. The elite looked like uneasy relatives. Rabbi Bender, as usual, orates in a polished style but lacking conviction – yet he seems to have a goal in mind. He obviously intends something positive, as signified by his ability to move these cold Jews to contribute to this magnificent building. The only beaming presence was Sternthal, he is the main campaigner and is soaked in enthusiasm. He speaks English that sounds cold and distant, but his English retains something of the folk idiom. No Yiddish word was heard, neither was Hebrew, except for the cantor who chanted beautifully and with dignity a poem from Psalms: "Unless the Lord builds the house, its builders labour in vain." May God help this frigid Judaism to survive. There were no children present. The whole affair felt like a campaign-awards ceremony. A bunch of ignoramuses all about, crawling from one honour to the next, pleased with their recognition, waiting to be photographed and be done with it. On the other hand, who knows what they are really feeling. Maybe the photographs just catch an everyday pose, while inwardly they are truly joyous – because if not, why would they put themselves out? They nevertheless help build an institution. Even though it is in a language they don't understand, they still believe it is the only way. In this way they bind themselves to a creative Jewish life. Without understanding the concept of survival, nevertheless, they still come.

Mendelsohn sat up front, perspiring, but wasn't given a chance to speak. Has he nothing to say at this celebration or are they ashamed to present him to this audience? They already presume to speak for him. But it doesn't seem to me that he is bothered by it.

All the school principals were present except for the Westmount crowd, who sent a telegram. Magid with his cane and his self-satisfied but bitter smile stands on the platform, something of an intimate yet estranged. Wiseman, with tight-lipped slyness in his entire demeanour, sits at the rear and can barely contain himself. He doesn't look well. Something gnaws at him that he can't conceal any longer, especially when he doesn't speak. For lately when he does speak he disguises himself with a thousand words, Biblical quotations, and snatches from the liturgy, on the morality of human relations. In silence he gives himself away.

I stand at the rear in order to see better. I envy them – but yet do not. All those sitting in places of honour, the community leaders, show no enthusiasm, their *yarmulkes* cover it all up and they rejoice coolly. Good for them, but it seems a pity that they can't derive any satisfaction as they should. I didn't detect one gleam of real happiness at the performance of this dedication amongst the activists or the teachers – whose presence was totally overlooked. No students at all. How different it was at our celebration some six or seven years ago. The happiness of the folk, the lay leadership, and children. It was a moving experience. So should we too be pitied? Is our warm flame now unnecessary? Is this now solely an Outremont celebration? I am ashamed of my own attitude, that at the building of an institution I should feel this way. Yet without the common folk I remain chilled, despite the sunshine and the heat.

On returning home, I couldn't help being troubled by this picture: here, a large, fully equipped building, but cold and desolate, without a public that would rejoice openly and sincerely, while on Duluth, with all its warmth and enthusiasm, there is sadness under the threat of being shut down. At best, a friend passes by and sympathetically shakes his head. Maybe it's time to search for the meaning of these events.

MAY 15, 1951

The kindergarten registration for the next school year is very brisk, more than any other year parents are hurrying to register their children. Each one has a different story to tell. They have gathered here from all corners of the world, and in their eyes there shimmers a flame of sadness and an odd kind of happiness at being able to register their child in a Jewish school. They can't believe that the community elite are totally opposed to their sending their children to us.

Yesterday a letter was published in the *Keneder Odler* by a father, and in the *Montreal Star* under an assumed name, that questioned the community's silence. Hayes was furious and indignant. Wrote me an insulting letter with copies to Miller and Zuker, claiming that we had betrayed his confidence by divulging confidential information, since the anonymous author of the letter to the *Star* refers to minutes that pertain to matters in the Congress Bulletin. And since we receive the bulletin from Congress, he assumes that we released the information. I answered as he deserved and pointed out that his accusation is groundless, and that he ought to treat us with more respect.

Hayes let Zuker know that the Combined Appeal had rejected their request for a subsidy. A rapidly convened lunch meeting was called for 12:30. Nachum Meyerson, who was at the Combined Appeal meeting, was also there. He reports that the issue was not presented to that meeting as originally agreed upon. Congress apparently asked the Combined Appeal to provide money directly to the school from their funds. The Congress didn't even propose that they would borrow the funds, as they had told us. It would appear that they are fooling us, and behind the scenes they are planning something that we know nothing about. Zuker fought with Hayes, and refuses to see him again; broke off relations.

In the evening, there is the committee meeting that must make the ultimate decision. According to what Meyerson also reported, Michael Garber had proposed a motion to reject the Congress plan. This means that even before the meeting they had changed their plan and claimed that our board of directors is not competent to run the school, and therefore cannot be trusted. So apparently he is the main antagonist. He seems unable to wash away his former radicalism and seeks to impress the "cocktail circle" that he is now kosher and can even lead in the closing of the school where he himself had been active at one time. Not the first time this has happened in community life.

MAY 16, 1951

The meeting of the special committee, after a lengthy and heated discussion, decided to submit an open declaration to the newspapers. Zuker and I were assigned the task of preparing our position for the *Keneder Odler*.

MAY 17, 1951

Without sleep all night. Zahler came to school very early and we discussed a new budget plan for the upcoming year. The cuts are extensive and painful. Based mainly on the teachers' salaries and freezing of all the debts owed to the *chaverim*. Following another consultation with Miller and Zuker, it was decided to present the new budget to Hayes. Possibly he will help. Rabinovitch's opinion is that we should come out with a proclamation. The *Keneder Odler* will help, but is reluctant to call for a public campaign. Who knows if the response will be positive? He doubts whether we, with our limited strength, can arouse the community. It might simply result in tumult for its own sake.

The lawyer, Rosenheck, called to say that he is prepared to take a stand on our side if an open battle is declared.

Attended the meeting of the Histadrut campaign. L. Segal was the guest speaker. Asks in passing how things are – and nothing further. Our *chaverim* don't inquire at all.

Registered several children for kindergarten next year. The total nears thirty. All of them at reduced fees.

Received an invitation to the meeting of the Dominion Council of Congress. The school question is on the agenda. An opportunity to put our position forward.

MAY 18, 1951

Sent out a mobilization notice to all the school committees for Monday the 21st. So we will able to gauge the response of our own people. Parents are restless, make inquiries, but do nothing. Hayes had promised to convene a special meeting of the Congress executive. I reported the whole situation to the teaching staff. The atmosphere was unpleasant. Chose a committee to work alongside the board of directors, another committee to study the new budget.

MAY 21, 1951

At the meeting of the special committee we formulated the agenda for the general meeting. H. Miller will be chairman, L. Zuker will present the report, and I will read the resolution that will express our protest against such treatment. To establish a committee to lead the action. Thanking the teachers for their cooperation to date, and to the select group of activists for their efforts. The proclamation should be such that it conveys all the facts and calls for a struggle with the community leadership based on our principles. The financial campaign should be put off until we see the public response. After the meeting went to visit Zahler, who is the main adviser about extracating ourselves from this difficult situation. He is not well and couldn't attend the meeting. In recent months he has devoted much time and thought to these issues. Had a lengthy discussion with him. He is quite worried but still believes that the new plan along with a sharply reduced budget for the coming year can possibly save the situation. I read to him the proclamation, which he accepted after a number of very important comments. So now we must prepare for the meeting.

MAY 22, 1951

Once again, couldn't sleep the whole night. Returned late from the meeting with the school board and tossed from side to side. Whichever way you draw up the account – it never balances. One thing is clear: we have reached the climax. The meeting was well attended. Almost all those invited were there except for a number of relatively new board members who didn't identify with us in the time of danger, and some old-timers who were angered because of principles, for them we were insufficiently progressive.

Miller, in an animated and very effective manner, pointed out that the issue is one of principle. They – the Congress – are dragging their feet because they do not wish to help a Yiddish school. Zuker delivered a brilliant report on the development of the education issue for the last two years. In the discussion, a number of people spoke critically against the committee for allowing the matter to drag on for so long. There was also a sense of bitterness directed at the Folk Shule for their failure to offer moral support (although they did extend a loan of $2,500). It even appears that a number of their *chaverim* in fact secretly strengthened the hands of the opposition by stating that this neighbourhood could no longer support such a school, signified by the fact that they are closing their evening school branch on St. Urbain.

The general summary: the meeting is prepared to fight publicly. In my response to the charge that we had delayed too long, I indicated that despite everything we did actually receive partial help so that at that point we were in no position to undertake public opposition. Even when we realized that they were stalling – as long as they didn't refuse us categorically – it would not have been prudent to declare open warfare. It is truly a battle for principle. We have the feeling that this is part of a desire to destroy Yiddish and to denigrate our approach to Jewish life. A battle against these beliefs is imminent, but we wanted to avoid being the battlefield. In such a war we would suffer the most. Now, however, we have no other choice; tomorrow evening at the Dominion Council the battle must begin and then be carried through the newspapers. The resolution that I proposed was passed. The proclamation will be approved by a special committee that will include all the support groups of the school. The executive committee is authorized to deal with and execute all matters pursuant to saving the school.

Many embittered *chaverim* took comfort from this decision, as if the decision itself marked a victory. I, however, remain heavy-hearted. I am still afraid of the conflict. I don't see the forces required to lead us to victory.

Enrolled two more children who were born in a concentration camp. They can pay very little. Should I refuse them? If we are forced to do this there will no longer be any justification for our struggle. I won't be able to do it. Community leaders must understand this and respond. This evening we must address the community with candour and ask them in simple words: Do poor children have the right to an education? And does the responsibility for this lie with the teachers alone, must they be the only ones to make sacrifices? This starvation-budget gives me no rest.

MAY 23, 1951 (IN THE MORNING)

Since I've been active in community affairs I've never experienced such a meeting as last night at the Dominion Council and never felt so degraded. It was a well-attended meeting. Until the agenda-item on Peretz Shule everything went smoothly, although there was a difficult matter to approve the decision to disallow the "Progressive" organizations from standing in the forthcoming Congress elections. The argument was that they disrupt the harmony of the constituent elements that make up the organization. The resolution was moved by a rotund Jew with a shiny, smug face. Opposed to him appeared the representative of the "Progressives," nervously stuttering, pale and thin. The resolution was adopted without discussion. They really deserved it; still I couldn't raise my hand to vote for exclusion as if I had the right to chastise them. It was pitiful to look at their stammering representative who warned and threatened them. I had the feeling that this wasn't pleasant for anyone.

An official report was presented of the trip to Boston to see Ben-Gurion. The historical significance of this was lost on them.

Fearful that it was getting late and that our item would not be heard, Zuker asked the chairman to bring the item forward and bypass the other items on the agenda.

This motion was accepted. In a brief and precise report, Hayes accounted for the Congress's action to the present, and that now they could do no more because the Combined Appeal refuses to allow the Congress to include a specific sum of money in its budget for us. The assembly listened attentively to the report. Seated opposite me was the lawyer Marcus Sperber, a pleasant face with an animated smile. He glanced about the room ironically, as if he could not believe his ears. Near him David Kirsch, lean and well-groomed, sat silent as usual with a melancholy, sullen expression, as if something extremely serious preoccupied him. To the left of Zuker and myself, Abe B. overflowed the chair with the expansiveness and confidence of a millionaire, looking about at everyone as if it was his victory that nothing had come of the whole issue. Zuker was given the first response. He began with an acknowledgment to the Congress and the Combined Appeal and several individuals for their efforts on our behalf. He demonstrated the basic conditions that led to our difficulties: poor neighbourhood, new immigrants that the richer neighbourhoods refused to accept – while we did, and rejected the arguments that this was just a local issue or solely the concern of our board of directors. It made a very good impression. Miller elaborated on the financial aspects, clarifying certain figures of the budget and deficit. Several people added their names to the speaker's list, but at this point Michael Garber, red-faced and excited, moved up to the podium and began to leaf through the papers, pointing out that the real issue was our incompetence and we were no longer to be trusted to balance the budget. In other words that we had come to the meeting to waste everyone's time. The neighbourhood is exhausted and in this matter the Congress can do nothing. Zuker and Miller responded sharply and rebutted his facts, which enraged him all the more and he continued to create the impression that they had done everything and that we were entirely guilty for not having reduced the tabled budget. In my remarks, I underscored clearly and forcefully that it appears that only because these are poor children do they demand the school's closing. I provided them with several cases of immigrant and local families: a child of a former war veteran who had died in the hospital; a newly arrived child who was smuggled out of the ghetto at birth. Should they now be sent away?

The millionaire rose in all his witless presence and spoke so naively that everyone simply hung their heads at his argument that a business that cannot support itself must be closed. Several questioned the assertion that no money was available, claiming that if money were needed for public relations it would be found. No one answered these objections, but the chief antagonist continued his charges, repeating candidly that our board of governors lacks credibility to maintain the school and therefore if the Folk Shule wished to absorb us they would be able to convince the Appeal to provide the necessary sums to cover the deficit. His motion was carried. Wiseman then sarcastically asked: I suppose so. And what will you do in two years when we both come to you for aid? At this Garber smiled and answered that he doesn't believe that this would occur and if it does we would deal with it then. Zuker then declared in his own name that if the amalgamation option was the only way to save the school, he would defend such a union at a Peretz Shule's board of director's meeting. Due to the late hour the meeting dissolved in a spirit of exasperation with an announcement from the chairman, Monroe Abbey, that the issue could be resolved in one week and if required he was ready to convene a special Dominion Council meeting.

That I couldn't sleep all night goes without saying; however the other *chaverim* didn't sleep either. By nine o'clock Zuker was already in my office, dejected, his face creased with worry. His first thoughts were that we should approach the Folk Shule and begin negotiations immediately. I pointed out to him that this would lead nowhere. We would only waste time. Above all, I felt that the Congress's strategy was to toss the whole matter on to the Folk Shule and thus justify themselves doubly: if the Folk Shule rejects the proposal it will mean that even the Folk Shule refuses to help us, so why should Congress be faulted? And if the Folk Shule does agree and we don't, then that is unquestionably in their favour. In my view we should make it explicit to the Folk Shule that they should turn the whole matter back to Congress. In his desperation Zuker had other plans that could lead only to liquidation, including the sale of the building, paying the teachers' salaries, closing the day school and retaining only the evening school. I pointed out to him that none of this would help and it would be more effective to consider a public battle. We do not want to close the school. If they refuse to help us, let the community close the schools. Amalgamation now also means our liquidation. The teachers refuse to make further sacrifices that the new budget projects in the event of an amalgamation. In general, our entire structure would be destroyed. We went to consult with Rabinovitch and his publishers. They understand too that this is an issue of principle and that it concerns their cause. They promise that they will lead an open opposition and organize a financial campaign. Earlier, Rabinovitch had spoken to Mr Myerson, who had attended the meeting and is also a member of the Folk Shule's board. His opinion is that we should simply accept the resolution to "unite," obtain the funds, and then dispose of things to our liking. It's with a bitter smile that one contemplates how lightly and without seriousness certain activists advise us on this matter. M. Wolofsky phoned Hayes to inform him that as a newspaper they have a duty to report and take a position but he doesn't want to do that until he knows what Congress intends to do. Hayes' answer was that Congress is sending a letter to the Folk Shule to discuss the matter. It remains for us to delay the public declaration until the union issue is clarified. Wolofsky and Rabinovitch promise to give us their unqualified support in case we have to resort to an open declaration. In the evening we held a meeting of the special committee, where it was reported that the Folk Shule was holding a meeting of their board of directors at the same time.

MAY 24, 1951

Last evening the meeting of the special committee took place. We reported on the Dominion Council meeting and the talks with the Combined Appeal. The mood was turbulent. Yisroel and a number of *chaverim* spoke bitterly against our management of the whole affair. It looks as if we have to justify ourselves before our own *chaverim* as well. We pointed out – Zahler in particular – that open conflict is the last resort, and that we have much to lose in a premature attack. In particular, we have to remember our own weakness; nor can we foretell as yet where our support might lie. Zuker speaks for union, as he had promised. But we cannot permit discussion of the issue since we have not yet received an official invitation. We select a negotiating committee in case we are summoned. We'll wait until next Thurday, the 29th of May, and see how things develop. Everyone was enormously disappointed and embittered. After the meeting Miller, Zahler, and myself went to Horn's for coffee and to make sense of the situation. We sent Zuker home because he looked done in. We sat there until 2:30 in the morning. Zahler proposes a new plan with which to approach the Congress.

The budget for the upcoming year is to be established according to the prospective income of $66,000. This will result in fewer classes, fewer hours of instruction, and a reduction of expenses. Of the debts incurred earlier, only a small number would be repaid now, with an arrangement for a five-year moratorium with our directors. Twenty-five per cent of teachers' salaries to be withheld for this year, and will be repaid in the event of a surplus the following year. In addition, he and Miller should guarantee the sum of $10,000 each to cover any deficit. As I listened to the plan each word cut me to the bone for I instantly realized that it would demand an immense sacrifice from the teachers. As for myself, I would sustain a significant cut in salary, aside from the $3,000 loan due me that would now remain as part of the guarantee. The remaining sum to be obtained from our own *chaverim* who would choose to underwrite Miller and Zahler's guarantee. At the same time the scope of the plan encouraged me because it demonstrated a strong will to save the school. I sit and observe Zahler. Usually he is tired, grey, and reserved. Now he is animated and can't sit still. The plan means the following: if Congress accepts, it will be difficult, but the school will continue; if they don't accept then we have a basis for an appeal to the community, which will place us at the centre of a righteous cause. They won't be able to squirm out of this nor find excuses. Miller, who rarely shows his emotions, and who has recently cooled off to the extent that he must be dragged to the activities – it seems that he is concerned with school matters only at meetings – is too involved with his own affairs. He too smiles oddly and I sense that we all share the feeling that this is a master move. At the end we looked at each other and smiled knowingly. We had the feeling that an important strategy had been formulated and that we had reached mutual understanding without a word being spoken. Tomorrow we will have to prepare a detailed plan on paper and go to meet the chief antagonist. To attack at the centre. If we win him over, our victory is complete. If not, then we will inform him of our intention to publicize the new plan that he has rejected. We departed in good spirits.

I couldn't sleep after all this, but not for the usual emotions: this indicates that at the ultimate critical moment, people summon up undetected resources that surpass their former expectations. Will this work?

On arriving home the whole family was awake. I had forgotten to telephone that I would be late and they couldn't fall asleep and were waiting. From my explanation they gathered that something new had been devised and this calmed them.

Early next morning I went to see Zuker to outline the new plan. He was most satisfied. He concurred with us that we would find *chaverim* who would underwrite the guarantee. We jotted down a list of names. They won't be approached until the matter becomes a reality. Heard nothing from the Folk Shule all day. Looks like they too have decided to remain silent. Or possibly they haven't even dealt with the issue.

Brought all the papers to Zahler. Tomorrow is the day.

Kronitz telephoned. He is amazed at the Movement's coolness to the whole affair. He plans to bring it up at the Actions Committee meeting in Toronto next Sunday. He advises me to travel there. I don't feel that I have to do that. I did enough knocking on doors in the Movement last summer.

Zuker has a meeting with the secretary of the Movement to inform him about the situation. We have to begin preparing our forces in case of need.

MAY 25, 1951

Zahler just informed me that he and Craimer had had a meeting with Garber. At the last moment Miller couldn't make it. This angered Zahler, yet his mission was successful. After much discussion, Garber conceded that the whole idea of union – which he supports – was really put forward to embarrass the Folk Shule. In the meantime he revealed that the *chaverim* of the Folk Shule, behind our backs, had not said a good word about us. They said that they always maintained that we didn't manage our affairs well, and they had warned us not to build in that neighbourhood. When he heard about the guarantee he became more amenable and he immediately called Hayes and told him that the situation was now totally changed and that a special meeting of the inner executive of Congress and the Combined Appeal should be convened. Things are beginning to look brighter. The plan appears to be workable. We have to put aside the idea of amalgamation with the Folk Shule and speak to the other Congress members.

Garber and Hayes inform us that Dickstein said that there is no need for a school in this neighbourhood. Sternthal of the Adath Israel said that if the school did not exist, one would have to be built. They also said that Wiseman had told them that in the case of amalgamation, they would close the school on Duluth immediately and transfer the children to the school on St Urbain, which they intend to close in the next year. That is their idea of helping us!

MAY 26, 1951

I happened to run into Sam Harvey and he invited me to his home for a chat. In the discussion I felt that he was trying to gather information. I found out that they had discussed the issue including the question of the value of the building and the possibility of finding a buyer. It became clear to me that in the case of a union they were prepared to liquidate the school. It looks like they are in agreement with the Congress people about getting rid of the poor. Spoke too about the Teacher's Seminary. As usual he gives the impression that he bends all his efforts for our institutions, which we don't appreciate sufficiently. As a result of our discussion I am better informed about one thing: their plan is to drag their feet on the whole matter. We'll have to take the bull by the horns and approach them directly about ceasing their delaying tactics.

Received a copy of the letter the Congress sent to the Folk Shule. It's diplomatic and they commit themselves to nothing. We have to see that they respond immediately and not throw stones into our spokes.

Helman reveals that Wiseman is trying to help us. That's the impression he makes on his innocent people. Helman is a naive soul who accepts all things as God's truth.

Was a guest at the Bornstein's, a strange gathering. Merchants from the old country, intelligentsia without culture. Little more than clever witticisms and drinking. Most had interesting faces, particularly the men, but their mouths were twisted and cynical. An evening wasted. The host too hovers between earnestness and acute cynicism. Possibly one has to assume these attitudes in an embattled world.

MAY 27, 1951

A meeting was held of the special teachers' committee regarding the budget. In principle, all feel that there is no other option. For the teachers this will mean more belt-tightening. Not only forsaking a salary increase but facing an actual reduction. But we must save the school. The main opposition, voiced by some, concerned the termination of teachers. Certain teachers won't have any work at all since the number of classes is being reduced. A difficult and agonizing matter that should really be addressed at an open assembly. I'm afraid that this is unavoidable. The helplessness of the situation is now increasingly evident. It would mean discharging teachers without any compensation whatever. And through all this they still maintain that we can attract young people to the teaching profession when it offers no security now and for retirement. But they still go on talking about the importance of education.

In order not to prolong the issue of amalgamation, I called Wiseman and asked to meet with him. At first he was equivocal, nevertheless decided to see me. Entering his office, his bearing indicated that the entire issue was distasteful to him and he let me know that he hadn't expressed his views nor spoken to anyone, except for his attempt to call a meeting of his *chaverim*, which was not possible in the immediate future. This one is out of town and that one is busy; at the same time he disclosed his own severe difficulties with his board of directors. They also have a deficit and many of them have deserted us and are not interested in building a new school, etc. He also added, in these exact words: "In any event, you probably don't believe anything I say, but I'm telling you that that is the way it is." He was very keen to know about my discussion with Harvey and wanted to leave the impression that he had little regard for him, etc. I therefore had decided to make it very clear that I had not come to discuss the amalgamation nor to ask for their help. I was primarily interested to see that they did not prolong their response and that their answer should be one that would indicate that they have no responsibility in the matter. We are not interested in giving the Congress an alibi. And that we don't intend to wait any longer than Thursday, the 30th. If no answer is forthcoming we will make the issue public. We are most reluctant to address the Folk Shule position publicly. He immediately became more pliable. Called in his secretary, Zingman, and enumerated all the difficulties with regard to convening a meeting. But finally he promised that their response would be given within the next two days. Their approach would be, more or less, that the Congress had no business taking up the question of amalgamation before officially investigating the feasibility of the arrangement. Nevertheless they are prepared to hear the proposals. The critical issue is that this would require too much time. I added to this that we would be prepared to discuss a joint financial campaign. Amalgamation would only bring harm because both organizations would be weakened thereby. It's like a forced marriage, which can lead to no good. Nothing was said about the new plan.

MAY 29, 1951

Zahler and Miller met with Hayes and he too feels that the new plan might work. He promised to convene a special meeting of the inner executive of Congress to study the issue once more and to call a special meeting of the Combined Appeal. Meanwhile he divulged confidentially that Wiseman had told him that in the case of amalgamation the first thing they would do is to close the Peretz Shule for there is no reason for a school in that neighbourhood. Zahler calls this an "as if" proposition; however, we cannot at this time utilize the information. Today the Folk Shule meeting will take place. Hayes knows more or less what the Folk Shule's answer entails. Something similar to the approach that Wiseman had discussed with me.

At the meeting of the Teacher's Seminary trustees it was revealed that Congress had taken a decision to close the Seminary. Wiseman speaks on behalf of the Seminary, but explains that their standards are not sufficiently high, etc. This is meant to denigrate the Seminary, even though the language remains positive. The representatives of the Adath Israel and the Shaar Hashomayim are extremely angry with the Congress, but don't perceive that Wiseman's words help to bury the Seminary. Why is he doing this?

MAY 30, 1951

Couldn't reach Wiseman. Zingman summarizes the general thrust of the letter to the Congress. This will clear the way for us to be able to deal directly with the Congress.

Zuker tells me that at the special meeting of the actions committee of the Labour Zionist Movement, Bobrove and Dickstein spoke adamantly against giving direct help to the Peretz Shule. Uncovered all sorts of faults about the neighbourhood and that we oppose amalgamation. Dickstein doubts whether the new plan will be approved. It was decided that the Movement would participate to the extent of guaranteeing the sum of $3,000. I inform Rabinovitch about all that has transpired. He thinks that we should postpone the public announcement.

MAY 31, 1951

The inner executive of the Congress decided in principle to accept the new plan and to approach the Combined Appeal. The meeting should take place when Klein, the chairman of the Appeal, would be back in town.

At the meeting of our special committee we presented a full report. During the discussion we offered some facts about the new plan and the budget that would greatly affect teachers' salaries. Some are very dissatisfied with this. Appreciation was expressed for the committee's leadership to date, and authorized it to continue in the same direction. Some felt that especially the final plan demonstrates that a number of our *chaverim* rose to new heights in their readiness to save the school. The truth is that only with a great moral effort were we daring enough to propose such a plan. I feel that morally speaking, we rose to a high plane.

Last night the closing meeting of the parents and teachers of the Peretz Shule was held. A large audience was present. In my brief remarks I pointed out to the parents that they have to shoulder more responsibility. I emphasized the enormous undertaking of the teachers, and told the parents that we were not begging but demanding. The school will continue. Will they understand this?

JUNE 2, 1951

I notice that Yechiel seems to be quite agitated, although at the last meeting he was rather enthusiastic and self-confident. I had a discussion with him. It appears that he too is making his own arrangements, so it looks as if we are really alone. On the other hand, maybe we have sacrificed too much while other teachers have managed to build a pretty good future for themselves.

I answered him that it could be that we have sinned against the Biblical injunction, "And you should protect your own being." We always considered ourselves envoys of continuity, and the community would therefore take care of us. It turns out that we are alone, neglectful of ourselves and are looked upon as ne'er-do-wells. In any case they don't appreciate our worth, and poverty drives us into a concern for petty matters. Aside from the bitterness that we experience we almost lose a sense of our own worth.

We have to raise ourselves above this, although I can no longer advise any student to become a Jewish teacher. Yechiel is thinking of learning a trade, but understandably this arises from despair. He can be nothing but a teacher. He tells me that Shmerl, his son, asks him: "Who will become Jewish teachers, Papa?"

This is indeed the central question. But I fear that we are no longer able to be as confident as we once were.

JUNE 7, 1951

The school issue drags along. It looks like it will eventually come to a conclusion. The establishment types make promises, even compliments, but meanwhile prolong the matter from day to day. In the meantime we are preparing the necessary documents. Every time I glance at the documents that we must sign and the sums to be relinquished by the teachers as well as the *chaverim*, I am rendered cold and warm. Cold – because it cuts to the bone. After all, the *chaverim* will not be destitute – God forbid; for the teachers, on the other hand, it means food torn from their mouths. I don't doubt that the sacrifice is valuable and necessary. But it's heart-wrenching that this is required. An outsider would hardly believe that this has come to pass. Warm – because of the fact that we have risen to the occasion and have accepted the task without a murmur. The teachers are even making an effort to smile and try not to talk about the issue at all.

Last Tuesday, Rosenheck invited me for lunch and we talked about amalgamation, Folk Shule's attitude, etc. In the Folk Shule he is an activist but knows hardly anything about the issues involved. And because he finds it difficult to comprehend the Folk Shule's cool attitude, he wanted to have a chat with me. I tried to clarify the issues but left him more confused. He can't conceive how we put up with it and the reasons for allowing it to continue. He makes a good impression but because he is a novice in our circle it's difficult for him to grasp how we continue to withstand it and remain so stubborn.

Meanwhile we are preparing for the graduation. The truth is that I am lacking the momentum to celebrate, even though it is the largest graduation in terms of numbers. Within myself I seem to lack the appropriate words or the vigour. Not even the perpetual *niggun* comes to my lips. Could this just be fatigue?

Yesterday we had field day together with the Folk Shule. It's hard to look them squarely in the eyes. The children actually excelled and each time that they won, a look of envy crept into the faces of the Folk Shule teachers. A rather foolish envy, bordering on pettiness.

Zuker tells me that he has almost succeeded in having the Movement give the $3,000 as a guarantee. Oddly enough, each time the question is raised at a committee meeting where a Folk Shule *chaver* is present he equivocates and delays the decision. What a sad state of affairs we have reached. Who has so polluted their minds?

A special meeting of the Teacher's Seminary took place. The Talmud Torah was represented by their board members, none of their teachers were present. Is it that they have no say in the matter there, or is it simply that: "Leave me alone and let Ivan blow the '*shofar*'?" Only heaven knows. Could it be that they feel that they are only subservient to another's will, and they are content with a *yarmulke* on their heads and a cheque in their pockets. Argued all evening and finally elicited from them an agreement that the future plan for the Seminary would include the day school and the evening school. The Congress representatives were hesitant and in the end promised to support the Seminary if the concerned institutions were wholeheartedly in support.

I pointed out that the question of attracting students was closely related to the situation of the teachers, who are never certain of the present and certainly not of the future. We have to change the approach that sees education as a business governed by costs. Subsidies must be provided and the social status of teachers must be raised. No one reacted to this. It still falls on deaf ears, even among school activists who are well-intentioned. Hyperbole still reigns, and flowery speeches on education are easier to hear than actual facts. A decision was taken to hire a new director and to make plans for the coming year.

EREV SHAVUOS, JUNE 9, 1951

Finally things have begun to move. The meeting of the Combined Appeal has already taken place. Hayes, it would appear, is seeking support in public opinion, in order to pass it. Since the plenary session is to take place shortly, it wouldn't be politic to appear at the plenary with a record of closing a school. So he wrote a letter to Rabinovitch, praising him for clarifying the issue to the public and in vague terms he lets him know that the plan for amalgamation has far-reaching implications and they don't intend to blame the Folk Shule. Meanwhile they are trying to implement a new plan. This gave Rabinovitch the opportunity to editorialize and to caution them that the Congress now has the possibility to demonstrate that they are sincerely interested in education and feel responsibility for it. In *IOI*, Congress' information bulletin, there is no mention of this. That too is a good sign. They had invited our representatives to the meeting, which is really a good sign.

The greatest difficulties will now be internal ones. Will we be able to maintain ourselves with reduced salaries and with children who are primarily drawn from the poor and the newly arrived who can afford only a reduced tuition. We'll have to bear the yoke and survive.

JUNE 14, 1951

Sholem Aleichem says: "When things happen, unexpected things follow." There is enough hardship all around. Still more blows descend, unexpected and fatal. Danielak, the director of the Jewish Public Library, always a man of good spirits and seemingly in good health, who had made peace with himself and all others, died suddenly, leaving his wife and two small children like flotsam on the water. Disrupted their world and marred the *Shavuos* holiday for all of us. It was as if our whole group sensed that we were implicated, that our turn had come. And beyond that we saw how unrewarded is the lot of a public servant; struggles throughout his lifetime and leaves no security for his family. The final reckoning has become more and more difficult.

Right after the holidays troubles are multiplied; Gittel catches cold and it looks like pneumonia and a blood-clot – doctors, specialists, and within a few hours she is taken to the hospital critically ill. She is like a mother to me, and if one can say this, much more than that. Due to her, it became possible for me to reach this stage in life. I owe her everything. If not for her I would have perished in the black year, 1919–20.

I am so agitated that I cannot work at all. I am at the hospital more than at school and this is graduation time. So much work to do, but I can't concentrate. Today is the first day that the doctor has calmed us with news that the danger has almost passed, so I was relieved a little. But a great fatigue overtook me. Haven't experienced such fatigue in a long time.

To exacerbate all of this, the Combined Appeal meeting about our issue was held, and they postponed it once more. After all this, it now has to go to another committee. Miller and Zahler report on their reception. They felt a deep sense of shame and humiliation from those who call themselves "leaders." They report that the "leaders" speak openly of closing the school. It appears to them that our situation looks both tragic and insignificant. To the world at large, it appears that they are doing everything to help, but in reality they are cold-blooded scoundrels, without any feelings for what they are doing. Strangers have control over us and all the *chaverim* look on in silence and even take pleasure in it. I am told that even our own *chaverim*, so to speak, have not a good word to say about us. Could this be because we are out of step with them, that we don't parrot what all the others say, at the right time and the right place?

Last night attended a Farband meeting, which I addressed, unburdening myself a little. They feel guilty. Maybe that's why they are searching for excuses for their inaction. They are trying to uncover our sins. Possibly we are no longer really part of what we call "the Movement." I feel sorry for the few individuals who support us, and have little understanding of what is taking place. They are now determined to save the school; however, if they had devoted their time to the previous campaigns we probably would not have reached this crisis.

The atmosphere at school is embittered. I cannot look the teachers directly in the eyes. I feel that the morale is so low that we can barely face each other. The teachers are afraid to meet together. Their year-end get-together will be a miserable affair. It had always been festive, but now teachers are unwilling to contribute their share. Once something gives way, everything collapses. This is the bitterest pill I have to swallow. The graduation is next Sunday and I must prepare. I perform all my tasks mechanically.

JUNE 15, 1951

The *chaverim* have now seen the important personage, Klein. The entire matter is in his hands and he is a cold fish. As much as we pleaded for a reply before the graduation, to no avail. He won't call a meeting before Tuesday. Possibly he may not be entirely at fault. He has to take others into account. And the others consider the whole matter nothing but a nuisance, and little else.

God knows how we will be able to carry out the graduation in this atmosphere. We will have to summon up all our courage.

Today there was a disastrous fire in the French old folks' home and orphanage. Many were burned to death. One shudders at the thought. In a seventy-five-year-old building they housed more than 400 children and aged persons. Their philanthropists claim insufficient funds for these institutions. The point is, however, that these do-gooders act without heart or soul. Indeed didn't our do-gooder, Abe B., express himself at the Dominion Council: "Your school gives the best to the poor and the refugees, while we can hardly afford to provide them with bare necessities." In other words, those from the second rung don't deserve more. All the do-gooders have one face. They don't see the living soul in their midst, just a business to attend to. It seems as if all these matters are interrelated and tend to look alike.

JUNE 16, 1951

Gittel is improving. She will probably be able to get off the bed today and this calms my spirits. The fate of the school still hangs in the balance. On the one hand, it is hard to imagine that they will simply close the school in cold blood. Yet, on the other hand, it drags on; they have postponed the meeting once more.

Yechiel is enraged. He speaks of us as being the guilty party, and as a person of faith he questions why he must endure more than the elite and why we should suffer for the sins of the rich. At our father's *kiddush* he openly repeated his charges. Father, as is his habit, does not answer directly, but launches into a story. At the end of the story Father became thoughtful and continued: "Not too long ago I was shown in a dream that I stood with all my children beside a burnt out ruin, a hill of ashes, and opposite stood a well-lit house with open windows. Someone asked me, what is this? So I answered: This is a part of the Garden of Eden and we are only worthy of looking upon it. Again someone asked: Why can't we enter? So I responded: Primarily because we are alive; and secondly, because here rest all the souls of the incinerated, according to Hitler's edicts, may his name be blotted out, who have not intentionally entered paradise. They await the coming of the Messiah, and only then will they enter the true paradise."

Yechiel became enraged and he burst out, "I would rather that the establishment be put to the test, why is it always me?" So Father responded again, "It is written in *BaMidbar* that Dathan and Aviram, who held themselves high and suppressed their *Yiddishkeit*, were aids to Pharoah. When the Jews left Egypt they didn't go. Only when Pharoah and his army had been drowned did they arrive and commanded the sea to part because they were also sons of Israel. And that is what happened, all because they should be able to annoy Moses. And this continues to this very day."

I couldn't contain myself so I asked, "Where is this written?" Father suddenly showed great dissatisfaction and replied, "If I say so, it is written." And quickly began another story.

This story was obviously meant as a reprimand for me. So I justified myself by saying that I never questioned his memory, but when a holy text conveys such a critical pronouncement about Dathan and Aviram, then there must be similar matters that I would like to scrutinize. He then told me that the source might be in *Yalkut Shimoni* or *Yalkut Meiri*. Yechiel was overjoyed and I placated my father by saying that his storytelling offset his reprimand. These Sabbath stories should be noted, for there are pearls to be found among them.

JUNE 23, 1951

Was so upset and preoccupied all week that I had no opportunity to note things down. Today is the first day of summer vacation and the haze has not yet cleared from my mind. On the contrary, fatigue has set in and spirits are embittered. But at least I can find the time for these entries. I begin to feel a need to write. I'll begin by continuing the chronology.

The graduation ceremony was festive. A large audience attended. All felt the gravity of the situation and among our closest, one could sense their shuddering at the thought that this might be the last celebration of this kind for us. In my words to the assembly I spoke openly and candidly about the reasons for the crisis and why the community wishes to "punish" us. Spoke about the dignity of Yiddish and the ordinary simple folk, and the right of every child to a Jewish education, and the community's responsibility for this. The response from the audience was enthusiastic, but this audience has no influence and we doubt whether we can inspire them to take significant action. On Tuesday the 19th, we finally received the "good" word that the elite had decided to provide $31,000, which is meant to achieve the "great goal" of refinancing the school. Finally the school has been saved. Whether it can endure with the same spirit and drive is an open question. The conditions are onerous and partially humiliating. First of all, the teachers have to renounce their unpaid salaries of about $7,000. Of this year's salary, twelve and a half per cent will be withheld for one year and will be paid in the following year on the condition that there is a surplus after covering the annual budget. The budget for next year is reduced by $13,000. This means a reduction in school hours and the number of classes. It turns out that teachers' salaries will be reduced by 10 per cent. And this at the same time that other schools are awarding raises of 30 per cent to the English staff and 10 per cent to the Yiddish teachers. It looks like the community has decided that since we are what we are we should hunger a little. It is painful and bitter to swallow. The teachers will endorse this. Some will probably leave and the entire atmosphere will no longer be what it once was. We feel as if we have been condemned. In addition, Congress will install two of their representatives on our board of directors, evidently to keep an eye on us. And we have to promise to negotiate an amalgamation with the Folk Shule. All these things would not affect me were it not for the cut in teachers' salaries. While it amounts to large sums of money for some teachers – for myself alone it amounts to over $1,000 – it is more our feeling that the entire community, especially the most affluent, have decided that we must remain poor and be thankful for it. The press, no doubt, will have to report that a great deed has been accomplished. There is, of course, some truth to this. Especially the gesture of the *chaverim* to underwrite next year's budget to the amount of $10,000. It also marks a precedent that the community cannot allow itself to close a school. However, the cost to the teachers will probably not be reckoned by anyone.

    Wednesday and Thursday Zahler and I worked all day to prepare the documents. We spoke to people who were signatories and others who had to waive debts and loans. The same applied to the suppliers and creditors, to arrange payments over four years. It was easy to deal with the merchants, more difficult with personal loans from *chaverim*, and the most difficult for me was obtaining the teachers' signatures. The first to sign was Chava Singer, a dear woman, and when she had to write off the sum of more than

$500, I took it to heart and burst into tears. She attempted to calm me! With the others it was also difficult and some convincing had to be done, especially with those who had only spent one year with us, but in these cases I held firm.

The closing affair with the teachers was enjoyable for I had in my pocket the cheques that Zahler had signed. He told me: "This is the most gratifying signing of my entire life and I can now go peacefully on vacation." His face was radiant. I understand his joy, and rejoice with him, for it might have been far worse; we would have had to close up and gone on our way empty-handed, and suffer hunger too. There is not a great deal of joy left in me. I can't work myself into a happy mood. The pleasantries of the gathering, it seems to me, were a way of disguising our true feelings. It is even futile to bear the anger, since it won't alleviate the situation. We'll simply have to gird our loins for the next year and extricate ourselves from the feeling of bitterness.

Yechiel also spoke and told an interesting tale, which we'll have to retell in an artistic manner. A symbolic tale related by the Rizchiner Rebbe. We parted from the teachers who were setting out on their travels and those who were leaving the school. The most difficult was to say farewell to Chava. She will be sorely missed next year.

Closing the school on Friday morning, which is usually a pleasant task, I quickly said goodbye to the children in the classes. Even the distribution of the cheques gave no pleasure. The first reverberation of the salary cuts came with N.D.'s resignation. Reason: she can't accept less than teachers in other schools. Her husband earns little and they will look for work in another city. My impression is that she will actually search here and will find something. She simply says: "You want to maintain the school. I've been with you for only one year and am not obligated to take a reduced salary." One must also swallow this and it is most difficult. This poses a problem for me; if I were to fire a teacher without notice after having contracted with her earlier, wouldn't the whole world condemn me? And this is permitted to a teacher? In truth, in these circumstances I bear her no grudge and see it as part of the bitter pill I must swallow. Is all this worth it?

However there is one joyful event in all this: Gittel came home from the hospital yesterday. At least one happy event in such a long, long time. Had a lengthy conversation with Shoshana Deisenhaus. A dreamy young woman who sees the world so rosy. An only child who left her home in Toronto against her parents' wishes to study at the Teacher's Seminary. Now she is going to study at the Hebrew University in Jerusalem on a scholarship and won't complete her studies at the Seminary. I tried to make her understand the position of her parents and some of her teachers who disagree with her decision to leave the Seminary. Today a diploma is the main route to success and we must take that into account. Without a degree these days one is condemned to remain on the sidelines and left behind all the time. For myself, I feel that she ought to leave, but she must take care not to create a precedent of starting something and not completing it. She has already done this twice before. Among other things I told her that if she conceives her leaving for Israel as *chalutziut*, she must consider whether it is the *chalutziut* of settling the Negev, in which case she should not complain if refrigerators are not available. If, however, her *chalutziut* is in Tel Aviv, she should be disciplined in the work she undertakes and not flit from one project to another. She has matured considerably since her arrival at the Seminary. She is very idealistic and stands by her convictions, but I am doubtful whether she can stick to a single goal. Any strong spark can ignite her and draw her in various directions. It is a pity for her and us that we have nothing to entice her to stay here.

JUNE 25, 1951

Yesterday, the *Keneder Odler* came out with the headline: Peretz Shule is Saved. Reported in brief the details. Only now, when seeing them in print, the issues look so demeaning and difficult that it is a wonder we had the strength to accept. We were able to endure it because we wanted to avoid a catastrophe. The public has no inkling of this and sees only the facts – saved, and that's that; and pays respect to the "saviours." Even Rabinovitch, who knows the whole story, cannot do otherwise than pay compliments. The catastrophe is ended. Now begins the real work of maintaining the school. Once again, the teachers are the essential element. Our survival depends entirely on them.

JUNE 14, 1954

It has been three years since I made use of these journals. Was preoccupied with other matters, but in order to remember, and at least pour out my heart on the paper, I return once more to this form of writing. Once again a crisis. Possibly the most severe that I have ever experienced. Three years have passed with difficult financial and spiritual struggles. It has become more and more difficult to be a Jewish teacher and writer. So much of the banal all about and so much dishonesty amongst our inner and outer circles. In Montreal I often feel that I'm back in Tishevitz, Ustilla, or Ludmir. These last years have seen the arrival of Hungarian Jews in their full traditional costume with their fur-trimmed hats and long black coats. Accompanied by their energy and scorn for their surroundings, together with their extreme and incomprehensible piety that leads them to complete isolation, even from the Lubavitcher. With their cleverness and agility – supported by their Rebbe's force – they are toilers and are unafraid of manual labour. It's an odd experience to see in Montreal such Jews entirely outfitted in their ancient garb, lifting rocks at a construction site, riding around on a bicycle delivering parcels, or driving a truck.

They are a totally separate community, do not interact with anyone, and on a Sabbath day the whole neighbourhood between Fairmount and Bernard looks like a world of long ago. Children with long, curled earlocks are strolling with their fathers in their fur-trimmed hats. Small children play in the parks speaking Yiddish with their distinct dialect, which has a thousand charms and flavours. The Lubavitcher are more elegant and the *Merkaz HaTorahniks* are close to being modern-enlightened. They've all built *yeshivas* and offer accreditation for the rabbinate. They manage to attract a large number of the genuine orthodox, who are warmed in their presence, especially those who seek paradise and a good word from their Rebbe that will intercede on their behalf for their ordinary transgressions. These orthodox support the Chasidim financially and represent them in the community. And the whole to-do of artificial piety is once again in the saddle, precisely as it was once in Tishevitz. The manner is the same. They are always at each other's throats, plotting and scheming. The *shtreimel* quivers with arrogance, and the honest folk among them go hungry and are miserable. The glib-tongued poser sits front and centre, giving advice. Exactly like our circle, which has become so devitalized that there is no one to discuss anything with, it appears that they too are at an empty trough. They beat and claw each other over rotten eggs.

The educational institutions have actually climbed to new heights in these years, particularly the day schools, however a sadness and despair eats away at everything. Homes are arid, all parents crave a higher social status. Often you feel that you are surrounded by strangers; estrangement pervades all. The parents desire something, but can't describe it. From the State of Israel and Hebrew cultural groups, cold winds blow over our schools. Once again we will have to unfurl the ideological basis of our outlook – but we lack the energy to speak or to act. Somewhere along the line we obviously miscalculated. The Talmud Torahs have sheathed themselves with Hebrew, and try to espouse a kind of modern religiosity. Similarly, the congregational schools, which have expanded tremendously. They teach "Hebrew" and "Religion." In fact, this means mostly English, and the bit of Hebrew is dull, yet complies with fashion. The Folk Shule tries to adjust, chases after, and tries to outbid the Talmud Torah in Hebrew and even religiosity. We are left isolated with a complete Yiddish program and an orientation toward the common folk. All have converted their Hebrew studies to the *Sephardic* mode. Until this year we have not succumbed, but the pressure is great from parents as well as some new teachers who had been educated in *Sepharadit*, and we will have to follow. How this will affect the Yiddish studies remains to be seen. We have introduced a complete course on prayers. This came as a result of the gradual introducing of traditional subject matter into the curriculum. We feel that this brought us closer to the real prototype of a people's school. This cost us the support of a number of activists who were unrepentant radicals.

The danger to a school such as ours lies in the fact that the general public demands less studies so as not to tire the children, heaven forbid. Secondly, only a few children arrive with any knowledge of Yiddish, so that the evening school cannot manage to teach the language as it should. As for Hebrew, that's out of the question. The day schools are still able to achieve much. However, the larger the school grows, the more difficult it becomes to maintain it financially. The school system has outgrown the organizational capacity of their institutions. The teachers become more and more despairing. Their faith in their teaching leading to a creative life is diminished. They grow older, the new and younger teachers are not prepared – neither spiritually nor practically – to give some impetus to this matter. Meanwhile, the cynicism that is evident in the Hebrew system has not yet affected us, but we must fear it as well. We feel the need to make major revisions in our program, but don't know how. The activists have lost their faith in their mission; they recite as if in slumber the slogan "Jewish Education." Only a few individuals give the maximum effort, others comfort themselves with much less.

In the last three years I've had the feeling that we are slowly approaching a catastrophe that will either lead to the awakening of the small remnant that still takes these things seriously, or to mark the end of the Jewish school based on a folk philosophy with its support coming mainly from the people. Bit by bit, the neighbourhood surrounding the school is emptied of long-time residents and is filling up with new immigrants, harshly battered and deeply embittered. At the same time they are very concerned with the education of their children. From a financial viewpoint the position of the school becomes worse day by day. The number of children increases while the number of activists diminishes. They are exhausted by the constant battling with deficits – so they quietly leave us. Others have prospered and it embarrasses them to serve as leaders in an impoverished school. This, in addition to the spiritual crisis, makes it inordinately difficult to maintain the school. We are constantly having to defend ourselves before everyone for our Yiddish as well as our poverty.

Following our "rescue" by the Congress, which left us to struggle on our own in a pared-down condition, the teachers met the challenge – two years without a salary increase while all other schools provided raises. The new teachers acclimatize well and we appear to be one family. They help one another without complaint. They take pleasure from each other's achievements.

The atmosphere in general has been crisis-laden these last few years. It was evident that the affluent were dissociating themselves from the school. Only the poorer remain. Parents are for the most part newly arrived. Yiddish returns to its dominant position, but the financial resources continue to decline. The school's officers – except for Zuker – have somehow also lost interest. They are becoming more prosperous and are drawn to other social groups. And it is difficult to attract new people.

Among thoughtful teachers there is the feeling that it is not only a financial crisis. It is a spiritual crossroads and we must undertake a re-evaluation and we don't know how to go about it. Introducing a consistent program of prayer doesn't please everybody. The new problems of teaching; the pressures of Hebraism. All of these and more indicate that each one of us must make an individual accounting, while taking into account the consequences for the school. To some degree, and possibly to a much greater extent, the factors that have led to our depressed state derive from the veteran teachers' feelings that they have laboured for a lifetime barely supporting themselves without any security for the future. I myself share these dark pessimistic moods. A twenty-five cent piece still has value for me and I have remained a teacher of beginners. Only elementary teaching. I remain at a beginner's level, never having developed my own potential. Soon it will be too late.

An entire generation of Yiddish writers has died in the last few years. I am left alone – who knows for how long – and I haven't achieved anything yet. The book that I wanted to write remains unwritten. The children have grown up and I can't do anything to help them establish themselves. As a person, I wanted to provide for the whole world; as a father, nothing was provided for the children. Similarly, all teachers have their own private problems, aside from the general ones.

JUNE 15, 1954

Today received an answer from Congress that they cannot help us cover the $20,000 deficit that has accumulated over the past three years. They claim that we haven't kept our word and haven't balanced the budget. They will, however, negotiate with the Combined Appeal. But they themselves do not believe that they can accomplish anything. The general view amongst the opposition to the day schools is that since all the schools are in financial difficulty, now would be the time to squeeze out the weakest. It is too expensive an undertaking and the community cannot afford it. Parents alone must support the schools. Those who can't pay should be sent away; an end to the matter. This means that the schools would become institutions for the rich only. It is almost a year that we have been negotiating with them and detailing the reasons for our deficits. In addition to the basic poverty there is the issue of survivors' children. From 1946 to 1954 over 700 children of survivors studied in our schools at the cost of $115,000, while the income from their tuition amounted to $25,000. The school system is precarious because of the financial uncertainties. There is no united community fund for education. Each school acts independently. The wealthiest, the congregational schools, receive funds from their congregation; the Talmud Torah is supported by a number of wealthy men; the Folk Shule also has a number of the more affluent, while we have no such sources.

As a matter of fact, those schools hardly accept any pupils without tuition. It turns out that they conduct campaigns just for the well-to-do. Children of the poor, apparently, must remain outside.

For the last five years I've been warning our own Movement about this; I've written articles, but no one pays attention. Rabinovitch of the *Keneder Odler* helps, wears out his fingers, but no one listens. A kind of apathy has befallen everybody.

The *chaverim* from the Folk Shule haven't aided us by a single word in demanding some sort of unified community effort. There is even a suspicion that some of their *chaverim*, who are at the head of Congress leadership, are giving the impression that they too believe that our principled stand against sending away children for an inability to pay, and not to desert the neighbourhood like all others did, is not a proper one. They abandoned their evening school in this neighbourhood two years ago. Undoubtedly, with time, this neighbourhood will be emptied of Jewish children. But in the meantime we have over 500 children in our school, the majority of them, close to 70 per cent from this neighbourhood.

How can we refuse them when a large number of them are orphans, from broken homes, born in the displaced persons camps, or in Siberia. Some were rescued from the claws of the Nazis by devoted acts, or miracles. Their mothers are marked with numbers, crippled and disturbed. When I can free myself I will sit down and write about the histories of some of them. Every time such a child enrolls in this school it is both a celebration and a sadness. A celebration because I can provide them with some warmth, and a sadness because I know that finally we will arrive at the point when we will have to give in and close down. It is increasingly difficult for me to bear and to constantly drag along the teachers in the same uncertainty.

Before my eyes I see Sorele G. who was born on the night the Vilna Ghetto was liquidated (this was told me by her aunt, who brought her to us on a winter evening). A Christian nurse saved the infant in a sack, the mother perished. When the partisans entered Vilna years later, she gave the child up to them. Through many wanderings she ended up here. The aunt and her husband, the son of a well-known activist in Vilna, brought the child with the big brown eyes to me. Should I ask them if they can pay tuition? There are many such cases. I know that I am jeopardizing the school by accepting everybody. The greater the number of pupils the greater the risk of closing.

For an entire year I exhorted those close to the school: Do something; do the very utmost to prevent this. The parents, who remain active, are a loyal and devoted group, ceaseless in their efforts. But all this is insufficient. The "leaders" of the community declaim their support for education while demanding the closing of the school. At all the public assemblies of the Congress, I spoke, argued, and explained. So they regard me as nuisance, an incompetent, a beggar.

The other schools – especially the principals, Magid and Wiseman, who are devoted teachers – see that even a minor crisis or the anger of a prominent supporter can endanger their schools. So they too are frightened. However, they are fearful of community funding for education since it might diminish the independence of the schools. So they seek other options. A theory is postulated that since the majority of children find the day school program difficult by virtue of its four languages, only the brightest should be accepted, the others sent on to the afternoon schools. They choose to forget that those children will neither go to the schools nor benefit from them. The result will be that only the poor will not be accepted and they will be rejected by the day schools. It will not be the *IQ* but the dollar that decides. In this way they plan to save the schools, and give the elite an excuse to conceive of the day schools as exclusive. Their theory helps the opponents of the school system who have not for a long while dared to raise their heads. They now have a justification for not helping us tear down the walls of resistance to the school system. The rejection from Congress has therefore left me in a state of demoralization. The teachers wander about lost in anxiety since the majority of them face unemployment. Other schools will have no need for teachers since they too are reducing the number of classes and are dismissing a large number of their own teachers. We are instructed to balance the budget, which means closing the school piecemeal or completely.

JUNE 16, 1954

Today a meeting of the school board will take place to report on the negotiations with Congress. We were dragged along for a year and now no one knows what to do. The teachers haven't received any salaries for two months. There are no prospects for any funding.

From the Restitution Conference where we had applied on behalf of the refugee children, we were informed that this year they can do nothing for us. Possibly for next year. Only our dire needs brought us to them but there too the promises of help lie in the future. Meantime, all we get is sympathy like that from the local philanthropists. They offer sympathy but no help.

All morning I talked with Zuker looking for an alternative. He is totally lost, feels that our own Movement is apathetic and will not stand up for us. *Chaverim* Dickstein and Harvey, who are on the Movement's executive, have not only not helped, but intending to place the Folk Shule in an advantageous light, have distanced themselves from our principles. Doing so they actually harmed us. When I accused them and demanded that they deny their harmful actions, Dickstein brought a complaint against me to the Actions Committee and summoned me to a hearing of the Movement's court, to which I will gladly go. But they haven't called me. It is as if we were surrounded by nightmare. They, wishing to ingratiate themselves with the wealthy whose help they need in financing their new building, are evidently ready to sacrifice us. Is this being done with clear intent?

Zuker doesn't believe that an open conflict with Congress leaders will result in any benefit to us. Ordinary people will also not be ready to support us. According to him we should accept the decision to close the day school or leave a nucleus and wait out the crisis. He feels that in the end a community fund will be established; or the new council for Jewish day schools, which is mandated to discuss all matters except finances, will eventually receive a subsidy from the government. If we still exist at that time we will be able pursue our program – so he thinks.

My feeling, however, is that this will not save us. I can't and I won't accept this. His despair gives me more pain than all the rest. He is truly one in a generation who has shown such devotion. For over forty years he has been serving beyond his strength, and now in his discouragement he wishes at least to save our name. And how he was preparing himself to celebrate our fortieth anniversary, which should take place at the end of this year. Some celebration!

JUNE 17, 1954

Certainly this has not been the first sleepless night of this year, or of all other years that I have experienced at the Peretz Shule, but this night for me is a watershed. I am in the midst of drawing up my balance sheet as a teacher, a Yiddish writer, a member of the local community, and as a servant of the community.

It is three days before the graduation. Possibly the last one that I will attend. These words are now being written in tranquility. Inevitably, a last time must come. May it arrive while I'm in full consciousness. I'm soon going over to Rabinovitch to invite him to the graduation. The press should be present at such a splendid finale, and he, who understands the issues at stake, certainly should be present.

Last night's meeting was the most excruciating I have ever experienced. When I came home Sorke could barely recognize me. I could sense it in her stare. For the meeting had rendered such a hammer-blow to the core of my deepest feelings that it made my whole being feel on edge, not merely my teeth. There wasn't one voice of true protest or readiness to fight. Even those who protested could only shout helplessly. The others as if at a funeral were eulogizing a whole generation. The proposals to close or to cut the schools reverberated in my ears, heard as from a far distance; echoes of clods of earth falling into an open grave. That is how I felt last winter when clumps of frozen earth struck the plain casket of J.I. Segal. At the same time, right there and then, I began to make my own reckoning, which had already commenced three years ago. Then I agreed to cuts, slashes, compromises – as long as the building would remain. At the time I still saw a number of supporters for the school and saw the possibility of waiting out the bad times. The school remained intact; so the sacrifices were not in vain. Now, however, the majority of our supporters are exhausted, others cry out helplessly. The main leaders, like Miller and Craimer, would like to wash their hands of the entire matter. Things will become so reduced that they will not be blamed for their inactivity. Miller didn't even attend the meeting. Zuker, unfortunately, is completely lost; I actually fear for his health. What is the point of arguing with him. Zahler is ill, labouring to breathe.

Finally I took the floor and proposed the formation of two committees. One to investigate whether the following motions would be accepted: Is it possible to cut another $15,000 and still have a viable school? And second, what would be the consequences of closing down? The second committee would plan to arouse the entire community. Possibly, they might be able to effect a revocation of earlier decisions. If not, at least it will give us the opportunity not to close in silence but allow everyone to bear witness, in full view of the people.

All night long and all day today I keep asking myself one question: What is our sin? Why should we have to close? Aren't we still morally entitled to exist? When these are answered then my reckoning will be concluded. As is usual in such spiritual questions I turn to Yechiel to hear what he will say. But he too, at this moment, is depressed. Understandably, in contrast to myself, his faith is not undermined. He believes that in the end there will be a positive outcome, although he has no plan. He has no doubts about the moral value of the school and its principles.

So I start my reckoning from this point: Why did I involve myself with Jewish education for thirty-six years, almost thirty at the Peretz schools in Canada? What was I thinking of? In brief it meant: to further continuity, to become a link in the chain. All the means, and even the content, methods, and principles, were only there in order to achieve that goal. As a result, my pedagogical objective is that every child who wishes to enter the school, and thereby participate in this goal, must be accepted. My duty is not to ask for a passport or about finances. If I send away a child for these reasons then I am a desecrator of holy things. Where have I sinned? I have only carried out the mission that I assumed. This means that I am to be punished for realizing what the community, without asking or commanding, directed me to do. This could mean that even now the "leaders" are ignorant of the consequences of their actions. This has to to be openly stated. And if they are not listening, this would signify that a community doesn't exist. And if there is no community then I have no one to serve. So I have to abandon teaching.

In order to analyse these things I am obligated to wage a war of clarification. It is no longer an issue of $20,000 to cover the deficit, nor a question of balancing or not balancing the budget. The real issue is whether Jewish children should be driven out of a Jewish school. If that is the community desire, it certainly is not mine. I would leave, but before I do the community will hear me out. I owe an explanation to my colleagues, my pupils, and the entire community. From this moment on I have begun to know how to proceed. I instructed Tencer to assemble all the teachers to have a discussion. I hinted that the time had come for the teachers to issue a declaration to the press. I will not attend the meeting. It will be the first time the teachers have assembled without me. My reason: I have not yet formulated my stand, so my presence there would be of little help. Let their outcry come from themselves. I must have at least one free evening after these last few weeks of intense negotiations. I have to formulate specific strategies. At one time I was able to wage battles with other antagonistic parties and people of influence. I have to start thinking of this again.

JUNE 18, 1954

Said goodbye to the pupils of the evening high school, a well-knit group despite the limitation of their knowledge. Their development and interests are on a high level. They sensed in our tone of voice that this was more than a simple farewell of the teachers with their class. Bracha began her speech and burst into tears. Bit by bit the plans are clarified in my mind: at the graduation we have to reveal everything and call on the parents to write letters to the newspapers, telephone the Congress, telegraph the leadership of the Combined Jewish Appeal, picket the Congress, use the radio, and alarm the Jewish press outside Montreal. We must not close down in silence.

Tomorrow at the committee for public action I intend to make these proposals. We have to be careful to avoid debates; only explanations. At the budget committee I will oppose any cuts that will reduce or diminish the school by sending away children. The teachers have already prepared their declaration. I. Rabinovitch will write a column on Sunday. Lermer and Rabinovitch will try to become the mediators. The problem of unification with the Folk Shule has cropped up again. It would be very harmful if the Congress people succeeded in turning this into a feud between us and the Folk Shule. We will have to reckon with them at another time.

JUNE 19, 1954

Last night the Budget Committee met. Zahler came in from the country for this purpose. He looks extremely tired. They applied themselves to the cuts. The entire matter appeared to me as if each of them was trying to outdo the other with deeper cuts, thinking thereby that these measures would be our salvation. Even Zuker seems to have forgotten that this is really a slaughter rather than merely a contest to see who could make the greatest reductions. Someone proposes to send away all children from grade four and upward. Zuker states that even though this would mean that his grandchildren could no longer attend the school, he would be prepared to support it in an effort to salvage something. Another suggests eliminating the evening school. Miller is neither for nor against. Zahler is silent.

I had to speak candidly: this is not the way to save the school. It only means that we ourselves are closing down the school. Accepting this plan would mean the saving of just four walls. They oppose this strategy of struggle since it would most definitely lead to the closing of the school. I had to respond: if things are as they describe them, that everything is against us and no other road is open to us, then the only avenue left is to speak out about the issues. Let the people hear us and judge our case. And if there is no community – then there is no point at all in our struggle to exist. I would never agree – nor would the teachers – to drive away Jewish children from the school. Those who can do this are free to do so. We will not be there. If they want to accept such a plan they will have find a principal and teachers to carry it out.

Zahler proceeded to summarize our situation: we have no choice but to inform Congress that we cannot carry out their plan. We would then be left without a school. Let us, therefore, allow the teachers to continue their work as they see fit. Everyone felt, it seems to me, as if a yoke had been lifted. At the graduation ceremony all the speakers will clarify the situation. That will be the occasion to call on the parents for action.

JUNE 21, 1954

The graduation ceremony had many stirring moments. We made every effort to avoid turning it into a sad or protest demonstration. The speeches explained the situation. Zuker, in sorrow; Miller with a few strong words. I spoke firmly about the principle that is involved in our case and called upon the leaders of the other schools to recognize that we are fighting for all the schools. Why are they looking on from afar? Are they all so afraid? My main theme was that if there is no community and no one cares, then "Berel the tailor" can no longer serve. There is no one left to serve. I called on the parents to take the initiative.

Speaking as a teacher who candidly expressed his personal version, they told me that mine was a proud speech. The children also spoke impressively and it was painful to consider that this might be – God forbid – the last time.

All day today our *shtetl* was in an uproar. Parents are organizing themselves, phoning the Congress and other institutions, and writing letters. Rabinovitch and Lermer are negotiating with the Folk Shule and with Hayes. Nothing has changed there. Telegrams have been sent to prominent leaders, including one to Bronfman. Plans for further public action are being prepared.

JUNE 22, 1954

All day my office looks like a military headquarters. Every group that is involved comes in to give reports. The parents work very effectively. Congress responds clearly. They recognize that the matter will not simply disappear. Hayes sent a clarification to the *Keneder Odler* explaining what they had done in the past and that it would be impossible for them to do any more. The community has no funds.

This response is beyond laughter. They are not even ashamed. We are forced to balance the budget. Reduce the school population, etc. I'll answer and give them my view on the way they saved us! That the teachers and individual school activists did more than the entire community. And question whether $15,000 is such an enormous sum. Still, we must not let ourselves be drawn into a public fight.

Lermer tells me that when Bronfman received the telegram he phoned Hayes from the airport and advised him not to take any hasty steps. To wait until his return within a week.

Pressure is put upon me to see Hayes. I'll see him only when he has made some proposals. The delegation of parents who saw Hayes made an impression on him. He promised them that he would have a meeting on Friday and would report back to them.

JUNE 23, 1954

There was a large gathering of the school's committees last night, the atmosphere was tense but serious, ready for action. It was decided that if by Friday there was no answer we would begin to picket the Congress building. Utilize the radio and the English press and raise the alarm in the foreign Yiddish press. No children should be used in this campaign. The gathering was very angry with the Movement and with the Folk Shule.

All week no one from the Movement even called me. From the teachers, only one, Mendelsohn from the Adath Israel. Quite an honourable city, it turns out to be. Are they all afraid? Or do they consider that we are wrong? How can that be?

Looking for outside help it occurred to me to approach L. Segal by phone in New York to ask Dr Nahum Goldmann to intervene. It turns out that Goldmann is not in New York and through the World Jewish Congress nothing can be done. However Segal will see if something can be done. He was very disturbed by the whole affair – "Oh, what a catastrophe" – he exclaimed when I began our conversation. "You will hear from me today." At five o'clock I received his telegram informing me to contact Judah Shapiro, director of the cultural division, of the "Reparation Conference" at once. Judah wanted information about the justification for their granting us a one-time sum. Despite the fact that they had previously rejected us, they would now see what they could do. I pointed out to him our expenditures for the refugee children. This year alone approximately $30,000. Previous years about $115,000. He promised to do something. He will let me know by this Friday noon. It begins to be brighter now. Today we ended the evening school term, let's hope this will not be permanent. We must keep the pressure up locally, but we must restrain ourselves from taking the issue into the streets. We must not overplay our hand.

JUNE 24, 1954

Chaver White has become the unofficial mediator between the parents' committee and Hayes. He let Hayes know what we plan to do if they don't accede. Also intimated that we would stop at nothing. The Yiddish-Anglo press supports us editorially.

The situation is tense. The politicians who received telegrams want to know what they can do. Crestohl, the member of Parliament, is angered, but his anger happens to serve our purpose. He wrote a silly letter of protest to us and a copy to Hayes.

This evening the farewell to the teachers will take place. The mood is joyless. I'll have to outline for them in brief that there appears to be a way to strengthen the school.

Meanwhile Shaffir has gone to the hospital for an operation. Tomorrow Soreh must undergo a serious operation. May it all end well. When things happen they come from all directions.

JUNE 25, 1954

This morning we closed the day school with a short address out in the school yard and the singing of the anthems. I hope that we will open the schools in more joyful spirits. The children were playful as they always are on the last day of school. Holiday-spirited, exhilarated, but the gloomy atmosphere remained. In the minds of most were the same unexpressed thoughts. The gloom was manifest at the farewell gathering and the exchange of gifts. Last evening the teachers' farewell was also sad. Yisroel, as is his nature, was angry at everybody and everything. I had to serve as mediator; one has to see all this retrospectively and in perspective. The fate of Jewish schools is inescapably like the fate of all things creative. It is a bitter fate but it is also the strength that sustains everything of importance. In ambivalent terms I related the more positive outcome. The essence is: We are morally justified and therefore must persist.

Today at noon, Judah Shapiro telephoned. The National Foundation for Jewish Culture will provide $10,000 as a special grant. Future subsidies will depend on formal application. This is an unexpected source of aid. When we receive it we'll be able to negotiate once again with the Congress.

Meanwhile, Hayes responded to the Parents' Committee that the Congress meeting had made no decisions. Unless we balance the budget they won't be able to cover the deficit. They are relenting slowly. Soon we'll be in a better position to negotiate. It looks like they are waiting for Bronfman. In the evening Zuker called from Philadelphia. He is attending the Poalei Zion conference. Shapiro promised him that the arrangements he spoke of would be honoured. Chaim Pomerantz let me know from New York that he would see to it that a group of writers and the Congress for Yiddish Culture would intervene on our behalf. In the interim no drastic measures will be undertaken. We must give them the opportunity to wait for Bronfman's return. My answer to Hayes is prepared and will be published on Sunday!

JUNE 26, 1954

The first day of vacation, but still no feeling of holiday. I am calmer and more confident but, as yet, still far from being able to relax. The entire matter is ultimately tortuous. Is this the way to build a Jewish life, which is disintegrating in our hands? With these resources? Like pulling teeth.

Went to visit Rochl Korn at the convalescent home. She had heard what was happening and about our conduct. She is ecstatic. She stated that she is encouraged whenever she sees that there is still someone capable of standing up for the Jewish child and for matters of principle. The more she praises me the more I sense her own despair. The despair of the Yiddish poet and Yiddish artists.

Simple Jews, ordinary women, came in to console me all this week. The sense of helplessness spills out of everyone. There obviously are still Jews who hold us in respect, but they are without power. They cry out and then crawl back to their corners. A parents' delegation had a meeting with the chief rabbi of the city, Rabbi Herschorn. He told them that he has no influence at all. Who would listen to a rabbi anyway? And why don't they build a school in a rich neighbourhood. What a stroke of genius! He suggested that if they could find another rabbi who was willing, he would accompany him to plead our cause.

Lermer, who has extended himself on our behalf, is also dejected. Each time he calls his voice sounds mournful. So I console him. Just as Sholem Aleichem's Tevye consoles Menachem Mendel in Yehupitz when he discovers him disillusioned and starving. A pitiful sight.

Zuker telephoned from Philadelphia to say that Segal had arrived from New York and told him that the arrangements have been carried out. We will receive $10,000. Now we must try to reorganize the school for the coming year. It will be difficult to hire teachers. Many have already taken on new positions. Others are afraid to crawl into such a shaky edifice.

I guess Zuker was right when he introduced me at the graduation as the captain of a leaking ship. At least the loyal teachers remained. Nevertheless several left because they left the city or are giving up a teaching career. It is difficult to find new teachers.

Meanwhile we have to encourage the New York writers to speak out. I contacted Selchen in Winnipeg, asking him to participate.

JUNE 27, 1954

Had a committee meeting where it was decided that until Wednesday nothing more than letters to the editor. Letters are appearing in the English press. My declaration made an impression. Someone sent me a box of candy. Parents don't believe that the school will close. They are registering their children, particularly for the afternoon school. We are preparing our plans for next year. I telephoned Schneider of the Farband. Why do they remain silent? It turns out that he knows nothing. I phoned Cheifetz of the Actions Committee. How come they do nothing and some of their leaders are actually doing harm. His answer was that their main leader, Dickstein, refuses to take up the question. So I wrote to them and that's how matters now stand. The bureaucrats are fearful of the boss. At the same time I was invited to participate in a conference on education sponsored by the Actions Committee. A fine comedy.

JUNE 30, 1954

A meeting was held of our administration committee. Zuker reported that Shapiro promised that the grant had been processed. Any day we should receive a letter confirming the grant. We decided on our strategy – decided to wait till Friday. If Congress does not produce a plan we should reopen the negotiations on the basis that we can assure next year's budget. They should cover the current deficit. My point of view – that we can't compromise the principle – was adopted.

All day tried to locate Hayes without success. Turns out that he had simply taken his daughter to summer camp. For him this is not a burning issue; what transpired between him and Bronfman we don't know. We'll have to wait till Friday.

JULY 2, 1954

The letter from Shapiro arrived. We'll receive $5,000 now and $5,000 in September. They obviously want the assurance that the school will definitely reopen. His letter states that this is a non-renewable grant, so we should not expect them to provide funds in the following year. But privately he told Zuker that we should reapply and request further funding. He should be supplied with details and he'll see what he can do. Zuker called Hayes about this. It seems that Hayes knew about this arrangement and would like to see our committee on Monday. Our bargaining is just about to begin.

I wrote letters of appreciation to Segal and Shapiro.

Received a telegram from J. Pat saying that they had appealed to Congress in the name of the Congress for Yiddish Culture signed by Leivick, Opatoshu, Niger, and Pat. This is splendid. Let them know that the address of the Peretz Shule is not only on Duluth. It is an address for Yiddish culture in general and touches everyone. We are not as isolated as they think.

Spent all day convincing the newly hired teachers that they have no reason to fear.

Soreh was to be released from the hospital but the doctor decided to keep her there. We are very worried. May everything turn out for the best.

My fatigue is becoming more evident. It seems that following great tension comes the aftermath. As usual, it drives me to melancholy. I cannot discern what presses on me the most, and can find no inner peace. Reading is beyond me. As if a heavy stone were pressing on my spirits. Who knows what awaits us.

JULY 6, 1954

Yesterday the cheque for $5,000 arrived from New York. Immediately we paid the teachers' salaries for the month of May; several for June. This lightens my spirits a little. The mood among the teachers is slightly improved. But we have difficulty hiring new teachers; they have no confidence in us. I still need an English teacher for grade 7.

Zuker met with Hayes. It looks to him that they haven't made any definite decisions. The argument that the $10,000 that we received will make it easier for the Congress to cover the deficit has not yet had an effect. No assurances were received. Zuker is pessimistic, but not as bad as earlier when he was ready to give up, and now maintains that we should continue to fight. We should start to adopt bolder methods so that they won't think that everything has quietened down.

At the meeting of the Administrative Committee, Zuker gave his report. He recommended that we wait for Hayes' answer, which is promised within the next two days. Following the discussion it was adopted that a committee of Miller, Craimer, and myself would meet with Hayes and state clearly that we can no longer wait and must have a decisive answer. Most importantly, two issues must be clarified: First, that the $10,000 is not sufficient to allow us to open the school; and second, failing their help, we'll be forced to condemn them harshly in the Yiddish and English press. They clearly understand that we will not remain silent. They will be responsible for the consequences.

A resolution to discount the second post-dated $5,000 cheque in order to pay the teachers' salaries was postponed until after the discussion with Hayes. The teachers as usual bear the burden of the school and its difficulties. The atmosphere is once again gloomy. Those parents who telephoned the Congress were told to phone the school and the school would tell them that they can survive. An odd tactic. I told the parents to write more letters, this time especially to the *Star*. In any case letters appear daily, but more are needed.

This afternoon we were supposed to meet with Hayes, however I was in the hospital all morning during Soreh's second operation. Yechiel is terribly upset. I had to sleep at his house last night. I couldn't sleep at all, because of the new developments, Yechiel's condition, and the stale air in the house. They even have a cat that performs all her functions in the house.

I was so exhausted and mentally depleted that I couldn't gather my thoughts to participate in such a meeting with Hayes. Although the doctor reassured us that Soreh's illness was caught in time, nevertheless our anxiety is overwhelming. A hidden fear oppresses us. Despite this I accompanied Miller, but sensed in his words that all the confidence that he showed at last night's meeting had totally evaporated and he is no longer prepared to transmit the decision of our meeting as we understood it. He said that it seemed to him that it would be advantageous if I wasn't present this time so that there would be one person who remains unimplicated in the case, and at the last moment he could reopen negotiations. I allowed myself to be convinced and remained in the car.

I realized that when the staff of the Congress left their work, they would see me sitting in the car and it would appear very strange. So I went out for a walk. But ironically those whom I especially wanted to avoid were the ones who noticed me. Hayes came out with Dr Horowitz and jokingly said: So you are gaining entry through the back door. We both smiled and Hayes said if you are waiting for Miller and Craimer, they will come out soon. I thanked him and walked on. From his tone and flushed face, I felt that the answer had been negative and bitter. Ultimately, it looks as if I'll have to speak to him face to face. Miller and Craimer emerged in a distraught state. Craimer with a certain satisfaction: "I told you that without cuts, funding would not be made available." "They have no other plan," Miller added. We must now seriously consider what is to be done. From the details of their account it became clear to me that in Hayes' dealing with them he is very formal, deprecated them, and is patronizing. Because they too are concerned only with the financial picture, and do not defend the moral principle properly, they could not justify the reasons for our opposition to certain cuts. He runs circles around them and they are left in the rear. I told them that it looks like we have to fight publicly and fiercely. So let it be! A meeting must be called tomorrow. But before that meeting takes place, I must meet with Hayes to be able to gauge where we actually stand.

They did not serve the ultimatum. Hayes simply said that on the 14th the inner executive would discuss the matter once more. A positive decision is doubtful; according to them, near negative. We must be prepared for that.

JULY 7, 1954

Contacted Hayes for an appointment. He said that he would be pleased to see me, and we met at 4:00 p.m. I explained the true reasons for not meeting him at the committee meeting yesterday and that I would like to clarify certain matters that our representatives were unable to clear up.

Met with Rabinovitch and thoroughly reviewed the whole situation. Gave him the telegram that the Farband had sent to the Congress for Yiddish Culture signed by S. Niger, H. Leivick, Y. Opatoshu, and J. Pat. The publication of this document should initiate the revival of public action. Sent letters to *Der Tog* and the *Forward* in the name of parents. We must publicize things in the "broader" world. Rabinovitch also believes that we must return to pressure tactics, but doesn't know how to proceed. The attitude of our own Movement is also incomprehensible to him.

Met Berman in the street, but he turned aside. Not the customary greeting, when he seeks to display his learning and his cultural attainments. They must be ashamed of their treatment of us. By contrast, the ordinary folk and those far removed from our cause find ways to support me. A strange world.

Wrote an open letter to all school activists, teachers, and community leaders. It had the tone of farewell after all these years of work, and it pointed out that this was actually a struggle for the existence of the entire school system. It is a fight for the principle of community support for day schools. Let them not deceive themselves by thinking that the reason for the lack of support is simply incidental; this is the way that the anti-Yiddish, anti-day school, anti-community school supporters find their opportunity to destroy the school movememt. Their silence, I openly charge, is the way in which they participate in the undermining of the school system. It marks the beginning of the end of the whole affair. I hope that this letter will never have to be printed, but in case it does, it won't bring happiness to anyone, nor honour either. I must be prepared to tell the truth as I see it.

Zuker suggested that we summon the Relief Committee to the Rabbinical Council to expose the fact that the fund has money but uses it for other purposes rather than education. What a scandal would result if this were known to the general public. I greatly doubt whether the rabbis would choose to stand up to the Establishment. I don't know a single one of them with the courage to take up such an issue. I don't have the sense that there is anyone we can turn to, who would risk taking our side, who would be unafraid.

Such a still silence, such hypocritical pretense, and no one except the ordinary folk want to change the "reign of silence." Everybody acts friendly in this hypocritical atmosphere, and that is difficult to change.

JULY 8, 1954

Spent about two hours yesterday with Hayes. He received me in a very friendly way, and wanted to convince me of the difficulties he has encountered in this matter. His version fits well with my own assessment of the situation. Certainly it is not a question of the hardship of raising funds, but rather that the leadership that he meets with are not interested in Yiddish, are opposed to day schools, are against the principle of community responsibility, and the idea that education should be available to all regardless of their ability to pay. Precisely my words. He is therefore convinced that on the local scene nothing can be achieved. Unless Sam Bronfman gets involved. He is inclined to help but is out of town and by the time he returns it will be too late.

He tried to convince me that he is attempting to get money through the Relief Fund. Next week there is an official meeting where this question will be definitively decided. He hopes that he will be able to get results. He reviewed all the plans that had been proposed and he acknowledged that all of them would result in the crippling of the school. I indicated to him that if the plan includes the sending away of children and teachers then I will leave with the teachers and pupils. He let me know that indeed I was right but that's how things stood.

I informed him that he should know that the school would not be closed in silence and the entire responsibility will be theirs. It seems to me that he has a good grasp of the situation and would like to avoid an open fight. I immediately related this discussion to Rabinovitch and it seems that he too had learned from other sources that the whole matter was one of principle.

JULY 9, 1954

Today Rabinovitch published his "Good Morning" column in which he doesn't mince words, stating that the matter is one of principle and can no longer be postponed. He argues sharply with them and promises that he will not let the issue rest. He is inspired by a letter received from a parent that asks accusingly: "Has he become weary and abandoned the parents?" He reassures the parents that he will stand by them. The letter was inspirational and it was effective.

Sent letters to *Der Tog* and the *Forward* with clippings from local newspapers. I feel that a bit of external pressure will encourage them to agree to accede to our demands. Morally they already see that we are in the right. Hayes acknowledged this himself. Our own *chaverim*, however, still have no courage. They refuse to discuss the other $5,000 that would enable us to pay another month's salary to the teachers. The satiated have no empathy for the hungry. The Farband has finally decided to publish a resolution calling on the Congress to act.

JULY 12, 1954

The end of the week turned out to be more difficult. A meeting at Unzer Camp of the Actions Committee. They discussed the school question. *Chaverim* complained about the fact that there was insufficient religious teaching and not enough *chalutziut*. Some thought that the Talmud Torah was adequate for them. After so many years we still need to sell our school philosophy to our own *chaverim*.

Had a sharp exchange with Wiseman and Dickstein concerning their attitude toward day schools and afternoon schools. Wiseman seethed with accusations that he is misunderstood and lies are actually circulated about him. The more he denies, the more one can see how harmful are his actions. He puts words into the mouths of the enemies of our school system and day schools. They also took up the Peretz Shule problem. Zuker bitterly accused our own *chaverim*. Dickstein spoke overheatedly to the issue, but his words went unheeded. A resolution was passed to send a committee to Congress in the name of the Movement, demanding aid. The meetings were agonizing, as if our own *chaverim* desired to see our demise. And the Torontonians who were present remained silent. And they call this a unified Movement. Quick to offer advice.

Sunday met at Ivry with a few of our school activists to respond to the memorandum that Hayes had prepared and to decide on further action. It turns out that they are calling a special meeting about the matter, so we must supply more statistics, etc., and I worked on this all day. What disturbs me most is the fact that the school activists no longer seek ways to help us but put all their faith in the negotiations that drag on and on and on. I am so tired of all this that I can hardly concentrate on anything.

JULY 16, 1954

This afternoon the special meeting with Congress was held. The whole congregation was there: M. Garber, Lavy Becker, M. Robinson, Rabbi Schuchat, B. Beutel, S. Harvey, A. Bronfman, Y. Reich, S. Hayes, Unterburg, and our representatives, Miller, Craimer, and me. I. Rabinovitch represented the press. Right from the beginning Garber conducted the meeting in such a way that put us on the defensive. We had to demonstrate to them that we have the ability to function. All the arguments point in one direction: day schools are a luxury. The fact that afternoon schools also create a deficit was not seen as an issue for them. Poor children need not receive such an education. Beutel, the leading Talmud Torah activist, maintains that we should discontinue parallel classes and send away children, thus reducing numbers. The community has no funds. Garber asserts that poor children have always received a lower quality education. And he was once a socialist! The $10,000 we received should be used for this year's budget. It looks like the aim of the meeting was to show that we have to finance ourselves and we are incapable of that – so we are to blame for closing the school. They are insulted by our publicizing the matter in the newspapers. All our claims that the issue must be discussed in its entirety fell on deaf ears. Bronfman mutters that there is no need for any of this; it's a bad business. Beutel speaks and speaks without saying anything. Becker actually said a few words in our favour but he left, so he could avoid standing up for them. Rabinovitch remained silent. He appears to be tongue-tied in their presence. Harvey wanted to give the impression that he sided with us, but everybody could see that it was just talk. If it wasn't so tragic it would have been comical, the manner whereby the "leaders" couldn't find a solution for this miserly sum. The child is entirely lost from view. No one takes heed of this. It is merely talk about Jewish education. The meeting sort of dissolved itself without results.

Spoke on the phone with Hayes to make sure that I had understood correctly. If we found a way to cut expenses by another $5,000 they would cover the deficit. He confirmed that that was a correct assumption.

JULY 17, 1954

The more I think about yesterday's meeting, the more I hold myself guilty. Although logic dictates that I couldn't have acted differently, that I could not have influenced them with emotions but only with arguments based on statistics and down-to-earth facts, nevertheless I feel guilty that I didn't reveal to them the whole truth as I see it, as it lay on my tongue: that Jewish children are not to be measured by coins, a selection is not to be made. Others have done this for us. It is true that I did tell them that I didn't become a Jewish teacher in order to drive away Jewish children from school, but that wasn't sufficiently pointed. I should have told them that they weren't equal to their roles. But each time I wanted to say that I saw before me the children's eyes and the broken spirit of the teachers: Don't break the last straw, maybe something can be rescued with gentle words, with a convincing, business-like approach. But I am not convinced that I did the right thing by not banging on the table, foaming at the mouth. These doubts make it difficult for me to decide on the appropriate action for further negotiations – to speak out harshly or to continue the negotiations through arguments.

JULY 19, 1954

I wrote a letter to M. Garber setting forth our arguments and the moral principles that uphold them. I pointed out that I consider this a private letter, but if the negotiations went nowhere I would make the letter public. I also informed him that I will revise the budget but not by cutting classes or sending away pupils. I hope that his ego will counsel him to renew the negotiations.

JULY 20, 1954

Today received a letter from Garber. Jokingly he wants to give the impression that the letter did not influence him. Nevertheless it is clear that he was affected by it, since he is ready to take up the problem again if we will revise the budget so that it is more or less balanced. So the letter worked.

I didn't tell anyone about the letter to Garber and his reply. It's a pity that I must play politics with my own *chaverim*.

JULY 22, 1954

Miller has made the contact. Garber has called a meeting of the Congress for next Wednesday. It looks brighter than it was. He told Miller about the letter. So obviously it affected him.

Now is the time to travel and take a rest. We'll go down to the ocean for about ten days. I hope we'll be able to rest. Soreh has also returned from the hospital. She has to take special radium treatments. Their summer is already wasted. As long as she regains her health. Tomorrow we have the opportunity to get a ride to Old Orchard on the Atlantic.

AUGUST 6, 1954

Last Monday I returned from our ocean holiday. The route is beautiful. Mountains, valleys, and cliffs, mute and white, that seem to speak in their silence: See what you are missing by remaining in one spot. And see, too, how worthless are all your thoughts in contrast to my eternal silence.

The sea in particular is a mute narrator that loses all control twice a day and still remains in the same place. Leaves room for thousands of naked bodies to oil themselves in the sand and bake in the sun.

It was not a restful trip. Too great a tumult. Dismal surroundings with petty distractions to while away the time; and still my mood was restless. Especially since my writing was completely blocked. I can barely write a letter. And when there is no writing there is no rest. There is no inner peace. It seems to me that I am even more tired than I was.

According to Miller's telephone conversation, the meeting with the Establishment once more came to nothing. The same charges: keep on cutting, you haven't cut enough. We have no money. Try to continue to swim against the current. For how long?

AUGUST 13, 1954

Last Sunday we held the consultative meeting in the country at Zahler's house. Indeed, a wonderful house right on the lake with a view that is rare even for the Laurentians. Such a restful calm. It's a pity that they came to this only in their old age and can hardly enjoy it now. It was a bitter meeting. We will use this half year to continue pressuring the Congress, to obtain from them what is possible. If we are unsuccessful then we will be able to give the teachers enough time to look for new positions. Following a proposal by Zuker, that we immediately inform Congress of our decision in a memorandum and publish a declaration in the *Keneder Odler*, the motion was adopted.

Tuesday, Sorke and I spent several hours at the Zahlers at their invitation. It was most pleasant. Simple, intelligent people of the highest moral standing. Zahler remains one of the few recent supporters who thinks about the school and not only at meetings, and who is prepared to face the consequences of the situation. His influence on Miller and Craimer is always beneficial.

Today I submitted the declaration to the newspaper, which I composed with the help of Tencer. He has a good sense for clarity and the precise expression of ideas. Also sent out an application to "The Conference for the Rehabilitation of Nazi Victims" in New York. In principle I believe that we should take money from Germany. Nevertheless I would not wish this money in particular to be the salvation of the Peretz Schools. Montreal should be supporting the Peretz Schools. I will not forgive any of the local leaders or my own *chaverim* of the Movement for the fact that we are forced to be beholden to these monies.

I was invited to speak on education at the Congress conference in Western Canada. The Actions Committee is holding its conference in Winnipeg at the end of this month, where they will be discussing education. I can't convince myself to attend either of them. I am too tired and embittered to be able to speak calmly on these matters. No one is prepared to listen to my words. Even our closest can't tolerate it. Lately I sense this every time I speak. Everyone utters clever words to calm the conscience of the Establishment – who get away only with words. But I'm not obliged to join them. I don't have to be present at the Actions Committee in order to protest their handling of the affair. I have prepared a letter to them explaining the reasons for my not attending. Before I do, I would expect deeds indicating their seriousness. I refuse to serve a Movement that is not a Movement, nor a community that is not a community. What I can do in my own corner I will do. Enough of helping to enhance the prestige of those who only talk.

SEPTEMBER 9, 1954

School was opened yesterday. The number of children has diminished. Many parents found it tiresome to be constantly associated with poverty, which involved continual begging. Others would rather not fight for survival and have stopped coming. And others simply can't pay and put off registering. The result is fewer children in the day school and kindergarten. The afternoon school has lost more than ever before. The increase in the beginning classes is quite good, but this won't cover the loss. We'll have to think seriously about building afternoon schools in new neighbourhoods. Unless we install a taxi service for the afternoon schools as well. The afternoon school diminishes by the fourth year. The senior classes have few pupils. The school board meeting took place. Not well attended, but there is a sense of determination to do something and survive.

SEPTEMBER 16, 1954

Received a letter from Hayes complaining that we had sent the declaration regarding the opening of the school that states that we hadn't received any help from the local organizations, when, according to him, we received funding years ago. According to him, it would appear that we should have acknowledged their past contributions, and the fact that they aren't helping us now is not relevant. But if our stating that they have not helped still causes them discomfort, this is a sign that there is still a beating pulse.

OCTOBER 10, 1954

Now Y. Opatoshu is no longer with us. The last giants of a great generation, which had a lovely and glorious beginning, are passing away. Departing with question marks on their lips and on their faces the fear that they have no successors. Their treasure remains – but for whom?

We are already so few in number that there is no one to cling to. Since Friday, when we first heard about the tragedy, I've been going to see Rochl, who waits impatiently, and we both look like frightened lambs on whom fate has already passed judgment. We can't even bleat. We can only remain silent.

The few years that still remain should be devoted to writing that which nobody who follows us will be able to write. Where does one obtain strength, patience, time, and a bit of faith?

OCTOBER 22, 1954

H. Goldenberg, a member of the board, persuaded me to speak on Jewish education to his branch of the Unitas Lodge of the Knights of Pythias. Lately I've had no desire at all to speak in public. I have too many doubts myself to be able to speak to others, especially before assimilated Jews. On the other hand I reconsidered: let them hear a Yiddish word. Probably the first time they were addressed in Yiddish. I arrived only to find a locked door, with their emblem on it. Looks like an antique coin signifying fraternity. The uninitiated may not enter when they are conducting their affairs, which involve their charitable projects. Each of those present wears a ribbon or a medal according to their rank. Looks like a costume drama about the caste system. Finally they concluded about eleven o'clock. Which means that the secret meeting was over, and the outsider was permitted to enter. So I entered. The chairs were set up on either side in rows, in the centre a table. On the table lay a family Bible (New and Old Testaments) in English, edited by some reverend, published in the eighteenth century, bound in leather with brass clasps. On both sides of the Bible, two tin swords. They swear on these and perform their rituals. At the front, a table with the chairman and a book of instructions for the lodge on how to open and close their meetings with the proper rules of order. Banal prayers and phrases. Facing the chairman, another table for the second-in-command, who is wearing a heavy brass emblem with a sash. Games for grown children.

When my turn came to speak to them I couldn't control myself and told them that they ought to have their own Tanach. All of them understood Yiddish. They knew about Jewish education and a number of them send their children to Jewish schools. Most of them are hard-working businessmen and professionals who want to relax for an evening and are not interested in serious matters. They want to indulge in a bit of philanthropy and be done with it. Only one of them asked a question about *Eretz Yisroel,* which had not behaved properly toward Jews who had come to fight in the war against the Arabs. The entire evening was bizarre. Lost Jews who are totally confused. But they do want something. If there were some sort of serious cultural organization with an ideology, it could attract such Jews. They were attentive and many later told me that they long for a Yiddish word. But others barely comprehended. Look what happens here to the Jewish people when they actually aspire to something Jewish.

OCTOBER 31, 1954

Today was the formal opening of the new Folk Shule on Van Horne. A magnificent building. A pleasure to see how the aims and actual accomplishments have brought us out of the cellars to these heights. Even more joyous was the sight of some of the founders, like Parnass and Dickstein, on the stage. It can also be seen as a kind of achievement because amongst those who brought greetings were the establishment figures, many of whom had recently looked down on schools of this kind. Also Rabbi Herschorn pronounced the blessing, a sort of prayer in the American style. Today, this is required. Present too were a few politicians, which indicates that they are needed.

NOVEMBER 21, 1954

Yesterday I spoke at the memorial meeting for the town of Shebreshin. The audience numbered about twenty or thirty. In their town they were in the Bund, Poale Zion, Communist Party, and in the Jewish library. They were community oriented and were preparing for an active role. Here they are scattered like dust, lost. They gather here to remember their home with its nearly thousand years of tradition, and now they must be beginners again.

That region was both geographically and spiritually a symbol for all of Eastern European Jewry. It defended itself against the Asiatic hordes and spiritually bound Jews to past generations. In those forests and caves lie hidden the harsh life endured by Jews among the indigenous peoples, as well as the hope for salvation. As it was in Tishevitz with her mythic Messiah ben Yosef, so Shebreshin with her cave that led to *Eretz Yisroel,* and also Zamosz with its fortress. In modern times Zamosz produced *maskilim* like Peretz; Shebreshin gave us Yaacov Reifman and her youth, which announced: Our Movement is the new house of prayer. And in the time of our recent destruction the Jewish officials did not collaborate but died the death of martyrs. That's more or less what I tried to express. Did they fathom this? God knows.

DECEMBER 5, 1954

I no longer have the desire to conduct a prolonged struggle that leads nowhere, nor provides the possibilities for tranquil educational work.

Lately, I have felt that the parents – even those who ostensibly consider themselves well-educated and have a received a taste of a higher social status – feel that they are not sufficiently elevated when their children attend a Yiddish school. Hebrew is now in style. Naturally, they don't devote much time to master the language, they are clearly not at that stage, but they are ashamed of Yiddish. You can even find some who unashamedly state that in such a school their children won't make the right friends, referring to the absence of children from more affluent homes. And this is being said by those who were only recently in circumstances of poverty. The desire for social climbing is an affliction that infects everyone. A sense of inferiority gnaws away at us all. This entire picture leaves me heavy-hearted. I only refresh myself in teaching a class or when I come upon a well-taught lesson. But this too is increasingly rare. Only a few good teachers are left. The new ones are still inexperienced, while the veterans are tired and seldom give off flashes of youthful sparks.

DECEMBER 15, 1954

Last Friday the symposium on education was held at the Workmen's Circle. About eighty people were gathered. Lermer, characteristically, chaired the proceedings with enthusiasm and spoke in abstractions. Grossman relied on conventional rhetoric, summarizes the entire history so that when he arrives at modern times – he has nothing left to say, as if he had not thought it through. It remained for me to address the present condition of Jewish education in Montreal, where there exist great possibilities for development but the trend is toward reduction. This is due to the fact that there is no sense of community responsibility and the institutions can no longer support themselves. The poor child becomes estranged from the school and Jewish education serves only the middle class. I pointed out that the afternoon school has become the main "pretext for education" and described its attendant problems. The audience was attentive. In the discussion and questions one felt that people were still thinking stereotypically. They are still afraid of day schools and try to convince themselves that the fault lies with others. They themselves are not prepared to do anything. The comprehensive Jewish school no longer finds the base for support among the so-called masses. Strength has ebbed away.

Sunday, the twelfth annual Congress conference took place. A large audience was in attendance. The dominant subject on the agenda was formal and informal Jewish education for youth and adults. The audience was anxious to listen and to express themselves. One felt this immediately when the Federation was accused of placing orphans in Christian homes. And also later when the speaker on the youth panel pointed out that the leaders of the youth organizations hardly know anything about Yiddish life. The atmosphere became heated when Wiseman spoke fervently about the fact that the community can no longer support the day schools and that is the reason preventing their expansion. They must be restricted and only select individuals be admitted. In its place, the afternoon schools should be expanded. As if that were possible. As if he believes that those who enroll in a day school would all register in the afternoon school. His fear that there are no prospects for a united community ever supporting maximum Jewish education leads him to pessimism about the survival of the day schools, while he maintains that education will be rescued through the afternoon schools.

Finally, received a promise from Hayes that he is convening a meeting of the inner executive of the Congress to study our memorandum. At the last meeting of our committee on Monday evening, our total helplessness was evident. Our "leaders" are no longer ready to do anything except to tell the Congress that if they do not offer help, the school will close in a month. Arriving today at five o'clock to the meeting in Hayes' office, there was only him, Unterberg, and Harvey. Other members of the committee were either sick or out of town. There was no other choice but to review the issues with them. We made it explicit that if we did not receive any help from them, the school would have to close in a month or two. Since Hayes stated that he would like to obtain a picture of the present situation so that he could present it on Friday to their meeting, our discussion turned into an exchange of information. In practical terms this means nothing. Things are just at the very beginning. The problem is further aggravated by the fact that we will not be present at that meeting and will not be able to convince anyone. It appears that only a miracle can save us. It does not look as if they have changed their minds at all.

DECEMBER 25, 1954

The answer from Congress came in the middle of the Chanukah celebrations at the school. Children are full of joy experiencing the holiday. Along with them, parents and teachers are celebrating – the latter despite exhaustion. They don't know that the "leaders" of the community in their negative response – "No money for those who have none themselves" – have condemned them to the last Chanukah in the Peretz Shule.

I don't have the heart to tell them. How can I spoil their holiday? Let there remain a little hope.

Zuker, in his misery, goes about grim and despondent. We are truly helpless, there is no one to turn to now. The Talmud Torah announced their campaign for over a quarter of a million dollars. They say that Jewish education is growing in the new neighbourhoods and more funds are needed. It is as I predicted: for the affluent money will be found, but for those most in need – there is nothing. And our "people," so to speak, observe, hear and keep silent. Moreover, the Folk Shule *chaverim* maintain that they cannot discuss amalgamation in case their situation becomes like ours. They think that they will be exempt.

DECEMBER 31, 1954

Bronfman is out of town, nobody to talk to. Wednesday evening there was the executive meeting where the situation was dealt with. The letter that Craimer had prepared for Congress could not be tabled as written because the tone of his preface stated that the school should be closed immediately. This made a bad impression on everyone and people became anxious about the severe tone of his letter. Everyone wanted us to address the Congress in firm language, but not in a way that indicated that we were to close the school immediately. In principle, it was decided to summon the United Jewish Appeal to a Rabbinical Court.

According to our accounts, we will be able continue for another two months. The executive is no longer considering any new initiatives. I will have to effect things by myself. The only one concerned with thinking, worrying, and looking for solutions is Zuker. He does not look at all well. I simply quake at the state of his health. Let us hope.

JANUARY 8, 1955

All week I was occupied preparing letters to the Congress and the Relief Committee informing them that we are compelled to summon them to a Rabbinical Court; memorandum to the cultural department of the Conference for German Reparations, and a letter to the Rabbinical Council.

This week I met with Dickstein. My intention was to explain the situation to him that as the chairman of the Actions Committee he should know that if we are forced to close down in mid-year, that he, and the Movement, will be morally stigmatized. Spent the whole evening with him. He is the same cynic he always was, but much cleverer. It looks as if he took the issue seriously and would like to do something. He does not believe that the Movement can be of any help. He doesn't support the idea of a Rabbinical Court because they will prolong matters and it also involves the question of Relief support; for if they fund us then all the groups, especially the *yeshivas*, will demand the same. This funding is part of a national plan and the other regions would oppose it. He does not approve the amalgamation with the Folk Shule. There would be enormous financial and administrative difficulties. The central issue would be the appointment of the principal. It was useless to explain to him that I would not be the cause of any difficulty. He has his determined point of view and it was useless to counter it.

Congress called a meeting for the 6th of February to continue the discussion on education. This means there will finally be an open confrontation with our eminent educators.

JANUARY 20, 1955

The discussion took place as I had anticipated. Only a small audience convened, our teachers, school activists, and several teachers from other schools, and a few from the Poalei Zion. I spoke only about the aspects of organization and financing. I left the other issues for another occasion. I indicated that with the new organizational format of congregational schools, our type is pushed aside. Only the united strength of the Movement could accomplish anything. Provided statistics on student enrollments that indicate the necessity of enlarging the school system. But due to financial restraints they are going downhill, and the outlook of some educators that the day schools have to be reduced will lead to a catastrophe. The raising of tuition leads to the fact that the child of the working poor drops out of school. The afternoon school won't grow because of the inherent problems affecting it: inconvenient schedule, tired children, and other factors that prevent the child from seeing the afternoon school as a normal part of his life. The catastrophic situation of the high school is also due to the fact that it is an afternoon school. The only solution is community responsibility.

On Tuesday the 18th, in the afternoon, Zuker and I met with S. Bronfman in his office. What a spacious, well-designed place of calm. The wealth is not apparent. Simplicity and refinement in the furnishings and the walls. He received us graciously. He is acquainted with the problem and cannot understand why the leadership of Congress could not find a way to help us. Hayes, who was present, tried to explain their point of view, and he interrupted him. "It looks like they are just searching for an excuse." He feels that a vital institution should not be allowed to disappear for $8,000 a year. Our claim that we should be receiving relief funds for the refugee children we have taught is one he agrees with. He almost completely agreed with us and promised to take up the matter at the national executive next month. He asked us unequivocally to withhold any planned action until he had a chance to raise the issue.

Throughout the discussion we had the feeling that we were speaking as equals among equals, as community activists both interested in maintaining a community institution in need. At all other meetings there was always the feeling that we were the beggars who were imposing ourselves on the community. He appears to be someone who sees things in a broader perspective without ulterior motives or bias. He is definitely inclined to help us, and knows that we can't balance the budget and won't send away the children and thus cripple the school. We left him somewhat encouraged.

Our visit was supposed to last fifteen minutes, but was extended for over an hour.

FEBRUARY 16, 1955

The days and nights of the last two weeks were difficult. Father suddenly took ill with pneumonia and had a heart attack. This upset all of us.

Precisely on Sunday the 6th, when I was supposed to lead the open discussion about the school problem at the Congress, I learned that he was ill but had no idea how serious it was. I could hardly gather my thoughts, nevertheless I was able to express my intended meaning. The ordinary person saw that Magid and Wiseman did not have any clear ideas and how incorrect their arguments were. But the Establishment enjoyed seeing the whole matter sidelined, replaced by personal feuding amongst us. I left in the middle and arrived to find that Father had been taken to the hospital. He is now feeling a little better but is not out of danger. It is pitiful to see such a brilliant mind unable to express two thoughts clearly and he is as feeble as a child. Only the mundane physical functions are functioning and they perform according to their will. It is fearful to watch and to think our thoughts to a conclusion. Almost all of us are devastated. I have to control myself and make myself strong. I am at the hospital most of the day and have become quite a nurse.

On Monday the 11th of February, Rubenstein called from New York to tell us that Louis Segal had telephoned him to let us know that the conference in Paris had allocated $18,000 to us as a one-time grant. This means that the school is saved. Of course I had wished that the funds would have come from another source, but if this is the only way, it cannot be helped. I have no moral right to complain about this. The refugee children were the cause of the crisis, so refugee funding should save the school.

MARCH 12, 1955

Last Wednesday we ended the *Shiva* period. After much suffering Father died on Wednesday, the eighth day of Adar at three o'clock in the afternoon.

After several days of improvement, he took a turn for the worse and lay unconscious for four days. He never believed that he would regain his health, as we had convinced ourselves. It was impossible for us to accept. We did all we could. Held watch over him night and day for the three weeks. All to no avail; his heart could not withstand it. Until the last moment, amid his confusion, he would constantly argue with someone, in particular with the "elegant" Jews. He spoke continuously but left no final message. He spoke openly only on two occasions: "The time has come." And "undoubtedly you cry at home," he said to me. With Shifra he talked about piety. In his thoughts and fantasies he was already distanced and separated from us, but could express only his physical needs: to be cleansed, to urinate, and so on. He tried to formulate clear Yiddish words but could not.

The community arranged for a fine funeral. *Chasidim* fussed, performed *hakofos*, and treated him like a holy man – although when alive they barely took notice. Such a fate. And he so longed for a bit of recognition. From all strata of society people came to console the mourners. Now, when it is all over.

The last morning, on Wednesday at eight o'clock, he still asked to have his hands washed but was unable to say anything or dry his hands. At three o'clock a kind of serenity settled on his face. He had made his peace, it would seem.

Mother is certain that he was summoned to fulfill the role of *Rosh Yeshiva* in paradise, and Yechiel encourages her by claiming that he already hears him instructing *Torah*, although Yechiel felt that Father was displeased with him especially because of his rigid position on hastening the coming of the Messiah. We are all devastated, and can't seem to recover. We miss him at every step. It is impossible to believe that he is no longer here, no one to bring a query to or seek advice from. Formerly, when some pressing issue arose there was someone to ask. Now, I literally shiver when I have to seek advice. The wound is once again opened. Mother is sustained by her belief; the daughters are trying to become more religious, as is Yisroel. I go to pray three times a day. The *niggun* is within me but I am not at all stirred as yet.

In observing the ordinary Jews, who would have nothing to cling to, adhering to the synagogue for the *Kaddish* and the rapidly rendered prayers, I recognize the value of these acts. I am still not at home in this setting. It is a burden but not too difficult.

APRIL 4, 1955

The thirty days of mourning have passed but the grief remains constant. It is still impossible to accept that Father is no longer here. Often, when I glance at scriptures and a query arises, my immediate thought is: I'll ask my Father. Then comes the realization, accompanied by a heart-throb that pervades my whole body – there is no one to ask. Bereft of all desire, as if part of me had died. I would simply wish to be left alone; but being alone is hard, almost unbearable.

Sunday we went to the graveside. It is so silent, it makes one shudder. It appears to be so senseless. Yechiel, who is so confident in the approaching redemption, and even interprets our Father's death to be somehow related to this, threw himself onto the snow-covered grave. As for myself, I can only keep silent. If I do attempt to speak I cannot control myself. In the evening at the end of the thirty days of mourning we gathered at mother's and read from his books. Mother was certain that he was with us and heard everything. Mother can barely catch her breath. We are all devastated. Tomorrow will be the first Pesach without Father.

APRIL 9, 1955

Yesterday the third world conference of the Bund opened here. An odd feeling for me, a non-Bundist and certainly not a party member. The past was with me, and my conflicts with them, and remembering them in their glory with roots and branches and the sun shining overhead. I had so many good friends amongst them, now martyrs. For me it was like meeting my former self. Doubtless I knew that I would not meet Mottel and Shmaya of Ludmir, or Artur, but through their friends I will see them. What they might say is not important, but to see their friends linked to their past would be like being with them.

A large audience was present. The whole gathering somewhat pathetic. Full of reminiscences of past glories and the reunions of those who have gone through the fires of hell, meeting once again in the name of the past. In addressing the future they fumble among archaic rhetoric and unclear phrases full of flowery language. Nevertheless, it was rejuvenating for Jews from the earth's four corners who seek only one thing: to survive, not to disappear.

From the platform only one face shone forth that retained the aura of the former Bund, *Chaver* Oler. He still looks like an authentic Bundist: erect, bitterly stubborn, with a gaze that speaks of deep sectarian convictions, ready to transform everything without knowing whence it will lead. The others: tired faces, or just reduced to the ordinary. Still, they looked like a single family excited by this reunion. Not a single new word was heard. Merely the past glories and a need to identify themselves as martyrs. Now they hold on to the horns of an empty altar.

If one closes one's eyes and tries to forget and just listen, it seems as if committed Jews have assembled to search for a bit of strength, and even though this contravenes all reality, they still desire to serve the belief in their hearts. Where does this strength spring from? Will it all finally end up wasted? What weighs even heavier on the heart is the sight of their archives. From the mute documents arises a flame of pure martyrdom. Did they only manage to save these written pages? Can this be so? After such impressive generations, will only some dry pages remain?

APRIL 15, 1955

Spent a good number of hours at the Bundist Conference. There were many sad moments observing how worthy Jews speaking in rich Yiddish idiom and with sincere anxiety about the break-up of Jewish life, pour out their hearts, and in their many speeches, it seems to me, finally arrive at something positive. Suddenly, the old slogans that preceded "the Flood" emerge and they do a complete turnabout and we are back at the old "anti" positions that, in a void, float alongside their beliefs.

Also tragi-pathetic was the appearance of the representative of the German Social Democrats. Of all the socialists, a German comes to present greetings – that alone is sufficiently sad. He addresses the charred firewood saved from the flames that his nation ignited. However, one does not sense in his voice or in his words any true feeling of profound human experience. Just dry words and political slogans. Bones that no spirit can revive. These dry bones weigh on the spirit like dead baggage and obscure everything.

Seated amongst them I thought: the folk tradition recognizes the thirty-six holy men who sustain the world. These thirty-six are from diverse sources: from a water-carrier, to a wandering beggar, a chimney sweep, and even a confirmed drunk. Each one of them, however, fulfills his mission to uphold the world. Who knows, possibly they are included in the notion of "universal peoplehood" that the Bund still acknowledges and clings to. They are found in all corners of the earth, sustaining survival through their different activities and guises.

MAY 6, 1955

Going to *shul* to pray awakens my old forgotten enmity to the old-timers of the *shtetl*. Their same restrictive customs were brought here. In fact here they are worse, because there one could assume that they were sincere, that it was a part of religious faith, or ingrained fanaticism and superstition. Here it is totally bad, all is formalistic and empty. Sometimes there is ceremonial value, mostly though it is just words that are recited and not meant. Carried out rapidly. Insulting a person is amongst the least of their sins, and they distribute honours around the Torah, which they no longer follow. An unbearable cynicism. And their money goes to the orthodox.

Yesterday there was a meeting with the Congress people. They are not prepared to do anything now. On the contrary, it has become clear to me that if our own people won't undertake to do something, we won't get anything from them. They emphatically let us know through their spokesman, Lavy

Becker, that it is time to liquidate. Our type of education is no longer required.

Last year this still upset me. Now I simply heard them out and feel that it was a mistake to expect any help from them. They don't want us and don't need us. We're just an obstacle in their way and their actions will eventually lead to the liquidation of the whole school system. Our refusal to capitulate prevents the powers-that-be from realizing their own ideal conception of the school system, which shrinks year by year.

MAY 30, 1955

Blows come from all sides. From all the fuss with the reparations money, we received only $5,000 with the possibility of an additional $5,000. That is what happened to the promised $18,000. Their excuse is that they do not give funds for previous deficits. B.Z. Goldberg used the occasion to scold us and me especially. The "Holy-man of this Generation" cannot abide an injustice. Had we not, according to him, admitted all the refugee children, like the rest of the schools, and now be prepared to dissolve rather than take the money, that would be morally correct. But the whole moral issue has lately left me with a strange aftertaste. It was certainly morally correct to take in the refugee children and thus endanger the entire school structure. If only the refugees had appreciated it. But as soon as someone becomes more prosperous and has to make an effort to pay tuition, he ceases to speak about the need for Yiddish and Yiddish education. Public school is sufficient for them and they depart without even a thank-you. They leave just as it is said: "The Moor has done his work, the Moor can now depart."

JUNE 24, 1955

Graduation took place on June 19th. Tried to instill a more optimistic tone. After all, it is fifty years since Zuker arrived in Montreal, which literally means: fifty years of community activity – the origin and growth of all that we have today. Possibly we might be able to realize the construction of a new building for the Peretz Shule to celebrate this occasion. If the activists would understand this, they might desire to perpetuate the school on their own. The atmosphere was buoyant.

JUNE 28, 1955

Today received a letter from Neumann in Tel Aviv, that finally the first book, *Ish Haya Ba'Aretz*, has been published. I have waited so long for this. However I don't feel as overjoyed as I think I ought to be. Even the compliments that I have lately received about my writing hardly affect me. Is it because it already follows deep despair, or is it because I'm older? Had this happened years earlier it would have strengthened me and I might possibly have accomplished something. Now it seems to pass me by.

My single pleasure is at my writing desk. The new book that I'm now writing about Tishevitz completely overpowers me. And my pleasure is also complete.

SEPTEMBER, 1955

All summer I was in a tense and anticipatory mood.

a) There was the uncertainty of the school's survival and yet I had to prepare everything as if the future were assured. The moral responsibility regarding the teachers gave me no rest. What if, God forbid, the plans for receiving aid do not materialize, which would mean that they are left afloat on the waters. It was impossible to explain the situation to them. The question is: do I have the right to gamble with their livelihood? No other alternative than the hope that eventually a way would be found. Still I found no peace in this.

b) Because of Ode's decision to complete her courses at Columbia and Chana's work as a counsellor at the Workmen's Circle summer camp of New York, we went down to New York to visit Chana and to find work for Ode. Fell into the heat wave, which was extraordinary this year. Had discussions with writers that were only lamentations about the fate of Yiddish and our cultural path, which founders. Salted and peppered with gossip, one about the others, so that the metaphor of a sinking ship emerges clearly before one's eyes. And all the sailors are transformed into befuddled mice, may heaven preserve us, who cannot save themselves, so they bite and tear each other to pieces. It was painful to be in their presence.

c) And after all this, Ode's sudden decision to marry Motty Garfinkle. We had known of this for a long time and expected something like this, but it still came as a surprise. The problems in this relationship are substantial. He is undoubtedly a fine and lovely young man, capable, responsible; still it is barely a year since he became a widower and the child is now his most important concern. Who knows how this will turn out?

It was a quiet wedding, for the family only. As is always the case in matters like this, we do things according to formal pattern, like a play. Not according to your wishes but as it must be. It is strange how the conventional seeps in and binds you on all sides, and you even take pleasure in this. In some ways you are not alone. Generations that preceded now accompany you – affecting your actions. Now they are back in New York. A fine couple. My heart trembles – may it all be for the best. May they overcome the difficulties. It was a real joy that our friends and dear ones were so warmly devoted and helped us celebrate the wedding. Especially Berl and Issachar.

MIDDLE OF DECEMBER

Due to the great crisis that has developed around *Eretz Yisroel*, once again there has emerged the warmest sentiments and sincere, deep anxieties that the people feel for the State of Israel.

Sharett came – greeted by a crowd of three thousand people. But when the crowd gathered the organizers failed to inspire them. The enthusiasm the crowd had brought with them grew even weaker in the large echoing hall. The chairman, a *nouveau riche*, a coarse figure, couldn't arouse the crowd. M. Sharett spoke diplomatically to the press and a warm Yiddish word was not uttered. The Jewish heart could not respond. It became a matter of "investment." But there are better investments for wealthy Jews. And simple folk have no savings for investment.

It seems to me that these words from Bialik are fitting: "I have seen you in the shame of your assemblies." It seems that we deserve no better.

DECEMBER 27, 1955

Now Sh. Niger is no longer with us. Between one meeting and another, he collapsed. His heart stopped on the subway. It's over now, gone is the address for Yiddish literature. An end to controversy; and there is almost no one left to look up to with respect or in anger. Door after door is closing in Yiddish-land.

From all the obituary notices that I managed to read about his sudden death, there is a cry of fear from Yiddish-land and the final agony of one's own mortality. Some simply say *Boruch dayan ha'emes* and others try to philosophize about death. The sorrow for the individual who has gone is not felt in any of the obituaries, only the fear of the group for the survival of Yiddish. Is this the price paid by an artist or socially committed person? He is not remembered for himself but only for what he represents. That is where they seek consolation, but where is it to be found? The mourned person, it seems, remains only with his closest, with his family.

DECEMBER 30, 1955

Zuker phoned to say that the Folk Shule committee with Berman will have a meeting with our representatives next Sunday to discuss unification. As much as I know of Berman's approach, he is seriously for unification. His outlook, however, is to solve the financial difficulties and divide the leadership. It seems to me that they, especially the top leadership with Wiseman at the head, are not so inclined. So concerned are they with maintaining their positions that they can no longer see the importance of amalgamation, which would essentially save our school system. We will see. Indirectly, I'm told that Wiseman is afraid of working with me. If necessary, I will not stand in the way; I had already informed Zuker and Berman of this a long time ago.

MAY, 1956

At a meeting of the Peretz Shule, the committee reported on its negotiations: after Wiseman's speech opposing, because there would be no possibility of working harmoniously, the issue was struck from the agenda. The end of the unification matter. Total blindness. They do not perceive that our school system will disappear over time. The pressure of artificial religiosity and the opposition to Yiddish and our way of thinking are now too strong for us to withstand on our own. Possibly they are aware of this, and yet we must maintain the external semblance of "friendship."

NOVEMBER, 1956

These days are perilous ones. Truly, days of trial. Israel is fighting for its very existence. The helplessness of the local Jews is even more acute than ever. There, they at least have the sword to defend themselves; here, merely some words, which they hesitate to utter.

To hear what is occurring at the United Nations, where tyranny speaks in the name of justice, is agonizing. We are alone. Our predecessors believed that they understood the meaning of things.

There, they can at least weep over their sacrifices and feel that they have brought matters to a conclusion. Here, we are so small in our own eyes. Not even the role of servant who leads the donkey for him who moves toward his sacrifice. Here, all we hear is the roar of words: heroic and grand. Maybe this too is worth something. But how small we are, helpless and fearful. Both the leaders and the led. And in the synagogues they proceed as usual: Bar Mitzvahs, weddings, and old Jews are studying about temple sacrifices and altars.

DECEMBER, 1956

It has been a long time since I have made any entries. A difficult time. Barely escaped going under. The Reparations money saved us, but this leaves a bitter taste. But not accepting the money would have meant that we remain righteous but the children would have been left on the open sea. Louis Segal was the only one of the New York *chaverim* who really helped us.

On the eve of Rosh Hashana Mother, after grave suffering, breathed her last. With her went the illusory home that we still maintained here. Now we are alone. We must now begin to keep our own accounts. It is now nearer than farther. To make the accounting in accordance to whether it was all worthwhile is irrelevant. I must simply try to complete what is possible, according to the dictates of my feelings.

DECEMBER 21, 1956

Had a lengthy discussion with Hayes last week, he sees no way whereby we can save ourselves. His unchanged viewpoint: can't you see that while your way may be just, your work is a mission, but those who have the say in the city want neither you nor your mission. They are unconcerned with the poor children in general, and with Yiddish in particular. In effect, his tone informed me: Why make a fool of yourself? Why are you sacrificing yourself? No one will bewail the closing of the Peretz School except yourself and possibly a few others. Even your own *chaverim* won't be too saddened. It is hard to listen to these words and even harder to admit that they are not far from the truth.

FEBRUARY, 1957

The organization for the Zuker jubilee is having difficulty. At the meetings there are so-called activists, in reality, talkers. They are earnest, but it seems that they have insufficient faith that a new Peretz Shule will result from the campaign. So I myself go to speak to *chaverim*. Some of them encourage me, others are doubtful, but they all make promises. There will soon be a sufficient sum to buy the land. One of the first pledges, ironically, was from Moishe Dickstein. Had a serious discussion with him that lasted late into the night. He is a much deeper and more honest person than I had previously considered. He believes that we must undertake a novel and large-scale project, like the building. This will draw money and new supporters, etc. Sarah Caiserman promised to help and to contribute. She is enthusiastic about commemorating a worthy person like Zuker during his lifetime.

APRIL, 1957

Finally purchased land in Cote St Luc. An area of 30,000 square feet, enough for a building and a playground. It is both an occasion for congratulations and for raising questions: when will construction begin if for the land, which cost $26,000, we barely have pledges for $16,000, and only half of that is cash. Still we have to have faith; our appetite grows with every bite. However we are out of funds to conclude the year. We will have to mortgage the building to provide for it.

MAY, 1957

It was a joyous hour when we signed for the land purchase. *Mazel Tov!* I already imagine the building full of children and the Peretz Shule lives on. May it happen as soon as possible. In the new neighbourhood we'll once again be involved in pioneer work. Have we the strength for this?

JUNE, 1957

Hired a person to conduct the campaign and prepare Zuker's jubilee banquet. Celebrating his 70th birthday and fifty years of community activity is by itself a special holiday, which he rightfully earned; and if in addition the school is saved – then it is truly an occasion to celebrate. All of this means that summer will not bring any time for rest. We'll be involved in campaigning. Too bad; what else can I do?

SEPTEMBER, 1957

At the school on Duluth, the number of children diminishes. The local population is moving away. On the other hand, in the new neighbourhood even the day school is growing. This year we are likely to have close to one hundred children in quarters rented from the public schools. We have a good reputation there.

Taking advantage of a free day to distance myself from my own preoccupations, I suddenly felt unbelievably sad; I had so immersed myself in school affairs in recent years that I hardly see the world about me. As if everything is passing me by. I've detached myself from things and from seeing people. Everything is focused on one point. Even the most important events don't inspire me to record them or to devote one moment of thought to them. During this time we lost Moishe Dickstein. He too now rests in peace, and they didn't even mourn him properly.

Chana and Mark's wedding was celebrated in fine style. Spent a considerable sum; all the money from the sale of the house. This bothers me little. But it is rather lonely in the house. Now we are back where we began. Only on Friday nights is the house full once more. It is fortunate that Ode and her family have settled here. May they be blessed with good fortune. We have to adjust to the fact that from here on we are "departing from the Fair."

OCTOBER, 1957

When things fail to work, nothing remains but to raise the alarm. Zahler took ill when we needed him most. And Mrs Zuker was suddenly stricken with paralysis as she came home from a meeting honouring Zuker. Who knows whether she will recover? A good soul, a true mother of Israel.

NOVEMBER, 1957

One had to be a cold-hearted villain in order to "compel" Zuker to endure the jubilee banquet under these circumstances. He demonstrated great hidden resources not to surrender to all the difficulties and ordered us to carry out the celebration, because the entire fate of the school was threatened.

The children presented him with a beautiful album of drawings and greetings. A gigantic audience was present. A sum was raised that allows us to seriously consider building. Just a little more and perhaps everything will be resolved. About the agonies of mind and body that this involved it is best to remain silent.

DECEMBER 10, 1957

One of these days I will enter the hospital for an operation on my lip. The doctor assures me that it is not serious but there should be no delay, since it could become serious.

The plans for the building are almost ready. Good health is what we need.

DECEMBER 15, 1957

Montreal General in the evening – first night in the hospital.

A strange feeling; all day busy with attending to routine details. All petty things loom large when you know that tomorrow you will be unable to perform them or possibly they will be left undone.

At the moment you cross the threshold into the room where you will be spending some time, all those matters swim away. The doctor, the nurse, the roommate in the next bed become the centre of interest. After the farewells with the family, who smile but cannot disguise their own anxiety, they too float away from immediate memory. You are alone. On one's own. Somehow you are more or less losing touch with the outside world.

The nurse is friendly. Wants to put me to sleep with a pill and informs me: "No liquids after twelve, the operation is scheduled early tomorrow. You'll be thankful for it."

The slow entry into the world of surgery for healing embraces you.

DECEMBER 17, 1957

I lost a day. They woke me early Monday morning to bathe and prepare for the operation. About eight o'clock they gave me an injection. Sorke and Ode were there, and I remember them wheeling me to the operating room. I don't remember losing consciousness. Someone asked me something and I couldn't answer. A better way of putting this: the answer remained on the tip of my tongue. Later the nurse stood beside me; and then Chana, Ode, and Sorke. Was still drowsy and told them to leave because they had to go to work. Only then did I become aware that it was almost nine o'clock at night. The entire day was erased from memory.

DECEMBER 20, 1957 (NOTES IN THE HOSPITAL)

All day yesterday the wind was howling. From my window I see the rain flooding the mountain. Thick clouds passed rapidly in the greyness over the trees of the mountain and constantly transformed the trees into different forms that were continuously erased by the fog. Looking down where the cars are moving and pedestrians try to cross the road with a stooped helplessness, everything looks ghostly and presents a picture of unreal patterns of movements. At the edge of the mountain where a new structure is going up, men are working on the roof in the wind and rain. They move from place to place with great care, like the priests at their services. Rarely do they raise their heads. Their stooped posture fits the whole mood. The lip causes much pain. Already four days without food and without the body's normal functions. A feeling of being cut off from one's senses, and a kind of inner deafness accompanies you during a walk in the corridor, while you conduct a disjointed conversation with a visitor or stare in wonderment at the play of city lights observed from the fifteenth floor where you find yourself. The varied lights from near and far blink, speak, point out openings; but still the senses are closed off. The doctor says that things are proceeding normally and it will take a few days before the senses are fully recovered.

JANUARY 20, 1958

I greeted the new year in the hospital. Spent a few weeks at home. The lip is healing. Meanwhile it is difficult for me to enunciate all the sounds. I must have sinned with my mouth and words. During this time I wrote several chapters of the new book. Something redeemed from this illness.

APRIL, 1958

Spent a few days in the country. The sun and the fresh air rejuvenated me. I literally could barely drag myself around.

Wrote a little, so that was obviously a pure gain. While engaged in the building activities around the school I have come to know more about the outlook of the different circles in the community. The desire to build and to continue to maintain these institutions is strongly felt. And yet the negative forces are just as strong. Very often I too wonder if people who are totally immersed in their business affairs can still be drawn away from the market place. The process is not easy but later they are grateful for having been drawn away.

JUNE 16, 1958

Yesterday, with good fortune, we turned the sod for the new school. There was a large audience with special guests who spoke our praises. It was carried out smoothly, in good taste and respect. In my few words I spoke of the school's background and the ideology on which it is based. Originally I was supposed to speak in English. But at the last moment I decided to speak Yiddish. It was correct to do so. But there should have been copies in English for those who could not understand. We will send them a copy.

I can already see that by next year at this time the building will be ready. The honour of the sod-turning was given to M.Y. Garelick. A dear and simple man, who contributes whole-heartedly. Now he is a manufacturer of furniture, but in his factory there is a separate room where he keeps the carpentry tools that he used when he first came here. Every morning, he tells me, before he enters his factory, he goes into this small room. He contributes large sums of money for education and *Eretz Yisroel*. At the beginning he was cool to the project; now it looks like he will be one of our main supporters. It gives me the greatest pleasure that such a simple person was the main honoree. It is fitting for us. His assistant at the affair is also a modest young man, Dan Freedman, a former pupil of the *shule* in its early days. His father was very closely associated with the school. He is actively involved in the building – and will learn to contribute as well. All in all it was a fine celebration.

SEPTEMBER, 1958

Rested a bit at the seashore in Old Orchard. Wrote a little. The book about Tishevitz grows slowly, but to those who are knowledgeable it will be a book about the *shtetl*. Both the form and the scope are contemporary and historical. It is more than a tale and more than a fable. During the writing, I often feel that I have uncovered the essential soul of the Eastern European settlement of which Tishevitz was a last remnant of continuous history, extending from the earliest beginnings through all subsequent eras. When I knew it at the very end, there were still signs of its beginning; and the end was already so near. Every page that I write is a relived experience for me, more deeply felt than any other of my previous works. I often feel as if maturity and knowledge lead me by the hand. Often I remain standing as before a solid wall. The difficulty lies in the fact that I can't develop my characters further, but must leave them as they are remembered.

NOVEMBER, 1958

Signed the contract, a time of good fortune. We must still raise $100,000 in order to complete the project. The architectural plans are ready. Our cash account barely amounts to $15,000. Only because the contractors are prepared to delay the payment of $40,000 for two years, and the bank will extend credit for $50,000, will we be able to begin. The contractor, Ain, is aware of this and wishes to help. This is a risk but there is no other choice.

DECEMBER, 1958

The winter has settled in – a harsh one, but the building grows day by day. The contractor works determinedly. The *chaverim*, however, are doing very little. Only a few individuals and Sarah and myself are working continuously to raise funds. The others are even lagging behind the amounts raised in the regular campaign. I am afraid that by the year's end the deficit will put in jeopardy the whole undertaking. The sense of responsibility among the *chaverim* has totally evaporated. There is much talk at meetings, but little is done.

MARCH, 1959

Was too preoccupied with thousands of problems to write at all. Running around all day to get contributions; planning and goading and praising the few available supporters, and in the evening more meetings. The educational work in the school is not proceeding as it should. The standard has been lowered. But it has to be left that way. One cannot do everything. We must find new methods for everything. The teachers on their own initiative are either not able to conceive them or they don't see it as their responsibility. Something has gone wrong with their attitude, even among the best. I hope that with the new beginning there, things will change for the better. The building grows and the debts along with it.

APRIL 10, 1959

It is a strange feeling to know and accept that everything that we do this year is for the last time; at celebrations as well as assemblies. Except for a few new things that anticipate our preparations for the new locale. A kind of conclusion, a commencement, but not an ending.

Started to organize the alumni. This proceeds slowly. The young ones are enthusiastic but don't know how to approach the matter. The fact that only sentiment ties them to the school is not enough. They are happy to meet us, and at the same time they feel sort of estranged when they meet each other. Everything seems much smaller in their eyes. The illusions of the past have vanished. Nevertheless among many of them there is a wish to do something. We'll have to work much harder at this.

APRIL 16, 1959

An important guest has been here: Avraham Sutzkever, a guest of Congress. He makes a deep impression. The person who was in hell emerged as a great poet and human being. In him there is found a mixture of *Misnagdish* and *Chasidish*, if such an expression is permissible or sensible. He speaks in the language of a *maggid*, with lightning flashes of *Chasidism*. When he tells a story it has the sharp quality of an image, yet mystical at the same time. His lyrics are less impressive than his manner of relating an incident. His narratives are more authentic than his poetry, which tends to be philosophical and often florid. He is difficult to befriend. The cloak of profound suffering is evident in all his utterances and his bearing. As a person he appears to me to lack some of the qualities of his friend Kaczerginsky, of whom he speaks very little. I find that strange. Kaczerginsky personified friendly acceptance without reservations. At the first meeting you felt as if you had always known him. He remained engraved in your heart without any barriers. But between you and Sutzkever there is always a wall. The more often you meet him, the stronger and more evident becomes the division. You need to constantly intellectualize in order to engage him. It seems that he has a special purpose behind every utterance and every meeting. That you should be doing something for him seems to be expressed without words. Still it was and is a deep experience to have met with him face to face.

JUNE 20, 1959

Tomorrow is graduation day. The last one in the neighbourhood where we have become strangers. Let us hope that the chapter on the Peretz Shule in the east side of the city is not an ending but rather a conclusion that leads to a new beginning. A class from the evening school, which was housed at the Protestant School Board, is graduating, the first one from the new neighbourhood. May our future home be more fortunate.

JUNE 23, 1959

The graduation went well, a large audience and good spirits. A holiday mood and everything in good taste. The president was absent. The pretext being that he was ill and very tired. My impression was that he simply could not appear before the audience and the teachers and say things that he did not believe. That too stands in his favour. We'll have to find a way to relieve him of his responsibility without alienating him.

JULY 7, 1959

A strange dream. Yarmouth, Cape Cod.

Finally escaped from the city, and grasped the opportunity to take a week's vacation. For three days we travelled around in the car, crossing mountains, valleys, and bodies of water. A breathtaking beauty on the side roads, combined with the human effort to make things comfortable for the trip. A mixture of noisy highways, busy suburbs, and peaceful sleepy towns. One night we spent at an old-fashioned motel, with sacred puritan names on each cabin, à la New England. On the second night, in an ultra-modern motel on the outskirts of Fall River. People are friendly everywhere, in a vacation mood. You see them once and you have the feeling that you have known them for a long time. You have met them somewhere. Motoring on, more forests, fields, mountains, and lakes. Thinking about this is difficult; too many impressions all at once. Nevertheless, some past remembrance lives within you that strains to emerge but cannot.

On Sunday night reached Newport. An old town. On one hand the palaces of the rich, set in lawns, and enclosed in quiet reserve. Only the tips of the palatial towers transcend the surrounding silence. Touro Street rings with the echo of the jazz festival. Black and white groups stretch along the street corners in their own festival of banjoes and cymbals. At the seashore in the black quarter, much carousing, crowded and very noisy. Girls are seated on the shoulders of blacks and whites, all limbs pulsating, and over all, a mélange of sounds giving voice to freedom from routine; the odour of different foods, sharp and peppery.

After much difficulty we finally arrived at a house, very pleasant and well-equipped with personal belongings, all in good taste. The owner, who is leaving for the city, receives us graciously. He speaks of his profession, he is a music teacher, and his hobby is boating. Recently purchased a yacht.

We fall into bed exhausted and this dream unfolds. This modern house with its stylized wood interior and fireplace, several doorways, its ceiling that gives the impression of age and artistry combined, enfolds you and leads you far away to a building with high balconies and strange doors, and windows opening on old shutters. Long rooms, one after the other, well-polished, shiny floors, which evoke memories of long ago. Herschel Brestacher with his golden beard is smiling at you, holding a well-rolled cigarette. "Very nice. It's been a long time since we've seen each other, Yankel. What are you doing here? Soon they will all arrive so you can see for yourself what has befallen us."

Something troubles my state of mind. Where is his daughter? For the life of me I can't remember her name. When the entire *shtetl* gossiped about his befriending me with the intention of gaining me as his son-in-law, I was actually involved in a one-sided love affair with Hodl, daughter of Leib-Ber. She didn't give me a thought. She was sunk up to the ears in a passion for Shikele Lattek from Lodz. And I never gave a second thought to Herschel's daughter. I taught her Hebrew and treated her as a child. So why is my heart haunted and full of regrets? She, as well as her sickly mother, an exquisite beauty, a modest daughter of Israel, whose appearance reminded me of classical polished glass images, shimmering and silent, treated me as their own child. And through all my wanderings I always remembered the aura of their house. What are they doing here now? Coming toward me with her maternal calm, she gestures me toward her daughter, who wanders about among a strangely dressed crowd, faces distorted, which suddenly appeared. She alone is dressed like a bride, strolling amongst them like a princess. She notices me and embraces me. She places her head on my shoulder and sobs: "Are you at least aware of what they did to us?" She points to a young man, thin as a stick, whose entire bearing is frightfully sad, and says: "Him too."

I cough and Sorke wakes me with the prod of her finger from the other bed. The whole picture stands before me, but the nightmare continues from the tip of the middle finger, spreading over the entire room, where the faint morning light steals through the narrow windows.

I realize that I am awake and want to hold onto the shadows of the dream, which disappear and disintegrate into the ever-present timelessness. It evaporates with such an anguished melancholy that I am afraid to raise my head. My flesh trembles.

AUGUST 21, 1959

Today we moved to the new school. Beginning next week the office will operate from there. For a few days I will continue to work in the old building. Somehow it is difficult to leave this place so abruptly. It is not only moving from the building but leaving behind this neighbourhood after so many years. Although all the surroundings are nearly empty of Jews, one feels like withstanding the changes a little longer. After all is said, this is the neighbourhood where the major part of my labours took place since my arrival in Montreal, approximately thirty-five years ago. When I can eventually have the time to write the book about that period, these streets, houses, and people will live again – so I'd like to absorb the atmosphere for as long as possible.

The new school is truly beautiful and comfortable, but whether the ideals for which we sacrificed all these years will be able to strike roots in this new neighbourhood, with new people – who knows? Who knows if we are the suitable people to begin pioneering here?

The Abels were here last week on their way to Israel. It was very good to see them. They have aged considerably. I guess one doesn't see the changes in oneself. Made a small reception for them in the new building, the first celebration there. May it be a good precedent for the future.

Recently I learned that Volodya Baronofsky is no longer with us. He was a classic type of radical, but also a warm human being, devoted to the school, which he had helped establish. Formerly a union activist, he was among the first to give Montreal the sense of a Jewish community. He too will have to be remembered when writing the Montreal book.

Only now do we begin to recognize how much beauty resided in these simple, often limited people, who were the original builders. Disregarding the poverty, they managed to raise themselves above the masses, and their fervent hearts had the effect of warming the frigid surroundings. Their glow is still felt today.

SEPTEMBER, 1959

Finally, we have lived to see our move to the new building, which is grand. I am still in disbelief that we really achieved this.

For the school-term opening several activists came, amongst them Sarah Caiserman and Zuker. And when we led in the children and sang the first Yiddish song, it seemed to me that all the years of anguish and all those who gave their support were singing along – I controlled myself, but those around me were all misty-eyed. According to tradition, this should be called a new beginning. But everything within me cries out and warns: Let this not be, once again, a beginning. It must be absorbed into the whole way of thinking that marked our past. Only then will it be of value.

SEPTEMBER 11, 1959

We have passed the first few hectic days in the new building. On Wednesday, the 9th of September, we assembled the children in the school and for the first time since the six days of creation a Yiddish word was sounded on this spot. It is such a deep and profound feeling that it is simply too difficult to express. In attendance were Zuker, Sarah Caiserman, the grieving *Chavera* Borodensky, and several other activists and parents. There were tears in everyone's eyes. Joy and sadness combined.

Not everything is in working order. Even the teachers are not accustomed to the new area, let alone the children. About one hundred new children were registered. The day school had fewer than the afternoon school. It will take a little time. Parents are coming in to ask questions and discuss programs. The more intelligent they are, the greater the confusion in their mind. The conflict they had with their parents when they were young interferes with their ability to approach the issues of Yiddish, identification, and religion. Some of them are so fearful of these issues – like a devil in the presence of incense. Others want as much of this content as possible in order to make things easier for themselves and to absolve them of any responsibility. It will take much work to clarify these matters.

END OF SEPTEMBER, 1959

Have also managed to survive the laying of the cornerstone. I couldn't imagine that everything would look so appropriate and be ready on time. There was a wonderful celebration. Aside from the honouree who laid the stone, Sam Steinberg, who donated $10,000 for the honour, no new money was collected. This means that the financial difficulties will increase. Nonetheless, the celebration was wholehearted. Into the capsule we placed the scrolls in three languages, written by me, relating all the phases of the school development. It made an impression. A number of the activists worked devotedly and well. Their joy gave me greater pleasure than my own.

ROSH HASHANAH. OCTOBER 4TH, 1959

The last few weeks found me so involved and so overworked that I still have not been able to regain my strength. The preparations for the laying of the cornerstone demanded so much attention, petty and important things, that I am amazed that we were able to prepare it all on time. I guess this points out that if we need to, we can muster such energies that we had no idea existed. The few *chaverim* who were committed worked loyally. This fact alone was supportive. The printed materials came out clear and artistic. Saul Pomerance helped out in this significantly. In this respect we have the good fortune that people with refined taste are ready to help us and contribute with pleasure. This celebration was most successful. There was a large audience in a holiday mood and the warmth was transmitted from one to another. Everything came together with respect and earnestness, as was fitting. It left a deep impression on everybody.

This year I must do a number of things: lighten the financial yoke of the school; complete and publish the book *Tzvishn Teichn un Vasern*; and travel to see Israel. Quite a goal, but certainly worthwhile.

OCTOBER, 1959

With considerable difficulty the school is being organized. A large number of children have been registered in the primary grades. The attitude of the parents is excellent. We still don't know one another, and a barrier exists between us. We are trying to understand each other. The language is an important issue. We are forced to use a considerable amount of English, which upsets the parents and activists of the former neighbourhood – including myself as well.

The sense of being back in the *shtetl* overwhelms me constantly. A kind of provincial aura hovers over the whole district. Wandered about for so many years and I've returned to the *shtetl*. We're looking for a home here, which will make things easier. Now the travelling to the school takes up an ocean of time and energy.

Received the first proofs of my book, but have no time to devote to it. Still have to complete several chapters. Even this offers little warmth. It seems that I am entirely depleted from the enormous strain.

NOVEMBER, 1959

Because of my workload, I have hardly written anything. Not even a letter have I written. Aside from the children, Chana and Mark, whom I miss terribly, I write to almost no one. The children are now in Israel. There, they are constantly taking their pulse: Is this for us? Does this include us? And without immediate answers they react critically. Seeing the negative side, they upset themselves for failing to see its significance. Very, very interesting. Only in regard to Russia and Israel did they react so intimately and personally.

The world situation affecting Jews, especially Israel, is quite dark. Israeli officials visit the major cities in search of friends, almost like wedding preparations – but what kind of wedding? It's meant to be a rapprochement in the cold war, but the cold surrounding Israel has increased. Even France grows cooler. Perhaps I see only the dark side, which fulfills the saying, "I feel it in my bones."

We have already moved here, close to the school. If someone, thirty-five years ago, had told me that we would be living nine miles away from the old neighbourhood, as far away as Montreal West, I would have dismissed the statement as a pipe dream. Truly, a small town setting. A ten-minute walk from school. When work is over there is a sense of being isolated from the big city. It is peaceful and beautiful, but detached. Will I be able to acclimatize?

DECEMBER, 1959

It is impossible to make entries more than once a month, there is simply no strength, no time, no patience. My health, too, is not what it was. So visits to doctors are part of my life. Aside from the eye doctor, none of them has found anything. They prescribe a long rest. The eye doctor thinks that one eye is developing a cataract. It may take years before it becomes ripe when it can be taken care of. Meanwhile my eyes are painful. He, too, advises rest – but how can one rest and be serene when everything hangs in the balance and there is no one who can share part of the burden. I often have pity on Tencer for having dragged him into this; he too labours beyond his strength. Without him I would just collapse.

My book waits but I can't get back to it. Maybe during the Chanukah break.

During Chanukah, a tiny miracle of our own. In desperation I called together several *chaverim* and related to them my fears about a financial catastrophe. Once again Sarah came to our rescue, borrowing from a loan company a sum that will, for the moment, cover two months of salary. Avoided a catastrophe! But for how long? We are accustomed to miracles, so this is a tiny miracle. We have to gain time, so Zuker can travel to Israel with the Canadian delegation, without care. How his eyes shone when Sarah announced what she could do. Truly, an angel, a saviour. She will be able to take her winter holiday and heal her legs. Others will also get a rest.

And I will begin to prepare the spring celebrations for the official opening of the building. Possibly, with another small miracle, I might be able to get some rest. As result of which, my health might improve. A happy New Year.

1960–1969

April 7, 1960

Barely survived to this day. It's already past the dedication ceremony. It was truly a solemn occasion. Bronfman was the honoured guest. A large audience in a festive mood. How much effort this took is another matter. Hershel Switzman and Goodkin were the main organizers. In the middle of preparations, Hershel left town, so I had to enlist myself. However, it was all worth it. The school and the people were decked out for the holiday. Our "friends" from the Folk Shule were there as well. They walked around pretending to be pleased, but muttered under their breath. They are welcome to their opinion. They have suddenly lost their "poor relative."

Today I was down at the old building. Every corner of the building seems to weep. It is impossible to make comparisons. For us it literally means "from darkness into light." Let us hope that indeed it will be light.

May 4, 1960

My eyes, it seems, have stopped rendering their service. I am still in disbelief that it is so. So many things to accomplish. I must complete the book in the middle of my school work. And other plans for completing *Tzvishn Teichn un Vasern* and the book "Montreal" buzz inside my head and begin to ripen.

Began to read Sholem's book. It includes wide-ranging thought, wonderful chapters, and much dry prose. Paying his dues to his Movement – in which he was never totally committed – as if a *dybbuk* had possessed him and holds him in thrall. Actually, the pathetic and tragic combined. It breaks my heart to see him dragging himself around to his private lessons, which are his sole source of income. And I cannot lighten his load. He is too deeply engaged with that "Party" and that can't be forgiven.

MAY 8, 1960

A bitter meeting of the Administration Committee was held. The new people were shocked to see how cold our "leadership" was and how they complicate matters by doing nothing. So it was the newcomers who actually passed the test by taking over the initiative.

After a sleepless night I decided that the time for new leadership is now. At this morning's meeting with the newcomers and several loyal veterans, a foundation was laid for a new leadership along with a plan to bring the school out of its predicament. If all goes according to plan this will be a historic date. Their devotion, it seems to me, is authentic and full of respect. They appreciate our work more than we felt or realized. After the change is implemented without too much pain, we will be able to anticipate better and quieter years of work. "Relief and deliverance will come to the Jews from another quarter" seems to be an eternal maxim.

JUNE 3, 1960

Last Wednesday Rivka Yaffe, very reserved and shy as she was in her youth when she would pour out her girlish heart to me, the "grownup," invited me to an evening that the graduates had prepared to honour my thirty-five years since coming to the Peretz Shule. They are calling it twice *Chai* – with a down payment for another year, so to speak. Doubtless they wish me more years. That something was brewing I realized some days before, but what exactly it was I didn't know. I didn't inquire exactly what they had planned. The graduates are marking the date with a gathering on Saturday, May 28th in the evening. When Sorke and I entered the school, it was brilliantly lit and so full of surrounding faces that I was blinded. In the office there were two new armchairs sent as a present by Mike Solomon – who is doing so much for the school just as if he were one of our own for many years.

Coming down into the hall everything surged toward me as from a hidden world. Shining faces from many years ago looked at us from all sides. So much light all around. From the earliest graduates to the most recent, as well as the whole family. The whole evening was like a trance. Photographs of the first radiant days, how many dreams, melodies from the class trips to the Mountain, everyone together. The first grade six that I had taught. With them I became very attached. Today they are amongst the closest *chaverim* and activists. Such intimacy. There come into memory those who have vanished, and all of them seem to be whispering continuously into my soul. The speakers were Rivka, Esther G., Esther Zuker, and Shulamis. And these were interspersed with song. Everything looks so far away yet near. Something has settled here, something saved. It is not a question of whether it was worth all the sorrow – could I have done otherwise? What comes to mind: my mission has fulfilled itself. A shudder passes through me, perhaps I'm at the threshold of the final reckoning? There is no help for this. I always knew, and always believed, that nothing is lost. In the hardest of times I felt that a great number of students have a special feeling toward me, that they retain something of the good in myself. But the warmth, the radiance, that flowed from that evening with such subtlety, was an overwhelming surprise. I don't know what I said to them, I still cannot find words to express my feelings.

They gave me three gifts: their own presence, an album of greetings that I still can't approach, and a cheque for $1,200 for a trip to Israel for Sorke and myself. How can one respond to that? Possibly in the words of our forefathers: With my staff alone I crossed the Jordan. Solitary and alone I arrived here and now I have a share in the things that are happening here. I shared with them the feelings that overcame me when I first traveled through the white fields of Quebec and asked myself whether Soreh bas Tovim would dance here or would Eliyahu Hanavi in disguise ever wander here. What could the answer be?

It's a marvelous feeling – strengthening and invigorating. My gratitude goes out to them. Often I felt that we were teaching the first generation of Jewish children here, and the last. But it now appears that the truth is that this is a mid-way point, and that which they have absorbed will be transmitted to others. There will be those who will succeed us.

JUNE 9, 1960

There was a grand celebration in school the last few days. The childrens' concerts went off very well. The work was appreciated. Somehow, in these spacious surroundings one's self-respect grows, and the responsibility felt by those charged with preparations is also different. The children feel uplifted too.

Yesterday we staged once more the Sholem Aleichem play at the annual board meeting. It was a dignified evening. The play contributed to this, followed by the election of the new board of directors with new people: Friedman is president and Solomon is chairman – this gave importance to the whole affair. Miller resigned in a refined manner and we accepted his resignation with honour and inscribed him in the Golden Book of the Jewish National Fund. I was pleased that he could leave on good terms. It will indicate that he led us to this point, and carried on with honour. After all, he did contribute a great deal to the school, according to his grasp of things. He was the first of the younger generation that joined us, and in the end he merited our goodwill.

After the meeting I was quite excited, which later caused me to dream:

there is a storm and a train roars into the snowstorm. I have to get off at the old *shul* in Tishevitz. The train gallops in the direction of the alley between Moishe the slaughterer's courtyard and the *shul*. I jump down and fall into a huge ball of snow mixed with straw that draws me toward the ring-road. An overhanging tarpaulin roof is ripped by the raging storm; other gusts pursue me, but instead of falling down I am lifted up, a strange image and inexplicable. I open my eyes to look at the overhang and see that it is day and the sun has risen. Was occupied all day with various concerns so I totally forgot about the dream. Now it appears clearly before my eyes, eyes that refuse to serve me.

JUNE 24, 1960

Today the day school closed; yesterday the evening school. Both closings were quite different than those of the past. The relaxed nature of the children has had its influence. In drawing up the final reports I could discern their individual abilities and, in turn, could perceive one's own worth.

The problem of the older teachers adapting to the new circumstances is also quite serious. The most difficult is Gaffney, he refuses to acknowledge his age so he and the classes suffer. We must attract new activists and new teachers and the adjustment is not easy. In the coming year I hope to be able to devote myself to the inner cohesiveness of the work in the classrooms and the extracurricular programs. There is a great desire on the part of the parents to identify themselves with real educational work, rather than the fundraising or social events. We should proceed only through education and coming into an awareness of our heritage. We must organize groups to study, play, sing, and read. In the meantime there is a beginning with a small group that is getting to know each other socially.

I hope to complete the last chapter of "Garbarnya Street," which proceeds slowly, and prepare the Hebrew translation. Then we will plan our trip to Israel.

JULY 19, 1960

I don't actually know why and for whom I write these notes from time to time. Maybe because I want to unburden my heart and don't have the courage to do so; or maybe I fear that in expressing these thoughts they would pale and the outpouring would harm the listener and do little for myself. Recently I have the sense of a curtain descending on me. As if everything is behind me and the truth is that I have accomplished so little. I try to take stock of myself. Where did I miss out? Which side-paths misled me so that I couldn't fulfill that which I still think I have within me? I haven't produced anything of great worth. Neglected material gain, while spiritually failing to realize my expectations. It seems to me that those closest to me know this better than I do, but remain silent. I am uneasy with myself and cannot concentrate on writing or reading, and the school work is no longer performed with the earlier ardour. Seems to me that I disperse my energies with petty matters.

AUGUST 30, 1960

In a little while we'll return to work with full zest. Spent two weeks in the mountains. Nearly completed the book. Just one more small chapter. It proceeds with great difficulty. I'm somehow too partial to the characters. I can't denigrate them. Too much sentiment in their representations. Lived too long with this book, it seems; the thread of the earlier truths has somehow become lost.

From all sides there are cries: Yiddish education is bankrupt; Yiddish is doomed. Only Hebrew and a smattering of religion are significant. Here, a new generation struggles and asks, in English naturally: Can you furnish us with new supports and identifications without dogmatism or artificial orthodoxy.

I spend many hours with young fathers and mothers who want to understand our basic beliefs. Many leave these meetings strengthened. But how strong are we? I am afraid that since we don't have suitable personnel to deal with this new generation we are liable to lose this opportunity, just as we had lost out earlier with excessive radicalism and the total abandonment of the tradition.

This is our last chance and we have so few forces. The supporters of Yiddish fight over a dictionary entry in a collapsing world. They wake up and kick at the broken trough! One has to literally plug up one's ears to get any work done. See how everyone has pounced on us to deny us our existence here.

SEPTEMBER 15, 1960

Opened the school with an additional 150 students, two kindergartens, and two pre-kindergartens. Four-year-olds to seventeen-year-olds study with us. It's a marvelous sensation. At last night's parents' assembly there were over one hundred young parents. Such enthusiasm to learn and happiness that their children are at our school I have not seen for a long while. A whole new list of activities, courses, and study groups for parents. Still my heart quivers; do we have the spiritual resources to maintain this and make it viable? Difficulties to hire teachers; also with the adjustment of new teachers. Seems to me that we are swimming too quickly.

EREV SUCCOS, 5721

School is expanding. We haven't attracted any good teachers. The veterans have difficulty with approaching today's child – who comes from a middle-class home and is spoiled. On the one hand he has all his needs catered to; and on the other hand, naturally he is anxious because his parents are striving to live beyond their means and are themselves nervous and over-stressed. It goes without saying that they have no Hebrew or Yiddish background. It is a foreign world. The older teachers have an antiquated standard and want to force it on the modern-day child.

With the new parents, too, we have to tread as if on thin ice. They do not know what they want, nor can we speak candidly to them about the fact that we do not share the same goal.

Concerning the new teachers: those in the English program are remote from our cultural ideals. They see the school only as their place of work. The younger ones hardly know much more than their pupils. They may be better prepared linguistically and psychologically to deal with the new student and his parents, but behind them there is no tradition or knowledge of a comprehensive Jewish nature. What will come of this, only God knows.

OCTOBER 17, 1960. 27 *TISHREI*, 5721.

Today the first child was born to Chana and Mark. So we have crossed over the fence to become grandfather and grandmother. Gittel became a great-grandmother. Joy and thoughts of fate intermingled. It is wonderful how Chana went through it, she wants everything to be natural and will nurse the baby herself. Her happiness glows from her face. Takes everything in her stride – naturally and with full joy. May they be well. They want to call him David, the second name of my father, may he rest in peace. They are still looking for an English name. The custom is to have two names. We are preparing for the *bris*.

NOVEMBER 27, 1960

The last few weeks have been very hard. The financial crisis of the school is reaching a climax. The new activists have become frightened and are discouraged. They don't know how to arrange the refinancing in order to continue. We can bring the parents to the large meetings to hear speeches, but they are still far from assuming their responsibilities. This week it will have to come to a climax: either we will be able to convince them to undertake their share of responsibilities, or who knows what the consequences might be. My sleepless nights have returned. The shadow of catastrophe hovers over all our work. The teachers are nervous and that is transmitted into the classrooms.

There is one source of pleasure: the Y. Friedland Fund for Literature has awarded me the prize for the short story *"Dos Emeseh Bild,"* published in *Di Goldene Kayt*, no. 36. I should be able to derive full pleasure from this bit of recognition. However, since I know that Bronstein was on the jury, and he was steadfast in his support, I received the prize. In all cases it is always necessary to have someone champion your cause.

Yesterday we had the first visit by our grandchild, Dovidl. It is such a unique feeling that I have not yet found any words to express it.

DECEMBER 27, 1960

The prize has been announced in the newspaper. Of all the local writers, only Yehuda Elberg called to congratulate me. Among the others, I suppose, the envy tips the scales. I guess that too is only human. I shouldn't take it to heart. I wrote some pieces about school and cultural affairs for the Wiseman book. They don't want to publish it, apparently because they consider it too critical. I can't speak false words. I must renew the conflict and express openly what I feel. Merely to gloss over the conflict makes no sense, and it is not my way.

Ode and Motty are now in Israel, benefitting from the charter rates for the Zionist Congress. Strange how both children are in Israel before us. The grandfathers have dreams, the fathers strive, and the children pick themselves up and fly away. Maybe they will find something there for themselves as well.

FEBRUARY 15, 1961

We have postponed the trip until the end of April. I would strongly dislike making the trip while half-blind, and the school's financial problems continue to be oppressive. We make plans, but the outcome is still obscure. And meanwhile, in this mood and situation, I have to work to hire teachers for the next term as if I know whether there will be a new year. There is such a deeply ingrained conviction that keeps repeating: Do all that you can. Whether I have the moral right not to tell the old and new teachers how matters stand afflicts me terribly. The only one who knows is Tencer. But he is merely worried; such a believer is he that he assumes that in the end things will work out. There is no rational basis for this. Everything that happened to the school was not realistically possible, but still was realized. In this case, what can that mean? We owe the teachers for two months. The contractors will soon demand their payments. What then?

FEBRUARY 20, 1961

There is a bit of excitement in the city with regard to education. All the schools have felt the financial pressures. The issue of community responsibility for education has ripened. It also helps that the provincial government has appointed a commission to examine education in the province, so the status of the Jews will also be addressed. We have re-established the Council for Jewish Schools with Harvey as president. The Congress had a conference and devoted a session to this matter. I took part in the discussion and proposed that we have a united campaign for education. The main issue now is an application to the provincial government for a subsidy. That won't go all that smoothly. The Congress leadership is not yet prepared for this. The Council has already approved it. It appears that the legal basis for this is weak, and most importantly, it is a matter that will extend over several years. Maybe from this will come government subventions for education. At the next meeting we will have to state this forcefully.

MARCH 10, 1961

It seems that things were going all too well these last months, so we were suddenly struck by such misfortune that who knows what the consequences will be. Last Friday, early morning, Yechiel's Soreh suddenly died of a heart attack. She felt poorly the last few months but the doctors maintained that it was not serious and that it wasn't her heart. When they finally diagnosed it last Thursday, it was too late. She was only fifty-four years old. The truth is that neither I nor members of the family believed that she was so sick. Now we all go about with guilt feelings. I can't forgive myself for the fact that because of my usual worries and involvements I did not take it seriously and did not devote myself to them. I did not fulfill my responsibility, which rests upon me as the eldest of the family. Who knows what else I have neglected?

MARCH 11, 1961

Finally received the first copy of my book *Tzvishn Teichn un Vasern*. Actually beautifully published but I can't take pleasure in this because it is not the time for joy. I have no luck for luck.

I consider it a very good book and yet am still not satisfied. Now I must complete the Hebrew version and tackle the second volume of *Oif Yener Zeit Bug* or rather start the Montreal era. If I am able.

MARCH 26, 1961

Today I canceled the trip to Israel. Because of this, my inner turmoil is of the type that words fail me. It was so near, could this be merely by chance? Logically it is self-explanatory and that can't be changed: Yechiel's tragedy and his anticipated operation. How can I travel and leave him? Would I be able to be there with my whole being? My eyesight grows worse. I see through a mist. Reading is very hard. It is a strange feeling seeing people and objects unclearly. People approach you and you don't see them. The previous fright has disappeared. I have become accustomed to it. But I feel myself cut off from things, almost totally external to everything. A curtain within blocks you completely. A grey darkness envelops you. How can I take a trip without sight? I have to make peace with this. Somewhere a fear throbs, it quivers – will I still be able to accomplish that which I desire? Strange, now that I have decided to postpone the trip all those who earlier tried to convince me not to postpone the trip now have a unanimous speech: "I have said to others, how come you are taking the trip in your condition." How little one can rely on other's statements. Yet, despite all, we must rely on others. Everywhere a dead end.

JUNE 26, 1961

Last week I emerged from my blindness with the help of the new glasses. Now I am totally dependent on my glasses. Without them I only see shadows. The last two months were very hard. I was completely helpless the first month after the two operations. One week I observed the world through one eye. Then through a slit, barely tolerating light. That which I could see was of a completely different quality. Brilliant colours emerged from the least bit of light. Everything that shines, even from the tiniest tip, illuminates the entire object. It is fascinating to look out on the city from the hospital: one mass of vibrant light, all splintered. Another reality that appears to be unreal.

Nearly half the city came to visit. It is fatiguing, still it makes one feel better. Not so lonely and solitary. The other patients envied me and shared the pride in the prominence of the visitors. I think I could write something worthwhile on the relationship between patients and the special embitterment and deep friendship that develops in several days amongst strangers. It is also tragic to witness the terminal illness of one and the recuperation of another. There are also plenty of well-wishers about. An interesting study. People are observed from another angle. One day I'll take this on.

The graduation ceremony took place last night, where I overstrained myself and for several minutes was left without sight, virtually blind. But it passed.

It was truly a fine evening and I didn't want to give in. It seems that the fear of becoming an invalid drives me to undertake too much. Is it also a sign of aging? Afraid that I would be considered spent? There was a large crowd, a holiday spirit from all quarters. The guest of honour, Sam Bronfman, became so enthusiastic that he didn't want to leave and stayed until the end. Such evenings occur only once. The children conducted themselves beautifully. It was worth my exertions.

The entire time that I was absent from the school, Tencer was in charge. It was extraordinary how he managed, and aside from one small matter made no mistakes, preparing all things as required. It is only thanks to such devotion that we can carry on.

JULY 6, 1961

Last night I attended the meeting of the Council of Jewish Schools. This was the second meeting where reports were presented about the informal negotiations with the government and the Protestant School Board. The representatives of the Congress are satisfied. The truth is that they accomplished nothing and nothing was promised. One thing was accomplished: the problem itself has been clarified for them and for the Congress delegation. Now they are ready to propose and demand that the day schools be included in the government subventions for education. But too much trust can't be placed in them.

AUGUST 6, 1961

A week has passed since we returned from vacation. It was a lovely place. Right in the middle of a forest, not far from Mallett's Bay on Vermont's Lake Champlain. Spent three weeks in peace and quiet, with close friends. Took long walks, worked a little, but the whole time was somehow very anxious. A kind of dissatisfaction gnaws at me. As if I have lost the thread that binds me to my life's work. I cannot say that it is an inner accounting that fails to balance, but it looks like everything ahead is obscured while the past seems almost worthless. I would call it: "Without a Vision." It is most difficult in the morning. Fearful of getting up; nothing seems worthwhile. Strange tangled dreams haunt me and spread themselves like autumnal spiderwebs through my insubstantial memory. Dreams that I had after the operation recur. I know that I am dreaming for the second time. Try to explain away the dream by attributing it to the heat and humidity of the last few days.

All at once we are in a large building. Looks like a prison, but with many glass windows and a dark courtyard where you can stroll freely until the gate. It is filled with familiar people, though I cannot remember names, only the faces are warm and friendly. Suddenly, we are told to look through the gate that is not a gate – just two posts at the sides tied with a rope. Two giant fellows stand on a platform, one with an axe in his hand, a medieval axe with a broad blade, and he hacks at the other's flesh until his bones are exposed. The observing crowd is amazed. The audience is screeching, as if they would hasten the conclusion of his act. I sense, for the first time, that this is a play and I can't watch anymore, seeing only the one with the axe standing robot-like as if he no longer knew what to do. I turn aside and stride away, the cries following me, and fall into a hurly-burly market scene. Wagons are being loaded with goods. A dwarf with a tiny wagon works at loading a huge truck. The truck moves away from him. He places one foot on the side of the platform, and the other foot on the wall of a high, black building. I am already in a field and wish desperately to return to the former location. Night falls. The grasses are covered by the darkness as if they were sucking it into themselves, becoming taller and thicker, blocking all paths. I wish to return to the earlier place with the friendly faces. I think I see the way back in the silhouette of the barred windows of the building. A dull concealed light shines out of the large windows and I cannot find my way back, and wander onward, with ambivalent feelings of regret. Other entanglements follow, but I immediately know that they will be forgotten, and this fills me with regret. But I wake up and the light of day kindles my anxiety and fear for the day ahead.

There were a few pleasant days on vacation when Chana came with her Dovidl and later Motty and Ode. I felt as in my younger years. Wheeling a grandchild in his carriage is an entirely unique experience. Speaking with him and playing with him is also different than with your own children long ago. This thought now comes to mind frequently, that at one time, when I wheeled my own children, I still believed and was almost certain that your children will have a better understanding of you, and you of them, compared with the previous generation. Now, with the grandchild: with or without understanding – let's take pleasure in the moment.

OCTOBER 27, 1961

Meanwhile the book, *Tzvishn Teichn un Vasern*, has been well received. However no one except Yishaiah Rabinovitch has fathomed the essence of the book. But everyone acknowledges that there is something new and original, different from the usual *shtetl* accounts. Sales are not too bad, and readers approach me with appreciation. There was a well-attended gathering – an assembly that Montreal has not seen for a long time. But I myself did not derive much pleasure from this celebration. A bitter mood tortures me. The mood of finality and having reached a dead end. My health, too, is far from what it should be.

There is also a philosophical pressure that emanates from some parents. A number of them wish to imitate the new "drill system" of the public schools. They think that by drilling the children in arithmetic they will advance; but about educational principles and the needs of the child, nothing is said. When they do speak they classify the children according to their talents, everything is for the gifted. It's part of a completely different approach.

All of these things combined to force me into a bleak corner and I simply can't concentrate at all. I'm frankly afraid of having a nervous breakdown, or something more drastic. I am struggling both spiritually and physically. I seek help from all directions – but meanwhile things are not very good. There is one hope. That the vitality that strengthened me in the past years will once again perform the miracle of revitalization, enabling me to pull along the others.

THE JEWISH HOSPITAL, JANUARY 13, 1962

Already the third day here. As might be expected, it happened suddenly, but recently I had a premonition that something was about to happen to me. That is probably the reason that I was unable to make any decisions for the last few weeks or to follow a thought to its conclusion. I was afraid to be decisive in a way I used to be.

Suddenly I was awakened by a sharp pain in my mouth. I had felt the same pain several weeks ago when I was recovering from a cold. Then I ascribed it to the cold and quietened the pain with an aspirin. So this time I went into the bathroom, took two aspirins and returned to bed until 7:30. I woke feeling tired but my mind operating clearly, making plans for the day, which included a lecture in the history course that I give willingly and from which I derive intellectual pleasure. One can speak and think seriously there. Washed and shaved, and while replacing the razor and picking up the lotion I felt a weakness in my left foot as if it were numb, as if I wasn't standing on it. And the same sensation in my left arm accompanied by a cold sweat; this lasted a while then I felt pin-pricks in my fingertips, causing waves of heat to cover my body. This passed; then returning to the bedroom to dress I felt such fatigue holding me down on the bed that all my desire to do anything disappeared. Sorke's remarks wake me out of my introspection, and like a child I obey and return to bed. Everything floats away from me, except the sense of being detached and paralyzed, warmed by waves of heat that flow through my body, carrying me off to semi-sleep.

After a while, almost two hours, Sorke manages to reach a doctor. Dr H. Segal came in the afternoon and offered this diagnosis: it is definitely not the heart but blood circulation. Rest is required and as a precaution hospitalization is recommended. I surprise myself that my first reaction is one of relief, as expected, and if one can put it this way, a sense of happiness that it wasn't a nervous breakdown, which was my greatest fear. The moment he gave this diagnosis all these feelings became clear to me.

Traveling in the ambulance to the hospital, wrapped in sheets, is a unique feeling. During the half-hour that I awaited them, I took my silent farewell of the house. It seemed to me that some token should be left behind. Who knows?

Without knowing why, you try to dispel any further thoughts. It is better that you still have the ability to know that you are waiting for an ambulance. Being carried down the steep stairs on a stretcher seems like one is being lowered into another world. But you are still conscious of everything. And when they push the stretcher in head-first, the world turns around and seems to stand behind you. But in the hurried ride it looks like everything is racing away from you yet is really at your feet, and the world spins away. Only at the entrance to the hospital do you remind yourself that all the places that you passed were unfamiliar. An entirely different dimension. The emergency door opens automatically like a giant entrance-way that has been waiting for you all this time. Arriving at the hospital and listening to the nurses call out to the stretcher-bearers the number to the room, meeting people, some of whom are acquaintances who greet you with wonder and astonishment, all of this appears to be spectral. But it is as if you had expected it, ordained previously without your knowledge. There is no clarity of thought.

JANUARY 14, 1962

The doctors were here. Once again they probed, scraped with dull needles, lead hammers, and pieces of absorbent cotton, cold and warm liquids, and in the end they indicated that there were no residual effects from the stroke. But they feel that it is a warning not to overdo it. It might return but in a more severe form, therefore I have to plan to take a long rest, then to lessen my workload or stop altogether. I can't allow myself to be under strain.

In polite terms this means: You are a broken vessel, and that's final. The children and Sorke, without hesitation, are in agreement. But how can I agree? Is the game over? I know that it is childish to resist, but it is still beyond belief. Is this the way one steps aside – so indifferently? It would be easier if I were able to accept this as a sort of descent that leads to an ascent enabling me to do other kinds of creative work. Meanwhile, considering the situation of the school and my own personal financial plight means that I have to impose on them the decision to keep me on. And what will the other teachers do who are dependent on the school? What is my responsibility to them? How can I simply throw off my responsibilities and concern myself solely with myself? To what end? But it remains difficult to think this through to a conclusion.

JANUARY 16, 1962

Yesterday Dr Segal said I could go home and recuperate for two weeks. After that, they will see. According to him I will be able to return to work, but I must be careful. Today I still have to see Dr Woolhouse about my lip, which swells up and causes great pain. Pills don't help. He doesn't know what it is.

I am familiar, from the previous times, with the feeling of expectation and joy that comes with going home from the hospital. Strange, that this time I do not have the same feeling. It's as if I were enveloped in fumes. Now I'm not at all sure of what I should do or what I can do. Does this mean that I have been let off lightly with this attack, or is this just the beginning of something. Everything remains as if behind a curtain. The desire to resume activities has not yet returned.

MARCH 1, 1962

There were days when I had the feeling that I was approaching a nervous breakdown. The hardest to speak to is my own family. I have to make the greatest efforts to smile and not reveal what is occurring within me. Why should I frighten them? But the desire to express oneself is just as intense. Even to allow myself to shed tears. A number of times I attempted to write these words but went no further than taking this notebook into my hands. What eats away at my innards and stands before my eyes are expressed in these words: why and wherefore? Everything disintegrates. The financial crisis at the school is only part of the larger crisis affecting all our endeavours. Even the most devoted no longer believe that it can be saved. There doesn't seem to be any road, and we lack someone who might accompany us in our search for help. It seems that no one any longer believes that it can be saved.

I felt this following the meeting with the Jewish teachers when I disclosed the whole truth about the situation, and hid nothing. It is true that in the midst of it I couldn't hold back and couldn't restrain myself for a few moments. It's probably immodest, but I felt as if I was the guilty party as I looked at the wrinkled and sorrowful faces of what might be the last group of Yiddish teachers who had so much hope and vision when they started out, and now they face the end, desolate.

The second time that I felt, once again, that I was on the road leading out of the consuming anxiety, was last Sunday evening, at the symposium or debate, between Dr Handlin and Judah Shapiro, on the subject of "Prospects for Jewish Life in America." This was the first time that I had appeared at a public affair. It intrigued me to see people but it quickly tired me. The discussion and their academic approach tired me even more. Their conclusions, which lead to fragmentation and decline, weighed heavily on my spirits. Yet something within me was scalded: are their arguments something new in Jewish life? Have all these dangers and fragmentations only befallen our generation? Are these things actually new to me, or for the many who are assembled here and have we made an effort to overcome some of the difficulties and dangers? The essential thing was not to stand by with folded arms and search for excuses concerning our decline.

Usually I do participate in such public discussions, but I intended to remain silent this time, yet when the chairman asked the audience to participate, only Harvey responded, asking a question about education. After they answered superficially and before I was aware of it, I was already on my feet and posed my question to both of them: Why are they afraid to address Jews as Jews; and since when had Jews survived on scientific deductions? Jews searched for the means to overcome their misfortunes not through the values expressed in the speakers' abstract rhetoric, which is detached from Jewish culture and organized religious and secular life. Only by considering ourselves as a people will we be able to act and overcome the crisis. Their response is not important. The discussion took off in the direction I had alluded to. The chairman had to interrupt and adjourn the meeting due to the lateness of the hour. So while I was tired afterwards, I still felt that I had made a breakthrough for myself.

JUNE 15, 1962

Today accompanied Ida Maze to her eternal rest. Her passing brings to an end an era in the Montreal that I knew. A Montreal that gradually became a mother-city of the Jewish people. Her house was the address for Yiddish writers. The threshold that all the oppressed and needy could cross over and pour out their feelings to an open ear and a warm heart.

Two weeks earlier we accompanied Gaffney. Quiet, reserved, and solitary, he too was a remnant of the beginnings of the decades that saw the development of Jewish educational institutions. He never veered from his position and remained the symbol of belief in the new Jew. He had a great love for children, and the changing life around him seems to have passed him by. He died after much suffering, all alone. He left no word about the disposal of his few saved dollars. His relatives will fight over them. Without an heir, without a legacy.

Altogether it has been a troubled year and we lost a good number of close friends. When we meet in our social circles we look at each other, thinking wordlessly: How much longer will we be seeing each other? I too frequently think this way. It's time to write down a few words in a will, but what do I have to impart? Thinking about it though makes it easier and gives expression to the feeling that the road is behind you and the present is only a summation. This possibly helped me overcome the "depressed mood" in which I found myself for so long a time. It is still difficult for me to be in company, however I do not avoid people. I no longer have to force myself to go to work, although there is not much pleasure there.

During Pesach in the country I nonetheless finished a Biblical story, "Yaacov Gayt Ariber dem Yabbok." I'm not satisfied with it but plans for literary projects are coming back to mind. Maybe the summer will brighten my spirits.

I have the desire to take a trip. It's too late to make the planned trip to Israel. I don't want to rush over there for a few weeks. So this year we will take some small trips in this area and also rest. I also have the desire to write down a few words, without knowing why or for whom. It is at least a sign of my desire to write. Am I just trying to convince myself that I am emerging from the crisis? The accounting that I want to make with myself, my opinions and my thoughts, I continue to postpone. That is not yet mature. Sometimes things look reduced and unworthy, and I am ready to dissociate myself and don't know where to begin; and sometimes it looks totally different, very bright and uplifting. The last word has not been spoken. One way remains, which generally is the way of the world: wait for ripeness, when all things achieve clarity by themselves.

JULY 1, 1962

Last Thursday closed the school. The mood is much better than before. First, the feeling that the loan has enabled us to conclude the year and begin a new one. Second, the registration for kindergarten and pre-kindergarten is outstanding. Third, it looks like the *chaverim* will work harder next year and consequently the results will be better. After the plenary session of Congress, it is obvious that in the next year the issue of community responsibility for education will be seriously considered. It might be that they will establish a central fund for education and something may come of the government funding. This has encouraged the activists. In general, the Congress meeting was one of the best in terms of understanding and the maturation of the activists throughout the land. They have become tired of words alone. Canadian Jews have become older and more mature. Returned from the plenary really tired but it was important to attend. It refreshed and strengthened me although I hardly participated in the sessions. Sorke took the opportunity to visit Niagara Falls. Still a wondrous sight.

The graduation and the end-of-year celebrations took place in a holiday spirit. There was a large audience and this too strengthens me.

Thursday night I spoke at the memorial evening for Ida Maze. There was a large assembly and a genuine mood of sorrow. It demonstrated that authentic deeds have their resonance. With her departure there went the type of Soreh bas Tovim of our generation. Only through such types is the bridge between the generations created. Hopefully, the artist who can see this will be found.

OCTOBER 5, 1962

The reason why I periodically take to writing these entries, I myself cannot clearly understand. Maybe it is simply to entice the writer's urge, which has been dormant for almost two years. Since I went into my emotional decline after the eye operation and the other experiences, writing looks to me like a desire for diversion, and anything that I begin seems insignificant and worthless. It tortures me just like the relentless doubts and questioning of all my work. The worm of doubt nags at me, so I snatch these moments to record the daily happenings as if for self-justification, and maybe it is a way of preparing material for future use.

This whole summer I actually felt more cheerful. Travelling around the United States to visit relatives was refreshing and re-established to some extent my mental equilibrium. I was also strengthened by the visit to Stratford. The urge to write again began to stir near the end of summer but not sufficiently to make me sit down and write consistently.

Opened the school with a healthier body and also, it seems to me, with enthusiasm. Many new children enrolled in kindergarten and pre-kindergarten. Had to divide the class into three sections. Had my first failure, when in haste and at the last moment, I had to hire a teacher who unfortunately was unsuitable. This was the first time that I experienced such a failure, and had to dismiss her after two weeks of work. It cost money and blood: I feel that I had humiliated a person in this way and for no good reason wasted school funds. In addition, this year's deficit exceeds last year's. Who knows how we will manage?

DECEMBER 29, 1962

So H. Leivick, as well, is no longer with us. The conscience of our generation has departed with him. He was the most eminent personality after Peretz and it was a privilege to have known him and to have been in his presence. He tortured himself searching for answers and we were exalted not merely in aesthetic realms. He provided meaning and justification for one's own inner struggles. He gave voice to the modern individual, searching for answers and meanings about being and creativity. Peretz had given significance to the generations past, but the modern Jew could not see his own meaning in this source. Leivick attempted to find meaning for our time in the ancient motifs. He did not attain a complete answer. He looked too deeply into the "Comedy of Salvation," so he intensified the tragic element and elevated the individual conscience to tragic heights. Meanwhile they mourn him with cliches, but the time must come when we achieve fuller comprehension. The sense of emptiness around us becomes deeper and more intense.

Amidst all this I had to do more than I was able, including the plans for a new campaign in connection with the fiftieth anniversary of the school. Several *chaverim* are working very hard and contribute a great deal of time. With the help of S. Kom we have a connection with the Steinbergs. Extending ourselves beyond our own circle for help must always lead to a change of tone, at least insofar as it affects public relations. The irony of fate, or the way of the world: that at the fiftieth anniversary, strangers and those remote from us will stand at the helm.

JANUARY 11, 1963

Meanwhile we are making plans for our trip to Israel. And this draws me as with tongs, yet repels me at the same time. The hustle and bustle around the trip frightens me. The fear of an obstacle eats away at me.

Received an invitation from Winnipeg to attend a Yiddish conference. At any other time I would have gladly accepted. At this point I can't accept the invitation – how can I offer support to others when I myself am in need of strengthening? I'm actually pleased that I can't accept since I must be here that weekend. In fact, though, I really should be going; even getting involved in discussions could be important. But what have I to tell them? I have always believed in what I said and that is why it had an impact. When our whole ideology now appears doubtful to me and no alternative is apparent, how can I come out and speak to those who expect encouragement from me?

Lying in bed I reread *In di Teg fun Eyov* by H. Leivick. All the queries for which there are no answers are the ones posed by him there. Does he now know the answers? Even though he gathered all the questions in one place, he still had to leave the living to their existence. Added to his ordeals – near blindness, despair and suffering – the natural order of things and his body did their preordained work. Thought and understanding dissolve into thin air.

JANUARY 19, 1963

Our small world is torn apart and shredded like a tired flag in the wind. All the battles have been waged and the last survivors are struggling to hold aloft the flag in which so much glory and hope are symbolized. The arms are weak and limp. It is almost a year since the *Keneder Odler* has been fighting for its existence. That is probably one of the reasons why Rabinovitch keeps collapsing. All the public podiums declare that this cannot be permitted and a committee has been organized to raise the necessary funds, which in these days should really be a minor matter – about $25,000. Just a few individuals should manage this, let alone the unanimous support of all the organizations. Yet there is no movement. The sum has already been pledged, but when it comes to honouring the pledge the Peretz Shule alone sent in our contribution. It looks like those who consider themselves guardians of the importance of Yiddish are really hypocrites; they are neglectful and replace deeds with empty phrases that they think are enough.

Was invited to Chicago to participate in a symposium on Jewish education at the Dolnick School. Fradle Pomerantz is the coordinator, which makes it more imperative to go. But what can I tell them. Their evening school is small and pitiful and yet they would like to draw spring water from it. Won't I spoil everything if I speak candidly? I can't hide behind woolly phrases or flowery rhetoric. And on the whole I find it difficult to visit there when Chaim Pomerantz is no longer living. It is hard to refuse, harder still to accept. I don't see any other alternative than to be a bystander for a little while until I regain my health.

Bashevis Singer was here. He gave a lecture and was pleased. He came to visit the school, was very enthusiastic but that's all. He confessed that in New York he had never visited a Jewish school. He was asked, how come? We need support, the Jewish teacher needs support. The question is left unanswered. These are the same limp arms that stretch into the void without reaching anything.

JANUARY 25, 1963

Monday evening I was the main speaker at a gathering at M. Steinberg's house, addressing an audience that I met for the first time since my arrival here. Each one of them is wealthy but with no relationship to Yiddish or our type of education. They came because their boss had ordered them, certainly not because of Peretz Shule. I was very anxious the whole time before the gathering. It was really an historical event in the city, especially for us. The circle we could never approach had finally opened their door to us. This could mean that in this way, once and for all, all our debts could be erased and we would be able to continue our work with untroubled minds. On the other hand, it is a new world that does not understand us, and opposes us, full of suspicions and fears. Our past comprises fifty years of prolonged struggle. How do we speak to them of our history in terms of dignity without denying our past, and still not arouse their fears too keenly. They should be made to feel that they may, and should, offer help.

I spoke for approximately twenty-five minutes. While speaking I sensed that the audience was attentive and was becoming more sympathetic, prepared to think about the issue. Briefly, I described the symbolic significance of the origins of our educational movement. The dates of the school's founding, 1913, a year prior to the First World War; and 1940, the opening of the day school amidst the great blood deluge of the World War II; and concluded with the chapter on the surviving refugee children between 1946 and 1956. I gave a picture of our struggles with financial hardship, and a number of our achievements. The response was particularly positive. A nucleus of a committee was formed, with promises of work and contributions. The mood was more relaxed and, one could venture, even enthusiastic. It might be that at this evening the plight of our building has been resolved. We will be able for a few years to look forward to internal educational enrichment.

FEBRUARY 2, 1963

Today, while reading some new journals that have just arrived, I found myself meditating in an unusual direction. For generations Jewish individuals, and even communities, wanted to disappear. It is referred to by many names. And here, soon, it will be successful. Rid of responsibility, the hardships, and misfortunes. On the other hand, there are individuals and groups that don't permit this. They reawaken the feelings of personal dignity and the sources of folk creativity. In the name of what? So that they will be destroyed in the future by a monster? Did this not occur in Babylon? In Spain? In Eastern Europe? And are we doing the same thing in the American community? What is the point of all this? Dignity, creativity; yet tomorrow is so black. Aren't the Messianic longings, which always accompany the movements of renewal, only an agent for preparing a blood-bath and destruction?

I am even fearful of speculating further and arriving at the inescapable conclusions. My embitterment renders me helpless. I search for ways to extricate myself from this, but am still unable to. In consequence I cannot sit down to write, despite the fact that there is so much more that I wish to say and tell about.

MARCH 10, 1963. PURIM, 5723

Last Wednesday I attended a testimonial evening for the *Keneder Odler*. It happened on the eve of the biggest snowstorm of the winter. It closed down the entire transportation system. As if someone had stuck out their tongue at all of civilization and its technology. They were halted in their tracks like the heathen gods in the satire of the Psalm-singer. A small audience attended the supper at the orthodox club, and this was comprised, oddly, of non-Yiddish speakers. The Yiddish speakers haven't even the strength for this. One outbid the other in making claims for their ignorance. All done in good humour, boasting that they don't read and don't know any Yiddish. Despite that, they would like to support the Yiddish newspaper for prestige and for their poor brethren, pity on them, who need it. They are prepared to salvage something that they themselves do not need. One, for his eighty-year-old mother; another, in honour of his father, may he rest in peace. I sat there, my tongue eager to speak, wishing to stand up and point out to them how petty and low they were with boasting of being a leadership that doesn't know who they lead nor in what direction. I controlled myself. What would be the result? First of all, they don't understand the language that speaks about the creative life of a people. They are accustomed to being dutiful in regard to their Jewish activities. Isn't it enough that they want to do their duty for Yiddish as well? Second, without their "rescue" the *Odler's* wings would droop and it would plummet earthward. So we suffered through the evening and "saved" the *Odler* by establishing an interim fund. Saved for the moment. I felt a keen pity for Wolofsky, who had inherited a miserable business from his father. He too has no need for the *Odler* as a means toward a life of creativity in Yiddish. He has to present himself to these Jewish businessmen as an ineffective businessman. And even more so, my heart bled for Rabinovitch, sick and demoralized, whose appeal was based on the fact that the French too have to save their newspapers. He had to listen to praise about his idealism, and how well he writes; and to swallow the implication that if he were writing in another language, he would make a fortune. Therefore, out of pity, the *Odler* must be saved. I know how he feels, to be saved by those whom we should be saving. But the inescapable facts are: we have no other people, and we probably don't deserve another fate. So we must swallow this with tightly closed lips and try not to choke.

MAY 22, 1963

Now I have been home for over a week. Spent only six days in the hospital. Underwent a hernia operation. The troubles with the urinary passage can wait, according to the doctors. That operation could take place several months from now, or it could be postponed for years. The time for patching up the worn-out machine has arrived. This does not frighten me. The whole internal management of the school rests on Tencer and he does this very well and with enthusiasm. During these days I even managed to do some preparations for the celebration, but always fighting the waves of inertia. Maybe it is the result of my general weakness – which has persisted too long – and this disturbs me even more. Somehow it looks to me like "beyond despair." The passing away, one by one, of the entire generation of writers and leaders eats away at me like a moth. As if I have already made the final accounting with myself and am just waiting for... Despite this I'm planning to begin work next week. Maybe the work itself will help restore my equilibrium.

MAY 24, 1963

"Where did I miss out in my life?" is the question that Sarah Caiserman keeps asking me. The horror of her daughter Nina's suicide has shaken everyone.

How can one reply to the grieving mother who has always provided the material means – over and over again – and was unable to transmit anything of a spiritual foundation. She always fought against her mother's spiritual convictions. And somewhere alone, at a barren spot, she brought herself to an end. It is horrible to comprehend and even more horrible that we are helpless to offer any comfort.

MAY 25, 1963

Today there will be a meeting at home with a number of *chaverim* of the school to consider the issue of getting protection for the school from the terror-panic in the province, which has been aroused by a nationalistic wave for separatism.

The last few weeks there have been incidents of explosions at government institutions. Of primary concern, the institutions of Jewish education have been intimidated. There was a fire in the Folk Shule and in a number of others as well. Last week we received anonymous threatening calls demanding the removal of the Yiddish signs from the school buses. It could be that the situation is being exploited by cranks or anti-Semites. But it could be from the same gang. After all, the Jews are associated with the cultural, economic, and social sphere of the English. The Jewish leadership is frightened. We among them. What one anonymous telephone call can accomplish! This has been going on for months and as yet the police have not made a single arrest. It looks like they are helpless, or that they can't provoke the powers that lie behind these groups. The police advised us to remove the signs so as not to endanger the children.

Surrendering to this lies heavily on my conscience. But a number of activists argued that we shouldn't take a chance because of prestige. I had to submit; but still feel that this is no way to confront a crisis. Out of the fear of causing a panic one has to stifle this within oneself. It is not possible to make this public either for one's own satisfaction or for fear that it could suddenly become solely a Jewish question. In this way we are once again caught between the hammer and the anvil. As usual in the time of crisis, the Congress is very cautious, and counsels not to shout too loud. In the meantime we have to look for protective means for ourselves. The police cooperate, but they are helpless and don't know what to do.

JUNE 5, 1963

Every morning when I see the buses arrive without their signs, I feel humiliated. It is now clear that the telephone call was simply from an anti-Semite, or a childish prank. Nevertheless the fear lingers; even though everyone feels that the fear is justified, and we must not jeopardize the children, it is a bitter feeling. Consequently we try to talk about this as little as possible.

There was a meeting of the council of day schools. Nearly all the leaders of the schools were present. A sense of relief was felt because the police had arrested some suspects, whom they think to be a "group of terrorists." Everybody tried to minimize the whole affair. The teachers and leaders of the religious schools tried to attribute the fires in their schools, to of all things, their own pupils! All of a sudden our children are the guilty parties. Isn't it an aspect of our tradition to take the sin on ourselves? As the Prophet said, "Our sins testify against us." Here as well, the rationalizations made a poor impression. On the one hand, there is a feeling that our situation is very precarious, and that sooner or later the separatists will utter words against the Jews, who are culturally and economically a part of the English sector. It is possible that the threats were a manifestation of this. On the other hand, people are reluctant to make this public as a Jewish issue. So they talked and talked without approaching the heart of the matter. What should be done in order to avoid becoming the lightning rod in this fight for principles was not touched upon. No one wanted to touch this issue. It can't be said that this was due to cowardice. It is the tragic situation that imposes on us the old attitude: Better not to make any premature disturbance – sufficient unto the day are the troubles thereof. So it was decided to adopt preventative measures and little else.

Privately, it was revealed that at the audience Congress leadership held with the Cardinal, he tried among other things to explain the unrest in Quebec in this way: After all, isn't it the case that the industrial and financial control lies in English hands, commerce in the hands of Jews. The Frenchman no longer wishes to remain a consumer. Naturally, they pointed out to him that the large department stores are not Jewish-owned. But what is the point of such replies? It shows which way the wind blows. We can expect some difficult times in the next few years.

JUNE 29, 1963

Another school year is completed. It was a very difficult year both spiritually and materially. The continual illnesses had a depressing effect and how I managed despite this to plan and execute a near complete program for the

Jubilee Year amazes even myself. The beginning of the Jubilee Year was inaugurated at the graduation with true dignity. We honoured the founders and the only remaining teacher from the original staff, Wolf Chaitman. The plans are ready for three more celebrations: for the women's auxiliary in September; a Jubilee banquet for all in November; and a theatrical evening in March. Another large celebration for the graduates, and an exhibition of the school's history in April or May – and the whole plan is complete. If only this will also result in financial support, it will have been worth it. And then I would be able to devote myself to the educational matters that must be addressed.

The issue of four languages in the school is becoming a serious methodological problem. We must strengthen French and Hebrew, and it is becoming more and more difficult to teach Yiddish as it ought to be taught. The teachers are not prepared for this. And the problem of time is also a critical issue. If the finances were less pressing, we could find a solution. We have no choice. As it is, I eat my heart out, and the teachers are getting on each others' nerves.

Yesterday attended a meeting of the *Keneder Odler*. Some came with the opinion to abolish the committee and let things take their course. Precisely those so-called lovers of Yiddish, who could organize the fund to maintain the newspaper, are the ones ready to forsake it; and what will happen, will happen. It was painful to sit and watch the hypocrisy of the so-called culturalists. Despite this, they adopted a resolution to organize a community-wide committee that will concern itself with the deficit, and to reinstate the newspaper to a six-day publication instead of the three-day edition that was to have started this week. But there was no one to take on the responsibility or to execute this. Just words. How impoverished in leadership and honest activists is our circle. The richer the individuals became, the poorer became our community.

AUGUST 31, 1963

It was a strange summer. The whole month of July was hot. Had to be in the city for school matters and, most importantly, Ode had to undergo an operation and we couldn't see ourselves leaving. There is always an element of fear where surgery is involved, especially when it's your own child. The young have no understanding of this. They were even angry with us for staying in town. I guess when they grow older they will probably understand.

Spent about four weeks in the country, a lovely and peaceful spot. Few people, so I enjoyed myself thoroughly. The truth is that I am tired of people. The isolation helped a good deal to calm my nerves. It has been difficult for Sorke and Gittel; they don't feel well in the mountains and getting provisions creates problems for them. Above all, the evenings were very lonely. Except for the weekends and the week that Chana spent here with the children. That was the best of the summer. We simply came to know the grandchildren better, and our attachment became closer. It is a special delight to be with grandchildren. Of course, the language estrangement in our own house is a source of pain. Still the warm caress and the good-natured games are the same in all languages.

Also got in a visit to Quebec City, and felt refreshed by the remnants of the eighteenth century side by side with our own environs. The narrow lanes and children begging and the wall surrounding the city with its ancient fortress speak to me in a language of the old country that lies within me. It makes me feel more at home, yet seems to raise fears. It seems that the ghosts of the Middle Ages are still walking about, recently awakened. Who knows when they might pounce, and from where, and on whom?

I can't write, even though my mind and heart are filled with a complete work that will sum up close to forty years in Canada. But the spiritual strength and the moral certainty are missing. Meanwhile I have snatched the opportunity to publish the Hebrew version of *Tzvishn Teichn un Vasern,* and in softcover, the poem *Ch'bin Vider in Mein Chorever Heim Gekumen.* Maybe this will result in my having a little corner of recognition for what I have convinced myself are worthy creations.

And it would appear that we have to hurry; our generation is rapidly moving on. There is almost no one left of the pioneers. Last week the estimable Lipeh Lehrer passed away. There was a notice in the paper and that was all. If the great ones are not remembered within a year, what should the less-known expect? So one has to make haste and collect what has been saved – just in case. As long as one is working, the illusion persists of being linked to the chain of eternity. I am sad at the threshold of the New Year. A restlessness drives me and prevents me from sitting down to do something worthwhile for myself.

SEPTEMBER 8, 1963

The last while I was so busy that I hardly had time to breathe. Opened the school on the 4th. An overflow of children. The day school over-subscribed. A certain number are children of former pupils. It appears that they seek the status of sending their child to a private school, rather than what we stand for. At the slightest doubt, the Jewish aspects of education lose their importance. Nevertheless, it is a joy having so many young people around us. Perhaps, despite all, there will emerge a group that will truly help to pull the wagon.

Each day my outlook changes: Should I make the effort to publish the poem and the Hebrew version of *Tzvishn Teichn un Vasern,* or not waste the money from my only savings. I don't want to organize any publication committee. When I decide negatively, an emptiness envelops me. Maybe the process of preparations will enable me to begin writing again. There is so much to write, but I'm not yet able to sit down to it.

NOVEMBER 9, 1963

The awards evening for the Shule's women's auxiliary attained a genuine intimacy, totally in keeping with the spirit of the school. Rivka Rubin contributed a great deal to this. Both because she was a graduate and because she struck the authentic folk note.

The Jubilee banquet, which we had feared, was celebrated in a wonderful festive manner. Once again, the fact that a graduate was the guest of honour and the Abels attended added a great deal. Nearly the whole city participated in the celebration, about 500 people from all sectors. Representatives from all the factions and groups were in attendance or sent greetings. It was a real festival, well-prepared and executed. It was widely covered by the Yiddish and non-Yiddish press, radio, and television. It actually became the sensation of the season and put the social status of the school in the very centre of city schools. Now those who didn't attend complain – one thinks that he wasn't properly invited, etc. Financially, too, it was a good beginning. Still, we require so much that even after all the efforts at fund-raising we can't manage. It indicates that without this, we would be totally wiped out. Now there is the hope that the results will become manifest in the near future. The *chaverim* who worked for all this don't realize themselves what a great piece of work they accomplished.

At present the Bachrachs are visiting. They are among the best of the Hebrew educators, and still a chill emanates from them. Despite all the fuss about Hebrew, they still feel that they have not raised a generation that truly has warmth and a positive relationship to them. Strange, how the best of them advanced themselves through the school system. They became solidly rich and complain about failure. They seek to save themselves by clutching the synagogues and completely abandoning modern Hebrew and Yiddish creations. He doesn't even understand why these are needed. A Biblical verse or a tractate takes precedence over all for him. But they do not address the present generation, which lacks its own modern idiom – so the matter rests. Insensitive and without feeling; these people are a riddle to me.

NOVEMBER 11, 1963

All day yesterday I ran around visiting our sick: Rabinovitch is desperately ill. The main thing is that he has given up. No longer wishes to fight. Rochl

Korn suddenly fell ill and is in great danger. This really struck a serious blow. Things are crumbling around us, and to such an extent.

Was also at the Magids' house in honour of the Bachrachs who had come to visit the schools here. They, the Hebraists, have totally given up the attempt to bind modern Jewish creativity, modern literature, etc. to Jewish education. Magid follows the same path, causing him great pain. Still, their disappointment is more acute than ours. This situation is not new to me, but it has been so long since I was in their company that it hurt me deeply how easily they have given up. And even the best amongst them desire no more than the "*aleph-beis*" and personal material gratification. At most, they make a pretense of being committed to something.

DECEMBER, 1963. EIGHTH DAY OF CHANUKAH, 5724

Today the Chanukah celebrations at school with the children and parents were concluded. There were about eleven or twelve such gatherings, hundreds of parents. There were many fine and excellent presentations that also showed the childrens' involvement and achievements. Still, all together there is something cold about it. The younger generation of parents has not yet warmed up, they are somehow cold masks, as if they were afraid to express an emotion. The children, as always, were spirited and joyful, and part of them truly festive, but the parents are inhibited. No authentic feeling is ever expressed. Perhaps I'm mistaken. But when I compare how at one time the parents' eyes would sparkle, revealing a deep experience, I don't think I am. This might possibly explain why it is so difficult to attract new supporters to our work. My own mood doesn't help, although I once again have the desire to plan for the publication of the Hebrew version and the poem. Even including some writing. Constantly scratching your wounds is not a solution.

FEBRUARY 1, 1964

Another year has passed, more than a month into the new year, and the world is still in turmoil. One blow follows another and reproaches are heard from all sides. Our local separatists have started up again with arms, who knows what we might expect here.

The worries about our family and school matters are on the increase. The atmosphere is bitter. To take up my writing, which had always been my only remedy, seems unapproachable now. I've lost my faith in my own powers. The everyday routines gnaw away at me. I squandered myself for small change it seems, and a hole in my pocket. The petty achievements of the school work bring no satisfaction, but pose the significant question: "For whom and for what do I toil?" Our assessment of the Jubilee celebrations is also dismal. Somehow things look so dark. With all my inner powers I try to strengthen myself, but it is very difficult. Very difficult.

FEBRUARY 20, 1964

The first teachers' conference of Jewish schools took place here. It was far better than expected. First of all, the response of the teachers. They attended and showed strong interest. It looked as if a similar mood was shared by all. People expressed what lay in their hearts. Everyone reported poor results. Magid tried to topple the day schools from their pedestal, but he didn't have much praise for the evening school either. From amongst the Hebrew teachers those who had the courage to speak openly were the newcomers and especially those from Israel. The others were frightened. Their fear of the employer and their helplessness were evident in all of them. They shiver in the face of the employers, influential people, and principals, who speak about the teachers in a tone of disparagement. The problem of teachers' benefits was forcefully presented. Maybe the Council will do something about this. Over all, it was worthwhile. There is a group of young people and for them educational matters loom large. If the stone of fear could be moved and community responsibility was more than a slogan – then a great deal could be accomplished.

This weekend the graduates' reception will take place. Anne Landi and Brina Rose, among the first teachers of the day school, will be present at the affair.

SUNDAY, FEBRUARY 23, 1964

Last night we had the graduate reunion. Over 150 graduates, most from the day school and from the last ten years. The older, and those from previous years, did not come. Consequently, the new type of person was evident, exuding a warmth and coolness at the same time. I can't grasp their spirit.

For most of them the new building is another school building and they don't remember much of the old one. Still it was festive. Everyone was eager to look at the photos of the past. We were somehow close and distant at the same time. Once there was more intimate contact, a language in common, a shared melody. This time only the *niggun* remained, is it sufficient? Some of them, however, experienced and relived things just as deeply as we used to. This encourages us a little, but raises the thought about whether we are doing enough to fulfill their needs, beyond the contents of elementary school.

I spoke about this and it seemed to me that they understood. This made the festivities more profound. Still it gave a strange tug at my heart when I intuitively felt that amongst the teachers and the majority of activists still involved, I am the oldest. And what I won't be able to accomplish will remain unaccounted for.

MARCH, 1964

The registration for the coming school year is proceeding very well. The pre-kindergarten and the morning kindergarten were filled within the first few days. Now the afternoon pre-kindergartens will definitely be over-enrolled. So all is well, especially because this year we have truly accomplished a great deal with Yiddish and Jewish content in these departments, reflected in the fact that the children can understand and absorb. There remains, however, a depressing feeling that over 50 per cent of pre-kindergarten stay for only one year and disappear, and also from the kindergarten there is a 20 per cent attrition. This means that even if we have them for one year, we are not successful in attracting them with our enthusiasm, convincing them to remain with us.

The project with the Folksbiene to stage *Der Maharam fun Rutenberg* by H. Leivick has gained much recognition and is seen as a celebration for Yiddish at the same time. The tiny group of people who are working with such devotion is wonderful to behold. Of greatest importance is the fact that in the largest concert hall in the city, at Place des Arts, a Yiddish play will be performed. It looks like there will be a full hall, an audience of nearly three thousand. When you consider that the Habimah theatre group will be appearing in the same hall that same week, it means that a Jewish audience of about nine thousand must be attracted. The Habimah is being supported by nearly all national organizations. We have managed the Yiddish play by ourselves using our own resources. The members of the Workmen's Circle helped us a great deal. Yiddish is still very important to them, and moreover a number of them are recent immigrants, parents at the school. The Labour Zionists, along with the Farband, didn't lift a finger. Our people have become quite lazy.

I submitted *Ch'bin Vider in Mein Chorever Heim Gekumen* to the printer. Pomerance wants to design it with illustrations, in a soft-cover format. He promises as well to get the finances for this, and this, oddly, does not please me. It seems to me that I am receiving an unearned gift. The desire to write has actually made itself felt just recently, and I see images and even complete rows of words running by me and arrange themselves in order, but still very chaotic.

MARCH 19, 1964

Today accompanied Yisroel Rabinovitch to his eternal rest. O how he suffered to gain this rest. They say that on the day his soul departed he was murmuring verses from "Here I stand, poor of deeds," and from *Hallel*, "I am your most humble servant." All his life he stood at the lectern and instructed our society about the events of the world and the history of ourselves. The things that he loved most – the lectern for the prayer-leader and Yiddish melodies – returned to him powerfully just as he took his leave from us. Will his humble lectern in that dark and dusty room at the *Keneder Odler* ever recapture its melody through the creativity of an artist?

He was one of the select few who embued his grey and dusty environment with a deep, humane melody and clung to it all his life. On the surface, unpretentious in word and conduct. But internally, complicated and troubled, just like the rest of us. For over four decades we walked the same path, sometimes as one, sometimes distanced, and yet we knew we were cut from the same cloth, and cultivated a small plot of a neglected field. Now, the prayer-leader is missed and the solitude and the reckoning of our generation begins to move to an accelerated closure. His children, David and Mottele, have some conception of what his *niggun* meant. But can they extend it further or refashion it for the future?

MARCH 30, 1964. PESACH, 5724

One of the miraculous things that has happened is the recovery of M. Menachovsky. A year ago at this time, after a severe illness, he was in such a mentally depressed condition that it looked like the end. Suddenly, it changed so much for the better that he is returned to creativity and full of plans like a young man. On May 10th they are celebrating his seventieth birthday and after that he is preparing to teach Yiddish studies in Israel for a year. They are publishing a collection of essays in his honour. It was a pleasure to write a critical essay about him. He was also one of those individuals who contributed to our community, both as a party worker and a teacher. A dear friend, despite the differences in our character traits. Although some of his views were narrow he broadened the boundaries of his surroundings. May he continue for many years.

DAY AFTER PESACH, 5724

It was an overcrowded Pesach week. First, the *Sedorim* with children and grandchildren. Festive, joyful, and also sombre. There is something inauthentic in all of this. A kind of play; the ritual an imitation. The children go along, but it is hard to believe that for them it is a true experience. Since they don't have their own mode of expression, it looks like they are imitating. Of course one can rationalize and explain that it is necessary in order to bind oneself to past generations. Still, if one's own mode isn't suitable it again becomes theatre that does not give warmth.

Then I spent the mornings of the holiday in the synagogue. They sing and they pray, but it is not personal prayer. What they omit is more than they say. A young man sitting beside me asks: he knows the value of tradition, but this doesn't satisfy him. He conducts himself according to tradition, but finds no satisfaction. He wants something more, so he seeks knowledge. The rabbi talks at length about belief in the abstract. There is no connection to present-day creativity or national cultural expression. An abstract Judaism with ceremony and ritual. It exudes no warmth and repels you. I try to explain the concept of folk culture, the expression of a vital way of life. He grasps this, yet fails to grasp it. The formalities oppress from all sides, and prevent the analysis of a thought to its conclusion. It often strikes me that my preoccupation with these thoughts is a waste of time. Still if the form is removed the tiny bit of abstract creativity falls apart as well.

After the first days of Pesach, there was a major cultural event for Grosbard. A well-attended evening, mainly Yiddish-speakers but some English-speakers too. A new program. He reads masterfully. The last and only master-reader of Yiddish. In his mouth Yiddish literature becomes more exalted and festive. He reads now with glasses; soon, soon he too will be gone. So we listen, look about, and note that hardly any young people are present. For them, this no longer exists. An echo of a vanished world. Where will a future master come from?

In mid-week there was the Habimah presenting "The Dybbuk" and "Six Wings." The Place des Arts was nearly full with surprisingly many young people in attendance. But the acting was not attractive. In "The Dybbuk," the language was foreign, and so was the atmosphere. Their production of "The Dybbuk" was alien, arid, too realistic for the presentation of its mystical world, and on the other hand too removed from the actual setting because of the mystical nugget that must be at the heart of the play. What remains is only style. Artificially directed, and in some places, simply comical and dated.

Days following Pesach. Di Folksbiene whom we brought to the city, are presenting *Der Maharam fun Rutenberg*. Very well attended. Literally an over flow audience. Truly a pleasure to see such an audience in a holiday mood. Our own circle is particularly overjoyed. The venue itself inspires celebration, especially since the efforts of a small number of people brought in close to three thousand people to see Yiddish theatre. As a result we are cheerful and excited. The play is thought-provoking, concerned with the very essence of our tragic history. It could have been an extraordinary experience. It is so occasionally, but their acting, on the whole, is feeble and amateurish, and in addition, they are accustomed to performing in a small theatre for a few hundred people. They simply couldn't be heard. Very few understood or grasped the theme, the issues, and the tragedy. The hall is not appropriate for dramatic theatre. This caused pain, touching one's very innards. Such an audience, but blocked by a barrier. You need to have world-class artists whose performance can illuminate the play's greatness. So you ponder, where are we to find such actors who can excite an audience? Still, I saw the audience leave with a new thoughtfulness. Those who heard and understood were led into the drama's tragedy. Even if you do not agree with the play's resolution, there is still food for thought.

MAY 4, 1964

Have survived the closing banquet of the Jubilee year, which included the distribution of honours. It turned out very well. There was a large audience and the atmosphere was dignified. It can be said that it was truly an artistic evening, with respect for ourselves and the others. I had great doubts that we might have gone astray, that due to the general situation in the country and in the province, we decided to invite a French intellectual as our guest speaker, the rector of the University of Montreal. Certainly a fine person, a friend of the Jews, of Israel, but a priest. Because of his presence we had to speak both English and French. As someone remarked, everybody there was translating for themselves. I spoke in English, and partly in Yiddish too. Others spoke in French, and the guest speaker in English. This was an indication that at the beginning of the next fifty years we must pay more attention to our surroundings. To make contacts. After all doesn't the curriculum of the school embody the ideology that diverse languages and cultures should live as neighbours and interact together? I spoke to this issue. Theoretically, this is ideal, with no contradictions. But practically, the dangers are very sharp. Might it not happen that your own identity becomes smothered and watered down? So one has to become more careful and clear-sighted with oneself.

The guest speaker, Monsignor Lussier, is truly a fine individual, who spoke very warmly about Israel, which he had recently visited. The ceremony and the participation of the children's choir contributed a great deal to the high standard of the evening.

With the conclusion of the term, we are finally beginning to prepare for our trip to Israel. Have literally waited a lifetime for this trip. In two weeks, if all goes well, we will already be there. In anticipation of this experience, we are overtaken by nervousness. Fortunately, there is so much to prepare and attend to before leaving that it distracts us somewhat, otherwise both of us would be on pins and needles. It is a pleasant sensation, but apprehensive. Even my chronic illnesses and spiritual lassitude slowly inch away. I hope that the trip will provide strength of spirit to my soul and body.

MAY 6, 1964

Lately, there have been several incidents full of pathos. Zuker's acceptance of his honour plaque in recognition of his pioneer work at the Histadrut, and his presence at our recent evening for honorees, where he participated in the ceremony of unveiling the donors' wall. Speaking of precursors, he is among the first to be summoned, his fate inscribed, and what stands before my eyes is the finality, the ultimate parting. Hard to reconcile oneself; and yet here he stands before my eyes. Will an artist be able to capture this in all its depth?

MAY 21, 1964

Two hours before the flight to Israel. There seems to exist a calm-excitement or an exciting-calm. Finally, we are taking the journey for which we have waited so long, and which had been delayed so many times. It is obviously not the journey that I was supposed to make in that distant past forty years ago. Now, I am coming not only with expectations but also as someone on the frontlines of Jewish survival.

It is a combination of anxiety and calm that speaks to me: the children are settled, many things have been accomplished, so I can only anticipate new and refreshing things. All things close to me here are in good hands. Let's hope that in Israel the past will come to greet me and new experiences enhance my awareness. I am calm but internally tense and highly sensitive.

MAY 15, 1965

It has been a long time since I noted anything. I don't even have the courage to tell the whole truth to myself. All things seem to be breaking apart. Returned from Israel and Europe quite refreshed, filled with impressions but tired. Managed to do just the day-to-day necessities. The trip did not furnish new orientations, new perspectives. Nor renewed energy. I'm drawn to rest, but when I lie down I am restless, which further agitates my listlessness. Everything appears to be futile. Made several public appearances, summoned up my courage, and in a short time was again enervated.

Recently attended the World Conference of Yiddish Schools in New York. Met with people from several continents, our so-called remnant communities. Tiny schools, broken-spirited and disappointed people. When they speak from the platform they blaze with a final flame and forget that it no longer provides warmth. They quarrel as in the past and utter trite phrases.

Now the Canadian Jewish Congress will be meeting, so once again they will talk and argue. The kernel is dried out. Without a vision everything is chopped up and shredded. The camp here continues to diminish. Every one of those remaining is either a half or completely broken vessel. They walk around with a hole in their heart and sadness in their being.

JULY 6, 1965

Yesterday was a very difficult day: arrived at the school about ten o'clock and didn't rest for a moment till after one o'clock preparing various routine tasks, answering letters, reminding different people about campaign matters, etc. In the afternoon I worked with Esther to organize Zuker's books and to examine documents for shipping to the Jewish Public Library. Rome speaks with trembling voice about Zuker and is prepared to do anything to keep his memory alive. Let's hope so.

With the work completed I was left exhausted physically and spiritually. How little one can do for another and how unimportant are certain things that a person accumulates in a lifetime. How petty certain efforts and struggles appear after the passage of years, particularly in the eyes of another. I literally collapsed. But had to get up to attend the supper campaign meeting. Routine plans that can be made without me. I am already a senior in the group. So I have to be with them to give courage and sometimes even advice. This lasted till eight o'clock then had a discussion with S. Rabinovitch about his problems with the Movement concerning the camp. He means well and works very hard. The leadership as in all cases has no understanding. And he wants to remove himself, but takes pity on the institution. From there went to a memorial evening for Louis Segal where I was the only eulogist. I had great respect for Louis Segal and often marvelled how he overcame his limitations with an inner zest. He was a man of many contrasts: sympathetic and harsh, dynamic yet punctilious. An organization man who could see beyond his desk. Belonged to that generation that worked sixteen hours a day. He was hemmed in on all sides, but tore himself away through a personal social rebellion. From the lowest depths he climbed to the top and always remembered from where he had come. Spoke on this and much else. The audience received it in good faith and found no artifice in it but saw my eulogy as a true description of the virtues of a man whom providence had done much to destroy in his youth and in his adult years as well. And still he persevered. But this so exhausted me that I barely made it home.

SEPTEMBER 9, 1965

Opened the school once more. The student enrollment about the same. Only in the kindergarten and the nursery slightly less. Whether it is the beginning of decline cannot be known. Because of the "education revolution" in Quebec, the younger element is confused and they take it out on Jewish education. The anxiety over French is very severe and everyone knows that we will have to devote more time to it. On whose account will this have to be paid?

This summer I worked several weeks at the ocean, made a number of notes about last year's trip to Israel, impressions and experiences there, filtered through ancient memory and present-day developments. It gives me the opportunity for introspective thinking and to draw up a sort of balance sheet for myself. They will begin to appear in the *Keneder Odler* and in the *Folks-Blatt* in Israel. Also wrote an essay about Eisenman's *Mazalot*, which Sutzkever has accepted for *Di Goldene Kayt*. I still can't approach the book about Montreal, can't find the form. Although the outline of its contents is quite clear in my mind: the solitary road of our group, straying from the path, self-sacrificing, failures, and deceptions, and nevertheless emerging on the high road of Jewish destiny. Maybe it will yet come to me.

OCTOBER 25, 1965

The campaign banquet is now over. Was quite successful. Leo Yaffe gave a very vivid picture of the Jewish situation in Eastern and Central Europe, as well as Israel. His conclusion is that in all these countries there is no hope for Jewish life as we know it. Even in Israel, where Jewish life exists and is so dynamic, something is being created that alienates them from us. The only hope, according to him, lies here, but his conception of Jewish life can be dispersed by the slightest breeze. The here and now, so to speak, can certainly not assure Jewish life in the future.

My remarks pertained to the great changes in Jewish life here and to the changes that are taking place all about us. The entire social order has changed. For the founders, the school had replaced the older religious and social forms. Now it is only a convenience, merely a place to impart knowledge. The school hangs in the air without anyone to lean on, neither socially nor financially. The organized community speaks of education but is far from taking any action. It is a profound crisis that does not promise much in the way of improvement. Only through a renewal of our approach and perspective will we be able to overcome. Who will do the renewing?

OCTOBER 31, 1965

Attended the first meeting of the Education Committee of the Congress. The only teachers who attended were Kronitz, Wilchesky, and me. A few businessmen and officers of the Congress.

Saul Hayes aptly clarified the problems of the day schools within the new situation in Quebec. French will have to occupy a primary position. The other changes will also greatly affect the schools. In consequence the schools must restructure themselves. In my contribution I supported him but pointed out that the time is certainly ripe for the idea of community responsibility, which will provide the means for these changes and not let each school struggle on its own.

Unless united pressure is brought to bear and a genuine outcry from the devoted school activists and especially the teachers, then we will be witness, God forbid, to the decline of the whole structure that has taken so many years and so many sacrifices to construct.

NOVEMBER 3, 1965

Held the first meeting of our Education Committee, which has to devote itself to thinking about the changes that must be made in order to face the problems that confront us.

It turns out that many do not see as tragic the fact that due to the new regulations the day school will become a six-year rather than a seven-year program. So the Jewish curriculum will cease in grade six. We will introduce more French, which will reduce Jewish studies even more. The plan to open a grade 7 and 8 high school together with the Folk Shule did not elicit great enthusiasm. Nevertheless it was decided to negotiate with the Folk Shule and to investigate the possibility of retaining grade 7 on our premises, and only special subjects should be taught in conjunction with Wagar High School.

NOVEMBER 23, 1965

Last week I attended the meeting of the principals. Strange how placid they are in the face of the severe crisis that the local schools are enduring. They speak in outdated rhetoric and seek to hide themselves behind old justifications. The old guard at least believed in their actions; the new administrators, it seems, accept the fact that they are "duplicitous" because everyone else is, so they are at peace with themselves.

The new situation brought on by the education revolution in Quebec is seen by most as an edict that has to be circumvented and met with a good facade. I left the meeting depressed. Look who is going to inherit the leadership of this entire structure that has been erected with so much effort. Not one solid promise of a person of stature amongst them.

DECEMBER 12, 1965

Last Friday had a lengthy discussion with Wiseman about opening a grade 8. He hasn't changed at all. Self-centred. Instead of discussing the possibility of building a high school together, he first shows off with his own accomplishments. And how can we help him to assure success. It is true that he has invested a great deal of work and daring, still it is unpleasant. He wants us to have a discussion with the lay leadership.

We spoke at length, with much candour, and still did not express everything. He feels this to be his last important undertaking. And in this he is certainly correct. He also seeks people to whom he can transfer his work, precisely like me. His sense of helplessness in this is almost the same as mine.

DECEMBER 18, 1965
SABBATH EVE, VaYayshev. 1st CHANUKAH CANDLE

Last Wednesday I attended the celebration for Alan Bronfman's seventieth birthday. Clearly a millionaire, but also an intelligent individual, to whom the community is indebted. A patron of the arts, and a main supporter of the Hebrew University. Nearly the entire community was present and such elegance is seldom seen by our kind. This crowd always makes me feel sad. The self-satisfaction and self-confidence that pervades the scene is like a kind of circle that makes them forget all else. This angers me. As if they had taken upon themselves the aura of closeness that they feel they have earned.

The evening was drawn out and the chairman, a judge, tried to create a light mood by telling jokes. For him this meant relying on some popular Yiddishisms. He mixed English and Yiddish, and this alone demonstrated his attitude to Yiddish and to tradition. There was not one dignified moment, despite the fact that representatives of Israel, the Hebrew University, and the Shaar Hashomayim Synagogue spoke in response to receiving the gifts that the Bronfman children had donated in honour of the celebration. Each one tried to outdo the other with witticisms and jokes.

Only Yigal Yadin's presentation with slides about the excavations at Masada elevated the evening. It felt as if we were walking in the footsteps of history. Ironically, had the deed performed at Masada been followed by everyone, two thousand years later there would not exist one Jewish soul who would want to hear and be thrilled by the exposition. But yet, because the exposition showed their tortured, heroic days, one shudders and can do nothing but remain in deep silence, contemplating how the ways of existence and human events are complicated and mysterious.

Today attended a Bar Mitzvah of a grandchild of the Bravermans. Our younger generation was there, so-called intellectuals. Rabbi Halperin, it seems, tried hard and in a pseudo-Freudian interpretation provided a glimpse into the story of Joseph and his brothers. He emphasized the character of Reuven and compared him to Judah. He touched on the mystery of the prostitute Tamar out of whose superficial sin emerged royalty and the

Messiah, who is also fated to descend from Judah. In general, he spoke like an intellectual. Created an atmosphere through special melodies. There is a solemn, warm atmosphere in his synagogue. One doesn't feel intellectually demeaned sitting in his *shul*.

Went to light the Chanukah candles at Chana's. The children took pleasure in the presents. Because of Sorke's birthday, birthday presents were also distributed, as usual.

JANUARY 8, 1966

Back in stride and what a stride it is. After the holidays a new year but with old patches that are unravelling. My mood is the same. Rozansky from Argentina was here. It's amazing how active he is. He has the illusion that a Jewish audience exists and desires something with a sense of direction. He finds significance in his seminar and also in his literary publications.

Spent a few interesting hours with him. At Husid's house he was praised and his work evaluated with appreciation, which simply caused him to break down and cry. The chill and bitterness that he had brought from New York, where there is no longer a shred of faith, burst out of him. And his whole pose of strength could not conceal the inner crumbling. When we become conscious of the fact that only illusions inspire our actions, this leads to self-pity, and this is terribly bitter.

This week I had two distressing experiences. For the first time in my experience I had to inform the second year of the evening high school that we are not opening the class. They were a difficult class ever since they had been at the school. Recently they had not shown any positive attitude at all. In general, the motivation for Yiddish studies has weakened of late. It is felt in all classes. They felt hurt, but nevertheless only one of them came to argue: Where will I be able to complete my Jewish education? And she is not to be taken seriously, because she actually bears the most guilt all the time. She always rebelled and did her utmost to see that nothing could be accomplished in class because, she said, it was worthless. It is a bitter pill, but it must be swallowed.

Also had to advise the parents of a grade 3 evening school to take their son out of school. He certainly is an intelligent boy who in a regular class for his age would have been good material. He is head and shoulders above the program for grade 3, as well as being different than the other students. It might turn out that when he looks back on this incident he will see us in an unfavourable light; that ironically he was removed because of his intelligence. His superiority disturbed the whole class.

JANUARY 9, 1966

Finally received the first few copies of the poem *Ch'bin Vider in Mein Chorever Heim Gekumen*. The printing and publishing dragged on for so long that I felt little joy in its publication. On the contrary, a sadness presses upon me like that which follows a great exertion. It is beautifully produced. I have no idea how to distribute it. I have no enthusiasm for this. I rewrote the poem so many times that it has virtually seeped into my bones. It is in the style of Lamentations, and still everything has not been lamented.

FEBRUARY 4, 1966

The poem is now in many hands. How many readers actually read it is a question. Meanwhile the response is enthusiastic. I haven't sensed any profound understanding. They read superficially. There were two evenings in private homes. These don't make me happy because the major issues that I raise are not grasped, it seems, by the readers. The cultural elite and writers remain silent. The sales are sluggish. There are few buyers amongst us. Many seem to feel that they deserve it as a present.

This week the study group at the school began. A small group, but very eager. They want to learn, and the approach to the Pentateuch as a work of literature from a civilization with its own morality and world view is totally foreign to them. One must brush away many layers until they can see the grandeur beneath the religiosity.

Today is the Tu b'Shvat festival, and in the morning I had to be present at the dentist. With a frozen mouth and stuffed with pills I led the festivities with the children. Despite all, things turned out fine. The guest singers that the Committee for Pioneering Israel had sent added a great deal of spirit. The children really enjoyed themselves. My pain returned only at the conclusion of festivities.

FEBRUARY 6, 1966

Just spoke to Wiseman. He is very upset. He had just returned from visiting Lukoshov in the hospital. A solitary man, all alone. He had come here two years ago as a French language specialist. An able person and good-humoured, but sly and closed in within himself. He fell ill last year but refused medical attention and worked until he could no longer help himself and had to go into the hospital. We don't know whether he has some family somewhere. He is dying with the same closed lips as in life. In the last few weeks we helped with money and visits as much as we could. Today I couldn't visit him, was busy at school and felt despondent myself. In addition, we are expecting visitors. A family gathering to honour Sorele's engagement. Oddly, I feel that I should be sitting there, despite the fact that one can't help anyway. But I can't go because I must be here. A crazy world, here we celebrate and there they die. That's how it has always been: somewhere there is birth and somewhere they pass away. And in between there is a futile happiness, a futile grief, a terrifying unknown, all enclosed in an armour of solitude. Does anything really have a meaning, as we try to convince ourselves?

FEBRUARY 9, 1966

A week of funerals. Yesterday accompanied Zalman Gordon of the Keren Hatarbut, a refined gentleman. He stood at the peak yet you didn't feel that he was above you. Reserved and modest, he lived a genuine cultured life, truly one of the chosen few in our midst.

FEBRUARY 20, 1966

The Husids organized an evening in honour of the publication of *Ch'bin Vider in Mein Chorever Heim Gekumen*. Our select circle was there. As was customary, Ravitch had to be the opening speaker. But as usual with him, everything is superficial, grey, more a counting of pages than insight and analysis. His small ideas, dry and arid, were ones that few relished. Husid comprehended the poem quite well. His remarks, however, were subverted by his high-flown phrases while the simplicity of an anguished cry is of the essence. This aroused Wiseman, Dunsky, Lermer, Shulamis, and Selah to dig deeper and there ensued a fine exchange of opinions about the fact that in recounting a deep experience the word obstructs more than it can express. It also inspired me to give them an insight into myself and reveal, if only partly, how I stand at the brink of chaos and cry out to myself in a still, small voice. I think that they understood my meaning. Selah, the Israeli consul, in particular experienced this very deeply. Quite an exceptional young person, and his wife as well. If only a large segment of educated Israeli young people would comprehend Jewish circumstance so broadly, we would truly sense a commonality between us.

There was also a harsh note present. Morgenthaler arrived, accompanied by his Chava, who is herself a poet. At the present moment they are so far from our world, seeking an abstract humanism with a neutral God or pagan deity. Without having heard the preceding discussion, he countered in the style of "What is this worship to you? Why should you remember and devote yourselves to this? Only the present is important, etc." He got his reprimand from me in a very cutting but tactful manner.

FEBRUARY 22, 1966

I receive simple, honest letters from readers informing me that they cry with me while reading. Restrained praise from writers; angry complaints from others about the hopelessness. No one remains indifferent. They confess that they had to read it more that twice. The "important" critics from New York are, as usual, still silent.

THE END OF MARCH

There were certainly more severe situations in the school over the years, but now it is hard for me to see a way out. It appears to me that if I no longer have the faith that our way leads somewhere, how can I bolster others and demand something from them. It often seems that I am more of a hindrance than of use, and the best, most honest way would be to resign and let someone else take charge. But I am afraid that this would really cast the school into such a crisis that it would destroy everything. The deepest agony is the inability to write. It feels as if I am short of breath.

APRIL 8, 1966

Several distressing gatherings of the school council and principals. Accepted the decision to introduce French from grade 1, and to prolong the teaching day. We will slowly have to change to a more French orientation. How this is to be done remains unclear to everyone. The so-called leaders are frightened and only speak of adjusting, and don't want to consider our perspective as a factor in the cultural evolution. Also the idea of community responsibility for Jewish education is still quite remote. Everyone knows that the whole school system is shaky, and they talk and cover up more than they reveal. It looks as if everyone is waiting for a miracle, but no one is ready to prepare for it.

Tencer has entered the hospital to undergo a difficult operation. I will have to gird myself and conduct things on my own to the end of the year. And though I feel I can't, I must.

The author of Proverbs described it well, this period of old age. Because of confusion about my papers when I entered the country, according to them I am quite aged and am entitled to the old-age pension. It really makes you feel that you are already at the God-granted years. One can no longer pretend that one can make plans for many years and there is still time. More the feeling that one must seize what one can. This might be the reason for the heavy moods that befall me and give no rest. Also bitter dreams torture me and I awake more fatigued than before.

APRIL 20, 1966

The Ghetto commemorations have passed. They become more routine, more a kind of mass assembly. This year it was concert-like. The *chazan*, Koussevitsky, showed off all his cantorial feats and encouraged the audience to sing along, which deprived the evening of its dignity, lacking identification with the horror and grief that befell every individual and the entire society.

THE END OF JUNE, 1966

Have already begun the vacation days. The salaries for the summer months are unavailable. No loans can be arranged. I bother the few activists and they feel bad. Can't even take pleasure from a free day.

Prepared myself to write this summer, and to prepare the memorial book for Zuker, may he rest in peace. Can't put my hands or mind to it. Oh, how he is missed now, in particular by me. He seemed to have the ability, with a glance or tone of voice, to transmit strength.

There was amongst us a lover of Yiddish – Engineer E. Neiman, he always insisted on that title, who meant well, but diminished his few good deeds through high-flown rhetoric, which had the effect of reducing them to small deeds. He was, however, honest, and often naive. Loved Yiddish and Yiddish writings. Like others, he attended to all the gardens except his own – he wasn't able to transmit any Yiddish empathy to his son and his grandchildren. It got to the point where, in his loneliness, he felt that even a tombstone was unnecessary. Who, after all, would come to see it. So he left instructions for cremation; the ashes to be disposed of in the most convenient way. He presented himself like a European, poised and self-confident. But basically he was a lonely person. Suddenly, he was taken away in an accident. While walking on the mountain, he was struck by a motorcycle, at night. Young people speed through the highways, no one knows their destination.

It was my first time in the crematorium, situated on Mount Royal, surrounded by an extraordinarily beautiful, well-tended park. Nature whispers quietly there, and enwraps all in peace and dream-like visions. In the hall, a board on the floor slides open like a gaping expectant mouth. The coffin is slowly lowered and the boards close one upon the other, as if nothing had happened. Descended into the underworld. Only by glancing through the window can one imagine that it is an underground entrance to the mysterious world of nature. In lowering a coffin into an open grave in a cemetery, each shovelful of earth that falls with a dull echo registers like a blow to the heart, but you can see how the deceased becomes part of mother earth. Here, it's as if one is suddenly torn away and disappears. Is gone, never to be found again.

JUNE 29, 1966

Was at the Council meeting. The change of government raises doubts about what the new regime will do in general, and particularly what it will do for our school system. This makes it possible, finally, to take matters into our own hands. It enables us to approach the new government with the demand for support since we are not part of another board, but Jewish citizens demanding our own rights. The Congress leaders realized that their tactics so far had led nowhere. The school representatives as well seemed to have become enboldened to speak candidly and to reveal their financial needs and what they should demand.

My viewpoint all these years was therefore now sanctioned. We are not neutral nor a part of the English sector. We are autonomous. I am far from certain whether it is already too late. Or whether those who are now responsible will have enough courage, that too is questionable. But it is a good beginning.

AUGUST 1, 1966

Yesterday returned from Boiberik. Was there nearly two weeks. When we were there some six or seven years ago, naturally Leibish Lehrer was there and ruled the kingdom authoritatively. Now he is present because at every occasion they refer to him, saying: this is what Leibish did; this is what he didn't do. He has become a sanctified tradition there as well as a calcified relic. They simply do not make a move without invoking him. But his smile and his deep seriousness is missing. Still it is the best of what exists. Cozy, even in its buildings, like a small town. Built in circular form, a ring around a centre, with alleyways and other necessary buildings and playgrounds. A cultural atmosphere with a definite style and manner governs the inhabitants all day. Amongst the grown-ups Yiddish naturally prevails without pretense. In the children's camp, which is a model of orderliness and planning, Yiddish was a tradition at Sabbath eve and theatricals. They read, speak, and sing Yiddish, but day-to-day life is in English. Of the 300 children of the camp, only 8 per cent attended Yiddish or Hebrew schools. A large number of them were children whose mothers and fathers had spent their youthful summers at Boiberik. The parents come as if returning home, and reside with the older generation, but secluded. They all eat together, but they are rarely seen "under the tree" – where Yiddish and Yiddish literary works hug each other in the shade of the leafy and spreading branches. All our leaders sat there at one time or another and dreamed along with Lehrer of creating a Yiddish secular culture. The adults, who are in the majority, give the appearance of a real old people's home. They derive pleasure, but no faith can be felt. In the city they have no influence and it doesn't look like there is any desire to do anything. Here it looks like they are fulfilling the obligation of that which they had once desired. They look upon us with envy and with a big-city disdain, and even openly say that they look to us for strength. Neither leadership nor renewed will can emerge from there, but it is possible to feel at home. In general it is the most cultural milieu that we have. There you can meet former activists, writers, and artists, and the pulse of Yiddish issues can be felt in every corner. The friendly, egalitarian manner, and openness, contribute a great deal to making one feel good there.

It wasn't that much of a rest for us, but it was a change of routine. Characteristically, in a dream last night back home, a muddled vision of a whole new way of life. And in the background, persistently, a sense that we were about to find a synthetic replacement for the past. I awoke with a gnawing feeling in my whole body.

AUGUST 18, 1966

Last week was packed with functions that I had to attend. First, the wedding of the Steiners in Boston. It was hard to give up four days for this, two of them taken up with travelling by bus, but we felt that because of the family and, most importantly, since they are the only survivors from my father's side, we should be there. On the whole, we are very pleased with our trip. Chiefly because the in-laws were fine people – and survivors of the camps and Partisan groups. Now they are well-to-do but still retain vestiges of folk culture and a sort of attachment to their Bundist past. They come from the same group as M. Bernstein – may he rest in peace. Many camp inmates from all corners came together here. Everyone felt at home and close. We were almost the only ones who had not shared that experience. The majority are well-established. Some are even wealthy. One general characteristic typifies them: no faith in mankind and organizations. They pay lip-service to Israel, but for the rest desire to remove themselves. But the sense of wanting to be among your own people was evident nevertheless. Beneath the American adornment lies the simplicity, slumbering.

Returned tired but satisfied with the new acquaintances. Immediately engulfed in the current tensions. Attended a meeting of the group that seeks to obtain "tax money" for the day schools. Young people who are looking for something to do. They mean well but have little experience with local community affairs. They think that through letters to this one and that one something will be achieved. They jump from one extreme to another; at one time a vociferous protest against Congress and everybody, and then prepared to go along with anyone who will give them a hearing. In my estimation they can be used as a group to pressure the Congress leaders to become a bit more determined in their demands to the government. Leaving them on their own would not be advisable.

Yesterday met with representatives of the United Jewish Appeal. We came in the name of the school to ask for their help in covering our accumulated deficit. We knew from the beginning that we could not receive a positive reply but we did not expect that they would start by placing our existence under a question mark. Their president, M. Loewy, a *nouveau riche* type who considers himself knowledgeable and is an antagonist of Yiddish, presents himself as orthodox yet eats without a hat, let loose with a diatribe against Yiddish and our schools that are not religious and insufficiently pro-Israel, etc. Our response was outspoken, pointing out what we are, that our program is integral, and rejected his remarks about Yiddish. He and others of his committee found themselves on the defensive and justified themselves by saying that at the moment they cannot help but will consider it and as soon as education becomes part of their domain they will certainly be ready to help us.

AUGUST 19, 1966

You wake up in the morning with a headache from hayfever and the confused dreams that convey fragments of our bloody days. The radio brings lists of new casualties – which no one can justify – in the unfortunate country of Viet Nam, and simply prefigures a kind of prelude to a world catastrophe. And then, depending on the day, another broadcast about a crazed individual shooting at random from a tower somewhere in Texas or some other city. A tally of the casualties of the riots in the war for Negro rights, which has transformed itself into an open racial conflict, that also threatens catastrophe. In comparison, the incidents on the Israeli-Syrian border are minor acts, but for us caught up in this bitter circumstance, it again signifies the horror of disaster. The travels of Shazar, and earlier of Eshkol, take on a symbolic meaning: they chase around the world searching for help, while the world is preoccupied with destroying itself. In addition, the wildcat strikes and the rise of prices on the threshold of inflation, all point to dread and insecurity in all things. And we have to prepare ourselves and the teachers to welcome the children to the new year and to say "Shalom! Man is good and his God is just." However, the young ones no longer believe us and the youth feel it and clothe themselves in the varied weird colours to attend the apocalyptic drama.

SEPTEMBER 1, 1966

Was invited to meet the president of the united Allied Jewish Community Services. He feels uncomfortable for his disrespectful treatment of our representatives. He lives in a veritable palace – such grandeur and good taste in design and furnishings is seldom seen. He has assembled a magnificent library of rare and modern religious books. You felt like asking him: You have the holy books, but what about the people you are treading on? In the discussion he continually apologized for his performance. And that he has plans for the future but the community is not ready for it. He actually esteems the worth of Yiddish, but only the early forms of *Yiddishkeit* are of value. All in all, he sits on high and is complacent both spiritually and materially.

SEPTEMBER 15, 1966

The wheel turns and the hardships remain the same. Had a chat with Shloime Wiseman. His is almost the same mood as mine. The burden is beyond our powers.

Because of the significant changes in the educational system of the province and the stress on more French, and finding time for this – at the same time that we must attend to the improvement of the English subjects – we are almost more occupied with the general subjects than the Jewish ones.

The worm of doubt nags at me, questioning whether we will be able to survive the pressure. Naturally, the parents and the children are nervous and the motivation for Jewish subjects in general, and Yiddish in particular, becomes increasingly weaker. There should be a revision of our entire outlook. But the spiritual strength to accomplish this is missing. The financial worries are relentless and allow no time for thinking the matter to a conclusion. It is nearly impossible to speak a Yiddish word at a parents' gathering. In this public I often feel alone like Choni Ha-Me'aggel – the entire world that stands behind me and the Yiddish teachers is foreign to them. They probably don't even know, possibly, that there is a Yiddish literature, nor what are its demands and what it has created.

OCTOBER 14, 1966

Today accompanied H.A. Miller to his eternal rest. Died suddenly early yesterday morning of a heart attack. He had not been active for years but the suddenness was still shocking. First, because he was so young, only fifty-six; and second, despite his accountant-type dull calculations there was at times kind and humane considerations. In my words spoken at the casket, I characterized him as one of his generation who came here as a youngster, with only memories of an integral Jewish life, and who devoted himself mind and body to integrating.

Our first immigrant generation was whole and was able to lead full Jewish lives, but impoverished materially. So everything that they built was miraculous. With their departure we were spiritually made poorer. With the passing away of the second generation we are materially poorer, coupled by the loss of personal friendships. So our spirits are rendered more dismal.

NOVEMBER 11, 1966

It became obvious that one shouldn't be overly influenced by one's own mood and preconceived judgments. The fear of turning to the parents and thinking that most of them are not ready to offer help is unfounded. The first gathering with a group of parents took place yesterday. Of the sixty who were invited, twenty-five came. Five or six who couldn't come donated on their own $300 and more. Several asked to be invited to the next meeting. Some were not in the city or couldn't come. Only two said they were uninterested, and these were parents of nursery school children. Of those who attended all pledged $300 to a $1,000, except two who wanted to think it over. From this group we received about $11,000. The atmosphere was generally very positive and encouraging. It gave the activists a new indication that their deeds were worthwhile and there is someone to turn to.

NOVEMBER 19, 1966

It is now past the teachers' conference. Originally we were opposed to calling this conference at the same time as the teachers' conference of the Protestant School Board. In retrospect it wasn't bad, but it underlined even more that the two divisions are two different worlds. This became obvious because the English-subject teachers hardly attended any sessions with their Jewish-subject colleagues.

The pervasive mood amongst the teachers is defeatist. They accomplish little and the Jewish subjects are not primary for the children. And by the time you reach the point where the child can comprehend basic values, he is so intellectually distant from required language skills that he cannot be reached. Doubly difficult is our situation with two Jewish languages, neither of which the child thinks in.

At the banquet, the guest speaker was Saul Hayes, who delivered a speech that stirred up everyone. His premises are such that the conclusion must be that the entire matter is a lost cause. According to him there no longer exists a Jewish life and all our desires are contrary to this time and this place. The majority of Jews do not want it, as signified by the fact that 50 per cent do not send their children to Jewish schools. It struck a dissonant chord that disturbed the dignified mood that prevailed for the acknowledgment of Wiseman's fifty years of educational work.

Magid appropriately characterized our whole generation and the environment from which Wiseman came and which he influenced. At first Wiseman enlarged the boundaries and now he defends the transgressions of the boundaries.

Hayes' nay-saying angered even Wiseman, who, in his response, warned that we must now take up the struggle for the basic principles once more, from the beginning. If it wasn't for the fact that we are so preoccupied, we should now begin the fight on both sides: against those who argue that today we need an education that totally faces the twenty-first century and an entirely open world; and against those who are bound to holy writ and can't make a move without tradition.

DECEMBER 2, 1966

Last Saturday, there was an evening for *Ch'bin Vider in Mein Chorever Heim Gekumen*, organized by the Zhitlovsky branch of the Farband. Chaim Spilberg ably chaired and read excerpts from the poem. Yehuda Elberg spoke excellently about *Geven iz a Mentsh* – proposed that I should enlarge and broaden it in a new edition. He is an elegant speaker and understands what a writer accomplishes. It seems to me that he is one of us, and still I cannot manage to be close to him. The very fact that a Yiddish writer wishes his book published first in English and does strenuous labour to shorten and edit in order to adjust to the taste of the translator is questionable to me.

Rochl Korn spoke about the poem with her usual warmth, but she did not fathom its essence. She is probably hindered by the fact that she herself has little Jewish knowledge and limited Jewish conceptions, so essentially her remarks were too literary. In my few words I tried to probe a little deeper, but it seems to me that the audience is far from ready for this. For them, a lament is enough. They don't have the strength to make a full accounting. Considering everything, it was a satisfying evening. Despite the fact that there were several other meetings of various kinds taking place – all involving our circle – still there was a crowd of over a hundred people. That too was nice. All of eight books were sold – that has become the custom.

I read the chapter derived from my notes on Israel called "HaKikar," which is a down payment for a new book that has been well received by readers. But everything superficially. They don't grasp the conclusions that I draw.

DECEMBER 9, 1966

Yesterday evening there was a meeting of the Council of Jewish Schools. The leaders maintain that they have done all that is possible and we must wait.

The representatives of the special committee for tax support of the schools were present. A young group of people but lacking in experience. They could be useful as a pressure group. They have already pushed the Congress representatives to demand at least something – their motivation and their conception of the issue are such that we cannot support them. They are on a tangent with their policy to incite the French against the English – positing that the Protestants are the ones who prevent the schools from receiving financial aid. Even if this was partially true, it can bring more harm than good. It places us in a very difficult position. So even the support they have earned can't be granted. So we sat all evening, spoke candidly of our feelings, and reached no conclusions. I couldn't sleep all night because of the chagrin.

DECEMBER 16, 1966

Yitzchak Korn, the secretary-general of the Ichud Olami, visited with us. Months earlier the press was announcing that he was coming for a special mission with plans for a joint program for cultural projects in Yiddish. It signified that the slogan "Facing the Diaspora" would become a reality, not merely words. The ban on Yiddish was being lifted and they intended to conduct a sort of partnership with us. So he came and met once again with the same people who have always been embroiled in this politic. There was a reception for a large audience. They pretended to receive him as an instigator of something innovative. I greeted him in the name of the schools, presuming that he had some sort of a plan. But in the end, he delivered the regular official Israel speech. In the present tense situation the speech was appropriate, but of the mission there was no mention. So everything is still at the point of mere words – getting away with a good word and a newspaper article – rid of the whole matter. He didn't even feel it necessary to meet with us for discussions. His whole plan was a cock-and-bull story.

Attended the Bar Ilan University banquet. They brought together so many notables – the Chief Rabbi of Amsterdam, the Chief Rabbi of Romania, Minister Burg of Israel, and Rabbi Lockstein of New York. It was the first time that a representative from behind the Iron Curtain attended a local Jewish gathering. That alone was a new wind that breathed a heightened solemnity. Both had endured a great deal, and were replete with the markings of our generation; in their words one felt a shudder. Even more so in what they did not say, one could sense the sadness of the ember saved from the fire, for reasons that remain unknown. The chief theme of the evening was to reconcile Torah and reason, which should be the aim of Bar Ilan. What this means, however, was not made clear. The well-groomed audience stood in clear dissonance to the weighty questions that confront this generation: How does one reconcile *Halachah* with the existence of the State; how does one build a country with a wandering people, fragmented and divided? How to reconcile the firmly held belief in the divine sacredness of the Torah, at a time when all things are relative and float around in an atmosphere of surrealism?

DECEMBER 28, 1966

Recently, I have been disturbed once more by such horrible dreams that continue to reverberate, even though the details are erased with my awakening, lurking in my mind all day and preventing me from doing anything. In their shadow, everything becomes insignificant. Here we are assembled in a large hall, a kind of amphitheatre. Gathered together is the whole community, all the non-Jewish neighbours, young and old, as if for a festive procession. Costumes and golden epaulettes glisten, and we are caught up in this. Into this there emerges a scene involving Cossacks with pickaxes and cavalrymen from another faction. Over our heads they throw the pickaxes, and before you know it the Jews remain alone in the hall. Clashes are taking place outside. Fearful cries break through the narrow windows and envelop everyone. The doors are wide open. But no one is allowed out. The Cossacks stand guard at the exits, chuckling and jeering, waiting for the moment of riotous outcry: "Get the Jews!" Families become flustered, running in all directions, and falling to the ground. I search for my family – and awaken. The fear dissipates but the angst lingers on.

JANUARY 3, 1967

And here is the New Year with the old worries. Wherever one lends an ear or casts one's eye there is an open wound. A raw and exposed world. In everything one reads there is a great cry of woe and helplessness. Even the perversions in literature and art are only examples of this. They write about an exhibition of new sculpture that is characterized by a distorted figure and empty space, despite the fact the it weighs many tons.

Wrote a few pages during the holidays. So many subjects plead to be transcribed but when I actually sit down it seems that all these things are no longer important. Only when I forget myself or am compelled to do it does the writing flow.

Worked mostly on the Zuker Memorial Book, which must be published. I feel, however, that something is beginning to grow within me and will suddenly emerge when I forget my doubts and express my true feelings. Last night was prompted by the impulse to record "The Final Hours of My Father" – may he rest in peace. It came out of me in a single breath. I don't even know why it came to me at this time. Maybe it is also a part of the confused state in which I now find myself.

JANUARY 14, 1967

Last Saturday night we were at the Lermer's house, a sort of literary evening in honour of Rochl Korn. Our circle, so to speak, was in attendance. A volume of her poetry, translated into Hebrew, was recently published. This was the reason for the gathering and to show our support. And to generously acknowledge her place within literature. It was most interesting. About seven or eight people spoke without anyone recapitulating the remarks of another. And it felt as if these words were spoken with intimacy, from knowing and loving her. My contribution was a short essay concerning her journey from her home and her return to the eternal Jewish landscape, transfigured through the pain and the difficult path she traversed. If I have the time I will expand it into a longer work.

In the morning we learned that while we were sitting there, Sarah Caiserman, one of the members of our circle, was brought sick from Miami and immediately taken to the hospital and Monday morning she died in her sleep. Tuesday we accompanied her to her resting place. After the demanding spiritual and physical trials that she had undergone in the past years we can truly say, "To her resting place." Along with her, there literally went the last living link to the beginnings of this circle, which I met here in the 20s, and which had the creative energy to construct everything that we have today. The Caiserman home, in particular, played the role of a cozy nest for all who had artistic aspirations. The "Caiserman choir," whose conductor was tone deaf, helped a great many to find their own voice. Wiseman eulogized her, a bit too prudent, and too cold. I only spoke a few chosen words and read J.I. Segal's fitting poem, "White World," which really was tailor-made to her final years and her passing.

APRIL 2, 1967

These were several difficult months. Physically and mentally trying. The financial situation of the school is literally catastrophic. Meanwhile there is no way out, although the few *chaverim* are still looking for ways and means, and it is simply a miracle that we are surviving. The mood is therefore a bitter one. On the outside the work proceeds as usual, but an inner fatigue eats away like moths. To add to this, there are the continuous natural blows. The older generation shuffles on and we meet lately at funerals more than anywhere else. And above all, if you look carefully you see instinctively – so that your tired limbs turn cold – that the whole group has lost the appearance that you always regarded as part of a living milieu. All at once you see everyone and myself as if waiting for our turn.

APRIL 14, 1967

Spent three days in New York City. Usually I am not too enthusiastic about visiting New York. Somehow I feel lost in this boundless yet circumscribed giant who seems to swallow you up and leaves you in the midst of a tumultuous world, alone and solitary. The people – even the closest, it seems to me – are looking for somewhere to run and hide. Except for a conference that I must attend I don't usually go there. The YIVO conference didn't even interest me strongly, but I decided to go because the Cherniaks of Winnipeg and the Feins of Baltimore asked me to make it a kind of reunion. A remembrance of the past, and without saying so, a kind of farewell. The Cherniaks are already in their eighties – may they live to 120 – and we too are not getting any younger. Meanwhile the people from Tishevitz promised to get together to discuss the "Pinkas," the community annals. Quite surprisingly, Aaron Berland turned up, he is from the Ustilla years, a pupil and friend. Even though we both had colds, we flew down. Hoping too, that this would interrupt the bitter feeling of helplessness that oppresses me and prevents me from working and being active.

The meetings were quite an experience. The sense of loneliness shared by all didn't allow for undiluted pleasure. And in looking deeper, I perceived how each in his own way had not reached his goal. We were all a threshold for our children to enter the new world. Whether they are at home in this world is still a large question, but Cherniak and Fein are living with memories, and are afraid to enjoy the achievements of their children. As a matter of fact this was also illustrated at the YIVO conference: youngsters are at the leadership – some of them children of fathers who had built the YIVO – but what they are saying and how they express themselves is something that does not encourage one to feel pleasure. Fanya Cherniak, pitifully, is near helpless, not even a shadow of her former self. Cherniak is still in control but cannot conceive of ideas beyond Zhitlovsky. This is the centre of his world and he clings to it still. He has no expectation beyond this. Fein is also disappointed in himself for his lack of achievement, and endlessly repeats stories, actually interesting ones, of his life as a Jewish teacher in America. These cast a dark shadow and clarify somewhat the reasons why the entire vision of Yiddish cultural acitivities was so rapidly abandoned here.

The YIVO conference attracts a large audience, but it seems that what they are offered is less than satisfactory. It seems to me that the gap between a scientific conference and the capacity of a lay audience, takes its toll.

The banquet too was more of a honorific occasion for one individual than for an elevated gathering of the community. Even the announcement that they plan to create a school of higher learning to train researchers and to coordinate research projects, which has the aroma of a grand scheme in the work for continuity, was lost in the "testimonial style" that we all suffer from. And when the amount donated by the honoree towards establishing the school was announced, the pathetic turned grotesque. The Yiddish crowd still wants to purchase a place in the world-to -come for pennies. So in consequence our own world is diminished. The few sharp remarks by Elie Weisel on the American Jews, who, according to him, have nothing to say or to offer to the growing Soviet Jewish community, remained as a cry into the void.

The meeting with my townsfolk was also most pathetic; we no longer know each other. Our common memories, as well, are distant one from the other. We recognize each other by the names of our mothers and fathers, and grandfathers. But once we recognize each other then we are truly strangers. Most of them live in the largest city in the world but none of them even approached the sector of creative Jewish life. They cling one to another because they are alone. Possibly they might begin to do something for the "Pinkas" and overcome their fear that too much might be revealed about their relatives. Our household in Tishevitz, it seems, was an exception, and so it remains here too. They want to bask in our reputation, but to get closer – not interested.

Met too with Eliezer Sheinman, who flew in at that time. A true warm humaneness emanates from him. The New Yorkers are unapproachable and are always concerned for what you can do for them. He smiles openly and inquires about your affairs.

The last encounter was with I.J. Schwartz. He is in better shape physically than we had seen him several years ago. But when you sit a while with him his loneliness is disclosed and you sense a dread. Somehow in the final analysis one reverts to the sense that all the creative effort and institutional activity are no substitute for the intimacy of family and friendship. If these fall away, then aging is solitude.

APRIL 21, 1967

Yesterday, at three in the afternoon, was the official opening of Expo '67. We received special tickets to the opening of the Pavilion of Judaism that evening. A tremendous throng of people – just as it says in Scripture: "So numerous they could not be counted." You feel like a grain of sand that is carried along with the momentum, and there is a sense of celebration and of something significant. The first impression is simple astonishment. The American pavilion dazzles and shines with many colours and gives an impression of an illuminated globe. The Russian pavilion, opposite, projects a rectangular mass of colossal whiteness that is closed upon itself. Around about are all the others, twinkling and shimmering like tiny stars, which emerge and then retreat into the shadows. The sea of people flows on all sides. Nobody knows where to go, but everyone is prepared to offer instructions. The bridges and passages connecting the islands beckon, and you don't know where to look first. The train runs overhead, just like the metro; on the sides, like a lit-up snake, runs a unirail train and the cries of panic and wondrous pleasure are heard everywhere. We push ourselves amidst the crowds and take rides on the big train and the minitrain. The feeling is one of being in a dream in an enchanted world. There is no time to think, and yet the whole world passes you by: the steel colossus of Britain, then Japan passes by, Asian and African colour schemes, Europe, images from the deepest jungles to the latest atomic breathtaking modern achievements. And we see all this from on high on the small unirail train, which is propelled magnetically by an electronic headlight.

When you descend you feel like making the blessing for having lived to see such sights, and because He "has shared some of his glory with those of flesh and blood." Especially when you know that only four years ago this place was not in existence, only a river. "From the foundation to the rooftop," – it was actually created by human skill and imagination – and a bit of goodwill. Something murmurs within you unconsciously: If things can be so good, why are they so bad?!

As for the Jewish pavilion – I had few expectations, since its very name, "Pavilion of Judaism," limited the whole issue. Still, one hoped, that despite this it fulfilled some plan that was acceptable. The exterior is actually not bad; modest in structure with a two-sided entrance, something like a synagogue. Quotations from *The Sayings of the Fathers* paraphrased in English, French, the holy tongue, and Yiddish. Within, museum-like, without any plan. Ancient sacred books, a few pictures, displayed without order. Busts of historic figures, in the same way. Some antique documents and holy artifacts. A wall with Anne Frank's picture with pages from her diary. A room with a model of the Holy Temple. It was as if "Judaism" had no origin, and no connection with vital Jewish life. In the small hall, there was conversation; sipped wine and tasted Passover cookies, and suddenly from the small chapel someone sounded the *shofar*, and the few rabbis strutted about with glowing faces, wishing everyone a happy holiday. I never imagined such ineptness nor such ignorance of the possibilities to mark this historic occasion.

By contrast, the Israel pavilion provided great satisfaction. Modest and understated, but with a broad scope, with artistic imagination and an eye for detail. From room to room the feeling grows of an intense, vibrant society, with a progressive ideology and practical accomplishments that arrest the viewer and transmit the sense of dynamic growth. Even their failures are displayed as stages in a difficult path. A mosaic of past and present amidst hints of problems and deep divisions. The *Shoah* was presented so subtly that it leaves a lasting impression: the air seemed to be thick and damp in an almost empty corner. The pinkish-green light creates a mysterious aura that you cannot approach. As you enter, your eye is drawn to a picture of a child – frightened to near-death – over whom hovers an armed Nazi, while on the other side – a petrified Jewish family. On a table, only two worn-out children's shoes. The people who designed this pavilion deserve our deepest appreciation.

MAY 2, 1967

Yesterday was a wonderful spring day. I simply didn't want to stay indoors, although the fatigue that remains from my last cold has not yet disappeared. Just then I had to be at the tailor's in the old neighbourhood around Mount Royal. I had the urge to take a walk through the neighbourhood, the dwellings of our youth, our beginnings here, which had resounded with the ebb and flow of Jewish life. The Yiddish language was vibrant, and the hustle and bustle of Jewish labour, trade, old synagogues, schools, clubs, and social halls sprouted in every corner. The appearance of the district has hardly changed. The same cracked sidewalks, the curved outdoor staircases of the dark, shabby houses that for a whole block seem to be poured from the same mould. Occasionally a spindly tree, several new buildings at intersections, and in the middle of the block some houses demolished to make way for a parking lot. It looks like the present residents need them for their cars and for those who still come here for the businesses that have remained. Very few Jewish names on the stores selling junk merchandise or on the small factories. And on St Lawrence even fewer Jewish faces – on the side streets I didn't meet a single Jewish face. The former synagogues are, for the most part, parking lots or apartment houses. The cornerstones that were in Yiddish, with the dates of the Hebrew and secular calendar, now have the Jewish letters effaced or painted over, leaving only the secular dates. That's the situation at the Peretz Shule and the Beis Yehuda Synagogue. Only the Keren Yisroel Synagogue, because it hasn't been sold as yet, still has the inscription "Keren Yisroel, founded in 5670, through the generosity of Reb Pinchas Parness." Children of all colours play in French, Italian, and in English as well. Suddenly a policeman appears and stops at a door. A woman sticks her head out of the window and argues with him as if she were excusing herself while all of Colonial Street looks on from their doors and windows. Children run and hide in the small empty playground with sandboxes – a new addition. The way I seem to remember it, there was a stable here. This was demolished and replaced with a playground with a few sandboxes and swings, but without a blade of grass. The children appear as grey as the playground, but they laugh and jump about in the dust with great energy. They keep looking at the policeman and as soon as he leaves they are back on the sidewalk at once, where all the adults have gathered in circles; it looks like they know why he was there.

You wander about and the years appear with their conflicts of Left and Right demonstrations: hopes, disappointments, achievements. The children educated here. Several generations celebrated and wept and tried to bind all their yesterdays to today – now, not a trace remains. Fletcher's Field, at the foot of the mountain, is just as it was, but others sit and stand there. They can easily manage without us. It gnaws at the heart; but still you don't have regrets, knowing that your children and grandchildren have better living conditions now. Nevertheless you suddenly feel that in this district there existed something we used to call the "Jewish Quarter" – and where there is a Quarter, there is also the sense of being at home. And this has been erased in the new neighbourhoods. You see individuals but not a Jewish community; it is not a Jewish Quarter.

The sound of our singing on the hills in the summer evenings, and the cries of our winter snow-games still ring in my ears. That which still remains here seems alien; the only sign of the past, the *Keneder Odler*, looks like an abandoned stump in a cleared forest.

It's a pity that until now no one has given that period its artistic rendition. Its spiritual essence should be kept alive somewhere. That is where we still dreamed our dreams. Certainly, that generation, in their poverty-stricken attics, had endured the successes and failures of the life about them. Some redress should be found for them; they should not be wiped out like the buildings.

MAY 13, 1967

The school is once more in an acute financial crisis. The bank has sent out letters to the guarantors of the debts that we owe, asking for payment. For months we have been negotiating with them and made proposals that they declined because the manager no longer believes that we will ever repay the loan. Among the guarantors are some who would literally be ruined, and the others will pay but the school would be left without income or activists. Some are really in a panic. A numbered few are looking for means – running to the "leaders" in the hope that they will obtain a further loan – to stave off the evil decree. Several are speaking openly about negotiating to amalgamate with the Talmud Torah. There were hints from the Talmud Torah a few months ago that they were ready to amalgamate. This will not happen as long as I am able to do something. The last accounting can't be theirs – this cannot be! Now everything is at stake. The main allies are Issie Engel, Craimer, and Motty Garfinkle, who are exploring other possibilities.

Even those who are undecided, like Mike Solomon and Sheres, are also exerting themselves. But we will have to raise the biggest cry amongst our own. After so many years of toil, and we still have to rely on crying out. I am truly very tired of this. Where does one find a bit of strength?

Today drove through Mount Royal. The scene it usually presents at this time of year – the whole area with its hills and dales packed with young and old, full of play and exuberant springtime happiness – is now, because of Expo, nearly empty. The mountain seems to be brooding and silent, absorbed in its own thoughts: Because of the world out there, they have abandoned me, the true heart and foundation of Montreal. It is as if the heights are looking southward with envy toward Expo, which is filled with the tumult of millions and all roads lead to the grandeur of "Man and His World." Beaver Lake in its solitude reflects the sun, and its waters, rippled by the caressing breeze, seem to say: We will wait this out in silence.

MAY 14, 1967

Today the *Keneder Odler* was officially closed, just several months before celebrating its sixtieth jubilee. The whole era is coming to an end. Two weeks ago B.G. Zack died, the historian who had actually begun his contributions with the first edition of the *Odler*. The reason for its closing is not necessarily that it is no longer needed. There are enough readers who need the newspaper, but the enthusiasm, faith, and strength required to maintain and make it effective are no longer present. There will probably be a weekly publication under community sponsorship. The era of independent growth is on the wane. This casts a dim light of loss on all of us. The remaining individuals begin to look like lost Choni Ha-Me'aggel whose surrounding circle has lost its magic power.

MAY 19, 1967

The days since the *Keneder Odler* ceased publication are somehow mute and blind. All the doors and windows that were open to the Yiddish-Jewish surroundings have been closed and sealed. In our institutions we are isolated as on an island. No longer do we have the feeling of belonging to the domain of Yiddish around the world.

Among the so-called leaders we gain a lot of sympathy but little readiness to undertake anything concrete. None of them see any possibility for community involvement. The only one who is prepared to do anything is Saul Hayes of the Congress. He is pessimistic about obtaining any financial aid from community funds, but hoped to influence Sam Bronfman privately to raise a sum of money. He has to meet with him next week after he receives a memorandum about the issue. I can still feel in my bones the negotiations and the cross-examinations of past years. But do we have any choice? After so much effort, to stand once again like a beggar at the gate, hoping to expect help from those who don't even consider the whole matter a top priority.

The last few days have been fateful for Israel. Nasser has found the right moment to confront Israel again, face to face. Everyone is mobilizing. The UN peacekeepers were dismissed. The only ones who felt that he should not be yielded to was Canada. Meanwhile the great powers are silent. Are we seeing a repetition of our capitulation to an aggressor? The rational view suggests that there will not be an open conflict, but the heart quivers. "Who will defend Jacob, since he is so small?" Still, in this situation, there persists within Israel a bitter conflict at the highest level, expressed in such petty ways and means. It calls to mind the saying: Why was the Temple destroyed? Because of pointless hatred. I am often more fearful of this than of an external enemy.

MAY 20, 1967

Yesterday evening at a gathering for B. Shifner I met Wiseman. He is mentally and spiritually broken up and agitated with our whole school situation. Their situation is almost the same as ours. At first, as is his custom, he wanted to pump me for information. Then he talked so much, as if the "end of days" had been reached, even though they are opening an eighth grade, which should be a cause for celebration. He is taking a great risk. His motto is: If he is going under, let it be with all the flags flying.

This week will be marked by the occasion of President Shazar's visit. Tuesday afternoon we are going to see him with our senior grades; the success of this is a matter of concern to us. There seems to be little enthusiasm for this among many children. Does this represent a reflection of the atmosphere at home, or is it because it is taking place at Expo, which for them is not a treat with an organized group. Tuesday evening there will be a reception at the Queen Elizabeth Hotel for the formal welcome. Thursday, lunch with writers. At five o'clock, tea with educators. For us this is definitely an experience. Only once in the history of our generation and in such a tense Judgment-day atmosphere. If not for this, we would really be dancing with joy for having lived to see this day.

MAY 26, 1967

Had another long discussion with Hayes. After sending him the memorandum he had requested, he informed me that he had taken it up with Bronfman but could not convince him to give us any help at all. The reason: since there can be no general or complete solution from the community planning for education, and a little help only means postponing the crisis for a while, therefore his advice is to negotiate with the Talmud Torah to have them take over the school and its debts. He advises that it might be possible to arrange for a certain degree of autonomy. They will look after the older teachers and as a sweet enticement, I, personally, would definitely be taken care of. He utters this with delicacy, diplomatically, and with a touch of cynical philosophy. The apex of his argument: this will be a complete solution. My answer was quite clear without entering into any theoretical or other explanations: I do not think that I can negotiate with anyone to offer the children or parents as a dowry; or to negotiate the pensions of individual teachers. We are not looking for a special complete solution at the moment, only help for the school, which they themselves say, has served the community for over fifty years.

Personally, I feel that if there is really no help available from any source for the school as it is, then it is my duty to preside over the liquidation myself, and not to transfer it to someone else. So he asked if he could come to the School Committee to propose his plan. My answer was that this would mean discouraging the enthusiasm of the activists who would do nothing but immediately consider liquidation. This way there is still a hope to find a temporary solution to gain time and to gather new strength to proceed further. Only then did he protect himself with an "open-hearted" declaration. Cynically, he added that the entire proposal was his own, and that he has no authority from anyone that they even want this, but he wants to help us so is prepared to take on the role of the broker. If I was younger and more impulsive I probably would have torn into him. As it was, I just remarked that the older one gets and the more one is involved in community work, the implication of the saying "Don't put your trust in wealthy patrons" becomes clearer.

MAY 27, 1967

Spoke with Bloomfield. The excuse that he offered was that the subvention of $10,000 the Lady Davis Foundation now gives annually to the community cannot be increased, and he himself is too involved with too many projects and can't take on education as one of his endeavours. There are still several individuals who could be approached by some of our activists, but they move as slow as turtles.

MAY 29, 1967

The last few critical days in Israel have unsettled everyone. You can't speak to anyone of anything else. The latest troubles make you forget the earlier ones. I myself can think of nothing but Israel. If I was younger I would certainly fly there myself. It is a horror to even contemplate where this might end. What does the "Guardian of Israel" really want, if he is guarding at all. It looks as if the "King of Israel" is constantly sacrificing us. My father, may he rest in peace, would end his letters in a time of crisis with: "There is no salvation other than our Father who is in heaven." A fine Father who is forever leading his child to the sacrifice. For countless times in the last sixty years. For how long?

MAY 30, 1967

The crisis surrounding Israel becomes more and more acute. Everyone is terribly distressed. Last night in the huge demonstration in and around the Mount Royal Hotel, thousands of Jews, young and old, were gathered and the anxiety was palpable. There is a discreet plan for recruiting volunteers and openly a campaign for funds to save souls. The call of alarm from Israel that we should send volunteers to take over civilian jobs and to send funds reaches us daily. This also signifies that from this time of troubles salvation will emerge. And this makes our school crisis more difficult.

JUNE 3, 1967

The fate of Israel hangs by a thread now. The Security Council meets today: it is not secure nor does it offer any counsel. Who needs their counsel? Even those who side with Israel speak half-heartedly and pressure Israel to restrain itself. The isolation of Israel is so visible, and even though everyone hears the cries of the Mullahs and dictators calling for a Holy War against Israel – they still don't think that it will be directed against them.

Israel's answer is self-restraint, but for a limited time, and the formation of a national coalition. Jewish communities throughout the world are mobilizing aid. Tomorrow a campaign is being organized here for $10 million. Volunteers are flying out. Will this be enough? Will every Jew here understand that this implicates him and that he must at least give money to redeem souls?

With our own crisis, I realized that the few *chaverim* have lost their direction and they can't be prodded into action. To approach any of the leaders now is pointless. It has now become clearer that help will not be available from any source. At the meeting of the school council that discussed the resolution of Congress's Education Conference to approach the welfare bodies to include the schools, it turned out that the *yeshivas* were opposed and the Talmud Torah was always opposed, as were the congregational schools. Which left only the Folk Shule and the Peretz Shule which favoured it. This made little sense. After an appeal by Wiseman questioning whether the schools would be allowed to collapse due to their current financial crisis, it was resolved that a committee of the Council should meet with the leaders of Congress to discuss the issue.

JUNE 5, 1967

Early this morning the war between Israel and the Arabs broke out. That which we dreaded has come to pass. The news is still unclear. It looks like the Israelis have the upper hand. Who fired the first shot is now unimportant. The great powers who led to this are acting in the Security Council with convoluted arguments, while publicly professing neutrality. Russia stands openly on the side of the Arabs. The western world is confused and hides behind rhetoric. Israel appears to be alone, but the people of Israel around the world have risen to the occasion. Help is streaming in, propelled by the deep disquiet of the hour. Do we really need a time of despair to arouse ourselves? Meanwhile there are casualties – for how long will they be sacrificed?

Even our school children sense that this is the hour of decision for the fate of Israel, the Diaspora, and the whole world. You can literally feel the beating of the Jewish heart. During the day several former students called to say goodbye before flying off to Israel.

JUNE 7, 1967

I have just returned from a special emergency meeting called by the Movement. Although I was dead tired I went. Thought that they would arrive with a plan for mobilization here just as they mobilize there. Coming in I saw Wiseman sitting half-paralyzed, pale as the walls, and beside him several other *chaverim* whose children are there. At first I thought that the *chaverim* were stirred up and ready to serve as an example for everyone as to how one should behave in such times. After only a few seconds it was apparent that this wasn't the case. There was a dispute about the method for conducting the campaign, including hidden manoeuvres for allotting prestige to those who would sponsor the campaign; to assure credit for the Movement, and even fear that it could harm the Histadrut Campaign. The whole tiresome politicking amongst the Farband branches, and the envy of one for the other, came to the surface. And of the suggestions that came forward one was more inane and irrelevant than the other. I was really stupefied. Are these my people? Is this my Movement? That which had been so visionary in realizing great enterprises here and in Israel. Lilliputians are at the helm and are performing comic theatre; they should be wearing the jester's cap with bells. Part of the audience began to leave unobtrusively. The remainder, except for two or three, did not rise above the usual contributions of a campaign with a lacklustre appeal. I could no longer contain myself, and in few words I tried to explain how critical was the hour that now confronted us: now we must speak in terms of the ransoming of souls. Individuals should contribute at least a month's salary, while businessmen should give a tenth of their profits – if not their assets. This fell on deaf ears. The Appeal chairman refused to consider this. So they got away with paltry sums. I did not announce my contribution. I had already sent my month's salary to the Appeal office, without waiting for this meeting. I still feel the pain and the shame of that occasion. I have never seen the Movement so degraded before the entire community in a time of tribulation. If the old guard could only rise up and see this.

JUNE 10, 1967

This week was so tense and horrible, literally apocalyptic, that there was simply no strength or time to try to arrange my feeling into the framework of clear thought. Words were of no avail, only Biblical verses came to mind seeking new interpretations.

I am sitting, as I was all week, in front of the television, listening and watching the Security Council meeting, which has been in session since 4:30 in the morning. It is simply impossible to attend to other things, even though we know exactly what each delegate will say.

The astounding miracle, a human miracle that nevertheless is superhuman, and apocalyptic. In a period of three days Israel demolished all her enemies. After 2,900 years Jerusalem is in Jewish hands. It is not the time to count casualties. The feeling of pride and happiness expressed in the saying "They fell into the trap we set for them" has come to pass. This is bound up with the deep sorrow felt for the terrible casualties on each side.

The pride of seeing Israel's Abba Eban and Gideon Raphael in their debates before the tribunal of nations, speaking with assurance and courage, is tempered with the deep pain that they too must lie and deny that which they later will have to admit. On the other side the debate was led by the representative of Russia, supported by all their satellites, openly against Israel and demanding she be charged as the aggressor. Accusing her of acting like the Nazis. Drawing on these lies that everybody, and they too, know to be lies, as truths. In such debates it is difficult to know where the whole truth and greater veracity lies.

It looks like our side failed to convince public opinion, sometimes due to certain tragic occurrences. Tragic errors were made even though the whole world, except for the Communist and Arab faction, sided with the Jews. Nevertheless Israel loses in world opinion because of these tragic mistakes. Meanwhile it is clear that a unanimous resolution cannot be passed, but at this moment they have forgotten the political aspect. They continue to insist, despite the fact that Israel has accepted the cease-fire, that she is driving Arab inhabitants from their homes, and bombing Damascus. They, who openly cried for the destruction of Israel, are now the champions of justice and fairness. The representative of Syria appeals to Israel not to destroy Syria since we all stem from the same race. It is truly a drama in which the players, although unrehearsed, breathe the words of past generations, from the highest moral precepts to the lowest of evils.

Russia has broken off relations with Israel and publicly threatens to help the Arabs. Yesterday the Russian delegate even spoke to the Israeli delegate as if he was his message-boy and scolded him. But one felt that he spoke this way out of helplessness and anger because of the failure of their beastly, inhuman conduct throughout this period. They hammer away at the notion that America is guilty along with Israel.

This morning America is silent; that is strange. Britain talks about justice, and France appeals to conscience. Now Goldberg speaks – he is always addressed as Judge Goldberg, rather than Ambassador, emphasizing his Jewish identity. He conducts himself with courage and is careful not to make his tone propagandistic. It is not really possible to know what America intends to do. Russia, however, wants a flash-point for its own purposes.

JUNE 13, 1967. EREV SHAVUOS, 5727

Only now is it becoming clear how great was Israel's victory. Israel is now four times as big as it was. All the historic locations have been taken. For the first time in Jewish history, the Sinai is in Israel's hands, as well as Jerusalem, Hebron, Bethlehem, and both sides of the Jordan. It is as if the Biblical saying: "And He confounded them," was something beyond our understanding and beyond reality. Entire pages of the Bible stories that were once considered to be exaggerations have drifted into the realm of reality. The casualties are enormous. Twice as many as in the Sinai campaign, I'm told by the Israeli consul, B. Selah. Jerusalem suffered greatly. Letters are beginning to come from Israel in jubilation and deep sorrow, but with courage and pride, because not only did the defence forces perform miracles but the entire population had suddenly shaken off the bitter mood of decline and depression of the last few years, and especially of the last few weeks. And even here, such excitement has never been felt. This week it was with deep feeling and wonderment that I saw the school children bring their savings and accumulate the sum of $500 in two days.

We didn't cancel the end-of-year celebrations. At such a time we need to gather together, to be close to one another. Former students come to say farewell before leaving for Israel as volunteers. Every evening several of them fly there. The people have responded. The sums being raised are absolutely astronomical.

I now remember incidents from these days that left a deep impression, but because of the unrest I couldn't dwell on them then. On that Monday morning, the 5th of June, just when I heard that the war had started, I instinctively walked over to the small Tanach, which always lies open in the living room. It is a residual custom since my childhood years. In times of severe crisis to take up the Tanach and open it and the first line that the eye perceives is something of an omen, a sign of strength. In all of us there persists the belief in symbols. Rationally it can't be explained, so looking for some means of support we revert to the mystical. Took the small Tanach in hand and began to leaf through it. It fell open at Isaiah. "Do not fear for I am with you." Turning pages further, the passage from Jeremiah leaped out: "I have built you up and will not destroy you." And on the third time the story in Judges about Sisera's defeat.

JUNE 17, 1967

All of the angels of hell are conspiring once again to tear away the victory and transform it into a defeat – God forbid. At their head stands Russia, who has convened the General Assembly of the United Nations in order to arbitrarily state before everyone that Israel be forced to return to its former borders. It sounds like the Psalmist's importuning: "Why do the nations rage?" The assembly lasted less than an hour and it was obvious what kind of conflict would take place. The heads of almost all the nations are assembling – Premier Kosygin himself, "the world saviour in all his glory," will present himself in the role of Haman.

Meanwhile it becomes evident that Russia exploits the fact that the Arabs are not selling oil to the West, so she herself sells it to them. The corruption of the world leaders is inexplicable. The assembly was postponed until Monday, probably so they can negotiate in secrecy how to sell out all the weakest nations.

Today China announced that it had exploded a hydrogen bomb. It looks as if the third great power is preparing itself to challenge the two great powers. This is the way the revolution rolls into the abyss – while the Devil laughs. The two powers that represent, so to speak, "revolution" and "reaction" opposed to those that represent "revolution" and "progress." That might be the reason Kosygin suddenly flew to New York. The Middle East situation is a good camouflage.

And we educators demand of our pupils to relate with respect to people and ideals.

JUNE 21, 1967

Letters arrive from Israel full of joy and grief intermixed. It is elation beyond our grasp. King Moloch is exalted through blood and gore.

The assembly of the UN has opened the floodgates of degradation, gall, and virulence – truly a hellish underworld. Rarely does one hear a civil voice from there. My Tanach is often thumbed through and roars back: "Man has stooped low and has become base." Once again the truth of the *Midrash* is confirmed: "The whole world is on this side, while He is on the other side." How isolated we are. The power of oil chokes, and gushes from their nostrils. Chmelnitsky's grandchildren in red coveralls rule the roost. And all of their most evil conceptions are cast onto Israel. Our so-called friends are stuttering – which is still better than their coming together to mourn over us, God forbid – and praise us as the sacrificial lamb. Let them howl! What nerve! The lamb refuses the sacrificial role! The total bankruptcy of East and West lies uncovered. And also "the saint" de Gaulle with France's typical moralizing dances along in the Devil's game, and eternal Albion talks on and on about justice and the law. In this mood, we carried out the graduation exercises this week. How distressing it is and how futile.

JUNE 21, 1967

It is after the meeting of the "leaders" Kosygin and Johnson. It looks like they have not come to any agreement, but who knows what these misleaders may have arranged. At the UN the same theatre continues, barking at Israel. The "saint of our generation," the Pope, has now also spoken out for the internationalization of Jerusalem – which all had been clamouring for earlier. Now no one can abide the *chutzpah* of Israel, which wants to keep Jerusalem.

But our Yechiel has a completely different version. According to him, everything had been ordained from above, so that everybody should suffer the consequences. The more they refuse to acknowledge Israel's rights, the worse will be the final judgment. He takes his authority from the Rabbinical strategy regarding the War of Gog and Magog. When he elaborates on this, he even intimates that the secrets that are revealed cannot be uttered. He says that the fate of Israel is becoming more assured. Until now the Jews lived by the power of faith. The last great victory was through *tikkun tefilah* – redemption through prayer. Peace can be achieved through *tikkun* Torah – redemption through Torah. All Jews should devote themselves to sacred study, even if they don't comprehend. This is a part of the secret.

JULY 2, 1967

Israel is once more alone, but the Jews of the world are with her unconditionally. It is actually horrifying to observe how everybody wraps themselves in righteousness against Israel. Even the friends are pressuring Israel to return to her former status. In Israel there is a growing realization that another conflict is inevitable. Meanwhile there is news that at the Egyptian positions on the Suez, clashes have occurred. Does that mean that they wish to influence the voting by this action?

Yechiel argues that the time of the final judgment has arrived, and that is why they cannot surrender, because it must be resolved in a final judgment and Russia, who is behind it all, must pay the full price. I don't know if I should admire or pity him. I am quite worried about him.

Last night was spent at the Elbergs. He convened the members of PEN to organize a local branch. Of all the trite activities of PEN, he thinks that this would provide better opportunities for writers to express their protest against the rape of the word, and in general, to have closer contact with the local English and French writers. I sense that it might be more about resolutions than about true writer's work and thought. The only immediate accomplishment, however, is worthwhile noting. It is the first time that Sholem Shtern was invited to such a gathering. After so many years of excluding him, and his self-exclusion from the group, this is quite significant.

JULY 3, 1967

Today I went to visit the uncle and aunt. I was a broken man when I left. Both are like worn-out shoes. The uncle looks after the aunt, treats her like a child, argues with her, yet feels lost by being so tied down to her, and can't even complain about his own ailments. They feel abandoned by everybody. And still we crave a long life – in order to become useless to oneself and a burden to our closest. It is a very bitter feeling.

JULY 5, 1967

Exactly one month after the outbreak of the war, the special assembly of the UN concluded its session with a defeat for the Arabs and Russia. They couldn't procure the necessary 2/3 majority that would declare Israel the aggressor and force her withdrawal without condition. Of course, the main reason for this is the opposition of the U.S. Still it means that the rest of the world is not totally corrupt, and cannot see the justice in returning to the former situation. The second resolution, which called for the withdrawal to the former borders, but not before negotiations at the table, also didn't receive the necessary support. Nevertheless, this means that Israel has the opportunity to hold on to everything that she has won, and to demonstrate how she can manage with these new, overwhelming problems. The resolution not to recognize the unification of Jerusalem only means that this too should be negotiated. Jerusalem is now once again what it was long ago. The holy places will probably be internationalized. The historic longing has burst all bounds, and let us hope it will be forever.

The deep shock that affects everyone is only an indication of the inability to be reconciled to the fact that before our eyes a new constellation is unfolding, and everyone must change their long-held historic and mystical conceptions. The main question, and the most profound reckoning that we must make, is whether our future path will only be like the other nations, and through power be one of them; or to realize once again that power is not forever and Israel must seek her future in setting an example of how to revitalize the Ten Commandments, and to instruct conquered nations how to live and create, and thus participate in the historic era of great events.

The upheaval in which the Jews here in Canada were caught up should not remain merely at the monetary level. In truth, the financial support has gone beyond all expectations – in Canada alone $25 million was raised – but the commitment should be deepened toward the recognition of a changed relationship with Israel. Can that happen? Meanwhile we are still astounded by the events. It is to be hoped that the deepening of new understanding will occur in the near future. Even though the dangers are still vividly present, nevertheless one now breathes easier in our world. The fateful feeling of always being destined for destruction has receded into the background.

CAPE COD, JULY 13, 1967

Everyone is still talking about the miracle of Israel's victory. Others are even stating that this is the beginning of the age-old reckoning for the past generations. In essence, however, a miracle is only singular and consequently occurs but once. In this case, a momentary security. And because it was accomplished through physical might by the only nation in the world that had sought the path to salvation by eschewing power, it indicates that this nation too has adapted to the ways of the world. What becomes of their mission to be "a light unto the nations"? All the controversy about the true Messiah and salvation are cut off by the security needs of the hour, and through power. The rational mind of the Rambam, it appears, has once more gained the upper hand over tradition: "In this world, there is no other way to the Messianic era other than serving the reigning power." And according to the current realities, this means that even after the victory there is only the illusion of freedom because, in truth, one must rely on realpolitic and align oneself with one of the powers in the world. And because of this, one must injure others and bloody oneself in endless battles and laud the military. The rest is merely poetry. Can the impure beget salvation?

JULY 18, 1967

The political struggle concerning Israel continues. The decree that Israel cannot keep Jerusalem is the only victory gained by the powers opposed to

Israel. In the meantime they are arming the Arabs again. Soviet Russia, the arch-enemy, does this openly, using the excuse that they are supporting justice in the world.

JULY 20, 1967

Now, when everyone sees that Israel's only choice for survival was through the miracle of might, it might be – and many already hold this opinion – that the future path is only might. Does this not mean that the ancient debate between Yavneh and Masada is now being decided in favour of Masada.

JULY 29, 1967

Letters arrive from former students who went to Israel, in which they state that only now do they understand what our school education means to them. And that they feel closer to the land than those who never had such an education.

The riots of the Negroes in the large cities of the United States like New York, Detroit, and others has taken on the character of a tragic, unresolvable racial civil war. In the aftermath there were scores of victims among the Negroes themselves, hundreds of millions of dollars of destroyed properties and plundered businesses – a large number being Jewish. Behind all this stands the "Black Power" movement, which states openly that their program is to demonstrate their power by destruction. It is horrible that a just demand and a true reckoning for hundreds of years of degradation and inhumanity should be healed solely through devastation, and postpones for years a real humane solution. The truly honest leaders stand by helplessly and are almost ineffective against the sea of hatred and disappointment that refuses to consider mere promises any longer. They have adopted a version of Samson's cry, "Let me die with the Philistines!" The open wounds that result from the white domination on the continent are also oozing among the Indian tribes that still survive in Canada and the United States. There will be years when the so-called peaceful continent will be covered in blood.

Amidst all this, the egocentric de Gaulle arrived for a visit and openly declared himself on the side of the Quebec separatists. Masked by the pretty words of self-determination and freedom, lies the black hand that stirs a boiling, turbulent cauldron in order to take revenge for an ancient score between France, England, and America during the conquest. Who knows what the consequences might be. Because of his insistence on restoring France as a great power, he uses Quebec as the open wound on this continent. It won't help to remind people that France did nothing to help Quebec to survive; it was actually the English government, with all her faults, and the Catholic Church, with all her twisted ways, that enabled the folk of Quebec to preserve their identity. With goodwill this historic fact could lead to a new situation whereby different peoples could live in harmony. The world political leaders, however, have their own agendas, and as usual pay little attention to the victims of the smaller nations. They are always ready to sacrifice them for their own purposes. Just as de Gaulle sacrificed Israel, he is ready to sacrifice Quebec and destroy Canada. To what end?

AUGUST 2, 1967

The powers of destruction are carousing throughout the world. Black Power states openly that they want to destroy America from within. Destruction in the name of destruction. The Arab world, with the blessings of the Soviet Union, cries out again: Destroy Israel! This is already evident in the country itself. In the first few weeks the Arab leaders and the conquered territories gave the impression that they were making peace with the new circumstances. Now, however, open signs of resistance are appearing; cracks from within. Israel will be compelled to take severe measures. They want to force us to be oppressors as well. The ordinary people will suffer and Israel too will have to set itself up in the mire of conquest. The weapons that hitherto were considered to be clean, they now seek to besmirch. The so-called "progressive" forces of Europe have, so far, been pro-Israel with minor exceptions. The new horrors, however, cut so deeply into the vision of Israel that we shudder to think of future eventualities.

Wonderful letters arrive from Israel written by former students. The events have evoked memories of their school years and the influence of teachers that they themselves had not acknowledged. It is as if these recollections had just slumbered; nothing is ever lost if done with integrity.

Spent a few hours at Expo. My first impressions are strengthened. A great accomplishment. The whole world displaying its best countenance there. The crowds who visit there also come on their best behaviour. Mankind and its creativity and vision are manifested in a wonderful manner. But if you delve deeper, lies and deceptions are evident in every pavilion. The horrors and omissions are blatant: all this is the illusion of belief.

The Indian pavilion was the last I visited. Artistically, it was extraordinarily beautiful and in good taste. They boast about their new constitution: equality and liberty for all. The ancient gods shunted off to the museums. Yet at the same time the hostesses – each more beautiful and stately than the other – bear the purple dot on their forehead, which in the bright sunlight looks like a bloody birthmark, a symbol of the noble position of the Brahmins. Is there among them a daughter of the "untouchables"? Have they also been cleansed of the ancient impurities? You wander from pavilion to pavilion and everywhere you see the running wounds of history's bloody horrors, amidst this overwhelming beauty. And in La Ronde the crowds carouse until 2:30 in the morning, and in their revels lose touch with the bitter truth that in this magnificent exhibition what is missing is a pavilion realistically presenting "Man the Destroyer of the world that he had not created." It is reminiscent of Sholem Asch's remark, given in the words of his fictional character the tailor: "The world has become so huge and unmanageable that, pitifully, man can no longer preserve it." All the powers of destruction stand ready to release their chaos.

AUGUST 4, 1967

Today we laid to rest the poet N.Y. Gotlieb. For close to forty years he languished in this mother-city of Jewry. Sholem and I had something to do with his coming here. We made every effort to ease his existence. But we never managed to establish close relationships. He arrived here as an already well-known poet, with recommendations from the Movement in Lithuania where he served as the itinerant teacher for Hechalutz. As a poet-writer he did not develop beyond the ability to structure a verse. He was sickly his entire life. If not for his wife Raya, who knows whether he would have survived for such a long time.

AUGUST 6, 1967

Yesterday I was at Camp Dan to attend the meeting of the National Council of the Movement. Of the old guard only Kalman Berger from Toronto remains, actually carrying himself like the "elder statesman." The "youngsters" who now lead the Movement tolerate him, listen to him, but still wait impatiently for him to finish up. It is a completely new leadership, at the moment still colourless.

Only one young man from Winnipeg gave the impression of a thinking individual with imagination and scope. I should take note of his name: Feldman. He is an intelligent person who dares think beyond the needs of the moment. He was the only one to steer the crucial, difficult, and fateful questions of *aliyah* toward a farsighted plan involving education and a method of organization that does rely on immediate statistical success.

It is interesting to note that the number of young volunteers for Israel during the recent conflict reached 7,000, but only 600 were sent over. Sixty per cent of these volunteers were former pupils of Jewish schools. Relative to the school population, our Peretz School ranked first.

There was strong criticism regarding Israel's conduct, its bureaucracy and incompetence. The demand to take responsibility for *aliyah* is very strong. In the same vein there were the cutting words and weighty complaints of chairman Kronitz concerning the disdain with which the Israeli leadership holds the American and Canadian communities. He also articulated the complaint that Israel does little and is not attuned to the dangers of the spiritual disappearance of the American Jew. Only a few short years ago it would have been impossible to speak so candidly and draw attention to some of their actions and approaches, to be so open and naked about their petty politics. The old guard would be rending their garments seeing how the veil of pure holiness is being lifted from those over there. But we must be mindful of bending the stick too far.

I introduced the subject of education. I presented the issue firmly and clearly about the profound spiritual crisis in the Jewish school system in general. Above all, of not having discovered the approach of transmitting the immense spiritual heritage and learning for the nuclear age in which our children live. The lack of real motivation for Jewish learning and Jewish life in our children. Our particular crisis arises because we simply no longer have a mass population to draw from, and the current Jewish leadership would like to rid themselves of us, totally. The great challenge of an educational institution built from the ground up, with a goal of creating a generation of creative individuals working in their own language – this has been completely forgotten. The fact that we are no longer educating the future leaders, teachers, and ordinary folk to be able to live their lives intellectually in a Jewish manner places the whole structure in jeopardy.

The struggle of the schools for Jewish education has hardly gone beyond the elementary level, and these too are at the point of collapse. The Movement is in danger of completely losing its influence on the schools, due to the new leadership in the schools who are in the same category as those "who did not know Joseph."

None of these points are new. All these years we have been warning the *chaverim* in the leadership. Now that they are no longer here, maybe the new ones will pay attention. With them we must begin to teach from the beginning, literally with the ABCs. This is actually the reason for my accepting to introduce the discussion. It looks as if it has left an impression. For the time being it is only a resolution, but there was a time when even this could not be discussed. The resolution states that a national education committee should be formed, with regional sub-committees, whose mandate should be:

a) Direct involvement in activities to help the schools financially according to the committee's capabilities;

b) On the national level, to approach the Congress with the request that they establish a national fund of $10 million for educational purposes. Most importantly the fund would support the founding of colleges and high schools devoted to the training of teachers and leaders for the entire community;

c) To form a special sub-committee that will investigate and analyse the major questions confronting education. Its goal should be to convene a conference on education that will examine in depth the entire complex of educational issues.

This is certainly still far from something practical. Still it is worthwhile to further the proposal. Its broad scope alone promises some positive result.

In the evening, Sinai, the consul of Israel, spoke about his experiences at the United Nations. He indicated clearly how divided they are, and where the word "peace" is so prostituted that the prophet's saying, "Has this temple become a cave of dissenters?" – is well suited to the gang who are ostensibly representing their nations. One is horrified by the cynicism and depravity. None of this was new, still when he illustrated the situation with facts, it made your blood run cold realizing into whose hands and minds the fate of the world lies, and to whom we must conform. He is not at all optimistic as to how long we can deflect the sword of destruction poised against Israel. The isolation of Israel at the UN has become more severe.

As much as you want to console yourself with the power of the spirit and justice, it nevertheless appears that only by taking possession of the land and holding on to it will you assure your partial claim to future existence.

AUGUST 10, 1967

Since June of this year I began to notice that my hearing is diminished. Even when one sits close to me but does not speak directly and clearly to me, I cannot hear. Due to the recent events and constant tension, I didn't pay it any attention. Then it eased up somewhat, but only in my left ear. For the last few weeks the right ear as well is almost totally deaf. My ear specialist was on holiday so I had to wait. The ten days of waiting were difficult. It frequently happened that when someone spoke to me, I could only see their lips moving. Along with the bitter, anguished sense of this, came the feeling that the world that moves about you has been silenced. Even the passing of a car or the fly-over of an airplane sounds like the flowing and drifting heard from a long distance. The telephone ring is faint, as if hidden away. Words reach you as a whisper. Thunderstorms play themselves out in the far distance and never come close to you. As if you are already standing beyond the region of noise. Bit by bit I found myself estranged in my own interior, even among my closest friends. Instinctively I stopped participating in discussions – can only hear my own thoughts. The agony of it all also becomes more silent. A barely murmuring stillness, within and about you.

Last Wednesday at the doctor's, he cleaned my ears and I immediately felt the world rushing in again. He maintains that it isn't worse than it was, although the hearing ability has weakened. The former state of hearing, as through a solid wall, has disappeared but I still have to strain to hear clearly.

The sound of running water is more natural and no longer so fluid or liquid-like. The sense of being enclosed in one's own interior is still with me. The doctor thinks that it is due to over-exertion. Could this perhaps be why I can no longer write? That I look for an excuse for not writing rather than simply sitting myself down and writing?

TISHA B'AV, 5727

Went to Lamentation services. First of all because in historically significant days, one should be amongst Jews. Second, I wanted to see how the Orthodox feel and behave on the first Tisha B'Av in two thousand years since Jerusalem and the Western Wall were in Jewish hands.

The Rabbi deemed it necessary to draw to our attention that there are those who think that we no longer need to recite Lamentations. He, naturally, says that we should, because Jerusalem has returned to Jewish hands in a damaged state. He gave a far-fetched analogy. When a child returns home disabled, the joy is not overwhelming nor complete. He did not feel the significance of the whole historic event, and no one else sensed it either. The *niggun* of Lamentations was somewhat feeble. The Lamentation mood of old was gone, nor was the new one a replacement. There is nothing in that synagogue for me to return to. The excitement about Israel seems to be superficial; they can't, nor do they wish to change.

AUGUST 20, 1967

I do not know where such dreams come from, but for the last few nights they appear in different variations. In this way I know that they are not part of a previous happening, but of the present, as a repetition of an earlier event but now somewhat altered. It is also not something that grows out of my literary preoccupations during the day, because lately I've been absorbed in a sketch about Safed, whose caves were as familiar to me as the cave in my remembered Tishevitz.

Out of nowhere a group of people appear, amongst whom I recognize only a few, but can't name them. I know that they are close friends and someone is driving us in a locked automobile, which immediately turns into a bus and then into a railway car. They bring us to a desolate spot. Large closets surround us, with open windows and doors, through which a weird emptiness stares and voices an outlandish explanation: "What was done previously will not happen now. There are better methods now." We hear this clearly and as we look around everybody disappears, except two or three, who remain seated in the middle of the yard in a gaping crevice, which looks like the opening of an underground passage. No one is near us. We are not afraid. But in the distance we see as through the beam of a searchlight an agonizing struggle between shadows that are illumined and extinguished. We chase after these flaming torches and fall into a crowd of people who are jostling each other in twisted alleys, making us dizzy with their strange grimaces; but we realize that they don't see us. We arrange ourselves in a line and snake ourselves through them, seeing but not being seen, but we feel we are descending from the dream into a waking state.

Sorke wakens me: "Why are you constantly groaning and murmuring?" I arouse myself and actually find that my feet are off the bed.

AUGUST 26, 1967

Visited Expo; there is something new each time. But the feeling persists that something essential is missing in many pavilions. Human suffering is omitted everywhere. Except for Israel – where along with human toil and achievement – you also feel the groans of bitter anguish. But here too it does not result in a terrible outcry. However I felt this in the pavilion devoted to the Indians of Canada. With very meagre and limited means they bewailed the anguish of a mighty nation destroyed by the white man, and remain degraded to this day. It is an accusation that one cannot pass by indifferently. The sense of guilt is aroused in you, yet you are helpless to change anything; and even the usual social measures are incapable of altering their fate or finding a way to restore them now. All the pervasive, lofty inscriptions of the huge pavilions pale in contrast to the howl emitted here by this cruel sentence of history.

Something awful is represented in the last section of the exhibit, "Man the Producer" – the automated machine that processes everything from the raw material to the completed product. It instills a dread with its monster-like totemic appearance, as well as the notion that human concepts have locked themselves in and are immobilized.

AUGUST 29, 1967

Today I attended a meeting of all the principals and chairmen of the day schools. This might become the historic meeting at which it was decided to utilize the new law that offers the Jewish day schools the opportunity to be supported through general taxation. This could be accomplished by signing a mutual agreement with the Protestant School Board whereby our schools would join with them for the secular subjects, to be supervised by a combined committee. This is a far cry from what we demanded, which was direct recognition. Now we are only recognized as part of their jurisdiction. There is still the question whether the Protestant School Board will want this and what conditions they will set. However, given the political situation in the province, this might be realized. On the one hand this represents a real deliverance for the schools that are struggling with great financial problems. We are actually at the brink of bankruptcy. But, on the other hand, it is evident that the principle that we have defended is being forgotten. Who knows whether this means the beginning of the end for our own school system. When I raised these qualms of mine, they looked at me askance, as if I was way off the mark. And I wondered how they could so easily accept such terms. The Talmud Torah has almost concluded such an agreement with Chomedey. Ironically, it is they, who were afraid to ask for anything at all, who are the first to run and grab leftovers through a back door and to give up their autonomy, which they would never do when it concerned Jewish community responsibility for education. They trust the Protestants more. I only wish that it ends well.

SEPTEMBER 20, 1967

It looks like the Protestant School Board will not agree so easily to grant the day schools the status that will enable them to be supported through taxes. There are rumours that the Jewish representatives barely defended this issue before the Board. There will have to be pressure brought on the government in order to convince the Board to accept this. Will our representatives be ready to do this? I have grave doubts. They don't even convene the day school council to seek advice on the action to be taken.

Our campaign has begun and so far progresses with difficulty. We already owe two months' salary to all the teachers, and to some of them for three months. I am embarrassed to look the teachers in the eye. Who knows where this might lead?

SEPTEMBER 27, 1967

Last Monday we were invited by the Cultural Ministry of Quebec to a reception in honour of Melech Ravitch at the Quebec pavilion. This was the first time that the government selected a Jewish poet for such distinction. Only fifty guests were invited – half were French and half were Jews. We don't really know who they were – probably artists and deputies of the ministry. From our side there were writers, teachers, and artists. The mood was very good, the atmosphere friendly. The minister delivered the main address in French in a cultured tone of appreciation for the contribution of the Jewish writers and the significance of the guest of honour. Ravitch spoke in English, read a poem in Yiddish and in translation. Naim Kattan responded in French in the name of our group, quite superficial and bland.

At the affair we felt both good and uncomfortable with the fact that, with the exception of two, none of us could carry on a decent conversation in French. So we shared one room but at separate tables, did not converse, just looked at one another. After the fine meal, the minister himself and a number of his assistants made every effort to be friendly and even spoke English. He assured us of his best intentions and interest in the circle of Yiddish writers, which is a creative force in the province. But it was so obvious to everyone of us that our cardinal error was not taking into account all this time the culture and language of the majority.

OCTOBER 20, 1967

In the last few weeks the issue of negotiations with the Protestant School Board has not moved an inch. According to a report by the Congress delegates at the last meeting of the day school council and of the Education Committee of the Congress, a meeting was held with the chairman of the Protestant School Board where he informed them that they are waiting for a declaration from the government before making any decisions. Meanwhile they are asking for more information about numbers of students, teacher's salaries and qualifications, and budgets. The government meanwhile is occupied with the strikes of the transportation workers and radiologists, which have been dragging on for weeks and have almost paralyzed the city. The issue of separatism has become real and acute and holds everyone in a state of tension. So we can't expect a definitive answer one way or another.

At the last meeting of the Education Committee of Congress the report on the negotiations with the Protestant Board was tabled. The Committee demanded that the Jewish members of the Board take an affirmative position. However they would not make that commitment. One of them, a Mr Godinsky, even asserted that we should not anticipate a positive reply from there. So the old story repeats itself; the "leaders" are not ready to do battle but simply wait around until their wishes are granted – then they are immediately ready to accept. This too marks an advance, since until now they have refused to accept even this.

Among the participants there was the old man, Mr Levy, a longstanding opponent of the day schools, who began to pose questions whether our schools would qualify for such status that would enable them to obtain government subsidies. It looked as if we had to demonstrate the value of the schools once again. Only after I asked whether this was the aim of our gathering did the questions of Mr Levy cease, along with the responses that sought to demonstrate the worth and the standards of the schools.

It is odd and tragic – the largest sector of schools face bankruptcy and the "leaders" know this, still they treat the whole issue coldly and without passion. About community responsibility, nothing at all is said. The whole school system is fatherless. Meanwhile almost two months have passed since we have paid salaries. The campaign is rather weak. The negotiations for a new contract with the teachers is up in the air. We can neither accept the new salary scale which would mean about a 30 per cent increase, nor can we reject it. How long can we continue in this way? The debts grow and are due in the next month. I have no idea how we will manage this.

Last week I received the first Hebrew version of *Tzvishn Teichn un Vasern* via air mail and I can't even take pleasure in this, let alone write anything. My whole frame of mind is depressed. It is fitting to say about us: There is poverty in the place of riches. It is as if everything has gathered into one enormous horror. The whole world boils like a vat of hot tar. Just as the verse from Isaiah says: "Every head is injured, there is no wholeness in the body."

DECEMBER 8, 1967

I receive letters from writers in Israel. One senses a deep fear for the future. Truly a voice of affliction. From the host of emissaries who continually arrive from Israel we can see too how apprehensive they are there.

Each morning at breakfast I swallow one bitter news item after another. After the horror of Viet Nam, the moral failure and literal disintegration of the so-called West, nothing surprises me any more. Even the bitter struggle here in our province that presently affects us – not tomorrow but now – is part of the world's decline. I come to school and look into the tiny children's eyes with true pity for the world that they will grow up in. I don't even have the heart to punish the serious sinner. I no longer have any measure of right and wrong in such an upheaval.

During this time we lost one of our veterans, *chaver* Switzman, who died suddenly. He was always young at heart until the last moment. He symbolically personified the whole generation that managed to create from simple folk culture a complete honest and humane code of behaviour, and respect for Jewish culture and Jewish existence. He, more than anyone, was honoured by his children, who despite his strictness held him in respect and carried out his every wish.

Finally, last week it became known that the Protestant School Board had decided to negotiate with the Jewish schools. At a meeting of the school council this week the Jewish representatives on the Board explained that the four conditions set down by the Board are very extreme and indicate that their goal, in time, is the complete takeover of the day schools and their amalgamation into the public school system. For this reason we have to be very cautious. In the discussion it became apparent that even though the fears were justified, nevertheless we cannot withdraw before we have begun any negotiations.

My approach was that on the level of principle we should not have allowed ourselves to be pushed into a corner, but should have negotiated directly with the government. Now it is a little too late to approach the government. But what is the point of reminding them that I said the same thing a year ago and no one paid attention. Now the same thing is happening. So it is not surprising that people left with their original views unchanged.

The first report on bilingualism and biculturalism in Canada has just been released. Whatever happens to the recommendations it is an important step forward in finding a way to prevent Canada from falling apart. The supplementary papers by members of the commission are interesting and well researched. They also address the issue of enabling the culture of other minorities to maintain themselves; but Jews as a group are not mentioned. The Jewish representatives never demanded this or talked about it. What a shame! And we used to criticize our grandfathers and great-grandfathers for being servile, knowing only powerless mediation, and letting themselves be led by the Establishment! You only have sit awhile with our so-called leaders to realize that the earlier generation was head and shoulders above our present-day men of influence. The past generation was self-sacrificing and men of faith.

And along with all this I have lately been dogged by the fear of losing my hearing. There have been days when I felt myself cut off from the world of sound. I was at the doctor several times. He agrees that my hearing is getting weaker but he offers no remedy at the moment. He gave me some medicine, which helps a little, but I have to make a great effort to hear a clear sentence. Only when I am addressed directly and clearly can I hear; if it is not spoken directly it is lost and passes me by. It is an agonizing feeling. Suddenly everything comes from a distance, as if from behind a curtain. And you yourself feel separated from everyone, pushed aside into a corner.

DECEMBER 13, 1967

Today we accompanied M. Lauter to his eternal rest. He was for many years closely associated with the Jewish Public Library but also had warm feelings towards our school. He loved Yiddish, was a sensitive reader, and also took pleasure in the use of the Yiddish idioms of the Polish Jews. At the end of the 1920s and '30s he was close to the left, but he quickly shook them off. He was an amiable man. His beginnings were somewhere in Poland in the socialist camp like many of this generation. His radical period left him with heartache and disappointment. His rise in business never satisfied him. The pillars of the Yiddish circle are diminishing. One begins to feel like a sole survivor.

DECEMBER 20, 1967

In the last letters that I have received from Israel there is a feeling of a powerful, tense shuddering. The casualties that fall almost every day and the open preparations for a new round of fighting with the help of the Soviets creates a feeling of being abandoned by the world. The victory that did not bring peace fills us with trembling and horror for that which is being prepared. Despite this they all end these descriptions with a postscript: Life is almost normal. Even the conflict among the leaders is normal.

DECEMBER 25, 1967

On the day of "Peace on Earth" proclaimed by all the radios and TVs. Lyndon Johnson has returned from his trip – a so-called peace mission – that took him to Viet Nam and Rome. The gathering of scientists, writers, theologians, and community workers for peace presented such a fearful picture of annihilation that it induces feelings of horror. Everybody knows: racism, hunger, and hatred of the other are the enemy. But the so-called "national interests" covers it over with appalling techniques that allow them to destroy under the banner of self-determination. Such cynicism has never been seen before.

DECEMBER 26, 1967

Today I meditated about myself, trying to draw up accounts about matters that are not easily accountable in any case. According to the changes that have transformed the world, I am really an old man. I belong to the generation that was born before radio, TV, the splitting of the atom, nuclear proliferation, and before astronauts; I come from a region untouched by the telephone and the automobile. Can we therefore measure the passage of our years according to the conventional historical eras? There are literally miracles every day – while we are involved with petty details.

JANUARY 5, 1968

After the bitter year of 1967, which marked a tragic and exalted time in Israel, fear for the new year falls on us. Reality, as it appears, promises little hope, but nevertheless we make our reckonings. The Israeli press mirrors the deep fear felt there about the future. The agonizing internal struggle caused by the fact that the victory has made peace seem more remote and the prospect of a great *aliyah* is still not present. Many are even questioning the moral right to be there.

Ironically, with the expansion of the territories and the occupation of the ancient historic areas, the very existence of the historic claim for a Jewish Israel is placed under a question mark. This fills me with a spiritual dread. Was it worth so many casualties to reach the point where the State of Israel can never again become "One people and one nation on its land." The Arab minority is on the brink of becoming a majority if no *aliyah* arrives. Is this, ironically, the way history evolves?

JANUARY 15, 1968

Last week there was a sudden change for the good about the question of obtaining special status with the Protestant School Board. At a meeting of the day schools a report was given that the Protestant School Board is prepared to negotiate with schools on the basis of their present state, and the conditions are less stringent than we had expected. Also the tuition per child of $300 annually is quite acceptable. This will allow us to balance the budgets and, in time, erase the deficits as well.

Yesterday was a festive time, we greeted Levi Eshkol. There was a crowd at the airport. We also brought along a number of children from the schools, but as usual the organizers were only intent on publicity and the visibility of the "elite." He didn't even meet with the children. He looks fatigued and the heavy burden of his mission is even evident in his ungainly walk. Ben-Gurion's stride was brisk, lively, and defiant. Eshkol's was somewhat restrained, belaboured, and guarded. In response to the English greetings of the communty's "elite," he answered with warmth and simplicity in Yiddish. As luck would have it the microphone didn't work well and he could hardly be heard.

A large crowd attended the public assemblies, but something of a joyful feeling was missing. We have grown so accustomed to this that we don't even realize that it is most extraordinary for our generation to meet a Jewish prime minister. And perhaps we are not even mature enough to grasp this and are not deserving of this, as we always have to account for it in terms of the number of bonds this will sell. And what political benefits it will bring. And maybe this is also part of the tremendous struggle for resolving the tension between the ideal and the realties that we see before us. Therefore we cannot feel the thrill to the fullest degree or depth. The generations-old position of standing alone in the world now takes on a different aspect where the idea of Jewishness has no place at all. On the surface there is the State, borders, airplanes, and economics. But the heart of the matter – the very reason for our being – is not even approached. It is like the saying: "Going around and around, without approaching the vineyard."

JANUARY 29, 1968

Something is cooking and brewing behind the scenes. Someone is preparing a dish that will be sated only by death and destruction. The Exterminating Angel is not yet fully gratified. Submarines, one of them from Israel's navy, have vanished. The American warship *The Pueblo* was captured by the Koreans. The world once again stands on the edge of the abyss. It gives one gooseflesh, and we must continue on as if nothing is happening. Hydrogen bombs were lost over Greenland. They fly overhead, and below we are paddling and escorting the wedding guests to the final wedding. Meanwhile we teachers stand before our classes and teach our children about the good, about human achievements, and that 2x2 is still four.

Soon the negotiations with the Protestant School Board will begin. They have approached us officially. We will soon see the result of all this. Let us hope it is for the good.

Last night I went to hear M. Shtrigler. It is always good to listen to him. He is immersed in *midrashim* and genuine Yiddish idioms. He touches on problems but conceals more than he reveals. It seems that he is firmly anchored in the sources and builds his theories on them; nevertheless the feeling remains that they are blossoms in the air. The faith in the sources is missing, but perhaps it just seems so to me. In this confused world, is it reasonable to rely on traditional sources according to which our forefathers clung to eternal life with the illusion of Messianic deliverance and hence interpreted verses according to their need for survival. The present generation must create for itself its own fundamental beliefs.

FEBRUARY 5, 1968

Days of tension. The world is turbulent. All the signs indicate that something horrible is in the offing. On all sides things are happening. Viet Nam seems like the final total strain leading to a global catastrophe. In the meanwhile they are expiring in bloodshed. A struggle is renewed in Korea. Not a day passes in Israel without casualties. And now the tragedy of the submarine *Dakar*. Who knows what devilish hand is behind it?

And here, in our circle, cultural activities still go on. An evening to mark the publication of Dunsky's *Kohelet;* Manechovsky came from Toronto to speak on the fiftieth anniversary of Borochov's death. I wait all week to rest on the weekend; but when the weekend arrives there are these cultural events. One must and one desires to attend, but where do I find the energy to do so?

FEBRUARY 6, 1968

Lately I have been meditating intensively, examining past deeds that cannot be undone. Still, keeping accounts preoccupies me. First of all, it perplexes me how I could have decided in the first years of my arrival not to pursue general modern studies in a systematic manner? How could I reconcile myself to not learning properly the country's language? And as to my literary vocation, I am even more amazed that during all this time I have not made a single genuinely creative effort to picture the life lived here. And even now I still look for ways to return to the old themes, and keep postponing for later the descriptions of our local scene, which is already part of history. And when will that actually be? And what is the deep-seated reason for all this?

Could it be that the illusion of being a designated carrier of a Jewish mission was so all-encompassing that the surrounding reality was not perceptible. Could it be that my preoccupation with saving my family, which I accomplished to a certain degree, did not permit me to look deeper into the issue? Or maybe somewhere deep in my being there lay the determination that this need not be the final station. Like a passageway to something greater and more important.

FEBRUARY 16, 1968
LAMAIE HOTEL, RAWDON, QUEBEC,
IN THE LAURENTIANS.

Feeling myself totally exhausted mentally and physically I had to make a stop and declare "No more" and literally tear myself from the city to the silence, the whiteness, and virtual solitude. I used a longstanding invitation from Chaya Heller's brother who is struggling to establish a hotel for people who are looking for peace and solitude. It is really an ideal spot for this. Off the road, in a valley surrounded by mountains. With all the comforts. It may be storming outside, but you are sitting beside a warm swimming pool, in the nude, while electric sun-rays warm and caress you. Already my third day here and the enveloping peace is slowly invading my being. Almost as if I have forgotten the city's tumult and the stress of the last few weeks.

It troubles me a little that the owner is a bit of an enigma. He has been all over the European world and Israel, and almost empty-handed built here such a miniature Garden of Eden. But how to make the place livelier is beyond his ability. There is no one here except myself, the non-paying guest. The three people who work here are also unusual. Ostensibly they are Swiss-Germans, recently arrived. How they came to him and what their connection to him is, is unclear to me. I cannot see how he is going to enliven the place so that it becomes profitable. His whole family is very energetic but lack perseverence. They all come from Israel, *sabras*, he is the only one born in Riga. He was active in LECHI, left Israel afer the War of Independence. He is very embittered by the current leadership. The family embarks on unrealistic business ventures everywhere. One brother built up several knitting-mills, lost them, and is now trying his luck in Caracas, Venezuela. The only thing that remains of their past is the bit of Hebrew they speak. Being the only guest here, and an non-paying one at that, spoils the full pleasure of the stay.

Before tearing myself away to come here, three representatives of the Protestant School Board visited the school. They questioned and spoke in a most friendly manner. They came as teachers to familiarize themselves with how and what we do. They were pleasantly surprised by the set-up, management, and appearance of the school. It looks like we can expect positive results.

I stroll about in pleasant areas amongst trees that are lost in whiteness. What do I know about them and the silence that hovers over the mountains, and what do they know about me? Rarely does one see anyone drive by, the summer cottages are boarded up. Only by the single footsteps in the snow can you tell that in one of the houses there is a caretaker who makes sure that the houses do not freeze over. The barking of a dog also indicates that somebody watches you from a window. I have a kind of lonely yet familiar feeling on my walk when I hear the dog bark. Is he also looking for companionship?

Today I took two walks. In the morning, a clear sun-drenched sky. I hardly felt the cold. Had the feeling that the surrounding quiet was drinking in the sun but could not quench its thirst. The solitary houses in the primeval whiteness seemed to have opened themselves to soak up the sun's abundance. A strange restlessness enveloped me, and unconsciously I found myself standing by a bend in the road with my face to the sun. The barking of a dog aroused me from my trance.

After resting for an hour following lunch, I was again compelled to take a walk. The sun was low in the west. The whiteness appeared worn out. Both the mute houses in melancholy isolation and the paths that lead to them in wavering shadows warn you not to leave the road. A restless dog barks so plaintively in the distance that it tugs at your heart. All at once the sun hides itself far in the west, with a purple hue mixed into the vast space, rendering everything unreal by its light.

I felt as if I was in the most profound depth of this silent life – which was continuously changing – and at the same time excluded from it. The stillness, which I cannot penetrate, propels me onward, and all the surroundings that stand motionless as they were yesterday and will doubtless remain tomorrow seem to speak to me: You do not understand the essence of our existence nor can you experience our being. Is this the existence to which we are fated? Only at the end are we at one with them? Do they know of this? Will we ever know? Is it even possible to grasp this? We have barely been granted the sense of movement and action – what we consider our real existence. What is the phenomenon that exists without us? Does it then cease to be real? What does all this have to do with the turmoil and clamour of the world? What, finally, is the presence that creates something that results in change? All at once the strange purple and blue vanishes as if into a concealed space and in its place a bright restful glow on the rim of the far side of the mountain. With quiet assuredness it is swallowed up by the dark of the evening.

FEBRUARY 17, 1968

Today I couldn't take a walk. Not a vestige remains of yesterday's stillness and silence. A whirling bluish-white snow that howls in the wind swirled all day in such wild gyrations interspersed with flecks of sun that it appeared as if everything wanted to tear itself out of its solidity and run off to other realms. Seen from the window, beneath which the stream lies riveted to the earth, the snow only managed to roll from one bank to the other, whitening the stream-bed and then continued to smooth over the banks with rounded heaps that blocked out the view. Now everything has become quiet and rests humbly under the cloudy sky.

Odd how this thought comes to mind: This senseless drama is eternal; it came before me and will go on after me. Is this the Creation? Are we the only ones to vanish without a trace, along with all of our commotion? Where is our eternal existence?

MARCH 2, 1968

The few days in the country were truly refreshing and for a while made me forget the daily routine. The stress, however, was only postponed. As soon as I returned to the city we got the news that Yanya Abel is no longer amongst us. With the departure of each one of the generation that I began with, the feeling of being left alone intensifies, along with the feeling that one must hasten to capture the shape of this generation in artistic form. There is hardly anyone left who can do this from the inside. A feeling of helplessness is also growing, of being on the sidelines, although we are still considered to be in the centre. Yanya's passing – although due to his severe illness he was already beyond reach for years – affected me like the final sealing up of a tomb. The whole broad sweep of those days in the '20s is gone. I can hardly discern a trace of that time. He was an outstanding example of the refined and beautiful dream of the Folk-intellect that arose at that time as if from nowhere. Only few remain who recall his influence. And certainly in California, where he had lived most recently, they clearly knew little of his life here, so in fact he departed a forgotten man. Not even properly accompanied to his final rest.

Yesterday we finally received a letter from the Protestant School Board saying that they are ready to sign the contract with us that enables us through associate status to obtain financial assistance from their funds. This event is truly the first of its kind: official recognition. It is very significant in enabling us to maintain ourselves in the future. But we have a bitter feeling that in time it could require us to adapt strictly to the public school system, which would then place under a question-mark the value of this whole arrangement. The main point is the manner whereby the contract was finalized. It was not a dignified national moment. It looks like a round-about recognition and not a specific right to which we were originally entitled. Meanwhile though, it illustrates the verse from the Book of Esther, "Help and deliverance will come from another place," since we could not expect anything from our own community.

WEDNESDAY, MARCH 6, 1968

Today our representative, M. Solomon, signed the contract with the Protestant School Board and tomorrow it will be passed on to the provincial government for approval. But on the same day the Talmud Torah received an official letter from the minister of Education that their application, which had been filed there since September, cannot be approved since a new law is pending. This means that it was just deception; they didn't intend anything by Bill 37 other than to mislead the public. Only now is it clear how right I was in my demand that before we embark on a futile venture negotiating with the school board and having to plead before them, we should apply pressure directly on the government.

A very grave situation is developing in our negotiations with the teachers. Spirits are inflamed on both sides. A number of schools who wish to negotiate a collective agreement with the teachers have approached the Talmud Torah representative, Ben Beutel, to join with them. Beutel's answer was that they do not want to negotiate together. Today he made the clear demand that he should be the chief negotiator in the name of all the schools and insisted that the schools write him a letter requesting this of him. This means relinquishing all the power to him and acknowledging that his style of negotiating is approved by everyone. His negotiations were always one of the chief deterrents in creating a climate for a united school system that was as much concerned for the teachers as for the schools.

THURSDAY, MARCH 7, 1968

This is the third day I've spent at home with a cold. This evening I have *Yohrzeit* for my father. It will be the first time that I will not be present at the gathering of the brothers and sisters. Neither will I be able to go to *shul* to say *Kaddish*. He doesn't really need it. But for myself on that day all my senses register the connection with his world, aware of the hidden threads that lead from there to the goals that I have set for myself. It is a difficult moment for me, a kind of sealing off of an underground spring.

MARCH 16, 1968

Last week at a special meeting of all the schools it was decided to see the minister of Education in order to present our demands to him. And simultaneously to begin a campaign of public pressure in order to influence the government to endorse the contracts. When it comes to pressure, however, there is no unanimity as to means and methods. Unofficially we will have to convince the parents to flood the ministry with letters, and letters-to-the-editor in the English press. But in this time of general instability, who knows if anything will come of this.

Yesterday I sat through a gathering of representatives of Keren Hatarbut and the Zionist Federation. Such a dreadful meeting, which so upset me that I have not yet been able to calm down. The leaders of Keren Hatarbut behaved towards A.Wilcher, their director, like our guild of tanners in Tishevitz behaved towards the learned ritual slaughterers. The Keren Hatarbut people called their director a free-loader, a good-for-nothing, etc. The truth is just the opposite. It was actually he who created a better atmosphere at *Keren Hatarbut*. But they want a "yes" man so they can do whatever they want with the money. We rejected their charges; but I'm doubtful if it will be of any help. How will he be able to work with them after such talk? The scandal demonstrates once more how thin is the veneer of culture. It indicates how the powerful are still in command and wrap themselves in a *tallis* of self-righteousness, when in truth it is really a sheet of thorns.

Last night we were guests of the Davangs in honour of her brother, Rehavam Amir's visit. A lovely person, a man of few words, like a true diplomat. After his previous diplomatic missions for Israel, he is now chief emissary of the Department of Culture for the Diaspora. He has direct knowledge of Yiddish life and is far from optimistic about the situation. Nevertheless one senses a deep confidence in him, both in his goal and in his capacity to support Jewish culture. And above all that it is worthwhile, that it is significant.

For me, on the contrary, this entire issue is in great doubt. I can't reconcile our whole way of life with that which is coming into being before our very eyes. Even the link in the chain of generations that we represent, has become loosened and I cannot secure it again. So we sat and discussed the old themes: anti-Semitism, Jewish hatred towards others, and taking vengeance like the case of Amalek, etc. The participants, all decent people and even intellectuals, cultured people – ironically they were people who only preached publicly. But in private ... It isn't worthy of a respectable person to report their deeds on paper. They were full of praise for everything that was considered Jewish and have an answer for every question and a justification for every problem. And I couldn't loosen my tongue to say anything.

MARCH 17, 1968

Last night the annual benefit concert took place. The artists from Stratford performed Shakespeare's *A Midsummer Night's Dream*. It was packed. A festive atmosphere. But I couldn't free myself from the feeling that accompanies me at every school celebration, that it is one of the last events at which I will be present or be involved in. I felt the same way at the last Purim celebration which turned out to be highly successful. That same feeling haunted me the entire evening of the reception at the school for the guests. The halls were wonderfully decorated with paintings that Chana Pofelis had organized and Sorke had prepared with her grade five day school class. Artistic and educational. Oddly, this feeling saddens me but is not frightening. It is even almost becalming.

APRIL 4, 1968

It looks like the world is not to be granted one moment of peace, and even less, security. The week began with hope. President Johnson withdrew his candidacy for president, and reduced the bombing of Viet Nam. This evening he was supposed to fly to Hawaii to meet the representatives of North Viet Nam. The hopes for peace grew.

But today a madman or a messenger of the devil assassinated Martin Luther King, the leader of the Negro civil rights movement. This opened a new horror for America. It is impossible to predict how many victims will result. The heart cries and shudders. What a dreadful age we live in. Ironically, the champion of non-violence dies by violence. From every corner of the world come cries of woe: What will come of this? It becomes darker and darker in every corner of our world.

MAY 22, 1968

These were such difficult weeks that I could not lift my hand to write due to the pervasive tension, and principally because of the negotiations of the day school teachers regarding a new contract. This has evolved into a situation where the two sides no longer hear each other. In essence the financial demands of the teachers are completely justified. The majority of the directors know this. But it is also clear that if the directors knew that the financing would be provided by the government or the community, they would immediately agree with the demands. But nothing has come of the government's subsidy. And the community is not yet ready for this. As a result, this means larger deficits and empty promises that cannot be kept. It is simply a financial impossibility to carry this out. Parents alone cannot bear the increase, which for us, for example, means simply closing down.

MAY 24, 1968

The world is under the sign of the rebellion of youth. The students of France, the country of revolution, is in the forefront, from both sides – east and west – the unpredictable revolt continues. Red and black flags are unfurled, but it looks like it is only the result of a deep disappointment in the old world and in the twentieth century with all its scientific achievements.

Returned this week from Toronto from the fifteenth session of the Congress, which also marked the fiftieth anniversary of its founding. Of the veteran activists that one was accustomed to see at the sessions, only a few remain. The earliest founders were hardly mentioned. Except for Garber, who tried in an intimate and honest way to describe the beginnings, no one else even referred to it, just as if a ready-made Congress had descended from heaven. Still it was one of the few sessions that provided a glimpse of the readiness to act and to persist. The present leaders, it seems, have nevertheless learned something and have altered their rigid conventional views that depended on what the gentile might say. The change is clearly witnessed in their attitude toward Yiddish and toward the day school as a factor in Jewish education. Despite everything the will of the people has penetrated their rigidity. The high point of the session was actually the discussion around these issues. This time the discussion was not about principles at all, but only how to find the means to realize them. The most heated meeting was the one devoted to the situation of Jews in the world, and about Israel and her isolation at the UN. The old saying was once again demonstrated: All the world on one side, while Abraham stands on the other. Once again we stand alone with very few friends who would really raise their voices and use their power to help us. On the contrary, all the dogs bark again, as in the past. All the world's wrongs are heaped on the head of Israel, and even great peoples – Israel included – are considered the only evil-doers in a world of complete "saintliness." One could have been crushed at that session by the heavy burden that unfolded as the vote moved from country to country. At the same time one could be filled with pride that once more we have become the indicator on the scale of the world's conscience.

It was worthwhile attending this session of Congress because of the reports and meeting with friends, old acquaintances, and to see that a new cadre of young leaders has grown up. They are intent on doing something, and among them some of our former students play an important role. It is a bit of a consolation. Of course we were not immune from the dirty politics when it came to electing the president. Instead of electing an individual with intelligence and knowledge, they chose a man who knows nothing of authentic Jewishness. The money-purse triumphed. It appears that a united front of the Orthodox and the leadership of our Histadrutniks made a pact each for their own reasons: the former to settle accounts with a secularist, and the latter for campaign considerations. On the whole, however, the session demonstrated that the public has matured and is more focused on its goal and how to accomplish this as Jews with backbone.

JUNE 5, 1968

Went to sleep last night under the echoes of the artillery barrages between Israel and Jordan. A tragic drama on the anniversary of Israel's great victory.

We awoke to the tragic news that another Kennedy has been assassinated. Robert Kennedy, who many consider the tribune of the weak, was shot by a Jordanian, of all things – the explanation being that Kennedy was the victim of a Jordanian nationalist who considered him a friend of the Jews. The pointlessness of this further underlines how the foundations of our world have been utterly destroyed. How the land of the free and the brave is defenceless against terror and ordinary violence. It is part of the gruesome events in the world and most of all in the tradition of revolutionary action from the beginning of time: By force shall you enforce your will. It has reached the point where both will and reason have disappeared and only force remains. I am ashamed to meet the eyes of the children. We still claim that the world can be a just place.

JUNE 11, 1968

At last, one begins to see a way in which the day schools will be able to breathe easier financially. Today there took place the mass meeting of parents organized by Congress for the purpose of pressuring the minister of Education to sign the contracts with the Protestant School Board. There was a large attendance, but instead of a protest meeting, which everyone anticipated – especially the group that had lobbied for the past few years and had created a tumult – the Congress leaders, with Beutel at the head, constantly rebuffed them. Then the Congress was informed by Quebec that they would not pay attention to ordinary lobbying and would not even meet with them. Only when the announcements for the meeting appeared did the minister receive them and concede that for the new school year he would recognize the contracts only for the year 1968-69. The reason being that they are preparing a new law. Meanwhile the deputy-minister came to the mass meeting and publicly declared that for the new school year every accredited school would receive $300 for each pupil. This means, more or less, that the next year will be easier. But it also means the beginning of official recognition. This will be the first time not only in the history of the province but continent-wide that Jewish day schools would be so recognized. Whatever one's doubts are, this is an exceptional event. The load is still heavy, especially for us with our great financial burden. But the possibility of surviving can now be seen. Now if the leadership would only comprehend the situation and plan a broad, many-branched project that would be concerned with the teachers and with activating the parents, then something significant could be instituted. Whether they will be equal to this is a large question.

JUNE 21, 1968

Gittel Gershonovitch who has worked at the school for thirty-five years is taking her pension. Other than myself, she is the most senior of those associated with the school. It is truly the end of an era. She was one of the first pupils of the school system to become a teacher. And if the students are already being pensioned, what can their teachers say? Only a single reason: we must still carry the burden. Saying goodbye to her actually meant leave taking from oneself.

And especially today in this unstable world of thought and deed do we really need the tested veterans. But all the true desires that still remain in me strain and beg to retire as quickly as possible. Maybe a bit of quietude and strength will remain in order to voice the creativity that never had enough time for expression because of the heavy burden and constant presence of the demand, "One must ... " On the one hand I would like to be able to celebrate my own closure of the era so that I might be able to relive the whole period artistically. On the other hand I am fearful of the moment that I so anxiously wish to hasten.

JUNE 25, 1968

Yesterday, on the day of Quebec's national holiday, the separatists led a demonstration against Prime Minister Trudeau because he opposes their goals. The first time in history that the holiday was ruined by riots. Over 100 wounded, over 300 arrests, and tremendous damage. Is this a preamble of what we can expect? The will to destroy now reigns everywhere and when it has a nationalist colour it endangers the entire structure. The destructive impulse wraps itself in many different mantles and never wants to build, only destroy.

Odd, how the times alter attitudes. We were brought up with a negative attitude toward the police. Our entire generation considered the police as a pillar of reaction. When I arrived here and found that the policeman was considered only as a servant of public order or as a protector of the children and the weak, it was difficult to become accustomed to this. In the social struggles of the recent years, the police were once more placed in their former position. Now, seeing on TV how the police tried to control the riot, and how one after another was wounded by the hooligans who broke into a peaceful parade where thousands of children and ordinary onlookers were present, the sympathy was completely on the side of the police. Even when they raised their clubs on high and lashed out left and right.

JUNE 27, 1968

Yesterday I was at the first meeting convened by Congress to choose a National Council. A large audience was in attendance. Also present and prepared was the group that had publicly agitated for financial support for the schools through the tax system. Even at the Congress assembly in Toronto they had allied themselves with the religious and para-religious to reject the nomination of Lavy Becker for president; and they succeeded. Their justification was that they opposed a rabbi as president. The main reason was that he belonged to the Reconstructionists. The Histadrut people also voted with them on the pretext that Lavy Becker was not pro-Histadrut. Now, the whole Orthodox faction, led by the tax activists, came well prepared and created a tumult.

Last Wednesday was the first meeting of the representatives of the day schools and a representative of the Protestant School Board. It was very friendly and informative. Questions were posed concerning the manner in which the associate-status would operate. We can expect that for the first year at least things will function smoothly.

JULY 1, 1968

Today, the Moscow rabbi, Yehuda L. Levine, is arriving here on his way home. He comes from New York, where he was received with open arms, especially by the Orthodox. It is actually the first time that an official representative has come from there. We hope, and want to hope, that this points to a new relationship. The scandal that broke out at his first appearance was arranged by the Council for Judaism – enemies of Zion and Jewry – with the assistance of N'turei Karta. Extremes come together. Understandable but regrettable. You can also understand the open arms of the Orthodox because they consider him a "wayward child" and it is a terrible pity on him and on us – we want to embrace him but are stabbed by the words that regrettably he must mouth. Here too he will be received in the same way. The bitter irony is that the Soviets are capable of this; they can mock everything and anybody without fear of reprisal. The world is such that evil can furnish its own "defenders" of its deeds. The victim himself gives evidence that he is not a victim, that everything is according to holy purity. Nevertheless, the Orthodox should be more courageous in their declarations and not leave the impression that they believe that all he says is actually so. It borders on servility. Is this in keeping with the old tactic of referring to a spit in the face as mere rainfall?

JULY 3, 1968

From the meeting of the finance committee we went on to the reception for the Moscow rabbi, Rav Levine, who had stopped off here on his way home. The *shul* was packed and hundreds who couldn't get in stood outside for hours. Everybody knew that he would not say anything, yet there was a Yom Kippur feeling in the hall. The feeling of confronting an historical event.

His patriarchal appearance was like meeting a great-grandfather. The fifty years of separation and the rivers of blood and fire stood like a partition through which one could barely see. A large group of young people looked confounded by the crowd, especially by the hundreds of bearded Jews in their ancient garb – all the rabbis, congregational, Chasidic, and the neo-Orthodox. The speeches, mainly in Yiddish – heard for the first time in this *shul* – sounded at home in these surroundings, and without being explicit revealed the tragic nature of the entire gathering. They praised the guest and considered him an envoy even though he has sealed lips. Even the words that he spoke so heart-felt and simple, lauded the situation that he had found here. According to him we have an abundance of Torah and *Yiddishkeit*, which is truly miraculous, a kind of renaissance. He said nothing about the conditions in the USSR. More was transmitted through the *chazan's* singing. The *chazan* was from Leningrad, his beardless face symbolized modernity, and he looked somehow as if he was the Rabbi's guard. In his melodies, sung with great emotion, was felt the outcry of generations. He sang, "See our oppression, heal us and we will be healed," and a part of the benediction, "When will You reign in Zion."

JULY 14, 1968

Today I visited Rochl Korn. She gets about quite nimbly now, but her whole reaction to things remains sickly. She is more inclined to hold onto the illness, or the weakness of her feet and bones, than in some other explanation. To tell the truth, I don't see why she needs any explanation at all. Her poems, due to her experience, have become deeper and keener, the image clearer, and the expression often breathtaking. Her stubborn fear of conventional superstitions, or unfulfilled promises, is simply boundless. Her new book of poems, *The Grace of the Word*, arrived, but since the publisher had promised to send her the corrected proofs beforehand and hadn't, she is convinced that it is full of errors and the books lie unpacked. By chance, while discussing with her my plan to publish a bibliography and some critical essays along with her own memoirs in honour of her seventieth birthday, I said that we should also publish a new collection of hers. It was then that she told me that her book of poems had been with her over a week and that she cannot unpack it. With some difficulty, I convinced her that I should open the parcel, read several poems to see whether there were any errors.

Incidentally, she has lines and stanzas that are truly unprecedented in our poetry. Such depth and clearly etched images are rare. She has no need to depend on hyperbole or witticisms as do many of our well-known poets in recent years. The jubilee-edition of *Zukunft* is a concrete example of the poetic fraud that now popularly passes for poetry.

JULY 19, 1968. THE JEWISH HOSPITAL

Yesterday I came here to undergo an operation on the same hernia on the right side that I was operated on five years ago. As soon as you step over the threshold of your room, a feeling of being locked in descends. Or it might be better to say, locked out, excluded from the ordinary, normal, and customary. From the first moment that you meet the nurse, you sense that from now on, somehow, they will be in control and will handle you without asking. After all, you signed a document in the office giving them the right to do as they wish. Bit by bit, nakedness and calling human functions by their proper names become acceptable. The inhibitions you had on the other side of the door begin to fade. Shame persists, but you can't hide anything from the doctor and his three assistants. You stand naked while they probe the organ that is usually most concealed. Strangers busy themselves with the most intimate organs. Pipes and plumbing, orifices and orifices are now essential and the most natural. Having a proper piss takes precedence, even though a moment's reading informs you of more important problems. But for you, and those who are attending you, there are no issues more important. The routine of various tests – breathing, moving the limbs – look comical as I perform them in my old age. Purging your innards with enemas, and constantly running to the toilet, is ritual preparation for the x-ray room, where the dark, black, heavy machines make an impression of mysterious hidden robots, controlled by a young woman in a white lab-coat or a young man who is girdled in a shiny apron that glows with an eerie light in the dark. While waiting between one x-ray picture and the next, you stand half-naked at the developing room where the nurses all come for the developed pictures in which all the nakedness, with various internal blemishes, are revealed. Often, one of them takes a glance and grimaces at what she had seen. Usually, though, they are unconcerned, joking amongst themselves in coarse language, including personal information concerning exams or get-togethers with friends. They are tense because the loudspeakers are always giving them orders, and calling them and the doctors to the sick who are waiting for them in different locations. A controlled world with voices that come from somewhere unknown to you. Everywhere, patients are sitting or lying contorted with pain, their sad faces under the shadow of the unknown.

JULY 20, 1968

Slept quite well last night. The heat broke after the rain. Except for having to get down from the bed a few times, everything went well, but at dawn an anxiety arose from some inexplicable source and I felt a pressure in all my limbs. It would appear that I had to rush somewhere but didn't know the destination. I had to meet someone but didn't know who or where to look for him. Something tells me that I have to report somewhere, and I think that I am standing at an address that looks like 12, but don't know what to say or what to ask. Still my anxiety continues to grow. The white day that fills the room gives itself up without a struggle to the rose-coloured horizon and they meet in a ritual of greeting. And the soft voice of a nurse wakes me through the intercom from some indeterminate place. The smiling face of a nurse greets me with a "Good Morning," and hands me a thermometer, saying, "How do you feel today?" How do you tell her that you don't know yourself.

JULY 22, 1968. IN THE MORNING

Yesterday they began to prepare for the operation. Even the arrival of visitors has a special quality. Of course nobody speaks of this, but it seems like a leave-taking from one situation to another. Aside from Sorke, there were my brothers and sisters. Sorke sits a half-day in silence, brings a little fruit as usual, this time most welcome. I'll have something before my all-night fast. Meanwhile, the visitors talk of other things in order to pass the time and to dispel the thoughts that are concentrated elsewhere. A feeling of liberation arrives with the announcement: "Visiting hours are over." You feel that you want to be alone. You are certainly grateful for their visit, especially by those closest to you; if they hadn't come, they would have been missed. You wait a whole day for their visit, but the truth is that you are relieved when they say goodbye and you are left alone once again in the grasp of the ritual that you alone must endure.

I try to read but it is difficult. Walk about the dark corridor. All the rooms are already closed. From some rooms comes the sound of groans and snores and coughing. From the outside the muffled noise of passing cars penetrates. How often have you driven by this place without recognizing it for what it is. A place with a life of its own, separated from the ordinary. Taking off my glasses, the electric lights once more look like one flame, guardians of the city.

JULY 31, 1968. BACK HOME AGAIN

Came home Saturday the 27th. Although all the important post-operation procedures were attended to and you were able to go home – which alone satisfies and restores the feeling of being a human being and not a medical record in another world – nevertheless the whole body is stiff and swollen and is painful to the touch. Everything is still focused on one area: performing one's physical functions. All other matters are secondary, floated off somewhere. You are not in control of your own thoughts. Clambering onto the bed you close your eyes and all your limbs are hugged by a childlike embrace, and you hover in a world of fantasy. The entire eight days are like this, both day and night. Even the waking hours don't restore you to yourself, but to a secret magician who leads from one reality to another, and everything is suspended in air. Only your bodily stiffness is part of yourself and holds you back from complete dissolution.

AUGUST 12, 1968

Yesterday we laid to eternal rest the oldest of the old-time group, Avraham Parness, who lived till ninety although for the last few years he was paralyzed and didn't appear in society. Still he was able to communicate through notes and gestures. He was the cleverest of the early pioneers and full of natural humour, yet he was extreme in his social outlook which, in the '30s and '40s, lead him into sympathy with the Stalinists. He was also the only one of that group who always had close relations with the tiny *shuls* of that era. If I am not mistaken he was even the *gabbai* of the Yavneh Shul. A devoted Labour Zionist and Yiddishist, he nevertheless helped split the National Radical School to found the Folk Shule, which, at that time, 1914, was considered to be a Hebraistic school. All his life he was an activist and leader of the Folk Shule, and the Jewish Public Library. Because of his leftist leanings he became alienated from active Labour Zionist participation. A clever person, with an epigram and folk tale for every occasion.

Odd too, that all the patriarchal Parness family were pillars of the local Polish-Jewish community but he was buried in the Spanish-Portuguese cemetery on Mount Royal. It seems that the former Yavneh Shul had united with the Spanish-Portuguese Synagogue. The chanting of the *El Moleh* was according to the Sephardic mode, which sounds strange to our ears.

AUGUST 30, 1968

The Russian paw has been placed upon Czechoslovakia, with all its might and power. She casts her shadow all around her neighbours, such as Romania. From the qualified language of the world leaders beyond the Iron Curtain, we are on the brink of a Third World War. The Czecholovaks accept their fate with resignation. What choice have they? The Dubcek leadership struggles pitifully not to become the perpetrators of the evil actions of their own comrades, not to execute and fulfill their dirty work. Will that be possible? The gall of lies and evil is boundless. The few Jews there that we are concerned about are in particular danger. They are the scapegoats. The Soviet propaganda maintains that the "Zionists" are the counter-revolutionaries who simply want to destroy Communism. The words are Hitleristic. It looks like dictatorship cannot rest easy as long as we are here.

AUGUST 31, 1968

Yesterday morning before eight o'clock Sholem called joyfully to inform us that his son Leo, and daughter-in-law Reva, had decided to send their eldest, Joel, to our kindergarten. Later Sonia called with the same message and the same happiness; that Reva had persuaded Leo with the argument: "You see that they still persecute Jews, even those who have identified with the host peoples so as not to be distinguishable. At least let him know why he is being beaten." How could one predict that the events in Czechoslovakia would have an effect right here under our noses.

OCTOBER 9, 1968. SUCCOS, 5729

The past few weeks were very trying. The mood is depressed. The atmosphere in the world, especially the US., is further darkened by the student riots everywhere – with our compatriots at the head – which are so chaotic that one is seized by dread. It looks just like the end of the thirties before the Second World War. The world-robbers don't even justify themselves; they assert openly, "These are our interests – don't mix in." The students and the so-called "new left" want to topple everything, and don't even have an inkling as to what they will build to replace it. The massacres in Asia and Africa take place openly and without excuse. Israel is alone. The race-agitators in the U.S. express an openly anti-Semitic sentiment. Here in Quebec we certainly don't know what the morrow has prepared. With the sudden death of Premier Johnson, everything is even more unpredictable. Who will be the scapegoat here?

And at the school the mood is one of resignation. For over two months salaries haven't been paid. I have no idea where we will find the possibilities for refinancing until the subsidy arrives. In the new surroundings the pressure from the public for a religious veneer and the reduction of Yiddish is very strong. The number of children in the day school barely equals last year's number. Even less in the afternoon school; didn't even manage to enroll a grade one.

HOSHANA RABA, 5729

Today we said farewell to Aunt Esther, the last family member on my father's side. With her passing there departs a particular character type that it is doubtful we shall see again. A type that was bound to the feelings and life of previous generations. In her early life she had to accommodate to a cruel, ignorant person. From an orphaned childhood and from the deep humane powers at work in her, she created a source of maternal protection for all those around her. In her could be found the complete *niggun* of generations of Jews from Little Poland. She did more for the family than anyone else. On the one hand she lived her whole life in the family's *succeh* of poverty, and on the other hand, became a protective wall for those around her. After many years of illness she expired peacefully, calmly, on the second day of Succos. We knew that she was very sick, but when it happened so suddenly it was like the slash of a slaughtering knife. You don't feel the pain at the time, still it is deadly and numbs the senses. The last ring of the family has been linked to eternity. We buried and eulogized her with the respect that she deserved, surrounded by the Uncle – may his years be long – her children, grandchildren, family, and friends. She was close to eighty, but her memory and her words were fresh and young to the end. There is no one else left to ask about the family and the old customs of the *shtetl*.

NOVEMBER 1, 1968

Last night President Johnson announced that today at eight o'clock in the morning the bombardment of North Viet Nam would cease. Could this be the beginning of an era when the world leaders would come to their senses and stop their slaughtering, murdering, and bringing the world to the point of destruction? According to the current response of the international press, it does not seem to be interpreted in this way. We are so accustomed to a fatal destiny and to destruction that we can't even detect the least hint of a ray of light. The darkness is so dense, both in Israel as well as on this continent, where racism in its darkest form strides about shamelessly and even under the veil of "progress." The youth rebellion too, which clothes itself in progressive feathers, is rotten with racism and nihilism. It is truly a paraphrase of the Prophet: "It is a time of affliction for Jacob" – but whether the verse "From Him will come salvation ... " applies as well is a big question.

NOVEMBER 9, 1968

Already a week at home. I am being targeted with honours for my forty years of being principal. I don't derive any joy from the school's use of this date for purposes of raising more money in the campaign, nor from the fact that at the annual conference of Jewish teachers, I will be their guest of honour.

I will not be able to express that which lies in my heart nor the doubts that plague me. Perhaps it is because I am a coward, and principally because I no longer have the faith that it will do any good. Even the things that I still do now are from inertia, rather than deep conviction.

NOVEMBER 22, 1968

Last night at the banquet of the conference, a mood was created that moved me deeply. Nearly all the educators of the local institutions and prominent leaders of the major schools and Talmud Torahs, with whom we had been involved in life-long bitter struggles, attended. Not only from their speeches but from their warm glances and festive spirits could one sense a closeness. It was certainly symbolic that Rabbi Lewittes was, so to speak, the one chosen to honour me with such familiarity and warmth. His remarks were based on recollections of my father's religious writings and to his own associations with me in recent years. And surprisingly he stated that I had given him strength and encouragement in his role as leader of the school council, where he had encountered more obstacles from his partisans, so to speak, than from our circle. Only then did he realize how honestly and seriously did we consider our work. He exaggerated a bit and almost blurred the distinctions between us. Therefore in my response I felt I had to correct this and stress that I considered his words today to be a redress of those injustices committed against us in the early years of our work by the religious factions when we were considered to be destroyers of Israel – God forbid. Although we no longer carry a grudge against them, still I am pleased by the symbolic accreditation, which I accept not for myself but for the whole generation that did our work and initiated a new path in education. This was not limited only to education but included the right of modern Jewish creativity and life to envision a reconstructed Israel and social justice throughout the world.

Briefly, I described how we taught and the kind of *niggun* we brought into the miserable houses of those years. How we had to create our own environment and search for ways of imprinting our Jewish outlook on the world. Not everything could be realized, nor could we get the community to comprehend us. But a beginning was made. I had to control myself from speaking about the heavy doubts that torture me now, and that everything is once again in the balance. With only a hint here and there. I felt that at this place and facing this audience, I did not speak for myself but for those who are no longer with us and who left us without being appreciated or acknowledged. It took me several minutes before I could concentrate and regain my composure when, after Rabbi Lewittes' tribute he handed me the scroll, the audience spontaneously arose in full song. I felt the warm sensation of being amongst family and was very moved. The accounting of all these years can still not be drawn up. I hope to have a few peaceful years to realize this artistically. Meanwhile I am still confused both by the occasion and by the fact that I am afraid that the difficulties and doubts hold me in a vice, blocking up the wellspring of creativity. It begins to dawn on me that lately I can no longer roar as I once did.

DECEMBER 4, 1968

In Israel the fighting has broken out again. The situation is so tense that the fear of a repetition of 1967 is realistic. The attacks are against Jordan. While the news is sporadic there is still enough cause for fear. The situation in the province here is quite perplexing. Today the separatists broke into McGill University, occupied a building under the slogan: Reclaiming the symbol of English colonialism which oppresses Quebec. The group that is against minority choice of the language of education is leading this demonstration in order to force the provincial government to withdraw the law it is about to introduce in the legislature. Meanwhile the Jewish viewpoint has officially not been mentioned. From the sidelines, however, there are accusations that the Jews are partners with the "Anglos."

Avraham Sutzkever is now in town. There has been a strain between us for several years. He is trying to make amends and lets me know that all this time he never realized that he was ignoring all of my submissions to him. Despite this I attended a reception for him at the Husids' house. Husid and Ravitch discussed his writings. He read poems from his new book *Signs and Wonders*, which were really wonders of the language, eloquent observations and images, but lacking substance. It seems to me that these are even a retrogression from his earlier works. He now seeks winged words rather than the deeper utterance and tragic insight. Unless I am mistaken, his habit of pursuing only the wealthy and obtaining ever more revenue is distasteful, even though we ought not begrudge him this. He wants to gain financial security while the opportunity exists.

DECEMBER 15, 1968

Gershon Pomerantz is no longer with us. He was always a stormy presence and was just preparing, as he wrote in his last letter: "to probe into the essence of Poland as it once was, and to evoke its bloodiness once more." And now he too is part of that past, the world of silence. The emptiness around us becomes fuller – if one can express it that way. Loneliness grows and the circle closes by itself.

His presence appears before me at our first meeting in the early thirties on a snowy day in Winnipeg. He literally burst into the room with a shining round face and fiery words: We will conquer Canada. With *Ink and Plume*, his literary journal, he thought that he could flay his opponents, but in the end he barely flayed anyone. Aside from his recent monographs on the generation of writers he knew, I don't think that he even came close to expressing or depicting the flame that blazed within him. The last time I saw him was in the spring. He gave the impression of an embittered dissenter who throws fiery invective – so he thought – from his tenth storey dwelling, but who remains lying cold in the cage that has imprisoned him for the past years due to his terrible illness. The evening with him was interesting, intense, sometimes even deeply insightful, however no light or any melody arose from that cage. When he accompanied us to the lobby and literally had to drag his legs with great effort, he began to sob at the farewells: "You can see how shackled I am. At the window however I see further and further." What is there to say, what words can one speak?

EREV CHANUKAH, 1968

Today is the school celebration. Last night Ravitch's evening in honour of his seventy-fifth. What does Tchernikhovsky say: All Israel is holy, you are the Maccabee. Looking at the remnants of the generation of Yiddish writers, they did not bring a Maccabean victory, but the courage of the Maccabees was in them. In Israel today this epigraph is truly fitting. Everyone there is now a Maccabee. Let's hope that the outcome will be the same.

DECEMBER 20, 1968

The technical advances of science have today enabled the realization of the greatest human imaginings: man can examine the moon's surface with his own eyes. Today the spacecraft *Apollo* 8 was launched on a seven-day flight to the moon. They will circle the moon at a distance of 69 miles. This is the last stage before landing on the moon. One could certainly walk about with heads held high in light of this achievement, if the earth itself and all her creatures were not in danger of destroying themselves, and if the cry of pain and misfortune did not arise from the earth with horror and anguish. If the expenditure and the enormous talent and imagination invested in this project had been employed for worldly needs, it would be easier to live on this earth. So together with the uplifting feeling, there is the sense of sorrow. Is it not the case where gain is overwhelmed by loss?

DECEMBER 25, 1968

The last few days were busy with moving into our own house. Sorke is so pleased with her own home that it infects me as well. The children too are overjoyed with our home, and this pushes to the side the logical knowledge that this signifies the last station. Also, the painful realization that the plans for settling in Israel, following retirement, have been pushed aside too. It looks like illusion cannot replace reality. So we must continue to hope that we will be in good health and be able to express that which I still desire to say and narrate. And no longer seek for new worlds. The pleasures of the present have conquered the dream. It was difficult to make the decision, still one has to make peace with reality. Until now, even though it appeared that my life followed a plan, nevertheless I felt that I could alter things. I felt free and still anticipated that something will and must happen to lead to further places. Now I feel as if I'm bound. Only the power to be able to create something can keep me free, and enable me to join in the happiness of Sorke, Gittel, and the children.

DECEMBER 27, 1968

This morning the eyes of the whole world were focused on the wind-swept Pacific where *Apollo* 8 descended from the heights almost on the designated spot carrying in its instruments the secrets of the lunar sphere. Etched into the spirits and minds of the first three men who with their own eyes had glimpsed the moon was the image they saw from up above of the earth sparkling like a star. Such a vista is inconceivable, and yet we are left to question what could be accomplished with this goodwill and true enthusiasm to ease the cry of agony that arises from this sparkling earth-star. The most exalted moment of the voyage was the moment when from on high they cited the first verses of Genesis and the blessing in honour of Christmas. It was so humane and humble that it was truly moving. From the endless darkness their human voices shone, literally, like a declaration of the infinite longing for goodness and peace. Not a particle of boasting and bravado. How different from their modest humanity was the vulgar impudence and foolish arrogance of Yuri Gagarin, the Russian, who crowed from the heights that he had not seen God anywhere!

DECEMBER 28, 1968

For two days now I've been trying to deny the death of Yecheskiel Bronstein. The tragedy was that he had been sick for decades with tuberculosis, and then with all sorts of illnesses and undergone operations on almost all his limbs – and he had survived all this. Even when he begged for the end, he rallied and always overflowed with creative ideas. Then, ironically he goes out to mail a letter and is killed by an automobile. How strange and bizarre.

Just that evening when Mordecai Husid informed me that he had read it in *Der Tog,* I had written him a letter and admonished him for writing in his last letter that he has no more strength and is ready to welcome the end. I didn't take this too seriously and even joked that if such thoughts were truly entertained, he wouldn't be making such plans for writing projects that he mentioned. "Creativity holds me by the neck and I can't free myself from her," he wrote. "I walk with a cane because I fell." Could this possibly have caused the accident? I still could not believe it, nor could I tell Sorke the terrible news. Now that I actually hold the newspaper in my hand and have already written a few words to his wife, Yehudis, another sickly person – there wells up within me his image, together with the grief, as if part of myself had suddenly been torn away. An image that has remained in my memory and my consciousness from the beginnings, back in the thirties in Winnipeg, when he appeared out of nowhere one morning early. It was his vagabond period, and he roamed across the continent like a nomad. "I would never have returned to Winnipeg which I had left fifteen years ago with a bitter taste in my mouth; it was only because of you that I have returned. From your writings, I feel that we can be friends," he declaimed while still standing on the doorstep. A tall, thin man with hollow cheeks, shaggy black hair that gave him the appearance of one who purposely adopts a disguise. His voice was warm and agreeable, one of those voices that conveys the feeling that you have heard it before, and that voice is dear to your heart. "I have just returned from my travels. Good people always give you a lift. From Los Angeles to here without spending a cent," he sort of boasted. "Came to see you on the way to the Rocky Mountains." He was only with us for a few days, and we became close for the rest of our lives. We never met again, but we felt ourselves to be close confidants.

There was hardly a Yiddish writer that he did not laud, and he was overjoyed with each of their accomplishments. Not profound, but delighted by the act of creation. Will someone now repay him in kind? Or will they remain silent as they did during his lifetime? In his loneliness there, he was pleased with the few friends around the world that he had managed to keep. Over the years I became so friendly with him that we corresponded almost monthly. Now there is an emptiness about me. I feel as if I am all alone, like a kind of Choni trapped in his own circle. So one must make haste and seize as much as one can.

JANUARY 1, 1969

Yesterday, at the close of the miserable year, 1968, Israel was condemned by the Security Council for its attack on the Beirut airport and the destruction of a number of airplanes. The decision was unanimous. Only the Canadian representative deemed it necessary to point out that even while he voted in favour of the resolution, he considers it his duty to assert that the act was not a one-sided event, but the result of terrorist acts on the part of the Arabs and a direct consequence of the attack on the El Al plane in Athens, with its victims. His appeal that both sides should reconsider, though possibly sincere, was left hanging in the air. The truth is that if the big powers really wanted quiet in the Middle East, it would take place. But to punish Israel, they were all in agreement. Israel stood and stands alone in the world. From the Russian saints to the American pietists. The moral bankruptcy of today's world has never been so blatantly apparent. Even the Pope rushed to express sympathy to the Lebanese. When they murdered innocent people in Jerusalem, and after the attack in Athens, he was silent. Now he too is a saint.

JANUARY 2, 1969

The new year began with the placing of bombs at the city hall, Mayor Drapeau's house, and a federal building. Only one exploded. There were no victims, but much damage and great fear. In Ottawa too, there were similar occurrences. One bomb exploded. It looks like it is being orchestrated by a single hand. The fact that the goal of the terrorist group remains unknown creates an even greater panic. Does this mean that this will be the emblem of the new year?

And things around Israel are not very joyous. It already looks like a minor war. The Russian bear seeks to exploit the situation and proposes a "peace" offensive, naturally, at Israel's expense. Now there is such tension that it is a miracle that our patience doesn't burst. For how long?

JANUARY 5, 1969

Today I was up until midnight at the school council, examining the new laws that are about to be enacted in Quebec. Oddly, and entirely tragic, our "leaders" think that by taking a position that is neither here nor there that they will fool someone. Instead of coming out openly against the language law that takes away the right of an immigrant to educate his children in the language of his choice, they try to circumvent the issue with a disguise that in the "language conflict" we are both English and French. There were many sharp words exchanged on this matter, until there was a consensus that the school council should demand of the Congress that they should express themselves unambiguously and not support the new bill. A second issue was almost decided upon that we should make an effort to renew the contract with the Protestant School Board for another year.

JANUARY 30, 1969

The past days were enveloped by anguished sorrow and impotent rage brought on by the gallows in Baghdad. The world was certainly shaken, but still it looks as if they are more frightened of the possibility that Israel will take revenge on Iraq, which might lead to a war. The newly elected President Nixon warns that this could result in a world war. Only Russia and France have not uttered a word against the barbarity of exploiting a scapegoat in the guise of espionage. In general, the world seems to be like a boiling cauldron – from the universities all the way down to the basement slum-dwellings. The disintegration of an entire civilization is taking place before our eyes. It is hard to face the eyes of a child, or to face your own image in the mirror.

FEBRUARY 15, 1969

Events are racing so kaleidoscopically that it is impossible to chase after them. We feel ourselves besieged, and even worse, because we don't know where and when something might happen. This week students destroyed the computer centre at Sir George Williams University. Above and beyond the damage and the fact that young people will have to darken their days in prison and to live forever tarnished by this misfortune, the whole event was of the kind that shook you to the marrow. It looks like the affair was organized by several experienced agitators. They enticed the naive who probably thought that in this way they were serving "the revolution." In addition, bombs are being thrown at public institutions. It is not clear whether these actions are related to each other. Totally perverted creatures exploit this and telephone public institutions and schools with the warning that a bomb has been placed there, which results in panic. We at school have begun to prepare the children to evacuate quickly without putting on their coats.

FEBRUARY 28, 1969

The past few weeks were hard. Anxiety about Gittel's illness, events concerning Israel, the intensification of terrorism locally – almost an atmosphere of panic. The destruction at Sir George Williams University, and a backlash with racist overtones. From this brew, which emits such a horror all about that "the hearts feelings cannot be uttered." This could return us to the situation of the '30s when the wave of nationalism engulfed everything in a war. The unexpected death of Eshkol places Israel before new trials. May they be able to withstand these trials.

Amid all this, they are preparing the fortieth anniversary of my being principal. I agreed to this because of the assurance given by the *chaverim* that they would be able to raise a substantial amount for the school. But now that a large amount has not been raised, I have regrets. I am not enthusiastic about this.

On the other hand it has created such a warm atmosphere amongst the teachers and children. Some, like Chana Goodfriend, gave so much time and are so devoted that it is reminiscent of the best of times in the school. For many of them it revealed the secret of why we were able to survive until now, and they derive satisfaction from this. Old and new friends have responded and it looks like it will be a true celebration.

For myself, however, I know that it is a conclusion. Concluding is a source of joy when it anticipates a beginning and a renewal. Still there is some encouragement that so many close acquaintances are rejoicing and seek to cover the sadness of the celebration with accomplishments of the past and with drinking a toast to the future.

What I would wish for myself: several more years to write the saga of our family, and thus make my peace with the generation with whom I shared nearly forty-five years.

MARCH 8, 1969

Tomorrow will be a week since the evening took place, and I still do not have the words to describe what took place in the few hours that this moving experience lasted. Moving experience is probably the right phrase. Truly an experience: what I witnessed and what stirred my soul, brought on by the large audience – over 400 people – of various ages and diverse social circles. The individual activists of the early days, teacher-colleagues, supporters and dissenters, so to speak, but unified in the struggle for something and always with mutual respect. Students who were friends came from various cities in Canada and the United States. All with joy and warmth in their eyes. An artistic play that Chana had prepared with her grade 3 both lauded and gave voice in the most distinct way to the experiences of the by-gone years. Through the images and songs I could find myself simultaneously in Tishevitz, Ustilla, Ludmir, and Winnipeg, and sat in the double-parlours at the beginning of those years. I was among the old gang, with Chaim Weinschel – who came here especially for the evening – and who represented the actual beginnings of Ustilla and *Oif Yener Zeit Bug*. And at the same time felt the spirit and the bittersweet taste of the whole generation, part of which has already gone, and those still here. Throughout this I was constantly troubled: Is this a farewell? Is it possible that I really experienced all this? How long will the traces endure? Would I be able to accomplish this today? And how can one detach oneself from this and still be able to render it artistically? And is it a worthwhile tale?

It actually felt as if the whole community was speaking through the mouths of those speakers who lauded me, and I myself, in my words delivered with great restraint, spoke not of myself, but as part of a generation and its dream to realize itself in concrete deeds and accomplishments.

The warmth of the experience pursues me all week long in my waking hours and in my sleep. And I keep receiving greetings from people whom I never thought took any notice of me. It troubles me a bit, and saddens me when I wonder where they would all stand in the struggles that lie ahead? In the main, I am bothered by the sense: Have I not lingered here too long, and in truth, I am merely tolerated because no one has yet appeared to take up the rudder? Have I seriously done enough to find someone to replace me? The bit of time that remains, I would like to hope, cannot and must not be filled with routine. The final years must be dedicated to the writer. Is that really the case? Even this is not clear to me.

MARCH 23, 1969

Last night Ida Kaminska and her troupe performed *Mirele Efros* under the sponsorship of our theatre committee. The theatre was packed with a most diverse audience. I was somewhat worried about the audience response. After all, the subject is dated. That way of life no longer exists and the audience generally, in its contemporary state of agitation, no longer has the patience for particular themes, compounded by the Yiddish factor. Their performance was so disciplined – in the classic tradition – where a character is rendered authentically and the dialogue is drawn from experience. The audience was held in suspense for the almost three hours and was unaware of the passing time. Further, one felt that the audience was drawn into the performance, empathized and identified with the presentation on stage. An air of dignity breathed from the stage. It was as if everyone felt that it could be the last time that one could be present at such a performance in Yiddish, which has both the charm and the integrity of a traditional, honourable style. Ida acted with such artistic restraint, like the very great. At the reception at the school, there was real joy in having experienced an artistic event. The school was beautifully decorated, thanks to the work of the last few weeks by the students, teachers, and our Chana Goodfriend. She is full of talent and energy. She carried everything on her shoulders. Whatever she undertakes is always fulfilled. Her youthful imagination was expressed artistically. This too had an effect on the truly festive atmosphere. The actors, with Ida leading, attended and were formally greeted. The crowd refused to let her go. The mood of celebration continued beyond two in the morning.

MARCH 28, 1969

Today, the march on McGill is to take place. Separatists, joined by activists of the left and the right, those who demand "French Only" in Quebec by force, insist that McGill should become a French university. A clash is expected and everyone states that this is their aim. The problem becomes more serious. Ironically, it is just at this time that the Protestant School Board is most interested that we become associated with them. They have agreed to the demand of the schools to receive an additional $50 for each student in the next school year. Meanwhile it is a financial aid to us. Whether, in the future, this will not result in its opposite is a major question. Without this financial aid we could not consider opening the school for the coming year.

Last night attended a symposium about school problems. The speaker, Dr Schiff from New York, is a polished speaker but complacent. He is positive that he is asking the right questions and providing the appropriate answers. In reality it is only an illusion. But the audience snatches at this and seeks to place the blame on the school boards, the teachers, or the so-called community, which does not exist.

The real question is what does one expect of Jewish education, and whether it has any relevance in the life of the child, and whether the parents really desire it. But these are the questions that one must not pose. They don't even understand them. If a people exists in a state of inertia, living from hand to mouth, compelled by external forces, how can one demand of them a clear decision and education programs of significant scope? I left the meeting broken-spirited.

APRIL 18, 1969

It has become clear to me that I can no longer delay my serious intention to retire from the leadership of the school. A clear break is necessary to give it further momentum. And the time has come for me to rest and devote myself solely to writing. I discussed this with our president, Issie Engel, and transmitted my intentions so that he should be aware of this and take whatever action is necessary. My intention is that at the end of the next school year, I will retire if they have managed to find the suitable people to take over the position. At the most one further year, but I would prefer the end of next year. It appears that this was no surprise to him. He had already considered it. This marks the beginning of my self-appraisal.

MAY 1, 1969

The crazed world in its madness daily finds new twists and turns. De Gaulle has passed on but the mad world remains the same, but with one less self-appointed world-saviour.

Last Saturday went to visit Vichna Borodensky at the hospital for the aged. It was an hour when, intuitively, one finds oneself in a reality that is beyond or apart from any reality that can be grasped by the senses. You observe it but do not believe what you see. In a bright room there were over ten women in varying positions. All in wheelchairs. They were all together, yet each was alone. A number of them seem to look at each other, but don't really see one another. They don't make the tiniest effort to communicate. Some are half-undressed without realizing it. Several bent over from the waist, others with distorted faces and extinguished eyes. Some are upset and simply shout, not from pain, but their loneliness, depression, and terrible helplessness cries out. Others just stare about them. Only one young patient constantly shudders and grasps fistfuls of empty air. Vichna, in a corner, smiles good-naturedly all about, and seeing us immediately called us by name, although by the time we had wheeled her into her room she could no longer remember who we were. Still she was overjoyed, chattered on, and continued to smile with her loving smile of old. "Thank God that we still see each other. I wanted very much to see you, *Chaver* Zipper," she says, without the least reproof for not having visited her until now. "I'm not lacking anything. Everyone is here – all my family, my child, my husband, my brother-in-law, and you." Shulamis and Philip had brought her a baked apple. She takes the first spoonful and offers it to me. "I should be treating you." When I tell her that the apple is for her, she puts it in her mouth and takes the next spoonful and gives it to her husband. In this way she ate it up and then prattled on about things that happened fifty or sixty years ago. She recalled names of people and then jumped back to school incidents, and all with a good-natured smile. She asks about family matters and you feel that her speech flows without her being conscious of it. Forgets her subject and drags in phrases and tales as if from a shredded ball of wool. Complains of nothing and incessantly thanks God for His benevolence, and us, for coming to see her. Like an old, grown-up, good-humoured child, who no longer feels the tragedy of the situation. When we began to take our leave, it left no impression on her, and without a remark she allowed herself to be wheeled back to the main hall, which was like a picture taken out of Dante's depiction of Hell – a picture that she did not see. With the same smile she returned to her corner and took to fingering her grey cotton dress as if preparing for some required activity.

And this is called living. Remembering her as she was and what she did and how devoted she was to what we call life and society, and how she "lives" now and is thankful for the kindnesses, places all things under the question mark: Does any of this have meaning, and does anyone really know what takes place here. And what is really the meaning of such destiny?

MAY 19, 1969

Last evening was the closing of the first conference on Yiddish convened by the Canadian Jewish Congress. At first the issue was forced on the Congress. But sensing that it was a critical hour to win over the Yiddish audience they offered a sweet token by addressing the question of what to do about Yiddish in an organized fashion. After that, they cooperated without hesitation. Much preparatory work was invested in the conference, and to the surprise of everyone, it elicited a great deal of interest. The meetings and the public addresses by notables were packed with close to a thousand people who sat through all of Sunday listening avidly to both the philosophy and the practical demands. One could sense a profound change in the attitude toward the issue of Yiddish: To consider the situation without exaggerating the limits of our possibilities, and with respect, to present the issue as a national obligation. How deep this sentiment is remains a big question: Can our present-day all-pervasive helplessness be transformed through active participation? The fact that they were satisfied with the reading of declarations instead of creating an organization to achieve what was required, and could be accomplished, indicates that the time is not yet ripe for significant deeds. But the fact that a huge crowd was present and were exposed to the great treasures of Yiddish is already of significant value. A bit of the inferiority complex that the Yiddish circles have suffered from these last years was wiped away.

Delegates came from all the large cities and from very distant points. This alone added to its importance. Unfortunately, the guest speaker, Yaacov Glatstein from New York, spoke at length but contributed very little to its significance. It appeared that he had not thought through the issue and didn't rise to the occasion, failing to comprehend the importance of the gathering. By connecting this conference with the Czernowitz Conference he really departed from the true historic meaning of this gathering: that at this time there are intimations of repentance for past attitudes to Yiddish. He talked around the issue and took more pleasure in himself and the praise he received as poet than being concerned about his role as representative of Yiddish creativity on the national scene. It appears that his New York cynicism and the attitude of "After me the deluge," had gained the upper hand. His two public appearances were a great disappointment.

By contrast, Professor Landis, who, despite speaking in English, provided deep insights into the value and creativity of Yiddish. If not entirely new, it was, however, refreshing. Especially coming from an American-educated intellectual, it was a good omen. In general the conference was worthwhile, even though the practical results will be few in number. The psychological worth for those close to us and those more remote was most valuable. It also gave an opportunity to the few young people, writers, and teachers to unburden themselves, and to create the "illusion" that at least there is still a crowd that can be summoned at the call of Yiddish.

MAY 26, 1969.
ON THE TRAIN BETWEEN TORONTO AND MONTREAL

The first time that a Toronto cultural group has invited me to give a lecture. The constant sense of superiority that claims that they are not provincials, and how unbecoming to invite a Montrealer, was finally overcome. They did it so sloppily, however, that the announcement for the lecture was issued late. At conferences they are big-shots and great talkers. They make demands of others, but they are so small-townish that they remind me of the New York cynics. The few people who are really intelligent have such an inferiority complex that they conceal it with flowery phrases and a dogmatic party line. A small audience attended, they seem to be from the Arbeiter Ring, not accustomed to hearing a lecture in depth, with a unique approach. Spoke on Itzik Manger and his status as a Yiddish poet. The few intelligent people who were there listened attentively. The poor and careless arrangements were evident when the readers who were to be the highlight of the evening did not attend. The "singers" sang part of a Manger song without feeling. Then they sang Lessin's *Der Kremer*, followed by *Jerusalem of Gold*, and *Shoshanim*. It had the feeling of a threadbare bridal ceremony.

JUNE 1, 1969

Today we accompanied to his eternal rest the uncle, Leib, whose grave lies beside the auntie, who died last fall. After the death of the auntie he could not regain his health. Somehow lost the will to live which he had always maintained. In addition, the suspicion of TB had him sent to the sanatorium. According to the doctors he was free of it but his general condition rapidly went downhill until a bout of dysentery totally dehydrated him. Tuesday he was brought into the city in a coma. Suffered till Saturday morning, and today he lies in a fancy coffin that is absolutely inappropriate to the spirit and the way of life of the person whom all knew as Laibl. Simple in his deeds, with a ready smile on his face, despite all his afflictions carried with him the scent of Zomlitz, the village in Volhyn. It had a deep river full of fish, a buzzing forest full of secrets, and velvet meadows where the watersprites dried themselves in the dazzling moonlit night after their seductions. He also brought from there the Ashkenazi custom that every villager's home is a place to spend the night for any pedlar or wanderer. He can rest, eat, and expect charity when necessary. That was the kind of house that the uncle and auntie established here. Theirs was the first home for each of the family members who arrived here with their help, as well as for *landsleit* and for anyone in need. In my words I referred to him as the Joseph of the family, and I concluded, "The last ring of the chain of great souls from mother and father's side has now departed, to lie with them and to join them for eternity." We part from the mortal remains but cherish within ourselves the light that emanates from them.

JUNE 21, 1969

Already the second day of the holiday but the spiritual and physical fatigue, the sense of being harried, has not diminished but rather increased. The last two months were very stressful, both because of the poor registration and the diminishing size of the school. The evening school has been declining for the last few years. It is a general plague. Only the synagogues have a large number of pupils. There, they need very little except for a few prayers and prayer-books – offered by the rabbi – and they're done with it. But as the day school does not grow, and loses children in whom we have invested so much, the issue is much deeper. The main reason is the changes in methods and approaches. It has become more difficult for the students to learn in four languages. With the emphasis on French, we have to devote more time to it. A large number of parents request more Hebrew to the detriment of Yiddish. We are constantly defending ourselves for teaching Yiddish. At all the meetings we are complimented for the fine atmosphere and educational achievements, but they send their children where they will learn only Hebrew. This year the Folk Shule will only begin instruction in Yiddish at the third grade. We are the only ones who begin with Yiddish. In general I am bothered lately by the feeling that the whole concept of the day school, which was supposed to give the possibility for the broadening and deepening of Jewish education, has recently placed its emphasis more on the general studies than the Jewish ones. Everything is focused on the general studies. If the financial circumstances permitted we might be able to think of extending the time so the Jewish subjects would not suffer. But the financial situation is such that the school closed for vacation owing the teachers three months' salary. Now instead of making an educational assessment, we must manipulate and search for ways of getting loans to pay the teachers. I often feel that I am no longer the person to lead the school. It is too hard to see the situation as it is, and then have the confidence to change it for the better. Now is really the time to retire. But I don't see anyone who can take over and direct things. And the school is in no condition to afford a bit of pension. This presses on my frame of mind morally and physically. Because of this I have not had a free moment of vacation, and it is hard to attend to the completion of the last term's routine and to begin knitting together plans for the approaching year. In this mood of mute bitterness we conducted the graduation exercises, and in this mood the vacation began.

JUNE 22, 1969

Last night attended an evening in honour of Shimshon Dunsky. He served the Folk Shule for forty-six years, and in his seventieth year he is retiring from his position as vice-principal – but remains a teacher for a single class. There was a large crowd, a warm atmosphere, because he is truly a teacher of supreme grace – as the saying goes, a fine person and true scholar. Our friendship extends for almost forty years. How much chagrin he had to swallow under Wiseman only the select few know. Naturally, this was not referred to; but his career included much joy and achievements, which were highlighted. Sitting there I had the feeling that I was attending my own departure from our entire epoch. We can't even call it the changing of the guard, since I cannot yet see the guards of the future. In the meantime we are leaving the scene. In the ceremony, children with candles circled him about singing; while I felt a cold chill run through me. In leave-taking we are praised, but soon we are forgotten.

JUNE 23, 1969

This morning I was awakened by a telephone call at 7:00 a.m. A neighbour who lives next door to the school informed me that during the night, swastikas, crosses, and vulgar slogans were painted on the school wall. When I arrived at school the police were already there. The graffiti in English: Jewish Bastards Out, Motherfuckers, Crucified Jesus Lives Here, and my name too was assaulted. The police photographed everything, made a report, and called it quits. The radio programs announced it. The enemy lurks here among us. The graffiti was not childish and could not have come about merely from child's play.

JUNE 30, 1969

Yesterday I was at the airport to say farewell to the teachers who were leaving for Israel. A happiness accompanied by a chill. A bit of envy was also present because they are able to go, while we would like to, but can't. The joy surpassed this, however. I had the same feelings last week while saying goodbye to Sholem and Sonia when they left for Israel. I have the strong desire to experience once more the feelings of joy and trepidation that one has before a flight to Israel. But when?

JULY 1, 1969

The vandalism of the school wall is also being transformed into a nightmare. Both the police and the petty journalists from the local papers, *The Monitor* and *The Suburban*, unfold the theory that the perpetrators were Jewish children and most likely pupils of the school who want to settle accounts with the school or with me. It is really nightmarish. Jewish reporters are ready to blame us, as long as they maintain the illusion that everything here is as it should be. And if, God forbid, it is really true, then it is surely woe to us.

As Husid and Rochl Eisenberg reported to me, the Grosbards left the city angry at us for not awarding him the annual prize for theatre. They no longer wanted to meet anyone. Mrs Grosbard was so deeply affected that she suddenly aged. Began to show her years. He actually called me before leaving and took my address, but I felt it was only tactful. In truth it was a farewell without the promise of further contact. Morally, I don't feel guilty for having defined the prize as recognition of substantial contributions to the Yiddish language in the city, and to attracting younger energies to Yiddish theatre. He did not satisfy these conditions, as did Dora Wasserman, the prizewinner. Their deep reaction in this case awakens doubts in me whether by this action we have insulted the foremost Yiddish performance-reader of our times. It never dawned on me that he anticipated receiving the prize, and that people in our circle had even assured him that he would be the recipient. The writer in me demands that possibly we should have taken into consideration the artistic contribution alone. Possibly the social dimension outweighed the artistic because I was so immersed in community affairs, and this made me overlook the artist's struggle for survival. I saw only the communal, which is an aspect of my own tribulations in the city.

JULY 8, 1969

Last evening Yechiel came for a visit. It was the first time since we moved to the new house. He is so removed from the reality of this world that he didn't consider it necessary to come to see Gittel and the house, over the whole winter. He was very talkative, alert, and at great length intertwined one Talmudic tractate to another. He speaks with great assurance, yet one can detect the weighty doubts with which he struggles. The essence of his words are that secularism and the entire way we deal with reality is nonsensical and leads to catastrophe. He had foreseen everything, and all our efforts to search for a synthesis are futile. Only living in accordance with the Torah assures survival, and has meaning. *Yiddishkeit* is not built on belief but on divine omniscience. Redemption is at hand – he casually informs us – and that the select few have attained true knowledge through the Torah. From his tone, you infer that he belongs with these knowledgeable ones. He remarks: "You know that I like to prattle. (From childhood we called him "badjger" which means "a blabbermouth.") I sometimes blurt out forbidden things that are unnecessary. Father, may he rest in peace, was the true initiate, acknowledged by the heavenly powers. He still had to complete a fourth sacred book, which he showed to no one but myself. The manuscript is with me; you never saw it. But the powers above did not desire this, and took him away." He mixes fantasy with Talmudic lore. And his eyes shine with a strange glow that truly frightened me.

Taking him home he continued in the same vein, wrapped in esoteric lore where everything that surrounds us is not worth a pinch of snuff. I felt so depressed and at the same time struck by his ability to tie and to bind wonderful ideas, and entangle them in hidden, bottomless worlds. I felt myself trembling, laughing, and crying at the same time. The fear that he evoked presses on my mood with an aching bitterness. He chases about in the cosmos, and yet can still maintain himself in mundane routine. He lives like a hermit, and still is part of the day-to-day activities. At least he is not embittered.

JULY 13, 1969

Last night I heard that on Friday the 11th, Shaya Belkin passed away in San Leandro, California. One of the last of that generation that, virtually empty-handed, established all the institutions that are to this day the basis of our local community life. He was a colourful personality, with multifaceted capabilities, and a dear person. Lived through hard times, and applied all of his organizational skills for the good of the people. Like many of his generation, he represented the socialist movement and, later, the Poalei Zion, which then identified themselves with the Jewish masses. Their ideals were formulated in the party circles, but their practical deeds were aimed at the people and did not merely express a narrow party ideology.

He was the most intelligent *chaver* of his group, but never pushed himself toward the highest positions. He wrote the history of the Poalei Zion, and the story of the colonization and immigration movement in Canada, with which he was personally familiar. In recent years he was embittered because the *chaverim* and the community did not appreciate him sufficiently, despite the fact that he knew he was held in great esteem by everyone. He was hurt that very little was done to disseminate his books, and living these years in California, naturally, he was all but forgotten. We shared many hard times together, and joyful ones as well. There remains in my memory the gathering of extraordinary elation on the night that the State of Israel was declared. Spontaneously, people went to his house to share the experience.

One of his closest friends, Louis Rosenberg, already aged himself, cried bitterly to me: 'Nobody knows us anymore." He too in his own way, through JCA, produced an enormous mass of work, and was the best statistician of the Jews in Canada. Now he is just a small cog in Congress, which only now finally agreed to a tiny pension. It was pathetic to sit with him and hear of his experiences of those bygone days. Viscerally, I respond to the passing away of this generation, and as it fast approaches those in the second row, including myself. Beyond control, his tears scald me as if they were my own. The sorrow of old age seems to become more acute as we see the specific individual passing away.

Belkin's death and my meeting with Rosenberg so depressed me that I can't gather my thoughts. Yesterday, by coincidence, I met Ravitch who is fading rapidly. Heartbreaking.

JULY 16, 1969

For generations the world has been enveloped in mystery. For millions of years the moon – the mistress of the night – has looked through silver veils on the good and evil, joy and sorrow, love and hate of the world. She has many divine names and just today they launched a spaceship to uncover the mystery. It is probably something that can't be expressed in words. Exultation, the apex of accomplishment, but yet spirits shudder: Is this for the best for man, of whom it is said, "A little of the divine should remain." The more formidable is his knowledge, the more dangerous he becomes. He is almost at the point of destroying all the earth and its creation. Is the earth now insufficient, that he has undertaken to despoil the hitherto inaccessible? Or will this be different? My conscience was troubled watching the lift-off into the heights. All human energy was concentrated to uncover that which is distant and hidden, but of the need to quell the obvious hunger and poverty of mankind you still have to beg and struggle in every corner of the world. We should really be able to free ourselves from material concerns and exult in such an event. It is no small matter to be witness to a new discovery in creation. But our shaken spirits and our fragmentary awareness of man's position in the world does not allow us to exult and rejoice.

JULY 20, 1969 (4:30 P.M.)

Of the exact time on the moon, no one tells us. But just 12 minutes ago the spaceship *Eagle* landed on the moon. A dream, a fantasy for millions of years and generations has been realized. In a few hours, the first man, Armstrong, will take his first step on the moon. Man has finally liberated himself from the chains of his planetary enclosure. The few seconds before the landing were extraordinary. No words could be summoned. Only the ancient saying: Silent amid the silence. It is impossible to utter anything, although many try to say things in search of some significant statement. At the program break the TV returns to its mundane commercials: naked girls dancing; the Bank of Montreal announces a new type of loan. Is this all they are capable of after what has just happened? Will the reality of bringing back a rock or something else from there cast a shadow over the Jewish ritual blessing of the new moon? Meanwhile the world awaits the first step, and then the lift-off to re-enter.

AUGUST 1, 1969

It has been a terrible week. While still not recovered from Belkin's death and Bregman's sudden passing, which still remains a mystery, bound up with bitter suspicions and guilt feelings – Moishe Manechovsky died suddenly. He left his house last Tuesday on July 29th for the laundromat to leave his laundry, and felt ill. He managed to speak to his family as emergency measures were being applied at the hospital. But they were unable to save him. He expired just as suddenly as switching off the light. This happened only four weeks before the wedding of his first grandchild. It was meant to be a joyful gathering of family and friends. He still had so many plans to study, read, and write. In his last talk, recorded on my tape-recorder when he was here last May, he spoke so heartily and cheerfully about his plans and had every confidence that he would live on and on. As much as he was in love with living and doing – despite his own inner struggles and continuous disappointments – he never allowed despair to consume him. A very complex man he was, among the pioneers of the Poalei Zion in Poland, toed the line and was loyal to the party. Still he could grasp an issue humanistically and overcome his ideological reservations.

We travelled to the funeral. We knew each other and were friends for almost forty years, despite the differences in our characters and our outlooks, and the difficulties we had in Winnipeg. How desolate it becomes all around us. As Wiseman wrote: "When the time has come for us to make our complaints known by pounding on God's table, how can we do so when there is no table, but only the throne on high." The funeral was large, dignified, partly secular, partly traditional. Nevertheless, I felt that the eulogies were incongruous with the mystery of death.

AUGUST 13, 1969

Barely managed to get away for a few days to change the atmosphere. We went with the Husids. In truth I wasn't eager to travel with them for two reasons. First of all, they wanted to go to Boiberik, and I felt that going there would not be restful and not much of a change from the atmosphere of the whole year. Especially when one remembers the Boiberik of former years, now only nostalgia can bring us there, and the feeling that we are going backward in time. Second, the couple is strange, opposites to each other in every way. He is totally introverted. Gives the impression of being in the midst of composing a poem and searches for a phrase that will further obscure the thought that he wishes to express. She is open and an extrovert. Still it turned out to be much better than I had expected. It seems that away from the city's tumult everyone changes and a sense of humour gets the upper hand. Liberation from the normal routine frees the introvert and restrains the more forward. We enjoyed one another's company. When we don't take ourselves so seriously, our spirits are lifted and getting along together is made easier.

SEPTEMBER 5, 1969

All the evil powers of the world are raging at Israel after the fire of the mosque in Jerusalem set by a crazed fanatic. The aura of 1967 comes back, but with one difference: Jews are frightened here and there is no longer the feeling of readiness to champion Israel as in those days. Only a sense of agitation. Only the religious react strongly through their days of prayer. The official protest meetings are somewhat sporadic, and the so-called secularists have found only little strength to call out the masses as they should. It is also the thirtieth anniversary of the outbreak of the Second World War – the world's and our catastrophe. So was anything learned from this? The world now stands before a new, even more gruesome, catastrophe. The atmosphere is exactly as it was then. Even worse: it is accepted as inevitable. A kind of Greek fatalism on the part of the older generation, while the young play the game of long hair and long-forgotten beads from the primeval forests, together with casting off every responsibility. Even the most serious among them intoxicate themselves with various drugs – once referred to as medicinal herbs – in order to escape reality. And those who desire, so to speak, revolution and change, conduct themselves as if intoxicated by force, without any responsibility toward the new society to which they ostensibly aspire. Truly the confusions of Babel are all about us.

Lying in bed at night taking stock of myself, I also think that perhaps I bear the greatest guilt. My own doubts and aging, and the continual preoccupation with finances, the constant demands for financial aid from parents, rebuffs many of them. No one wants to identify with a poor relative. What is needed is a new approach and a new face. This year we are introducing several new things on an experimental basis. More spoken Hebrew – we have hired a specialist from Israel. The teachers are full of enthusiasm, recognizing that efforts must be increased if we are to save ourselves. My doubts: will we, through these measures, reduce our educational goals. In general, lately the entire emphasis in all the subjects taught in the school systems is on tangible achievements and mechanistic goals. While in theory every child's ability is taken into consideration, the subject matter and the approach to it from childhood on lead the pupil directly to specialization. I have grave doubts about this being the road to true education.

SEPTEMBER 6, 1969

Added to my bitter mood, which literally prevents me from working – let alone writing – is the growing number of constant deaths of writers and activists. Soon there will be almost nobody with whom to exchange a word, or with whom to correspond. Yesterday heard that Dr Shlomo Bickel is also no longer with us. The entire Eastern Wall is now empty and even the farther wall of successors is also quite bare, its notables broken and sick. Yiddish culture in recent years is expiring before our eyes and we are expiring along with it.

SEPTEMBER 7, 1969

The first breech in our "family pedigree" – as Sholem had once called it in one his poems – has now occurred. Dovidl, Sholem's younger son, has fallen in love with a non-Jewish girl, and they plan to marry soon – so Rabbi Stern of the Reform Temple will marry them. Still, it is difficult to be reconciled to the harsh notion that the circle of generations now comes to an end. Certainly, in order not to lose him or her completely, some members of the family will accept the fact with compassion and hold them as close as family. But how can we begin to befriend her relatives: pious Scottish Presbyterians? The tribulations in this case are quite difficult. Logic, heart, emotions, historical responsibility, and the undoubted traditional customs are in conflict with each other. But facts remain facts. One fact is tragically clear: our family too has been drawn into the whirlwind of dissolution. Might it perhaps be a new beginning? From what source? According to some of the family, all previous generations are trembling, and therefore they feel that we must consolidate and have no contact or dealings with him or her. They mean to cast them out. I don't support this. If it could not be avoided, now we must hold open the doors and hold them close. Wish them the best of luck and help them along so that all might go well. In this case, the left hand repels and the right hand draws closer; still this is insufficient. Straightforward humane treatment using both hands might protect us from a deeper rift.

OCTOBER 13, 1969

Last night was the memorial evening for Shlomo Bickel, may he rest in peace. It was pathetic to see Melech Ravitch mourn him, an aged person who has to eulogize someone younger than himself. His weak voice and emaciated, shrunken appearance conveyed such fatal sadness and sorrow. It was difficult to look into his eyes and to face all the others. I read aloud Bickel's introductory essay to his book *Writers of My Generation*, which best describes his self-evaluation, and has all the qualities of his essayistic style. I also added my few words; I saw him as an older brother who is looked up to in different ways than a father or a grandfather. As close as one might like to be to a grandfather or a father, this relationship can never be as whole as with an older brother. An older brother is still your own generation, one who has managed to attain a different rung from the grandfather or father. His struggle parallels your own and you look to him for support and answers. It is sort of looking up to him and looking into yourself at the same time.

The last few days we find ourselves as if in a besieged city. The upsurge of Separatists on the one hand, on the other, demonstrations, strikes by police, firemen, and other workers, has this past Tuesday brought out the organized thugs in the name of chaos and "revolution." At the same time the dispossessed, with the primitive instincts of basic man, are embittered and in a period of unrest simply desire to shatter windows and loot. They seek to cast the guilt on the other – and everyone has his scapegoat. We are extremely anxious and fearful that this situation should not be directed toward the Jewish sector. Signs of this are already apparent. The general sense of things is somewhat reminiscent of 1929. Let's hope that there will not be the kind of counter-reaction that will wash everything away. I find it sad to look into the eyes of a child when all our quests and plans for advancement through learning appear foolish and tragi-comical.

OCTOBER 18, 1969

The forced rest and the deep introspection has still not banished the troubled mood of "it's all over." A frame of mind that now reckons the days, and at best, the years. Yesterday I turned sixty-nine, one step from the threshold of "wisdom years." Will there still be time for a personal accounting? I am constantly tortured by the feeling: You can no longer make any far-reaching plans. The book of your generation has not yet been written, and now no one will ever write it as you could and wanted to. In addition dreams plague me, but also quotations and Biblical verses contend with each other in my dreams and while awake. Today I woke up with the saying: "If you are confronted by the evil one, drag him to the study-hall." The interpretation of this goes: Immerse yourself in work even though your bones are aching and your mood is reciting *Neilah,* the closing prayer of Yom Kippur. "As long as he has not ceased his studies the Angel of Death shall not have dominion over him." The desire to work begins to return. Hopefully, may there be creative days and nights. "Don't make too many plans," scripture says, "because he who does receives less." The utter sense of futility and vanity that needles like the autumn rain must now be repelled.

NOVEMBER 25, 1969

The atmosphere around us and in Israel has become unbearable. My day begins unwillingly and things get done without enthusiasm. As if the whole world has lost coherence. Harnessed to my tasks, and literally with the last of my spiritual resources, I continue to make others feel that everything is as it should be. Both in the school and the community activities. Even managed to deliver a lecture in English to the students enrolled in the course for Yiddish literature at McGill. For the first time I had about me sixty or seventy young people between the ages of eighteen and twenty-four, who had come to hear about the *shtetl*, its external and internal characteristics. Had to speak for an hour, but they didn't let me go and it turned into two hours. Was invited to return. Next week I have to address the Hillel group about Jewish education. Surprisingly, after all, there remains a kernel that especially want to hear what we have to say. Where do I get the strength for this? Something is brewing among the Jewish student body regarding Jewish issues. It looks as if there is a will to know and to identify with Jewish causes. Oddly, we have become those of little faith.

Some days ago learned that Yitzchak Atlas from Kibbutz Einat is no longer alive. Pepeh is now all alone. I was preparing to greet them on the fiftieth anniversary of our first meeting in Ludmir in the winter of 1919. In my desperate loneliness, once a week I would sneak through the back alleys of Ludmir to the Hechalutz library where I met him for the first time, anxiously hovering over each book and modest periodical. Through him came to know the quiet, modest, unfailingly enthusiastic Pepeh. They led me to the Hechalutz nucleus who, under leaden skies, in their impoverished dwellings on frosty evenings, dreamed of the sunny *Emek*. In their room I drew upon a bit of comradeship that sustained me over the week in devastated and starving Zimneh. I still had hopes of meeting him in Israel. Put it off for too long. With his passing goes a part of my own beginnings. He was only one year older than me. Time is running out, and emptiness surrounds us.

DECEMBER 24, 1969

In the United Nations, which is dominated by the Afro-Asian bloc, even the ostensible friend America has now come out with a "peace plan," which Golda has correctly labelled appeasement and reward for the Arabs. The peace plan was released after consulting with the oil magnates in Washington. From this cabal there arises a stench that envelops the entire leadership of the world. And today they celebrate the day of "Peace on Earth" with plays and carols on all the radios and TVs. This leads more to the incitement of spilling blood and the casting of all horrors onto the eternal scapegoat than to true peace.

The real "time of tribulation for Jacob" is upon us now, but whether "whence comes my salvation" is also at hand, who knows? Compared to the plotting and machinations concerning Israel, all other problems and events seem insignificant. Still, even in our little world, we must attend to what is happening. It is difficult, but must be done.

Sitting at a meeting of the Day School Association last night, the fate of our entire institution was in the balance. We find ourselves caught in the conflict between the French and English sectors. It is hard to decide which is the best and most honest path. I feel though that we should not become an independent board, and we should make clear that we are not prepared to identify solely with the English minority. The question also arose regarding the community leadership's inclination to become involved in education through the sponsorship of a research project. And before you know what is happening, there are such fierce debates that the whole issue may come to nothing.

DECEMBER 31, 1969, IN THE MOUNTAINS
AT CHRISTIEVILLE

Two days ago came out here to be with Chana and Mark and the grandchildren for a few days. Partially forgot the city's din and the weighty thoughts. Was supposed to leave a day before but the snowstorm prevented this. It was impossible to get out of the city. I thought, as in the past, that as soon as I arrived into the fresh air and surrounded by snow and whiteness, that my spirits would lighten as well. But it seems that with age it is no longer so. The strain is too deep.

Yesterday was a cloudy day. I wandered about the neighbourhood but saw nothing. Read through a complete issue of *Jewish Education*, devoted to current problems. In sophisticated English the "specialists" hold forth – nothing less could be expected from directors of teacher colleges and educational bureaus of all denominations. They address what is required and what is needed. Their diagnoses send a chill down my spine, even those provided by the optimists, and more so from their proffered remedies. All of them conclude that everything stands in doubt, even their most positive statements. It is as if they are beyond despair about Jewish existence on this continent and in Israel. With all their knowledge and publications about Jews and *Yiddishkeit*, they appear like outsiders who are fundamentally untouched by the whole issue. They draw all their conclusions from foreign theories. And these are the intellectuals. Not for nothing do the community leaders reject their advice.

The bitter year of 1969 will soon pass. What will the '70s bring? There really is little belief in any improvement, however, we are permitted to have expectations and hope.

1970–1979

JANUARY 20, 1970

The cynics of the western world and the hypocrites of the Communist camp are overflowing with Christian pity following their own machinations which led to the fall of Biafra. They cry streams of crocodile tears on its pitiful fate and at the same time they allow the "courageous" Nigerians to continue their own plan of offering aid. The "saintly" UN representative certified that all was right and proper there, and this he discovered after spending a single day on the spot. Then he flew to the French saint, Pompidou, to celebrate the event. And this bunch wants the young to have faith in them and to hold their tongues. And the impoverished of the world should accept as truth their declarations about a world of justice and peace. These are the judges and denouncers of Israel!

It is no wonder that locally an audience of thousands assembled to listen for six hours to the monologue of the Lubavitcher, and they celebrate with exultation the writing of the final passages of a Torah scroll in anticipation of the Messiah. Meanwhile they assert that it is forbidden to return even one inch of Israeli land. God does not allow it. Their publicity is carried in all the newspapers with calf-like rapture, and a special telephone connection broadcasts this immediately over loudspeakers to an audience of thousands assembled for the same purpose in Israel. (How many poor *Chasidim* could be provided for with such expenditure?) And the president of Israel sends a special delegate to represent him at the assembly of overwrought and incited patriotism – which confounds a world. One must find a place to hide from the world's hypocrisy and cynicism.

FEBRUARY 3, 1970

Last Sunday spent the day with the advisers or leaders of the B'nai Brith Youth Organization. It is the largest youth organization and recently quite oriented to Jewish issues. The seminar was held in St Agathe. There were about forty young people, all students between the ages of twenty and thirty. In the morning I spoke on the *shtetl*, covering almost the same material I had used for the course at McGill. The impression was the same. A deep curiosity to know of the past and what values of that time are still relevant today. Most of them know almost nothing about Jewish culture and life – except for flowery phrases about Judaism. In their introduction they used a Question/Answer form addressing the subject of "What is a Jew, and what is *Yiddishkeit*" and a film about Tevya with illustrations by a Toronto artist, to create atmosphere. The impression made by my lecture was very emotional. The questions posed by some of them were quite profound. Only a few participated. It was also a stirring experience for me to speak, after all these years, to genuinely young people whose different thoughts and appearance was only temporarily a barrier. In the course of the discussion it felt as if I were sitting among the youth of Ustilla and Ludmir, or the first years here in Montreal many years ago. The same questioning, the same inner debates and searching for the fundamentals of a kind of world view. We still have much to impart to them and certainly can communicate with them, indicating that they are not cut off and can still learn something from our experiences.

In the afternoon the subject was how to adapt the Jewish qualities of Israel to the needs of Jewish life here. The panelists were a local rabbi, the director of B'nai Akiva, and a representative of Habonim. Although the questions from the more intelligent participants were pointed and provocative, the answers of the panelists were shallow and mostly defensive in response to the questions. Almost in the formulaic manner of the Haggadah. The rabbi avoided or simply did not want to treat the issues in depth. He was anxious to please and to create the impression that he was a man of today. As a result he spoke only in clichés. The other two essentially gave the Zionist party line, made palatable with tradition, religion, etc., but were feeble in offering answers or posing the questions sharply in a contemporary perspective. It was painful to see how they thrashed about on all fours in the shallow waters. I tried to introduce a keener insight, but it was left hanging in the air. There must be a more acute clarification of these matters in order to comprehend them. It is clear to me that if the Movement really wanted to play a role among the youth, entirely different materials from those now in use would have to be prepared. The Congress for Yiddish Culture should gather the essays of Dr Zhitlovsky and distribute them systematically in the campuses. If we were younger than we are, we would have dedicated ourselves completely to this work. We could establish a cadre that in time could properly lead and influence the young.

FEBRUARY 4, 1970

The issue of the amalgamation with the Folk Shule has become public knowledge, and essentially in a negative form that can do damage to the whole affair. It was understood that people on both sides would not speak officially, and for the time being would keep the matter secret. I don't know who revealed this. The rumours are coming from those closest to the Folk Shule, and they are well enough informed to speak about a complete plan which is labelled "Taking over the Peretz Shule which is bankrupt." Our activists and parents who had heard nothing from our representatives feel insulted and injured. I have a suspicion that those who are instigating this are purposely out to sabotage the whole matter. I was afraid of this eventuality and advised our people to keep our activists informed unofficially. But they in their wisdom did not think it advisable, considered it premature. Now that it is out in its false version we will be on the defensive. Next week both committees should be meeting with the community leadership to discuss the financing of the deficit. And this, according to my view, should have occurred following the agreement to unite the schools and not before. It looks as if it was one of their demands, and further, it weakens both sides. But the negotiators decided differently. They think they know better, surely a sign of their business acumen.

FEBRUARY 9, 1970

Last Friday we went to offer condolences to Melech Ravitch on the sudden death of his youngest and last surviving brother, Hertz Bergner. Brokenhearted and depressed, he nonetheless accepts it quite stoically. His hands tremble much more than they did when I met him some weeks ago, a bit more stooped and hesitant in his speech – almost a soft staccato that is hard to grasp clearly at first. Still, he wanted to listen and conduct the discussion about the symbols in the Jewish manner of mourning and their deeper significance. And almost nothing said about the brother. He was a very excitable and often agitated person and writer, as he appeared to us, when he was here a few years ago. Ravitch led the discussion simply to find in the Jewish view support for his current belief that there is some form of existence even after one ceases to breathe. It is pathetic to hear from him, the atheist, that he is unwilling to be satisfied with the abstract concept of becoming a part of the cosmos, but actually clings to something concrete. Even when it is only an illusion, it satisfies his artistic nature. When a number of Jewish symbols of mourning indicated such a concept dealing with the transformation from one state to another, he visibly brightened and searched for the apt phrase to express it. Not a single word to try and relate something about his brother, when alive. Everything was in the abstract. Is this the way of sublimating death, and freezing within oneself the pain of his being cut off so young?

FEBRUARY 15, 1970

The tragedy of Israel's situation takes on such proportions that it looks like a game played by hidden powers who want to draw Israel into a cul-de-sac that can only lead to a world catastrophe. Similar to the passage: "Let me die with the Philistines." The bombardment of Egypt, deep in the interior, must eventually lead to strikes on non-military targets which sharpens the hatred and creates a sense of guilt in us that this is not solely a defensive war. It is not the easiest thing to reconcile oneself to the idea of becoming a scarecrow. The fear of a kind of Spartan consciousness among the youth is already felt in Israel. Can this be avoided or erased with flowery speech? The whole spiritual image of the Jew stands in jeopardy. Could this then be the face of salvation?

FEBRUARY 21, 1970

Last Thursday there was the meeting of the executive where a report was tabled regarding the negotiations with the Folk Shule and the leaders of the community services. At the outset the mood was very gloomy. Almost as if everybody sensed the disintegration of an era. Issie Engel presented the issue as a businessman, that the financial requirements forced the issue. Only after the clarifications that the issue of amalgamation was necessary for our type of school system, and more effective for better community planning, did they begin to perceive the issue in a different light and gave the committee the authorization to negotiate officially and report back. The next day it also caused the teachers to be depressed. Even the assurances that all would be done so that the teachers would not suffer was of no avail. It is clear that being the weaker side, financially and numerically, we will have to concede more of our principles. Generally the attitude and tradition to human relationships are different in each school.

FEBRUARY 26, 1970

At the executive meeting of the Folk Shule it seems, as was reported, that the issue of amalgamation was rather coldly taken up. A committee was set up to look into the matter and to elaborate some sort of plan for negotiating that will have to be approved by the executive before the negotiations begin. It looks to me like a way of stalling the matter and looking for a way to place the entire responsibility on the leadership of the AJCS. We, however, cannot wait. It seems to me that my idea to approach the leaders of the community on our own was more valid. In that case we would have known much quicker where we stood. Now we are powerless to make any decisions on our own, and our few *chaverim* are traumatized and see no way of financing ourselves. It is even hard for me to think lucidly about an alternative.

MARCH 13, 1970

I was very upset all week. It becomes more evident that the few *chaverim* who are the so-called leaders of the school see no other option than amalgamation, which in actual fact means accepting their program and their management totally. It will also mean that they will decide which teachers will be kept on staff and which will be let go. There will no longer exist on this continent a school that teaches Yiddish from the first grade. Realistically it is not a new beginning, but rather a renunciation on our part of our right to exist. Meanwhile, no salaries have been paid for almost three months. I find it difficult to determine how we erred so badly that it had to result in this state of affairs. I feel that it is primarily my fault. But could I have acted otherwise? Does this mean that I myself, in the course of my life, nourished an illusion and also misled a number of dear teachers and colleagues? There isn't even anyone with whom I can discuss this in depth.

I will probably have to agree to remain for at least a year after the amalgamation before retiring so as to insure that certain teachers will not suffer too much. Met with Wiseman. He is physically shattered, but spiritually he feels that he has emerged the "victor." He will probably retire and leave for Israel next year. Our era draws to a close. He feels, however, that he has led the school – his life's work – to a safe shore with a new leadership suited to the new age.

Also met with Katzman from New York. He maintains as well that there must be an amalgamation in order to sustain the whole school system. He is even prepared that in the case where community funds will not suffice to ensure the continued existence of both schools combined, they will increase the mortgage on their building. He also proposed that I assume the chair for Yiddish and Yiddish literature at the Jewish Teachers' Seminary in New York. Should I at this point make a new beginning?

MARCH 25, 1970

For the last ten days so many things befell us that we are all dazed. It was bad enough with the difficulties at school where everything falls from your hands and one misfortune follows another – poor registration and the feeling that the few *chaverim* are discouraged and are even prepared to hand over the school to anyone in order to get out from under. My entire life's work appears somehow to have been in vain – a foolish stubbornness. In addition, the situation in Israel becomes more futile. It also looks like the great dream and the effort of generations turns out to be an error, a fatal misunderstanding of the way of the world. And now, Gittel fell and broke her hip and had to be operated on and although the doctors say that she is not in critical condition, she is in great pain and confused all the time and most of the time does not know where she is. This was more than enough to drive us crazy and we walk about in a stupor. It was truly tragic when a few nights ago she tried to tear off her bandages and they had to bind her hands. She constantly cried out to us to get rid of the chickens that were binding her hands. She begged us mournfully not to abandon her and called each of us by our name. And in our helplessness we stood there and could only console her by saying that it was for the best. It tore at the heart, but we had to let her cry out. Helpless cruelty. Her cry is constantly in my mind: "Yankel, why do you not help me?"

MAY 5, 1970

I don't remember experiencing such a month since the '40s, the years when all the lamps were extinguished in the world and for the Jewish people. The horror of that time grips me now when both the world and Israel struggle with their final strength, and on the personal level we are struggling to save Gittel and the school – which represents my whole life's work. The only school actually with a complete program for Yiddish is expiring, and I don't see how I can save it. As long as the enrollment was high I could still hope to overcome the difficulties. But since the community no longer sends its children to us and those who desire Yiddish becomes smaller and smaller, my own courage to struggle on diminishes. It is a nightmare in which I can see no ray of light. Even with the best outcome of our amalgamation with the Folk Shule, we have still lost. I am tired physically and spiritually, so more and more am I persuaded that I am not morally entitled to direct the school. However, how can I retire now? And the fear of being cast afloat on the waters never leaves me. It seems that people sense my predicament and even old friends avoid meeting me and inquiring. And very few of those who can't attend the public meetings make any further inquiries. The process of being forgotten is already underway.

This year, too, the J.I. Segal Foundation passed me by for the prizes, despite the fact that they encouraged me to submit a manuscript! There is always someone more deserving. It hurts, but I am not embittered by it. In these matters they probably consider the socio-political circumstances tempered by a measure of pity. In a certain way I am pleased since this may be the last opportunity for this year's prizewinners. I would have felt badly taking the prize away from any of them.

MAY 8, 1970

The negotiations with the Folk Shule are at a dead end. Dragged out for too long. The community leaders state clearly that if there is no amalgamation they will do nothing to help us continue further. The few *chaverim* have despaired and do nothing to arrange for a temporary loan to pay the teachers. I can no longer motivate them. Barely convinced them to assemble all the activists; the important representatives didn't come. When a ship is sinking there are those who don't want to be at the scene, and they even assist in speeding up the sinking. But those who did attend – about forty of them – showed empathy and appealed strongly that this should not be allowed to happen. However, nothing practical resulted. They were not the kind of people who could offer financial support. The only advice they could give was to raise an outcry in the city, convene conferences. For whom?

MAY 9, 1970

Out of desperation, I met today with Saul Hayes. I also wanted to see the president, Monroe Abbey, but could not reach him. Let them know what is taking place, and perhaps I will accomplish something. This cold fish and cynic, as he refers to himself, considers the whole matter less important than I do, still as always he is ready with advice and will speak to the appropriate people about what can be done. All his thoughts were how to be rid of us who are always underfoot, and who are creating unpleasantness for the elite of the city who speak so glowingly about culture and education. It looks like I impressed him with the need to get involved. But it is the eve of a holiday so he will have to wait until next Monday.

According to the mood of the *chaverim*, they would be very pleased if there were no amalgamation, but they will agree since they have no choice. The truth is that amalgamation in this spirit no longer means what I originally intended. By the way, Hayes presented me with the proposal that the Talmud Torah take over the school. Naturally, I rejected this. If we are to be liquidated, we will do it on our own.

JUNE 17, 1970

Last evening the board of directors of the Folk Shule unanimously accepted the detailed plan for unification with the Peretz Shule. This evening the meeting of the board of directors of the Peretz Shule will take place where the plan will also certainly be adopted. Had this taken place years ago as we had desired, I would be very pleased. Now the happiness is mixed with much sadness and anxiety. The amalgamation now is more a sign of fatigue than of vision. Others can even say that the abandonment of ideological approaches enabled a valid arrangement to be made by a third party like the Congress and the leaders of the welfare funds. But in truth it is a sign of the commencement of community responsibility for education.

JUNE 18, 1970

As was expected, our meeting also adopted in principle the resolution to unite with the Folk Shule on the basis of the letter from the Allied Jewish Community Services committee, which includes the Congress.

The discussion of the issue was very lively. The opposition, however, felt weak since the realistic situation was that without amalgamation there was no possibility of further existence. And even those in favour could not muster enough fervour and belief to be convinced that in the process we are not being wiped out anyway. The resolution was passed with a majority but the feeling was that the coming year, when we will work out the details, will be the decisive one. As the chairman closed the discussion saying: "This could be a historic decision from which we will all be strengthened." However the doubts are formidable. One thing is clear: an era has ended. If we merit it they will say about us, "Blessed be old age which has not brought shame on its own youth." In the meantime *mazel tov* wishes are exchanged.

JUNE 26, 1970

The mixed feelings about the amalgamation, it seems, are felt on both sides. We congratulate each other, but no enthusiasm is evident. Especially our people from the old guard give *mazel tov* with tears in their eyes. The younger element too, parents who joined us in recent years, have the sense that somehow it is their weakness that forces them to accept a "new" direction when they still have not accustomed themselves to the "old" way. They fear somehow that they are being treated like second-class citizens and are being patronized. Some unimplicated observers regret that our identification with the common man and woman will finally be wiped away.

Meantime we are trying to maintain a group of activists so they will feel that everything must be done to strengthen the organization for the benefit of both schools. Personally, I have the feeling that our representatives on the amalgamation committee are more inclined to dispense with the whole matter than enter into the issues. Consequently, every important issue remains in flux and hangs in the air. They concentrate on our weakness and not on our potential strength. This troubles me a great deal and they sense it and are constantly justifying themselves. I'll have to discover what troubles them.

At this time we are also extremely exhausted by Gittel's stay in the rest-home, which is very far and the day is taken up with travelling back and forth. All the efforts to transfer her to Maimonides Hospital, which is close by, are meanwhile unsuccessful. Here too the bureaucracy is in full swing and the arbitrariness of the bureaucrats outweighs the needs of patients. Every step is regulated and not one of them can be bypassed. One good thing at least is that she feels somewhat better and can be moved about in a wheelchair.

JULY 10, 1970

I just received the text of the agreement that the amalgamation committee had drawn up. The first impression is that all the clauses are so sharply phrased that it would be impossible to accept them. The Folk Shule simply takes over the school. No guarantee for our board of directors or administration. In both programming and matters of finance, they are the bosses. My own status is not even mentioned, as if it didn't exist. Time to adjust is not included. I simply can't understand how the negotiators agreed to this. It is really an insult from beginning to end. In political life this would mean "total surrender – unconditionally." Looks like nothing has changed. The older generation of Folk Shule activists had always thought this way. And the current generation wants to realize it. Nothing new under the sun. I will not go along with this.

JULY 12, 1970

In sleep last night a piercing thought flashed through my mind. I heard someone declare that I had killed someone. Shuddering, I awoke groaning: What could such a nightmare mean?

The continuous clarifications with the people on our side, and indicating the tragic dimensions to them, does nothing to ease the situation for myself or them. The best course to forestall my complete breakdown would be to retire now. I cannot do this; how can I abandon the teachers? After all, the justification for retiring is that an era must come to an end sometime – so why all the commotion? In our time we actually accomplished great things and a good number of people shared our dream and derived meaning for their existence. But somehow this fails to console. It is very hard to make peace with the fact that all the chapters of my life, in which I sacrificed everything, now come to a close, and no one even cares that it end honourably.

JULY 20, 1970

Today we brought Gittel home from the convalescent hospital where she spent nearly nine weeks. She can walk about a little with the walker or a cane. She is still very weak but we are so glad to have her home. As difficult as it may be, it is still easier than driving there twice a day. These two months were truly a nightmare. If it were not for the children's help, who knows if we would have been able to endure it.

Had my second discussion with Nachum Wilchesky on matters related to the unification of the schools. He makes every effort to ease the transition. Goes out of his way to give the impression that he expects no drastic change to take place this year and it appears that we will be able to work more or less harmoniously together. But now it becomes evident that the traditions and approaches of both institutions are much wider and deeper apart than was conceived. There, it seems that everything is directed from above and quite formal, which is not close to our hearts. His manner of speaking about "his teachers" and "his board of directors" is something that grates on the ears and my inner being. It will not be an easy task to find a common language.

JULY 22, 1970

Yesterday a meeting took place that was to approve the agreement. About twenty-five people attended. If these people had come to meetings in the last few years and participated, they would not feel as if they had been deceived and placed in a second-class position – as some refer to it. The atmosphere was oppressive and tense. Some even tried to renegotiate the terms and ended up in the dead end of the old debate of Yiddish versus Hebrew. But rational minds prevailed, helped by my explanation concerning the ideological background of the two schools and the changes undergone by both over the passage of years. Also of help was my decision to retire in the following year so as to help create a *modus vivendi* for a new school where the traditions of both would be accommodated. The consensus was that it was up to each individual and his participation in the new organization that would result in effective school work. In this way they would not be totally effaced.

During this dialogue the meeting, in part, because of the lowered heads and dejected faces, looked like a wake. When some began to defend Yiddish it suddenly struck me that people were enacting a grotesque play. They all spoke English, and if someone spoke Yiddish he was looked upon with pity. And they were uncomfortable for those who could not understand any Yiddish. Nevertheless they are still somehow championing the battle of a previous generation.

August 28, 1970

Managed to snatch two weeks in the country. It was an emotional experience to be in St Agathe after so many years. All the anguish of the past years swept over me. Every place brought back to me the early years, and the whole generation – no longer here – hovered over me kaleidoscopically. It was truly like a cemetery visit to the forefathers of our youthful days in Canada. Because of this the stress did not disappear, but rather intensified.

As time approaches for the opening of the schools, I am dogged by fright. It is hard for me to go to work and prepare things, as if the taste for such things has been lost. But one must stay constantly involved; can't let things decline further. Had several meetings with their principals and assistants, along with Tencer, who has returned and is able to express himself and relate his experiences at the school. The issue of unification is a fact and many details still hang in the air. They don't have any concrete plan and a large part of the financial pressures remain the same and perhaps even more severe. It looks like the activists did not bring their conceptions to a conclusion and made no plans to deal with the transition period. And under these conditions the pedagogical and administrative plans are being prepared and no one knows precisely what to do or not to do. It is a kind of leap into a fog.

The situation in Israel too becomes more and more difficult. The cease-fire appears to have been only an excuse to give the big powers an opportunity to enforce a patchwork solution. It will not lead to peace. From the Israeli press come weak, humble voices strengthened only by the fact that they have arrived once more at the moment of "no choice." If it was ever true, the folk proverb is now conclusive: "God, protect me from my friends; I can protect myself from my enemies." As my father, may he rest in peace, used to say, "From the heavens will come our mercy."

September 1, 1970

The idea of retiring troubles me greatly. It is difficult to express and to make explicit what essentially this feeling consists of. Meanwhile it leaves me discouraged and darkens the enthusiasm that was once present at the beginning of a new school year. Once the saying "It is not up to you to complete the work" inspired me, really furnished strength. Now I know that I am on the threshold and it is clearly the end. The knowledge that this is the last year that we can teach the beginner grades in Yiddish brings unimaginable pain.

SEPTEMBER 4, 1970

Three days ago, with the combined gathering of the teaching staff of both schools, the year of transition began. This concluded the period of separation and introduced the preparations for the new era that will evolve in time, leading to a complete union. It was fortunate that due to construction the Folk Shule building was not ready, so the majority of meetings were held in the Peretz Shule. Our teachers felt at home despite the fact that the planning and negotiations were largely done by them. But it became clear that the assemblies had given the teachers the opportunity to get to know one another, leaving a deep impression on both sides – a positive one in most cases. Collectively, our teachers were older and more experienced than theirs. Due to the rapid expansion, the majority of their teachers, especially in the English department, are inexperienced and unacquainted with the traditions of either school. Because of this they paid attention to what our teachers said. Our teachers felt that the methodologies and educational principles that the Folk Shule was experimenting with were quite chaotic. It strengthened their feeling not to chase after them and imitate everything.

But the difficulties yet to emerge are already evident. The dynamic of a large institution must lead to centralization and must compel the minority to accept its directives and lose its own initiative and independence. Even the petty details of acquiring materials from one central body creates certain administrative hardships that hitherto we controlled.

Other issues will undoubtedly arise. Especially difficult will be the fact that both the teachers and the staff still see me as their leader, when in truth, in administrative matters I am no longer in that position. Simply because in all financial matters I am no longer independent. The budget has been centralized. I also foresee that in many pedagogical matters we will no longer be able to act as independently as we would wish.

It is also very hard knowing that all this is for only one year, and will probably become easier with the passage of time. Yet, I am constantly observing on a daily basis that the Shule that was no longer exists, and I myself must participate in this process of its disappearance – all this is painful beyond measure.

Certainly, I had envisioned and hoped for a different way of retiring from my school work. Life, however, leads us elsewhere. It weighs on me like a haunting presence, both in the waking hours and while asleep.

SEPTEMBER 11, 1970

On my way to this year's school opening on Wednesday morning, the 9th, the continual ringing in my ears and all of my senses informed me that this is the last time that you are going to inaugurate the school year. Though I slept uneasily last night – mainly because I thought I heard Gittel calling –

and because of the confusing dreams and the discomfort of the usual tensions, particularly the recent hijacking of the three planes by the Palestinian freedom fighters and their threats to blow them up while the whole world stands by helplessly – what has the world come to? – all this was alive in me and pressed on my consciousness. Still, that refrain reverberated within me: "The last time. You have done your part."

It was both painfully haunting and sweetly caressing. Then calm descends. A strange peacefulness overtakes me as I approach the children – former pupils and new ones – as they were playing, and a good number of them did not even notice me. Pausing for a moment I was overcome by fear, and pity for them growing up in such a world. I pitied myself and the teachers – what can I say to them on the new year, since everything would sound so trite. Can I speak to them about humaneness in today's world? Since everything we wish to transmit to them and lead them toward dignity and justice is merely a soap-bubble in today's diseased atmosphere. They should throw it back in my face: Why are you uttering nonsense about a moral world? You are deceiving us! During the last three days of organizing the school, I am pursued by the question: What can be said to the children? Within myself I am ashamed that I do not have the courage to declare freely and openly that we have deluded ourselves that we can continue to educate with all our new skills – and convince ourselves that we know the goals of education.

Yesterday I was even more saddened by a visit of a former pupil from the mid-'30s. I rarely saw him all this time, though at each annual campaign he always sends in his contribution. He was not a great scholar nor interested in studies. His mother, a widow, really sacrificed herself so that he should study and graduate. Now, he tells me, he is prosperous and can afford to give his daughter all the things denied him. Primarily, he is looking for a school that would prepare his child for life in Quebec, to be bilingual French and English. He also wishes her to identify with Jews. Can I point out such a Jewish school to him? The naivety of his approach is astonishing. As if everything around him had passed him by without touching him. His children should assimilate to the local environment and still be part of *Yiddishkeit* – as he puts it. How can this be done, and to what end? This is likely another chapter in the mystery of Israel amongst the nations.

OCTOBER 4, 1970

The holidays of the new year, 5731, are over. As the article by Aaron Zeitlin mentions – it appeared on the eve of the holiday – according to the commentary of Isaac Luria, the Ari, this is the year of redemption. Blessed is the believer – who nonetheless must gird himself with great faith, for if redemption fails to arrive this year he should not despair but attribute it to an imperfect repentance – which is certainly an absolute truth.

Today the Lermers inaugurated the social season. It was called ostensibly to mark his return from a six-month stay in Europe and in honour of the guest from Paris, the daughter of the poet Waldman. A nice young woman, like our children she still speaks Yiddish and has respect for her father and mother. For how long? Arthur Lermer returned with a rounded goatee, now greying, which adds an air of gravity and something of a fixed sadness. Our circle convened, always ready to get together. It gives the illusion that we are still a community. Lately, however, I do not feel at home with this group. It seems to me that they are too self-satisfied: with their support for Yiddish, their attending meetings, their theoretical discussions, and their self-induced convictions that they represent a group that expresses their cultural endeavours through meetings and conferences. Whether they don't see or don't grasp it, or simply don't want to talk about the fact that the only school that championed Yiddish is no longer here and will soon be completely wiped away. That the *Keneder Odler* is expiring and there will soon no longer be a printed Yiddish word in Montreal. I am overcome by fear: Yiddish Montreal is mute. In none of them do I see trembling in the face of this. They console themselves with a speech, with a university course on Yiddish, and preparing another conference on Yiddish at a special meeting for Jewish education at the Labour Zionist movement. So I become sadder still when I meet with this so-called community. If I were younger and had more faith, I would probably stir things up. But my mood is not equal to this and my mouth does not open. It may be sinful, but I cannot overcome the weakness that has befallen me in the last few months and holds me in its grip, depressed and weighed down.

On the eve of the holiday there was an emotional experience for all the teachers. For the first time in years they received salaries on time and with raises too, in accordance with the contract. The only ones who did not receive the raise were Sussman and myself. We are not part of the contract, and on our way out. The justice of this is somewhat difficult to accept and make peace with. I was certainly pleased that the teachers now feel more secure. But I was not freed from the tortured feeling that this is a part of the price that we paid for our independence until now. Taking the cheque, I was chilled to the bone as if it came from a foreign place.

OCTOBER 12, 1970

According to the secular calendar, on the 10th of October – on Yom Kippur – I turned seventy. According to the Jewish calendar it will be the second day of Cheshven. Anne Landi and Alter Cherniak were ahead of time and sent telegrams. It touched my heart. Especially Alter's telegram, from a man over eighty to a seventy-year-old, a mere puppy. He is eighty-five with all his faculties, may no evil befall him. From what a distant world he comes. He came from the closing years of the nineteenth century, with the airy dreams of the romantic period, and marched into the worst nightmare of the present century. It seems to me that my world was always nightmare.

During the past few days, added to my own nightmare, is the public one here in the province where, in the name of fanatical nationalism, the separatists – de facto terrorists – are trampling on every human value by kidnapping local officials and prominent diplomats from foreign countries in order to demand the release of their convicted comrades. The helplessness of the powers-that-be and the insecurity of the whole established order, which wants to save the hostages but cannot capitulate to the will of the desperadoes, has thrust everyone into a panic and an oppressive nightmare. Everyone faces the dilemma: capitulation would mean the destruction of the entire legal foundation of the social order as it is constituted. Not capitulating means giving inflamed nationalism its victim – and there would be no end to that.

The tragedy is more acute because this group, like all the "leftist" upheavals in the world, sails under the revolutionary flag that knows only the ABCs of destruction and has no plan or vision of what comes after. Almost as if they themselves feel that their distant goal, and how to base it on a new value system, will never be reached. It is like the world of spiders where the stronger one rules and knows too that after mating with his female she will eat him alive. It will not help him to disguise his spiderwebs with green leaves from the twigs where he builds his feeding-nest.

It seems that the transition from being independent – though in constant financial need – to a kind of security in a partnership, but now dependent on another's will, is not the easiest of things. The knowledge that everything you do is for yourself and that you bear the responsibility gives you the strength to overcome hardships. But security through dependency kills the initiative and enthusiasm for work. I experienced this myself; as if the vision and consequently the enthusiasm and commitment to work became atrophied in the partnership with the Folk Shule. Rationally, this need not have been so. Nevertheless, it is not my feeling alone, but among all those around me. Is it only a question of time to become accustomed to it? Or is it possibly because I also feel that everything I now do in the Shule is under the sign of finality?

OCTOBER 16, 1970

Last night the War Measures Act was proclaimed. The first time that this law was enacted in peace time. The army has been called out and has taken up strategic positions in the city and throughout the province. The FLQ, a terrorist-separatist party, which sails under the wing of anarcho-socialism and extreme nationalism, was declared illegal and hundreds of people were arrested. On the surface things appear to be calm, especially in the suburbs where the English-speaking and Jewish populations live. But there is a depressed, heavy mood in the whole country and especially here. The fate of the two hostages is unknown. The terrorists did not respond to the government's alternative offer given them yesterday, that the government is ready to exchange the hostages for five of their imprisoned members. The mediator refused to negotiate further. It is very doubtful whether this will save the lives of the two and whether this will help to stop the FLQ. It looks like they have great support among the students and possibly among the French working-class.

Jews don't dare utter it but the fear that it could take on a Jewish dimension is present in everyone. Those who were born and educated here are the most perplexed. We who lived most of our lives in such an atmosphere are not so much frightened as disillusioned. The police-state follows us wherever we have come. As someone today said to me in the synagogue, "We have to start carrying our passports again." I feel like I am back in my youthful years at home. Once more, we have to look into all the corners and be careful with what we say. How quickly we accept the new situation and consider it just. All the talk about democratic institutions, it appears, is only superficial. Let us hope that the powerful fist will not lose control and thereby completely undermine the possibility of a democratic society.

One thing is certain, that the prospect of a fully developed democracy with its feeling of complete freedom and the enjoyment of human rights will not arrive here so quickly. The disintegration of our system is quite obvious. At one time we would have rejoiced in this because there was a vision and a dream for new world that would undoubtedly be better. Now, it looks like the opposite; a retrogressive vision. The so-called revolutionaries here are the fascists and force the government to adopt totalitarian measures.

OCTOBER 18, 1970

The worst of horrors has occurred. Last night they found the captured minister shot dead. The senselessness and outrageousness of this is shocking, even though it was almost expected. Canada will never again be what it was. You no longer know who your neighbour is, whom you may or may not befriend, and whom you may candidly look straight in the eyes. We have acquired another homeland to be ashamed of. People walk the streets with lowered eyes. No one feels like talking. The radio and television are naturally full of broadcasting, time and again, the same news and the shock felt by the population, accompanied by funereal dirges. They appeal for solidarity.

We are entering a new era of dire events. One begins with the dream of liberation and then descends into the web of the devil's deputies.

NOVEMBER 1, 1970

Today I entered my seventieth year. I begin the "greying years" with all my faculties still intact, with hope that there will still be time to accomplish satisfying and creative work, but with the clear knowledge that these years are gifts and I will not be able to do too much except bring things to a close. It is a painful feeling but also leaves the sense that one must select carefully what is important and must be attended to, and what one can assuredly put aside.

Last night the children and grandchildren brought their best wishes and a gift. We celebrated and drank a *l'haim* – to life! However, I saw in their faces and restraint the same feeling I had when we came with wishes for my father, of blessed memory, on the occasion of his seventieth birthday. It was joyful to be with him as he was, but accompanied by a shudder and fear: for how much longer? There were no speeches. That was fine, but I wished them that when they reached this time of life that their children would come with the same respect and attachment as they had, to extend best wishes. At the present time it is certainly a rare privilege to be able to face your children and know that both generations acknowledge that they are different but bound together and ready to do everything for each other. The distinctions and differences are not alienating or spiteful because they recognize the worthiness of each other. This brought me a great deal of pleasure. Today, too, is exactly forty-five years since my arrival in Canada. In those years, approaching this date seemed like a distant eternity. And here it is. We must begin to make the reckoning of the distance travelled. It looks like I should be able to apply myself properly to this task. Hopefully, next year I should be able to free myself from the routine, and harness myself to the depiction of the generation with whom I lived here, and in this way the reckoning will be made.

Strange that none of the brothers or sisters realized the date's significance, although they all know that my birthday is always the second day of the month of Cheshven. Maybe it is because they don't want to admit that they too are aging. And maybe simply because of the tradition in the family that seldom marked such dates.

NOVEMBER 30, 1970

The meeting that honoured school supporters took place last night. A large crowd. Many of the old-timers who had helped us all these years and many younger ones. The atmosphere was dignified and still everyone felt the sense of closure. I even tried to evoke the tone of new beginnings, but I don't know whether this penetrated deeply into their souls and hearts. The elders sat with tears in their eyes and the younger ones applauded with bravos but without enthusiasm. At the core of my being, I too have the feeling of a new beginning. It could and should be this way, but I do not have too great a faith that the overworked businessmen really mean what they say. A new beginning cannot be built on the basis of negativity. I often feel that I owe a candid, honest answer to the few seriously dedicated, and to the Yiddishists, why I had agreed to this. I essentially agreed because the options were either to lead a public fight with the city's elite while not having an army behind me; to liquidate by slamming the door; or to liquidate silently with all the teachers, and myself as well, left at sea. The so-called amalgamation is a kind of refined form of liquidation and permits the salvaging of what we can. This thought plagues me and eats at me like a moth. In this mood I must carry out pedagogic and administrative work. I can't get my hands or feet to enter a classroom and it is difficult to speak to a teacher. They have more pity on me than respect. It never occurred to me that this is the way it would be when I faced retirement. Seems that the cup was not yet full.

DECEMBER 19, 1970

So now Boruch Zukerman has left this world, forgotten, shoved aside in a corner, and deeply embittered. How happy he was to see us when we saw him for the last time five years ago in Jerusalem. He could not get over his amazement at our phoning him immediately on our arrival. "Not at all like all my good friends," he said several times, and next morning he came to our hotel and insisted that we go to visit the aged Yaacov Lestchinsky, who is so pitifully neglected, he added.

The meeting with him and his wife, and Lestchinsky and his wife, was even more pathetic. They both clasped us heartily and wanted us to feel that our remembering them was cause for rejoicing. It even felt that by our visiting them we had returned them to that time when they were the spiritual core of an entire generation. It was somehow more than mere nostalgia. While having a simple cup of tea, which we drank at the Lestchinskys, Lestchinsky suddenly seemed to collapse moments after his great excitement, and had to be brought up to his room. Boruch remained with us, very distressed. "He can't even tolerate a bit of happiness," he said hoarsely, wiping his eyes, "still we were right to come here. You don't know, Zipper, what loneliness means. Here, we are among *chaverim* who still know and remember what we had accomplished, but we are forsaken. We miss our American and Canadian *chaverim*." Then *Chavera* Zukerman added with great bitterness, "Even the bigshots who, in the early years, stayed over with us day and night, forget to invite us to their homes. We can sit around for months without hearing from anyone, let alone being invited to official receptions." Zukerman tried to calm her. "We belong to another era, every epoch is jealous of the other, Nina. But I'll never forgive Ben-Gurion. When he was a child he stayed in our home for so many years and now he doesn't even recognize me."

Before my eyes I could see the final years of the 1920s and the 1930s when a visit from Zukerman meant revitalization and warmth and a deep involvement with ideas, after which we took up our work enthusiastically. We possibly did not sing as much as when Kaufman visited, nor fly heavenward as high as when Greenberg came, nor breathed in the worldly airs as with Zhitlovsky, but it was comfortable to be with him and feel the warm thrust of belonging to the people of Yisroel. It always felt that his analysis of current objectives derived from some distant point in Jewish history and experience, and still remained contemporary. Our present mission which binds us to the eternal past, still lives on and thrusts bridges into tomorrow. When those in power today projected themselves into their formerly conceived future, then the Zukermans and his kind were left in a corner, pushed aside and forsaken. Is this actually the way of the world? Is this fate? Something of the same is what I begin to feel now.

DECEMBER 20, 1970

The closer it comes to implementing the plans for the total unification – and I know that I will be unable to insist on any concession to allow Yiddish a place in kindergarten and grade one – the more difficult and bitter is my mood.

Painful too is the cumulated awareness of my own life's reckoning. Because of the community responsibilities and, above all, the school, I let the writer in me atrophy. Will I be able to catch up now that I will be free? Once when I had a free day I would immediately get down to writing. Now I find all sorts of excuses not to write. This frightens me. Were all my efforts in vain? Meanwhile I have one consolation and that strengthens me: I am now so mentally and physically exhausted that it covers up the bit of creativity that still lies hidden underground. When I am free maybe it will emerge out of the spiritual peace. May it be so.

DECEMBER 25, 1970

Yesterday the news reached us that in the trial of the ten Jews in Leningrad who allegedly hijacked a plane to fly to Israel, two were condemned to death and the rest to years of imprisonment. The trial was conducted secretly. The world press was not admitted. How low have the "world liberators" sunk? The interventions and protests did not help. Moloch demands his victim. A new chapter of martyrdom: the prisoners of Leningrad. No country has so far condemned any hijackers to death, only these bestial world-saviours. And Satan laughs away at all of us, the naive misguided of the twentieth century. Today the Canadian Jewish Congress is convening a special meeting. They will again rend their mourning clothes and try to arouse the world to protest. How helpless we are!

DECEMBER 30, 1970

Finally, some miles from Montreal, they have caught those whom they sought as being guilty of the kidnapping and murder of Pierre Laporte. Strange how the population took this so unaffectedly. A kind of anti-climax. The government immediately softened its approach to allow discussion of the issue of granting bail for some of them until the trial. As if the government was ashamed for having imposed the War Measures Act and creating the panic about the untold powers of the terrorists. It could also be that the populace is tired of the whole matter and considers them to be political criminals who have the right to special consideration. Is this the end of it, or a new beginning?

DECEMBER 31, 1970

Last night the protest meeting at the Queen Elizabeth Hotel took place. More than five thousand attended – young and old. Most visible were the large number of young people, many bearing placards. An agitated atmosphere, but restrained in tone as well as response. Several of the French elite brought expressions of solidarity. Among them a letter from the Archbishop of Montreal, and Claude Ryan, the editor of *Le Devoir*, who spoke as a liberal. Rabbi Hartman wanted to speak as a proud Jew and called for action; but as is his custom, he is seduced by his own rhetoric. Also, a New York journalist tried to describe the plight of the Refuseniks among Soviet Jewry and their demand that we make an outcry. The audience was deeply moved by the report of Rivka Broder Shaffir on her meetings with Russian Jewish young people two years ago. Solemn, too, was the moment when the crowd sang "*Am Yisroel chai*." Somehow a spark of conviction was absent in all the proceedings, possibly because the large audience, in the main, is really disturbed and senses an obligation to express its agitation and solidarity. But to demand rights for Soviet Jewry's culture, for Yiddish, Hebrew, and religious freedom there, while here they don't even come close to touching the culture, prevents them from authentically expressing their inner feelings of sorrow and pain over the violent destruction of their brethren's culture. If you don't stand up for your own culture, how can you decry the injustice being done to someone else who is defending their cultural values?

This morning the radio announced that the death sentence for the two Leningrad prisoners has been changed to fifteen-year terms. A relief for the individuals. Also, that the groundswell of opinion in the world counts for something, but the tragedy of the situation is not changed by this. The so-called "transgressors" still suffer, while those who stand in judgment are "judges according to the law." And the whole thing is a satanic game of a grand vision that has been turned on its head. All the hopes for the revolution were a complete delusion, a seduction that continues to this day in the guise of different masks.

JANUARY 10, 1971

At the last meeting of the amalgamated education committee I felt cast out, at best tolerated, as someone who is still listened to but whose words place them under no obligation. In general, the emphasis of the leaders of the Folk Shule is on the non-Jewish studies. The very essence of the school's reason for being is shunted aside. Almost as if they can hardly wait for the old guard to retreat and be done with. Maybe my view is too pessimistic, but it seems to me that their people don't have the least desire to maintain what was the best of our era. They don't even know what it consists of, and are not prepared to listen in order to inform themselves. This increases my anguish. If not for my pessimistic outlook and my disbelief in the existence of a Yiddish force that would have been able to continue a while, we might have straightened things out. It might be that my fatigue was more of a cause than the actual financial situation. It gives me no rest while awake or asleep. I feel as if I have renounced my whole life's work under the delusion that I was safeguarding something.

JANUARY 27, 1971

I am so busy with meetings and the bitter aftertaste that follows. The majority of their younger supporters know absolutely nothing of the ideological basis of the Folk Shule, and certainly nothing of the tradition of the Peretz Shule and its outlook. According to them, the most important aspects are the general studies and the most up-to-date of teaching methods. The Jewish subjects are taught as if in a modern *cheder* where language skills are given the main emphasis. It is fortunate that financially they feel secure due to the influx of children for whom the government pays a considerable subsidy. They plan everything in terms of the immediate present without a moment's consideration for the local circumstances, which are constantly changing. Despite their complete devotion, it seems to me that our adherents, while not much deeper than they, are more concerned with the essential foundation of our school system, which is the Jewish studies, and built on content. Ours, therefore, are better prepared and have already survived crises – which they have yet to meet.

My own distress because of this is so great that I cannot read anything properly or follow the important events of the day. And things are boiling here in the province as well as in the world, and of course surrounding Israel, and the upheaval of the events happening in the Soviet Union concerning the Jews. All at once, a Jew has emerged there who risks everything and makes demands like a proud human being. Out of hidden sources, a creative wellspring has burst forth, gushing in wonder at the sight of people standing on their own two feet. And on this continent, there has suddenly emerged a generation – especially among the Orthodox – that does not brook any insults. We may not approve many of their methods, but it is a sign of vitality capable of initiating a new era.

Amidst all this, a few events made a deep impression.

A) Once a year I usually spend time at the Golden Age club, reading to them or discussing Yiddish literature. This time they requested that I read from my own works. Just meeting with people who are mostly beyond the threshold of the seventies, and even though they are on the sidelines of normal routines, they still wish to be in society and participate in it. Every time I go there, I have the feeling that I remind them not only of fragments of their own lives that had a meaning but also bring them back to the present. For some of them I am a kind of tie to their pasts – their children studied at the *Shule*, and they themselves were members of community organizations. They want to emphasize their former roles, boast about themselves, or, generally, savour again the taste of having been part of an active life with a future and not merely await the prospect of oncoming night whose shadow spreads over all their faces and utterances. This time I felt it more acutely. First, because the majority consisted of people whose children had been my own pupils, a good number had attended earlier lectures, or were *chaverim* of the same organizations that I belonged to; and possibly, too, the essential reason being that I, myself, have already crossed the threshold of the seventies and am almost a has-been as well.

The first encounter, still on the stairs, was with a short, compact person with a troubled expression. "Are you going to speak to us? Tell them something about the God who imposes himself on the world and his puny Jews. What does He want?"

The second person, a former activist in community organizations and a letter-writer to the *Keneder Odler*, has a complaint: "Why don't you respond to my letter about teaching Jewish youth agriculture? I am still ready to teach them as I did once in St Sophie. Mr Gallay, the editor of the

Keneder Odler, did me a favour and printed the letter, but no one responded. The wealthy Jews don't want this, so we have to cry out." As he runs off to the bathroom with his hand clutching his pants, he calls out, "I want you to talk about this!"

A talkative woman holds a newspaper clipping to my face that tells about her daughter, a former pupil of ours, and now a guitarist who is making a tour across Europe. "She writes me Yiddish letters – thanks to you and your *Shule* – do you remember her?" In a few moments I am surrounded by older men and women, each one with a different tale of their children's success. "I know Zipper since his childhood," boasts a woman from my hometown, and seats me at the head table. After an introduction about *Tzvishn Teichn un Vasern* and reading the section on the Long Bridge, a discussion took place about its content and their own personal stories and interpretations. It is hard for them to express themselves, but their eagerness to be heard is such that they overcome this and can hardly wait for their turn. Some of them get very upset when they have lost patience waiting to speak: "Give me a chance too. I'm just as important as him." It was very pathetic to see how they clutched at their portion of being heard and recognized, as if it were the very essence of their present existence. Several times this idea passed through my mind: Will I too not look and feel like this a few years from now?

B) A day later, the memorial evening for Boruch Zukerman took place. I had written down what I wished to say and emphasize. The audience was very small, literally fitting the image that stands before my eyes, of our last meeting with him in Israel. A lonely man, pushed aside, and forgotten by his own *chaverim*. I also made reference to this. It made a tremendous impression and the small group of *chaverim* sat glued to their seats. In concluding, I suddenly had the feeling that much of what I had said about the experience of his past years I now feel in my own bones. People are already quizzical about my own circumstances: "Are you still with the schools?" Even when I'm attentively listened to when addressing an issue, I appear to be a marvel from another age.

C) Finally, the establishment has reached an agreement to carry out the research project regarding Jewish education here. They hired people to obtain the facts and make recommendations. It took over a year. At a meeting of the general committee, they spoke again about this, as they have been speaking about it for years without end: with much hyperbole and euphemistically, so as not, heaven forbid, to offend anyone. So, once again, I had to lift the tablecloth and look beneath the surface and ask the old question, whether we are ready to act with breadth of vision – and who will do it. Or are we just talking and still afraid to create the organization that will be able to accomplish this as a community responsibility. They actually gave me compliments for saying this – a reminder of the past. The possibilities for this project look better now, but I think that the current leaders are also only concerned with putting their own clique in the saddle. Not much has changed. I still don't see the energy that is really prepared for a serious plan of development for education.

FEBRUARY 1, 1971

Had a long discussion with Yechiel, which should have taken place a week ago, but didn't because of the cold. I met him surrounded by his paraphernalia: a creased pillow with a pillow case of faded colour, a hot waterbottle by his side, and he was in the middle of preparing some sort of meal to be eaten later in the day. He had eaten breakfast late, he eats only two meals a day. Nevertheless, there was an assured sense of peace about him and within him in the ensuing discussion. For me, it seemed like the peace that follows resignation. He interprets it as his faith in personal providence. He bears no responsibility since, in any case, he cannot change anything. So if providence acts in accordance with its own will, why should he take anything to heart. Since he arrived at this conclusion he feels liberated and at peace. He even eats meat and digests it, which he could not tolerate for thirty years. He told me that all my problems stem from the fact that I believe that I am responsible and can do something about it. But in truth, things are done for me, and I too must divest myself of responsibility. I have done my share, and need do no more. I only have to be concerned with getting a pension, which is my due. My mission for the school is at an end.

Then he launched into a deep discussion comprising stories of his old teacher and of the Riszener, of blessed memory, and offered interpretations of Chasidic dictums, such as "Cancel your will in the face of His will" and what it means to be "one who opposes His will" or "one who complies with His will." In short, the responsibility is mine no longer, and I have to rely on providence.

Should I say that he is fortunate to have reached this point? I must confess that listening to him speak so calmly and yet enthusiastically lightens my spirits, and I begin to feel that in some respects he is correct. It might be that in circumstances of no-choice, this is the best way to survive and not be devoured by bitterness and guilt-feelings.

FEBRUARY 5, 1971

Our wealthy men, the elite of the city's best, who recently declaimed about Jewish education like all the bigshots in the community, have cut their contributions to the schools for this year by eighty or ninety per cent. The reason being that since the schools receive government subsidies they no longer have need of money. This means that Jewish schools have to remain poor so that crumbs can be thrown to them from the wealthy table. If they can manage even marginally to live on the subsidies then living in comfort is not acceptable.

The best and most tragic of all is that Saul Hayes justifies this. In his language: The Jewish schools are dishonest if they now demand the same contributions. They don't need it, and he knows that without the subsidies the schools would simply have to close. And if they take away the contributions of the campaign, it means taking away the possibility of purchasing the new machines that are necessary, paying the teachers a decent salary, and establishing a pension fund, which could never be considered earlier. O how we need a new Mendele to write a new fable about our "leaders." The more I attend meetings with the Folk Shule people, the heavier my sprirts are, and I don't envy our teachers and activists who will have to work with them. There too one must bang on the table and cry out: Have respect, you rascals!

FEBRUARY 20, 1971

The struggle for the rights of Russian Jews has become international in scope. The convening of an international conference in Brussels with the participation of the most important leaders of all the Jewish communities worldwide is considered by Russia to be an anti-Soviet Zionist conspiracy, and they have officially warned the Jews of the Soviet Union that being a Zionist means being anti-Soviet. The means employed by "The Jewish Defence League" to annoy the Soviet representatives here by disruptive actions play into the Soviets' hands. On the other hand, the opposition of that part of Soviet Jews who want to emigrate to Israel and are ready for any sacrifice seems to be widespread. This has confounded the Soviets and they seek by terror to intimidate them. It looks like the battle between David and Goliath.

The wonder of this is that after fifty years of revolution and the suffocation of every Jewish feeling a new generation managed to sustain itself and look for a road back to being Jewish through religion, Yiddish, and Hebrew. Truly an extraordinary turn of events. Especially since here we observe the manifest abandonment of Jewish life. How mysterious is the course of Jewish history, simply beyond understanding. Still it somehow looks like the deeper meaning of the concepts "Concealed face of God" and "Eternal Israel" are clearly part of a designated mythic plan. The upheaval of Russian Jewry is a new example of providence to which we are witness. It might well be that it could happen here too some time, but for the time being the route remains unclear.

FEBRUARY 23, 1971

A new storm and the schools are closed. The experts say that this is the stormiest winter in almost one hundred years. The snow reaches over the windows. Leaving the house is like walking through a tunnel.

The world too is stormy. Israel stands at the hour of great decision. The pressure from all sides is relentless, even the "friends" apply pressure. Standing almost alone, one must decide alone. The sense of a fateful decision is conveyed in every pronouncement that comes from there. The world conference of Jewish leaders from over forty countries opens today in Brussels. Tiny Israel in a dialogue with the Soviet Union before the whole world. The courageous stance of a segment of Jews in the Soviet Union is literally unfathomable. Is it out of desperation or is it rather a strong revival of national sentiment that is prepared for self-sacrifice? The response of world Jewry is surely the result of the lesson learned from the days of the *Shoah*; and the guilt feelings that enough had not been done then inspires the present activities – "No matter what the consequences." Truly extraordinary, but in our historic trials, quite understandable. At one time the Zionist prognosis of Moses Hess was the most current: that with a Jewish state, anti-Semitism and the Jew's role as scapegoat would vanish from the world. Now, however, it is quite clear that ironically the state has created more anti-Semitism and has become a ready-made scapegoat. Zionism and the state are a convenient target for the enemies of Jews, and they can be blamed for all evils. Even when Uganda has a revolution, they can detect the concealed hand of Israel. And if the Soviets need an excuse to oppress Czechoslovakia, the liberal communism of Dubcek becomes a marinade of Zionism and Israeli imperialism. "There are many ways to hate the eternal people."

MARCH 7, 1971

In the last few days we lived through a snow blizzard that paralyzed the entire province. Everything is shut down. It was a demonstration of the utter helplessness of modern man and his impotence before the elemental powers of nature exceeding the norm. For three days couldn't leave the house. Many suffered cold and hunger due to the disruption of the electricity. Primitive man was more prepared for this than man in the technological period. One screw comes loose and the whole system is in chaos.

Amid the storm we nevertheless went to the wedding of Zuker's youngest grandchild. The bride's side is Polish, and according to their name I suspect that they are somehow descended from Frankish or Shabbetai Zvi families. The father, a liberal Pole, whose two daughters both married Jewish young men. They converted to Judaism – and moreover in accordance with Halachic precepts, not with a Reform rabbi but a Conservative rabbi. It was pathetic to see the father and mother standing under the *chupa*, genuine Polish faces with upturned noses, picture perfect, as the Rabbi read from the *ketubah* the name of the bride, Elisheva-Elizabeth, the daughter of Abraham our Father. Later at the banquet, the bride's guests sat on one side of the hall in the grand hotel and the groom's guests on the other. They probably thought that the crowd of relatives would feel more at home in this arrangement. But symbolically it appeared close – yet distant. During the meal the Polish guests stood up and sang the traditional wine-song celebrating the bride with such fire and gusto as if they desired to sever the web of *Yiddishkeit* that was spun around them and their daughter since the *chupa*. Spontaneously, the groom's side stood up and raised their glasses. A little later while the *chazan* led the singing of "Let us all greet the bride and groom" and "Good fortune to the bride and groom," the bride's side also stood up. It was one good deed reciprocated. It was only with the dancing of the hora and the wreath-dance for the youngest child that both sides mingled.

Odd how we accept as natural the mixed marriages, and stranger still is making peace with the situation. Especially so in this case, with the bride's conversion to Jewish belief according to rabbinic law and her superior knowledge of Judaism compared to a Jewish girl – and in this case much, much, more than the groom. Still the sense of tragedy and alienation is felt.

MARCH 11, 1971 (PURIM 5731)

Two days ago was the beginning of the campaign under the sponsorship of the community leaders to discharge the school's debts and the building expenses. The Montifiore Club and its guests probably heard for the first time a speech in Yiddish. The speaker was Barney Aaron. The audience listened patiently but smirked inwardly; it touched no one. As for the others, who were concerned with the improvement of Jewish education, their solutions were honest but superficial. What they consider Jewish education is so far from our ideals – to which we gave our lives – that I felt like crying out in anguish. Certainly their attitude has changed for the better. At least they address the issue and are ready to make amends for former neglect. The current political policies of the community can be relied upon to improve the school's situation. Still, I was constantly troubled by the thought that their present identification with our way is a sign that they have very little fear of our approach. Indeed, if they did fear us they might be inclined to absorb us into their conventional approaches and be ready to accommodate us so that we too would vegetate along with everyone else. Several of the activists tried to strike an historic note that somehow sounded hollow. Only one, a sturdy young man whom I see for the first time, warmed the atmosphere with a few choice words, reminding the audience that we, as a nation, are beleaguered and that every effort must be made to help those who are working to maintain a self-assured Jewish life.

MARCH 13, 1971

Strange paradoxes: on one side a large segment of native-born Jewish youth see in the new left ideology the only way to serve the revolution and forsake totally Jewish life here and, of course, Israel as well. On the other side a small group strives toward direct action, including terror, to defend Jews and *Yiddishkeit*. Others identify themselves completely with the extreme Orthodox and feel totally redeemed by this. They accept the teachings of Lubavitch and even more radical factions as the only path to *Yiddishkeit*. In Israel too the same process is at work. From one hundred per cent denial to full orthodoxy and narrow nationalistic identification. In Soviet Russia a new generation has grown up that, in the struggle against a totalitarian regime, has found their revolutionary expression through fighting for open immigration to Israel and identification with historic Judaism – although they never knew what it signified.

MARCH 27, 1971

In the last few weeks there were several meetings where the plans for next year had to be made, including special changes that altered the status of several teachers. Some have to teach only Yiddish or only Hebrew, others have to transfer from one branch to another. In this way, with some difficulty, we arranged that everyone has employment but they would have to endure intervals between classes and travel longer distances. Naturally they are dissatisfied and their complaints are directed at me. The people on the other side are generally accustomed to the top-to-bottom outlook toward teachers and employees, including the principal with whom they have no relationship. He constantly has to defend himself and his actions. Often I think about the fact that the whole enterprise will have to burst. We thought that if we could not save the school as it was, at least the teachers would not be left afloat on the waters. But it looks as if the majority feel humiliated, as if they had fallen into a boiling cauldron of mistrust and uncertainty. Some are considering stopping teaching altogether. They hold me morally responsible for having abandoned them. It is a difficult issue for me although I know that I am not guilty. There was no alternative. They do not see the advantages of the change.

APRIL 13, 1971

Just now, Hertz Kalles called to inform me unofficially as a friend and a member of the jury of the J.I. Segal Foundation that they have chosen me to be the recipient of this year's prize. It will be announced officially only next week. Of course it is a good feeling and a pleasure to know that your immediate circle appreciates and recognizes your accomplishments. If it had come sooner, when the road ahead still stretched into the distance, then the satisfaction would be accompanied by inner determination. But when it arrives at the end of the journey, the feelings are mixed with much misgiving; another sign of the end of a creative era. As to the future, who knows? Especially in my present depressed mood, the joy is very much diminished. Had it been for my literary work rather than the education prize, it would have brought me greater joy and the doubts and the bitterness about the way things are ending wouldn't be present. Still it is a good feeling.

I had a painful experience last week due to the letter sent from the teachers to the board of directors, stating that if they are not paid the debt owed to them of retroactive salaries by the 16th of this month, they will begin "study sessions" – another term these days for refusing to work – immediately after Pesach. Essentially they are right. It should have been paid long ago. But since we awaited the result of the campaign, they could have postponed things for a few weeks. But the teachers are embittered about the whole situation, so they assume combative positions before they know the facts about the possibilities of being paid immediately. At one time in such situations they would have had full confidence in me and consulted with me before taking action, and heeded my advice. Now there is the sense that my opinion no longer bears the same weight as it once did, and at the meeting that I called to discuss this, it was clearly evident. If such a mood had been present years ago, we would have gone under earlier. Even before the new regime began to rule, the common bond that held us together for so many years had been broken. I barely managed to get them to agree that I should intercede to obtain a firm commitment that in mid-May they would be paid; then they would withdraw the threat of the "study sessions." At certain times it was distressing to sit and argue with them. In my subconscious the thought gnawed at me: Just look, everything you endured in the last year was to assure that the teachers should not be cast afloat, that they obtain the current salary on time. They don't even acknowledge this nor appreciate it, and accuse me of being on the side of the administration, which according to them, refuses to pay and seeks ways of putting it off. This in itself is hurtful. The administrative personnel have not deserved such recrimination after the investment of so much devotion and effort. The whole moral foundation that I have always built upon has been undermined.

APRIL 23, 1971

The bitter mood and the constant recurring of gnawing doubts concerning the necessity for the amalgamation – which erases almost entirely a large part of my whole life's work in education – follows me relentlessly. It returns in my sleep with awful nightmarish dream-images of chopping down trees, severed branches and leaves. I am tortured by a guilt feeling: maybe there was another option, which I did not manage to perceive on time. The real truth is that if not for the amalgamation the community would not have come to our assistance and the school would no longer exist. But this truth brings no spiritual comfort. It seems that the logical faculties are not enough; the emotions are too profound.

Added to this is that in the press the journalist Yunin of *Der Tog*, in a grotesque manner, and Shefner of the *Forward* in a milder manner, charged both schools with being no more and no less than the rejecters and gravediggers of Yiddish, cutting out the tongues of Jewish children, etc. If I wasn't feeling the way I do, it would probably bother me less, and I could say to them: Where were all of you when we were struggling and suffering? After all, what has been their share in the development of Jewish education? In this mood, however, it is difficult for me to respond candidly and sharply. Defending yourself against a false charge is painful. These days, looking at the matter in its entirety, I seem to feel that this too is some sort of punishment that I must endure at the end of the road.

Good friends continuously call to congratulate me on receiving the Education Prize, but somehow I am not warmed by this. I would certainly feel differently if it were not for my present mood and amidst my gnawing sense of doubt, and of course, if it had been a literary award. Still, I'm disturbed that I feel this way. It reminds me of the classic *Mishnah* moral fable: A servant pours a glass of wine for his master who then pours it in the servant's face. After all, these people have good intentions, as most certainly do my friends, so why can't I respond with greater satisfaction?

APRIL 26, 1971

In the evening we had to attend the annual school concert – the first one held jointly. I was under tension both because of concerns for the evening's success, and for the various greetings from people including those from whom I got the feeling that they pitied me. Also, those who congratulated me for the award unwittingly conveyed the regret that this was long overdue. Others commented, albeit in a friendly manner, and without my having the slightest idea about their intentions: "You see, at the reception they photographed you with the Wisemans but not with the principal and the president. Now they are seated at the special table while you are not." The truth is that I didn't see it that way. My feeling of being estranged at this special reception is simply because I am not used to this formality and having a fixed smile for everyone. Especially since I did not see the expected faces of our people in the large crowd. Came home at 2:00 a.m. and had to get up early to accompany our children to the Yom HaAtzma'ut celebrations of Israel's Independence Day at the University of Montreal's stadium. Only a small group of children attended, not only from our school – the stadium was half empty. The upper grades of the day schools barely participated. There wasn't a festive atmosphere, although the presentations were quite artistic. An ocean of work spent on details, but the essence was missing. So I was aggravated and then was tortured by the feeling: How little we touch the souls of our children.

Came home exhausted mentally and physically and had to get ready at once to attend the wedding of a former pupil whose family came from Tishevitz. In Tishevitz I knew about her grandfathers who, along with many other Jews, lived on the upper hill, where according to tradition Mashiach ben Yoseph dwelt in his day. He was a cobbler just like her grandfather. When I meet with the former townsfolk who were there, and a number of parents of former pupils who had attended our school without payment and who are now professionals, business men, and bigshots, their greeting at such happy occasions seem to be joyous. They boast of their children's accomplishments, praise me for what I had done for them in those days, and usually conclude with the refrain: "We will forever remember you for this. Are you still at the school? How are things? It's time for you to take a rest."

They even gave me the honour of addressing the gathering. An honour that costs them nothing and which enhances their status in this society. But one can't refuse. And added to this mark of respect, just this morning I received the first review of *Pinkus Tishevitz* in which the writer praises my compilation and elaborates on several worthwhile contributions. So once more in the mind's eye there stands a vivid image of the Holocaust. How can this be compressed into the pages of a book?

MAY 22, 1971

Last Sunday, the 16th of May, was a dignified and stressful day. In the morning, a breakfast with the pupils, parents, and teachers of the evening high school. The attendance was not that good. The atmosphere was fine. Our former students commented candidly about the curriculum, and some of them were highly intelligent. The former Folk Shule pupils remained silent. As if they weren't accustomed to speaking and thinking in the presence of adults. The confidence of our pupils impressed everyone. For the Folk Shule activists it was a genuine surprise.

From there I drove to the Zygleboim Chapter of the Arbeiter Ring who were marking the 28th anniversary of Zygleboim's death. The audience, as well as the introduction to the program, and the songs they sang, "Dear friend, when I shall die," and "Brother, we have taken a vow" – ushered in the sense of such a far, distant past, which today seems unbelievable. However, looking at the audience, for a brief moment the grey reality was erased. They were mainly survivors of the war – with and without concentration camp numbers – and veteran Bundists, who cling to their juvenile experiences as if it were the thread that binds them both to their youth and those days filled with hope and those dangers that tempered the will.

In my remarks I emphasized the idea that even if we accepted that eternal salvation could be purchased by one hour's deeds, and Zygleboim's act was exceptional, still his whole life was a preparation for his mission. And when his mission was not fulfilled he simply could not continue to live. His martyrdom cannot serve as an example for the general public, but it is exalted by his mission. I connected him to his time, his experiences, and how it does and does not relate to traditional martyrdom. This gave a deeper insight into his own martyrdom and the place it can occupy in Jewish martyrology. The impression this made was truly electrifying. The audience sat as if chained to their seats and deeply immersed in the real and metaphysical world – the mysterious forces that direct the path and the inner being of humanity. When I ended they remained in a state of suspension, in a mystical exultation.

That evening the J.I. Segal Foundation's awards celebration was held. A large audience ready for a dignified experience. The entire evening, although somewhat lengthy, left a deep impression. With minor exceptions, everything was in good taste, suffused with self-respect, for creativity and its creations. That is how it felt at the opening where a select group gathered at Congress for a toast, and continued at the theatre hall of the university. It was the first time that representatives of the community identified openly with our circle as "partners." The small J.I. Segal committee felt very festive because this time the prizes included Yiddish and Hebrew literature, as well as education and Jewish music. Really talented people. My remarks were directed to highlighting a whole generation and its accomplishments, to recognizing an era, and I tried to point out that the individuals were the expression and realization of that era's mission. I tried to lift the veil of reality and displayed the hidden forces that shaped the creative individuals, myself included. The intimacy and openness elevated the entire occasion beyond the simple exchange of congratulations. All week people were calling to say that everyone left stimulated and exhilarated. It really felt at times that the bitter feelings of loneliness and abandonment should have no place. It was, as the verse says, "I sit amidst my people," and this filled my soul. At least for a little while. A creative person in his complete isolation can still be privileged to realize a moment where he feels that his mission will be redemptive. Especially moving were the warm handshakes of pupils with their reticent greetings: "It was a pleasure, *Lehrer* Zipper."

This was followed by a week of dismal meetings and petty concerns. So now I am so exhausted that not only are my limbs weak but all my senses are unhinged and strangely turbulent.

Congratulations are still arriving. They don't touch me, as if I had removed myself from it and simply observed the era coming to a close, and just waiting for it to be memorialized. Will I be able to accomplish anything when I distance myself from daily burdens? Meanwhile I am just tired.

MAY 26, 1971

This morning there was a gathering of the modern rabbis of all denominations with the school principals. No one came from the ultra-orthodox. From our schools and the congregation schools, almost everyone was there. The question posed: How can we introduce more religion into the schools? The rabbis' pessimism regarding the indifference of parents who desire as little religious instruction as possible, and with the children – including those who have received Jewish education – who cut themselves off from Jewish life, is even greater than the pessimism felt among many of us. These doomsday words were evidence of despair and poverty of thought. I tried to lead the discussion toward a deeper analysis as to the reasons for the failure of the schools and synagogues to maintain contact with their constituent communities. There is a sort of inconsistency and sometimes a deception by the official religious curriculum that leads to the awareness that while maintaining the official seal of the Shulchan Aruch, they do not act in accordance with it. In consequence, the child does not see in life what he is taught in school. He simply doesn't believe his educators and rabbis. They simply hold on to crumbs of *Yiddishkeit* and there is no wholeness present. There are now so many versions of Judaism that totality has been lost. One of the reasons is that despite the fact that the synagogue is a central gathering place, it does not encompass the totality of Jewish life. Many failed to understand this point, and resumed the discussion without getting to the main issue. In addition, the matter of throwing away Yiddish is part of losing contact, but they certainly did not want to hear this. All in all, the outcome was that more discussions were needed and that the rabbis and teachers should help the Congress mount a campaign for Jewish education.

JUNE 4, 1971

Last Wednesday was the closing meeting of the parents' and teachers' group, which every year usually summarizes the year's work, but this time was transformed into a kind of farewell evening for me. I was totally unprepared for this. Only when I saw that pupils were also invited as well as a number of directors did I realize what had been planned. It appeared that the warmth and the public expressions of emotion came from a true sense of appreciation. So despite my intention to avoid this note, I had to evince some nostalgia along with an indisoluble bittersweet sense of the past, and the closing of an era. In places my remarks sounded like advice for the future and a sentimental acknowledgment of their work and their predecessors. I think it was a significant experience for everyone. Ironically, it was "good" that I had to speak to them in English because at a minimum this was the most obvious sign of the passing of an era. The closer I come to the end of my career, the clearer becomes the correctness of my decision – clarified only at the last moment before my retirement.

The next night we were at a reception in honour of Rabbi Mordecai Kaplan, who had turned ninety. It is an experience to see this man standing so erect, speaking for about an hour with the same clarity as in his younger years, and still with the same convoluted philosophy, *pilpulistically* argued, that the folk is the creator of all values and not some supernatural power. But why this is necessarily so, he still cannot explain. He acknowledges the tradition and principles of *Halachah*, but then everything must be reconstructed. It is also strange that at the same time as the Reconstructionist Synagogue attempts to be a *shul*, it is a modern assembly – eating and drinking without hats, without blessings, satisfying themselves with the singing of a few Yiddish folk songs. It dawned on no one to recite *Mincha* and *Maariv*, even though he had mentioned the value of prayer and the set times for prayer. In his critique of the denominations he was quite sharp. The reconstitution of being a single people with one ideology once more hangs somehow in a void, bits and pieces that do not cohere. Just seeing before one's eyes an intellectual at such an advanced age still planning and calling for reconstruction, that alone makes one feel that one is a witness to another mystery of our time.

Yesterday we were at Daniel's graduation, where he received his B.A. degree at McGill University. There was a large audience of contented and glowing parents in the huge Sir Arthur Currie auditorium. The presentation of the diplomas and the student march made an impression. Among them, no doubt, are to be found the future leaders of our country. Nevertheless it was sort of commonplace altogether, a cold ceremony. The speeches were from a ready-made text, assigning no moral obligation, as if we were living in a time that had not been shaken from top to bottom.

The only joy that was evident were the students meeting friends and family with handshakes and embraces. One was also struck by the fact how few non-whites there were in the audience. Are they excluded from the beginning or are they among the majority that fall by the wayside before completing studies?

JUNE 19, 1971

On the 10th of this month the banquet in honour of the closing of the united campaign took place in the large hall of the Shaar Hashomayim. An audience of three hundred had assembled. The head table was occupied by the campaign organizers. Those of us who suffered the pox and measles of the early days felt strange, a kind of "joy in trembling." Joy in the fact that finally the estranged elite, who had battled with us for years, are now those who praise us and have carried out a successful campaign raising approximately $450,000, which erases all debts and promises a future of untroubled work and the beginning of community responsibility. On the other hand, they take to themselves the credit and try to wipe away the merit earned by the generation of founders. Still it is all lip service, "from the surface outwards." The real issue still does not concern most of them. The guest speaker, Saul Hayes, really a devoted executive, but a stranger to us in his outlook. Wiseman and myself introduced him and thanked him, sort of aides rather than those who should provide the tone and meaning of such an event. It appeared to be not only a symbol but a distinct sign that our era had passed. The children's choir sang quite beautifully, and the dance troupe of the Folk Shule was excellent as well. It also served to repair the fortunes of Botwinik as music teacher. The things he accomplishes with this gang, with all its difficulties, is of a very high standard. At least for this year they will not let him go because of his stubborn behaviour at the time of amalgamation, which incited so much bad blood.

Left there with mixed feelings. It turned out that I sat with several wealthy people, a husband and wife, who certainly contributed money, but the whole issue hardly concerns them at all. They spent the whole time flirting, speaking about their golf club, and where else they might better enjoy themselves. It was distasteful even when they tried to explain how sorry they were that their children did not receive our kind of education. Everything was a sort of pretence and a desire to be in fashion. It was a relief to leave them and their chatter.

The next morning we flew to Chicago together with Ode and Motty for Fradle's son's Bar Mitzvah and her second marriage.

Spent an evening at the Hurowitz's. Some of our friends were there, wealthy Jews who are culturally active. There was a discussion about the state of Yiddish culture and secularism in the world. Someone tried to voice a complaint and I had to point out that even now in their circle they are still penny-pinching when it comes to sponsoring a cultural event. He thinks that he has outdone himself when he contributes $100 toward the Manger Prize. In his estimation, it is no longer necessary since there are no worthy candidates; the great ones have already received it.

JUNE 20, 1971

Last Thursday the graduation took place. My last public appearance as principal of the Peretz Shule. With that I concluded forty-six years of educational activity here. The first graduation of the Peretz Shule that I attended was forty-five years ago, as the guest speaker. From now on, once again, I will only be a guest at this celebration. Naturally, everyone referred to this fact, but the more profound utterance about this event – that they had sung for the last time the Peretz Shule anthem – was not mentioned. I had to make an effort not to transform this evening into a kind of farewell. After all, it is a graduation celebration. Still, among other things I mentioned: "For forty-five years I stood on the stage facing the audience, from now on I'll sit in the audience and observe those who are assuming responsibility."

Since yesterday, along with the heavy feeling of leaving everything behind me, there emerges in me a sense of anticipation at being liberated from the worries over teachers, children, and an institution. A tiny inner door opens and only the writer peeks out. The imagination leads to types of characters and situations that have to assume concrete forms so as to be made palpable. I hope that will lead to creativity.

Today Sholem called to tell me his stories about how he has received funds for his Hebrew book and how they esteem him here and there. This makes me feel awkward. Nevertheless, he is a poet through and through. It is strange too how things turn out in life. All his life he opposed the Zionist movement and its leaders. Now, with the publication of his Hebrew book, he receives a subsidy from Shazar, Israel's president, and he writes him letters as if he were a close friend.

JUNE 21, 1971

There was a large and pathetic gathering with Mrs Alexandrovitch of the Soviet Union, a mother travelling throughout the Jewish Diaspora, appealing for her daughter Rivka, one of the condemned for applying to leave for Israel and disseminating underground Zionist literature. The whole upsurge of the Jews in Russia is full of pathos and somehow inconceivable. Are we once again the first harbingers to raise our voices about the great multitude of peoples who are oppressed? Does the horror of today's world and the isolation of Israel also stand as signs of the mysterious game of our history. The native-born youth too are disturbed by all these signs. Cold reason and logic cease to be the chief authority. Because of this, many struggle to obtain more knowledge. Just as earlier generations, they are looking for an inkling, some indication in Yiddish texts. Could this be the beginning of a significant era, or a last flicker of a dying flame? Our civilization, which has been forced into this brutalized world, without a spark of morality, looks like it is hurtling toward its collapse. Then what do these rays of light symbolize?

JUNE 24, 1971

Yesterday was my last official day with the children and the teachers. In the morning the gathering with the pupils began as it always has at this time of year. The children assemble, expecting to receive their report cards, and pay no attention to what one is trying to tell them. In the middle of this they all arose spontaneously and began to sing the song that was sung three years ago at the special evening commemorating the forty years of my principalship. Then representatives of the classes came forward and handed me special albums full of many naive but well-meaning letters. Two of them were so choked up over the words they were delivering in the name of everyone that I had to exercise strong control to prevent my own sobbing. I thanked them and promised them that Tencer would conduct himself exactly as I had. Fortunately, tradition had prepared a means of sublimation: singing anthems. And the Peretz Shule anthem was sung for the last time. Symbolically, I responded on the spot to say farewell to Sujata Tiaga, the Indian girl who studied with us for four years and is returning home to India. I was able to convey to them the deeper meaning of studying in our kind of school. Just at that moment it seemed that some higher purpose than simply acquiring information had accompanied them throughout their school years. It might be that one of them will become an artist one day, remember this, and give it form. I handed over to *Chaver* Tencer, my successor, the role of leading the children up to their classrooms. Although he is supposedly under Nachum, the general principal, I feel however that if he so desires he could be the spiritual leader here. May it be so. The teachers' farewell was a kind of expression of genuine gratitude from them for the way I led the school, and also an unexpressed fear for that which is coming. The watch they gave me is also a kind of symbol – to know the time, but also time to leave. I feel that I can honestly say that I never purposely imposed myself on any of them, and even the fears that the amalgamation aroused should cause me no regret. As professionals they are now more secure in their positions and in the knowledge that school will continue. If not for the amalgamation, who knows whether we could have said farewell without an outcry of bitterness.

JUNE 30, 1971

It is a day of sorrow and another keen demonstration of how helpless we still are against the unknown forces of nature. The three Soviet astronauts who were in the stratosphere for twenty-four days, and carried out experiments with the same precision as done on earth, were, until their re-entry to earth, full of wonderment and confidence that they had inaugurated a new era of human endurance and greatness. Following their descent however, they were found dead. Whether their hearts could not stand earth's gravity or whether it was caused by the air or the heat is not yet known. Our helplessness, just as our fear of the unknown, is boundless.

JULY 28, 1971

Two days ago returned from a two-week vacation in Saratoga and around Tanglewood. It was more of an artistic vacation than a real rest. Still, a great experience to find a corner in a magnificently beautiful mountainous region where literally thousands of people of diverse ages and classes come from the four corners of the earth to enjoy truly artistic ballet, symphony orchestras, dance groups, and good theatre. Seeing how an audience of over ten thousand sits, reclines, and stands spellbound and caught up in the fantasy of "The Firebird" with Chagall's backdrops, or to a Beethoven concerto with Perlman's violin playing, or Ashkenazi's pianistic virtuosity, one imagines for the moment that the world is really a peaceful Garden of Eden where the saints enjoy the splendour of the *Shechina*. From time to time the idea strikes me: Could poetry or pure literature ever attract such a mammoth audience? Still, it was somewhat encouraging. Not everyone or everything has been rendered barbaric on this continent.

We also came upon so many marvelous spots: mountain ranges that left the eye craving more, while the heart trembles before the sight of primeval nature. If the mountains' greenery were stripped away, it would seem as if the Negev and its splendour stands before my eyes. We also met several very interesting people, and they are just as alarmed as we are about the things happening in our uncivilized world. During the entire two weeks it was hard for us to be without a Yiddish newspaper and it felt as if we were in a wilderness without any connection to home. It was strange, too, to see how at the motels' swimming pools, people sit around as if at a river. Even if the river is close by, it is polluted and pitiful to observe. So when people say, "Let's go down to the water," they mean the artificial swimming pool. The deck chairs replace the soft sand; the artificial and manufactured replace the natural. The various locales of the festivals are untouched by the artificial, as are the pretty towns like Williamstown, with its theatre and its museum holding the largest collection of Renoirs, a town with its extraordinary cleanliness, beautifully maintained, still authentic and natural. Give thanks for this!

AUGUST 1, 1971

We were visited for a day by Pinchas Landau and his family from Israel. They descended for a day, left again, as if they had never been here. With his being here, a feeling was once more reawakened that I ought to write something about that past. But the desire is extinguished almost immediately. I am now somehow so far removed from that time, that it was even hard for me to listen to him and Yechiel get involved in the details of the period and that life. Everything that happened there is remote; I feel as if I was floating around in a vacuum, and what the future holds seems to me only a rushing toward the final shore, which is no longer far away. I am not afraid of this, but it interferes with my wish to arrange things in an orderly fashion. So the days drag on listlessly.

This is the week that *Apollo* 15 flew and reached the moon. It's like a mysterious tale from an ancient book: they float over the surface there in the ghastly whiteness of the atmosphere. Their vehicle looks like a robot, and they themselves in their weird coveralls, belted and arrayed on all sides with straps and tubes, glow mysteriously as if emerging from the unknown. Still it leaves one cold, almost unaffected. No longer the shudder and excitement of the first times when we sat up all night and shared the emotion in a kind of phosphorescent glow – like the phantom of lunar sapphire of our youthful fantasies. My mind is continuously plagued by the thought: What are they seeking there? And if they do find something there, won't it be the end of another illusion, replaced by emptiness and oblivion. A planet rotates for billions of years, worshipped and lauded from afar, but when we land on it is barren and can't even reveal to us what it's doing there, how it got there, and for what purpose.

AUGUST 8, 1971

All day yesterday, these lines occupied me:

I will shed the mundane cares
And only glance at the morrow.
How many mornings still remain?
How many are foretold?

Even while sitting at the television watching the astronauts descend from the heights – the more obvious they become, the more mysterious it is – these lines never left my memory. Together with the wonderment of the technological achievements that enable us to hear human voices from vast distances, it seems to be a fantastical mystery. Even the language and terminology they use to transmit what they see and where they are located are mystical veils covering a reality that lies beyond our senses. Even their footsteps – in reality they are floating – and the outlandish appearance of their garb are more enveloped in mystery than open to rational explanation.

At the same time, our little world goes on as it has from the beginning. We weave webs, make a mess of things, and we stand before the final judgment. Today Gromyko arrived in New Delhi ostensibly to help negotiate peace between India and Pakistan. In reality it is a move to counter Nixon's preparations to go to China. How history positions her mannequins: China and the United States move closer; communist Russia looks for help to oppose communist China. The tragedy in Pakistan serves both of them to heat up the brimstone under the guise of bringing help, and thereby rehearsing the military drill for a greater catastrophe. In reality, the surface terms of the debate unfold to reveal the mystery of the last judgment – surely the final one for this era.

AUGUST 9, 1971

Yesterday we visited "Man and His World." It is not what it was years ago, and there is no longer the feeling that the whole world's population and its achievements are concentrated on these islands, and have no other concern than to display their bright side and their accomplishments. But it is still lovely and attractive. It stimulates elevated thought and sad musings: the world could be so fine and beautiful, but is harsh and messy. At night it looks like a mysterious universe, which in the silence and variety of lights suggests that the secret of the world has concealed itself behind opaque veils.

Upset by several pavilions that took the audience for granted and dispensed entertainment that gave no insight into the culture of the represented people and had no intrinsic value. Mainly a bit of nostalgia for the immigrants who come to make contact with their homeland. One feels cheated.

SEPTEMBER 9, 1971

Today is the first day that I remained at home and Sorke went to school to teach her class. Yesterday, at the school opening, I was only a guest greeting the children and teachers at the new school year as a former principal. I told them the tale of the succession of Rabbi Chanina bar Chama, a third-century scholar, to head the rabbinical college, and at the end of which I gave Tencer the key to the electricity panel. Psychologically and in fact, I had been prepared for this transition since last year, still, within myself, I am not yet at peace with the new status. All day I was both very sad and very disturbed, unable to find a place for myself, and made up an excuse that I have to attend to something downtown and for a few hours aimlessly rode the buses and exhausted myself considerably. In the evening I went to a meeting of the Yiddish Committee but couldn't open my mouth and was silent right to the end. All the questions that were considered seemed inappropriate and petty, and I simply couldn't comprehend the bickering or why they were pleased or displeased with former projects. Only at the end of the meeting did the chairman recall and honour those who had passed away: Sam Bronfman and Dr Emanuel Pat. They were individuals of varied worth and distinction, each in their own manner and potentiality had placed their stamp on Jewish communal life and with their passing left a vacuum, a deep wound. Then I too arose and recalled Chaim Tolmatch, peace be upon him, whom I had eulogized the previous day. Chaim was a true prototype of an entire generation that fervently desired and sought to express themselves through deeds and creativity. But they remained stuck in midstream – which appeared to them to be an ultimate goal. In the end, however, they had realized fewer fulfilled desires and hopes than they had projected. Even their fulfilled dreams reversed themselves and evoke horrible fears. "My generation flees from me," is fixed in my mind and gives me no peace.

DAY AFTER ROSH HASHANA, 5732

This Rosh Hashana passed without any sense of holiday joy, and didn't even arouse in me the usual agitation that I always feel while sitting in *shul* listening to the foolish words spoken particularly by the synagogue leaders. Except for the first evening when the children and grandchildren came to visit, which was full of the joy of being together. After the meal we sat until late and sang songs that we had not sung together for a long time. Beyond that, everything is somehow enveloped in a gnawing sorrow. This began earlier on the eve of Rosh Hashana when we had *Yohrzeit* for mother. On our way to the cemetery we heard the radio bulletin that a bomb had been thrown not far from the Western Wall in Jerusalem, an Arab child was killed and tourists were wounded. Walking around the cemetery, the thought and feeling surfaced again that here lie more people than those we used to phone on Rosh Hashana eve. In the afternoon I found out that I.J. Schwartz was no longer alive. The last member, I think, of Di Yunge. His handsome bearing remains before my eyes. Alone and solitary, he expired in an old people's home where no one knew what he had meant for Yiddish literature. How much happiness he would bring to our home in the years of our beginning. One door after another closes. I also learned that Chaitman had accidentally fallen in the street. For many years he always looked like a remnant, virtually like a protruding root of an ancient cut-down forest, when he attended a lecture. In the evening I recited the afternoon prayers like a petitioner, in the style and melody of the Hussatin *Chasidim*, it touched the hearts of the older congregants: "You should be hired as a teacher to instruct the Jews how to pray." "We felt ourselves back at home," several said to me, deeply affected. Afterward I sat among the congregation and everything seemed foreign. I know a good number of them for many years – I suddenly noted how old they had become. In the two days I also noted that everything and everybody had grown unfamiliar. Even the youngsters, with their long hair and beards, seemed older, and sit and stand as if they were in an unfamiliar world. Coming here without purpose, they don't pray nor do they articulate anything. A kind of artificial ritual of reciting, listening, and observing. Not part of a congregation. The dreary, contrived sermons touch no one and they do not excite or anger anyone. It strikes me that if someone were asked, "Why did you come?" he would be dumbfounded and reply, "You're right, why did I come?" Nothing here reminds one of anything having to do with contemporary Jewry or with the peoples of the world. Everybody around me has a dull expression. Even former students, who mainly attend the supplementary services in the adjoining hall, wander about aimlessly, lost. Some of them are from radical-secular homes whose parents still run off to the country for these two days so as not to sit at home alone. It looked to me like a threadbare bridal reception. Even the joy of greeting people that one had not seen all year seemed like a pretence. Is this really a community that has something in common? I couldn't clarify for myself why I felt this way. Is it because everybody who considers himself an acquaintance wants to know what I am doing with my free time? Thus underscoring that I am already a has-been? Or is there more involved than this. That those who attend do not have a real connection with the whole matter. Rather than be alone at home – an outsider – they come to *shul* to be together.

SUCCOS WEEKDAYS, 5732

Attended the education conference that the Movement had organized for the weekend of September 24-26. At first, I had no desire to go. I am tired of words, no longer have the belief that our people will want to do anything of value. But they insisted that actually one should not judge without seeing for oneself. I was pleasantly surprised for two reasons: the majority of the delegates were young people, about twelve or fifteen teachers and activists were former pupils of our schools and of the seminar. They were remarkably earnest. The discussions were honest. Aside from the main speaker, Dr Shapiro, who tried vainly to construct an argument based solely on current realities. The young want direction and are attentive. In all the committees that I attended, I tried to highlight the main thrust of our philosophy of education that still has a part to play in Jewish life here. They paid close attention and at certain moments an atmosphere was created like the one that existed long ago when we were a group with a vision. They also honoured me with the closing speech of the conference and my words had an influence on the older members who said that this awakened good recollections of the best years of our work. Regrettably, just then the tape-recorder malfunctioned. They had intended to publish the speech and distribute it to the schools throughout the country. A number of practical resolutions were passed. We'll have to see whether there is anyone to carry them out.

OCTOBER 9, 1971

The first time that we left home on a Jewish holiday. The first days of Succos we travelled to the mountains of Vermont with Rivke and Berl, the Kalles', and the Shainblums. It was sunny and as hot as summer and the mountains were fantastically beautiful in the various shades of red and yellow. From a distance the mixture of colours look like the Negev, but there it is always solidified gloom and stony anger. Here it is a mild peace-making with the change of seasons. From far, a kind of interplay, a fiery struggle between sun and shadow. Up close, dried-up sap from summer's vitality that is spat out as crimson and the bare treetops listen to the autumn winds that foretell a total desolation. I was able to clear my head and began to feel that the desire to write was returning. I felt encouraged.

Returned and the anxiety of the unknown troubles me again. First, I am tortured by the feeling that every time I go to school, it seems to me that the children feel forsaken. As often as I have been there, I have never seen a child going into Tencer's office to ask him anything or to consult with him. They look at me, it seems, with odd smiles that stand like a barrier between myself and them. They don't dare to approach and ask me anything, and others look at me accusingly: "Why aren't you with us?" The teachers, on the other hand, seem somehow frightened, performing their tasks perfunctorily, obeying the rules. There is no longer the feeling of being a free agent. Now they seem to be driven by a superior force that must be obeyed.

Added to this, my own close colleagues seem to have changed so that I hardly recognize them. They too no longer feel themselves to be leaders, but led, and hide behind their aprons saying: "They don't permit this." The pensions for Sussman and myself are still not determined. They make decisions without consulting us. Weeks have passed since I wanted to meet with the three leading initiators of the amalgamation in order to clarify my position, but cannot arrange a meeting with them. Privately, they admit that after so many years of service to the Peretz Shule I have earned a more honourable retirement pension that should assure a pension equal to my salary – small enough all these years. But they never carried this through. "They are opposed to this." This hurts me terribly. "Is this the reward of the righteous?" I would like to avoid bringing them to a public arbitration, but I will have to do it if they refuse to act properly. And they still complain why there are so few new, good, and devoted teachers! Everything changes but the miserable attitude to teachers remains the same. I would very much like to avoid leaving in anger, slamming the door behind me. But it looks like I will have no other choice. This hurts more than all other difficult experiences. I feel insulted but can't even cry out. It looks as if tranquility is still far off.

OCTOBER 15, 1971

Today I had to meet with our three directors regarding the matter of the pension, but it was postponed because of Sheres' illness. Dangling in mid-air is an agonizing and bitter feeling that keeps me from establishing a routine or a sense of composure.

Last evening was at a meeting of the day school council. It was obvious that there is a struggle between the powers at the Federation and the Congress about leadership. And that has an effect on the plans for the place of Jewish education. The new leaders of the Federation wish to become involved in Jewish education and Congress is very displeased by this. Still, Congress conceded to the forming of a combined education committee under whose supervision the research study will be carried out. But even before the research is completed, they are arguing about jurisdiction. Either through oversight or possibly calculated, they did not consult with Beutel, the chairman of the council, about their plan for continuing education courses for teachers, which both the council and the combined committee were considering. But they sent him a written notice asking him not to do anything until they had a discussion. He, as a veteran opposed to allowing any organization to interfere in educational matters, openly opposed any joint project with the Federation. He is ready to resign his leadership in council if his position is not supported. No one desired this because his role in obtaining associate status with the Protestant School Board virtually saved all the day schools, and with his leaving this could be severely threatened. On the other hand, the principle of community responsibility for Jewish education stands at risk. It is not only a question of a theoretical approach and principle, but a practical one as well. In the situation in which we find ourselves now, it is entirely possible that the government subsidies we receive could be revoked, leaving the community alone entirely responsible. Therefore my approach was that we must not allow the bureaucracy to quarrel and overlook what is at stake. The representatives of the schools however – even those who agreed with me – were fearful of losing their "autonomy" and resolved that the council conduct its activities independently, without partners. But they softened the resolution by stating that only the executive of the council can negotiate educational matters with other community bodies. It was quite evident that even if the Federation would be prepared to provide the funds, the majority of the schools would oppose it since it could effect the schools' autonomy. The religious schools, with Lubavitch at the head, state this openly and unequivocally. The others follow suit. Who will actually be able to execute that which must be dealt with now, who will establish a seminar, prepare educational materials, etc.? Things remain as they were. And what had led to this requires no explanation. Suffice to see that teachers with authentic Jewish learning are no longer available. In the meantime we live with remnants who will soon be gone; no teacher of Yiddish is available. Hebrew instruction is supplied from Israel, but the majority of the teachers barely adapt. How can they talk about renewal? It was distressing to realize that for all these years none of the delegates have evolved; they still see only their own little corner in the immediate present and overlook the future.

The same situation was evident regarding the demonstration in Ottawa at Kosygin's arrival. Rabbi Kramer demanded that in the announcement about the participation of the schools that their name should not be mentioned. They won't participate and will continue with studies as usual. Yet they are the ones who insist that the world conduct itself harmoniously and humanely, not petty, not everyone for themselves, but with a shared vision for all.

OCTOBER 21, 1971

The past few days were marked by protests against the Soviet Union related to Kosygin's visit. It began with a Simchas Torah march and will conclude this evening with a mass meeting. During this time there was a march to Ottawa and the closing of the offices of all Jewish institutions on Tuesday, the 19th. Monday, several rabbis and students fasted and held a vigil before the Soviet consulate. There were ten thousand marchers, including many from here that you would not have expected to actually leave their businesses for a whole day. It seems that this issue has deeply touched large sectors of the Jewish population. Other minorities, too, had protest demonstrations as well; the Jewish one was the best organized. A hot-head from the Hungarian minority even managed to attack Kosygin, which could have ruined the whole value of the demonstration to arouse public opinion. It might even have been a provocation. Kosygin, the boor, exploited this by calling the opposition "riff-raff," people of no account. According to the press reports, it appears that during the session in Parliament, he adamantly denied the charges of discrimination against Jews, and said that all the furore is being created by a few hot-heads. It also looks as if the members of Parliament were generally uninformed about the situation there. This was evident in the few questions posed to him. This time the Jewish leadership's organizational skills were excellent, but their information briefings limped badly. The slogan too, "Let My People Go," has not been sufficiently thought through, and in a broad national perspective is actually harmful because it indicates that after the release of those who wish to leave, the remaining Jews would be left on their own and would cease being Jews. The "boor's" brazenness seems limitless. He attacked the United States and wants to draw Canada into the conflict. It looks like Prime Minister Trudeau is playing high-stake politics, which can embroil the country in an enormous whirlpool. Let's hope it will all end well. Incidentally, the other minorities like Ukrainians and Latvians couldn't even forget their hatred of

Jews at this time, and unashamedly accused the police of allowing only the Jews the right to protest, while they were held at a distance.

NOVEMBER 19, 1971

Today Yaacov Glatstein died suddenly, the last of the Inzichists and a great poet. A real blow for all of us. I simply can't compose myself.

NOVEMBER 28, 1971

It has been such a crowded month of activities that I could barely catch my breath. It was really impossible to feel that I had retired. First, there was the teachers' conference of all the Jewish schools. There was a large attendance of local teachers and from nearby Ottawa. Among them were many former students of the Seminary. Seeing this large gathering, I had the feeling that something of substance has developed. But listening to the guest speakers and the exchanges that followed, the feeling of satisfaction diminished. Dr Judah Shapiro took the same line that he had taken at the Movement's education conference, that we can no longer educate with antiquated materials and everything must be adapted to modern times. The student no longer comprehends the past. Everything must be up-to-date, Jewish and general studies fully integrated. The issue of the approach to language acquisition must be altered. Of course this leads to the outcome whereby Hebrew, studied for one year in Israel, can achieve more than seven years of study here, but Yiddish, which does not have this option, will certainly disappear. The audience from the Hebrew schools were quite ready to agree with him. No one is prepared any longer to swim against the tide and to state that education is not based on submission to the present environmental conditions. Dr Chandler, however, took the view that the world may be changing, but that the "Torah descends from heaven," and hence everything is holy so that nothing can be questioned. The Hebrew teachers, mostly from the religious schools, did not dare to oppose him. So it remained for Dunsky and myself to be the heretics. The fear of the militant orthodoxy now casts a long shadow over all educational matters. And we barely make up an opposition. Totally isolated, along with all our achievements.

Then came the plenary session of the Canadian Jewish Congress. There was an assembly of almost one thousand delegates from all corners of the country. The majority were new people whom we had never seen before. A large segment were young, among them many of religious sentiments, and extreme nationalists. Again I had the feeling that the youthful crop of delegates were excited about Israel and the situation of Soviet Jewry in its struggle for the right to emigrate – almost a revolution. At the centre of their concerns was the education issue. This alone is of greatest value. However, there were no moments of exultation. Not one of the speeches by the invited guests, who were quite well-known, and all from Israel, succeeded in igniting the crowd. The plenary sessions and the workshops were full of interest and the discussions were reminiscent of the '20s and '30s. The most acute debates were at the education sessions where all the educational work to date was under attack and negated. Even the struggle in the universities and high schools was introduced here, and an objective evaluation of the situation was missing along with a plan of action. More confusion than realistic demands. Everyone saw only his personal experience and passed judgment accordingly. At times it appeared as if one generation was passing judgment on the next, ignorant of the facts and not even knowing what they want themselves. The positive aspect is: We have to get down to work and receive means from the community, which must fulfill its responsibilities. Maybe something might come of this.

In school there is also more confusion than a clear-sighted notion of what they want and where they are heading. Everyone is still salivating over the slogan: "New times, new directions." Meanwhile, no one is concerned about the loss of the basic tenets of education and the principles of our school. They think it is fine to be distracted by new technological methods and forget their own sources.

The plan for a high school meets the same confusion when discussing the curriculum. They are prepared to discard everything and are fearful of anything that smacks of an East European mode. We will have to resume discussions regarding the chief rationale of our schools and our approach to languages and religion.

My personal situation drags on. I am nauseated by their petty bargaining. Tomorrow I have to meet with the committee to present my demands. I am sick and tired of all this. I want to avoid public ridicule. It hurts me that after all this time they are still not mature enough to resolve this matter honourably.

Last night we were at the Lermers for the annual gathering to honour Ravitch's birthday. Usually it has been for our circle only, this time a number of our closest were omitted and in their place they invited several of the Federation leaders. They are clambering to reach high society. Ostensibly, the Lermers mean to use their social contacts to further our agenda. There is a certain amount of truth to this; recently the community leaders have softened their outlook and are more inclined to aid Yiddish programs. There was a very fine atmosphere. Instead of speeches, each of the writers read a poem from Ravitch's work. In this fashion, they avoided the envy and dragging out the evening with formal speeches. It certainly gave a better view of Ravitch's work and the diversity of his forms. The hostess spoke excessively, in the style of a patron and salon-matron, but that seems to be the recent style. So we have to forgive her for it. Ravitch was deeply moved by the whole evening. He is seventy-eight – may no evil touch him – and carries himself as befits an elder. May he enjoy length of days.

NOVEMBER 30, 1971

Yosef Kairler was here – the Jewish poet from the Soviet Union – who has now become the symbol of the Jew who struggles to maintain his humanistic-Jewish presence. His poems are pieces of the soul's outcries, verbally structureless and unpolished, but they are more than lyrics, they are deeds. With his tortured life in the Russian prison and labour camp, Lubyanka and Varkuta, he is an extraordinary example to us in our enveloping despondence. Over a thousand people came to the evening. There is still a great number of Yiddish-speakers who are present only when it comes to admiring something foreign; for something local, this audience is not to be found. Here, it allows its schools to disappear. There is not even a quorum to stand up courageously and ask: Why did the Peretz School have to succumb? Why does the *Keneder Odler* have to cease publication? Here, for themselves, they no longer need anything in Yiddish, while for foreign causes they are prepared to set up an outcry, and even to bear the financial costs. Also spent an hour and a half with him at a luncheon at Congress. He makes a very good impression. A person who grasps things instantaneously, and takes a position calmly and thoughtfully. It was difficult to reconcile his mild, smiling, expression with his stubborn battle in the years of toil in the coal mines of Varkuta.

In the past weeks there has been a sharp attack by the orthodoxy in Israel on the liberal, nationalistic outlook. They are fighting now with the same means and arguments that they formally used in Poland. The fight revolves around the "Who is a Jew?" question and concerns military service for religious girls. It has reached the point where Rabbi Kamenetsky has ruled that an Orthodox Jew who has daughters is forbidden to settle in Israel. The secular faction here is silent and dejected since they capitulated long ago to the skull-cap wearers. They take no cognizance of the fact that Israel is now in a perilous situation and isolated in the world. The old *Agudas Yisroel* stands once more as if Auschwitz never existed, as if a nationalist movement had not come into being that had managed with great anguish to save the remaining survivors and gave a purpose to the future direction of our lives. The culture-war that we had feared is now already full blown, and where it will lead to, only God knows. They are now fighting with the aid of well-educated rabbis and intellectuals. But if you scratch beneath their prescribed tasselled-undergarment, there springs forth the whole narrow zealotry of Tishevitz. Yesterday at a bus stop I saw this vignette: A young boy of about sixteen with thick hair flowing over his shoulders, but on the tip of his head perched a *yarmulke* held fast by bobby-pins. A fringed jacket that all the hippies wear, tight jeans, and unlaced shoes, but from beneath the jacket hung four tassels. Has this now become part of the amuletic dress-code of the new culture? Without the tassels and skull cap, he is one of today's youth. How he positions his phylacteries on that head of hair and how he sits in *yeshiva* in that outfit is beyond my comprehension. They concede the appearances and even allow the participation with activists as long as they can control them with the ancient interdictions: Thou shalt not. The Torah forbids it.

DECEMBER 4, 1971

Couldn't fall asleep for a long time and tossed from side to side until I was striding up and down the hills in Tishevitz, down to the pasture-bridge, which lies partly collapsed a few feet from shore. I jump over the breech and a small, stony path appears between a stone fence and a blind wall that looks like a prison wall with small barred windows right at the top. It leads into a broad courtyard where a crowd of people, young and old, most of whom I know but cannot name. And it is clear to me that none of them is of this world. They surround me with magic that holds me in its spell because I can understand everything they say, mocking the real world of lies, which indicates that they have certain knowledge and that they know the difference between good and evil. A tiny person – who looks like one of the brothers that were involved in Yiddish plays at the Monument National Theatre in the mid-20s – with a round beardless face smiles at me, saying: "It is a theatrical performance where everyone is disguised." A woman in a decorative shawl, with a child at her breast, arises from a grassy resting place, and intervenes like a sharp wind: "And do you think we are better off here? We don't know what anything means nor are any explanations offered." Strange that it does not occur to me to ask: "Does a 'life' of birth and nourishment exist here too?" It seems to me that she senses my query and manages a grimace: "This is how I arrived here after the earthquake; possibly you know the reason?" The courtyard expands and images moving about without purpose jostle me and recite something nonsensical. But it oppresses my heart with a gnawing and hollow feeling. Each phantom is attached somehow to an invisible shawl that prevents one from seeing the other, and my wonderment becomes expressive: "Why do I see them so clearly, and can even play with several children who won't let go of me? Who are you?" "This is only a play," comes the ostensible answer from afar. But one of them clings to me: "If you remain here, all will be revealed." "And do you already know all?" Opening my eyes in the darkness of the room, it seems to me that in my inner eye my memory is still unwinding the complete picture of that other world, which is being erased as it appears, carrying me back to the original entrance-way opposite the slit of white light reflecting the outside snow.

DECEMBER 17, 1971

Two days ago the matter of my pension was finally resolved. I did not accomplish very much, nevertheless, they did concede something, and thus chastised themselves by admitting that their earlier decision was incorrect and inappropriate. Ostensibly, this means that they have placed me in the same category as Wiseman's pension. (However, this is not exactly so, since he has a special private school fund.) Still this is a compensation. If I had insisted on my original demand it would have meant involving private individuals and that would have resulted in an adversarial situation, which in the end would have led to a rift in the organization. So I reconsidered: All my life I sacrificed for the school, so one more sacrifice is required. The truth is that it will be very difficult to manage with the pension and I will have to cut back my very important donations which I must and want to give. So I will have to deny myself too. But there is nothing to be done.

I hope that this will not interfere with the inner peace that I have yet to reach, and that the bitterness induced by their attitude will dissipate and I will now really get down to the things that I wish to do. Many themes attract me, chiefly the years in Canada. But the inner peace is not present. In the meantime I dribble away the time with petty issues.

All of this week, Rozansky of Argentina has been here. A man of significant accomplishments: the editor of standard editions of the classics, which have now reached the fiftieth title. What a stubborn individual can achieve! They might have been published differently or better but he has accomplished something that the entire community here did not even have the vision to desire. Each time that he visited here there were always those who could help him enlist subscribers, but now he is literally in a desert. The Library people, who are his official hosts, exploit him merely to have a guest speaker from abroad for Glatstein's memorial evening. When it comes to helping a person on his mission, they are not to be found. Only our generation tried to ease the collection of monies for such causes, when I.J. Schwartz and others came, and we opened our houses to them. Today's "activists" know nothing of this, and are entirely indifferent. Wiseman is in the hospital, and we can't have visitors because of Gittel, who can't cope with visitors. So there isn't anyone to invite him for a Shabbos meal. Aside from words of support, I can't even help now. First, because I find it hard to get around, and second, I am busy raising funds for Dunsky's edition of *Song of Songs*. So Rozansky is very dissatisfied and feels abandoned and unappreciated. I speak to him every day, and it is unpleasant each time.

After all, in the Tishevitzer house of study, a Jew would not be left alone on Friday evening. Indications of our cultural impoverishment whistle from all corners. No one is obligated to bear the entire responsibility for everything. Since we are no longer an integral community, we are like a leaf in the wind.

JANUARY 1, 1972

Dispatched another year into historic eternity along with many illusions and bitter disappointments. But this is the essential thing: the new year promises nothing, and the desire of anticipation has atrophied. Bitterness both near and far. And added to the bitterness of 1971, the year came to a close with the sudden cessation of the *Der Tog-Morgen Zjurnal* last Wednesday. It causes such pain and makes one feel so ashamed. How the era of vital Yiddish comes to a close. Only one Yiddish daily remains: the *Forwarts*. It is as if one has to observe the Yiddish world now with one eye. The pitiful weekly, *Keneder Odler*, is also about to expire. Who knows if we will be able to maintain it? Our marginality has become increasingly narrow. We all look like the condemned. There is no longer the spirit to do anything. It is even hard for me to read. It seems to be like walking in a cemetery where we stand about waiting to see who will be ushered in next. In the small periodicals and even the major ones, an anguished howl in a multiplicity of forms issues from the poetry. And from the prose too, only an elegy and voices bearing witness, which torture more than they uplift and stimulate. Nevertheless we have to steel ourselves, so we get together and try to publish something for children. And even here there are arguments. Still the feeling of helplessness does not abate, eating at us like a moth.

JANUARY 14, 1972

Last week I signed the contract for my pension with the school. It leaves a strange feeling. On the one hand it means a kind of security for the future – for as long as it is granted – and also a secure future for Sorke because it gives her a legacy of 50 per cent of my pension. On the other hand, it is a kind of signatory to one's own ending. While there, I expressed my dissatisfaction at their withdrawal of the special gift of $2,500 that they had originally promised. But because they had increased my pension by $500 so as to equate it with Wiseman's – or so they say – they withdrew it. This means that we will have to postpone the trip to Israel for a few months, simply because of finances. They resented my statement; they feel that they had done more than their circumstances allowed. Teitelbaum excused himself saying that he would have wanted to approve the sum, but had no basis to defend it to the others, and my supporters were guilty for not having arranged it at the negotiations for amalgamation. But he will keep this in mind and take up the issue at another occasion. Essentially, he feels that I am entitled to this, and above all he feels that I should be able to live unencumbered by financial worries after a lifetime of such significant work – his words. However, the truth is that when it comes to buying some equipment, or something that can be displayed publicly, then several thousand dollars is not an issue. Only when it involves the teachers, do they become scrupulous. The same old story.

Had a interesting talk with Laibel Krishtalka, who was visiting. He has developed into a nice, thoughtful young man. His studies in geology and zoology, and his involvement in research being conducted by serious professors, gives him a deeper and more comprehensive perspective. He is not frightened by the frothy politics bubbling away on the campuses, intent on bringing everything down. He maintains that there is a healthy kernel that protects and defends that which education should provide. He is also strongly interested in Yiddish cultural creativity. Throughout the conversation, he reminded me of Uncle Yonah, may he rest in peace. He resembles him and in certain aspirations he echoes his ambition to achieve something on his own. I only hope that his fate will be more fortunate. He said, "In your own writing, you have to provide an account of the generation with whom you constructed a community here. Both the light and the shadows." My conception that many current America-Jewish writers – and I include Isaac Bashevis Singer among them – write as they do about Jewish life in a negative mode in order to justify to themselves why they have abandoned it and refuse to identify with it. This appealed to him greatly. He elaborated on this by saying that the present upsurge of interest by the student body in Jewish issues signifies a deeper search and therefore he maintains that we must make the account in depth and with honesty. He thinks that I ought to have my works translated into English. There now exists a serious readership for this.

JANUARY 20, 1972

Last week was full of meetings, which take up much time and take a bit of my health as well. In conjunction with the plan to establish our own high school, all the weaknesses of the school program and organization are revealed. Complaints and demands of students and parents also surface. Among the activists, the differences of opinion regarding the educational approach of such a high school is very sharp. From the extremists who want to sail under the banners of the windmills of progress and all current experimental novelties, to supporters of the previous normative standards. We who place the main emphasis on Jewish studies, in accordance with our view, are always on the defensive. There is a segment that would enthusiastically like to reduce Yiddish to a minimum and transform it into a free option. There is a mishmash of approaches to the question of attitudes toward Jewish life and creativity. Eventually we will have to take up the discussion in depth. I often have the feeling that I am sitting among total strangers who are not even prepared to tolerate differences of opinion. It is painful to listen to some opinions where the manner of speaking about teachers of Jewish studies is really insulting. It often appears that in Jewish studies, the teachers know nothing about relating to today's children and attracting them to their subjects. They forget that the motivation for Yiddish studies is almost nonexistent. If Hebrew still has the aura of Israel, Yiddish recommends itself only by virtue of being a cultural treasure that neither the children nor the parents understand. There is the danger that the whole issue has become questionable. For this reason I try to attend all the meetings in order to influence things as much as possible in our direction. On the positive side of this issue is the fact that some parents and a number of students show great interest. They don't quite know what they want but they do want something purposeful. Because of this concern I devote so much time. Something does adhere. As much as I tell myself that it is time to retire completely and concentrate solely on reading and writing, I am still unable to do this. Despite all, people still listen to me. I also try to overcome the bitter feeling that I have not been treated properly until now. So why should I invest more effort? Still I can't leave everything to the half-baked who have mastered the rhetoric and are served well by the new style.

JANUARY 26, 1972

Abba Kovner was here. A fine poet. His language is picturesque, with a mystical aura reminiscent of Hayim Greenberg, may he rest in peace. In my brief talk with him, I was left with a good feeling. A friendly, simple man with no pretensions. In his dress and bearing there is something of the former Russian intelligentsia. An intellectual honesty that draws people to him without self-consciousness. Just the opposite of Sutzkever and his dealings with people. I must better acquaint myself with his work. Why he allowed himself to be introduced only as a partisan and not as a poet baffles me

Later, I drove to the gathering of canvassers at Issie's house. There was barely a quorum. By chance, a discussion developed about Yiddish teachers that angered me because everyone patronized them. So I gave it to them and showed them how false were their generalizations. Most importantly the desire to place the blame for many failures on teachers who have to instruct students whose parents, as well as they themselves, have no practical motivation for Yiddish studies. And all this without teaching aids. Even when a budget for aids is provided, it is so inadequate that it covers only a fraction of the need. And this condition prevails in the private schools as well as the congregational schools. It wasn't pleasant for the leaders to hear the account that I gave them. They will be searching for the footprints of a Yiddish teacher by candlelight!

JANUARY 28, 1972

Another link has fallen from our weakened and decimated chain. Just last Saturday I met Gittel Gershonovitch at a Bar Mitzvah. She spoke joyfully about travel plans and seeing things since she is now retired from the library as well. And two days ago she was cut down by a heart attack. Suddenly, in the middle of the street she fell ill and in a few hours it was all over. She was one of our first pupils here in the mid-twenties, in whom we took pride and saw in her the continuity of our educational philosophy. She became a teacher first at the Folk Shule, where she had graduated, and later in the Peretz Shule for about thirty-five years. For over forty years she served the Jewish child to the best of her ability. She was deeply involved in all of our social and cultural activities, especially the YIVO Committee, which she really carried by herself. She was always introverted, reserved in company, but did everything honestly and with integrity. She had a difficult life and departed like a juniper in the desert.

As things happened, Wiseman, who was her first teacher and principal, and a friend of many years, could not attend the funeral because of the misery of his own pains following an unsuccessful operation. And I too, who for many years knew her well from work, am in bed with a cold and can't attend the funeral either, to at least say farewell to one of our circle. Like a final symbol of her harsh life. How does one sort this out and make sense of life?

FEBRUARY 21, 1972

A person can live and create, love, hate, only when he believes that it has a meaning, and that there is a dream to be pursued. Without that, everything is empty, bare, valueless, and hence, without purpose.

The city is still crippled by the snowstorm. Because of a strike by the municipal employees the streets of Montreal have not been cleared. So everything is closed down. The only communication is via the radio. We can't get about anywhere. In the face of natural forces, human helplessness becomes evident.

APRIL 10, 1972

Lately I became involved in the preparations for the opening of the high school. In meeting the candidates for principal and teachers I became gloomy. Almost none were of our kind. It seems that none of the applicants had the secular outlook of our circle.

Finally, we settled on Dr Newman, who has, it seems, a thorough knowledge in Jewish and general subjects, experience in school administration in the Conservative school system. It looks like he will be able to adjust to our approach – though only God knows what our approach is – because the spirit in which the school is now being directed makes me feel like a stranger. It is the sort of fruit that has me questioning the appropriate blessing. It seeks to be a Hebrew school, but also wants to maintain Yiddish and folk culture, and leans socially and spiritually toward an upper middle class for its leadership, and a lower middle class for its parents.

Last night after returning from the meeting with the new principal and the parents, I fell asleep immediately. Although the evening was successful and practical, still I felt sad. Words of celebration were missing, no sense of uplift both from the audience or the speakers. A kind of arid spread of bookkeeping figures, which did not convey the purpose for which they were required. Suddenly, in my dream, I find myself in my own home, or so it seems, although the rooms and furnishings are a mixture of various pieces from different houses. Sorke and I are in a hurry to pack up what we can and to hide whatever we can. The same thing is now taking place in all the Jewish homes. It is the day commemorating the *Shoah* – I clearly know – and feel the all-encompassing terror of the need to hide and run away. Maybe this time too, as in other times, there will be a place to return to. But what shall I do with the manuscripts? Where are they? The terror mounts. The children hasten to leave, taking nothing with them. At this moment I know where the manuscripts are. Literally millions of letters of the alphabet fly off the sheets of paper and adhere to my exhausted memory, which rushes to meet them like a strip of film that absorbs everything. Confused, I run after the filmstrip and open my eyes to see the darkness of a grey morning in the house.

MAY 27, 1972

Finally, warm, sunny days are here and in just a couple of days nature hastened to plunge into summer. As if it were born fully ripe. Some difficult days during the last few weeks, an atmosphere that anticipated a revolution. A general strike covering the entire province. All the workers' unions and government employees supported by the private construction workers and longshoremen. A united front. It began as an economic strike and became linked to the political, although the demands are not clear to the workers and even less to the general public. The outcome: a new law passed in the legislature ordering them back to work is obeyed. Although an earlier court injunction was not obeyed and a number of union leaders were given prison terms, which they will not appeal. They prefer to go to jail. Nevertheless, the strike was broken and one of the unions is at the point of collapse. The leaders are ready to appeal and have been granted bail so they can contest the government, which is ready to soften its offer regarding the economic demands. Only the municipal workers are still on strike and the city is filthy. All the parks are full of garbage and nauseating odours. It is a kind of turmoil where irresponsible leaders exploit the situation to confuse the public even more. The public no longer knows the original purpose of the whole struggle. The desire to smash and destroy rises to the surface. A distrust exists from the top echelons to the lower ranks and vice versa. At such a time the intelligent man should remain silent. Who knows whether there exists an honest will to improve the conditions of the working man, or whether it is just exploitation which leads into a deeper mess.

Out of nowhere I find myself inclined to write metrical lines. I note several such lines:

> Suddenly enveloped in a deep silence:
> The storm now located beyond the door
> The distant echo rages within me
> Barely sensed, I cannot fathom its will.

I am alone, yet not all alone. A veiled *niggun* still comforts me. Somewhere the storm rages, but is not meant for me. All alone. Is this something of a premonition? Only in dreams do the entangled images appear that I cannot fathom, confounding me even more. All that I do unravels and I cannot bind them together again.

MAY 28, 1972

Last night I was at Shulamis's. She had invited some people in honour of Shimshon Dunsky, who received the J.I. Segal literary prize for his translation into Yiddish of the traditional commentaries on *Shir HaShirim*. Due to the mix of invited guests, at the beginning things did not cohere. But later, when Dunsky made a few remarks about *Midrash* in general, and *Shir HaShirim* in particular, things became very interesting. Both Elberg and myself made a few comments about the topic and Dunsky's work. So we sat around till late. Came home at 1:00 a.m. Found the nurse slightly upset, because someone kept phoning and hanging up the receiver as soon as she answered.

JUNE 1, 1972

Since yesterday when we learned of the tragedy in Israel, where "mercenaries" or misled "liberators" attacked close to one hundred people at Lydda airport, among them twenty-two dead and many more seriously wounded – it has been hard to regain one's balance. Engulfed by a sense of paralysis I cannot carry any thought to its conclusion. It is so senseless and chaotic and the Arab nations, with few exceptions, applaud approvingly. So the cultural level of contemporary man is contemptible, without a thought or feeling for the worth of a human life. There is not even a means to an end, only uncontrolled, animalistic impulses. How can we hope that anyone from the up-and-coming generation will be better? In one day he hears about purposeless and senseless slaughters. Inhuman acts on all sides. Then he walks about the streets of Montreal, which are full of garbage, all the parks covered with trash for weeks because of a strike. Everywhere it is said that this strike was imposed on its members by the same unions in which we had invested so much hope. In miniature this is part of the anarchy that has become second nature – almost normal.

Meanwhile the voices in opposition to this anarchy are weak. All of those who only two weeks ago criticized Israel for freeing the passengers of the captured airplane by "tricking" the hostage-takers are silent in the face of this bloodbath. They even admire the terrorists, who aren't even Arabs but Japanese. This chaos, it would appear, is universal. Before our eyes every form of human daring – even to the point of self-sacrifice – is transformed into the opposite of its original intent. The senselessness of risking everything unto death – the Devil's game – is sovereign over all. As Yechiel says: All this is happening because authority no longer exists.

In the meantime, what remains to be done? Until this authority appears how do we defend our own small corner with a bit of humanity? It would seem that those responsible for the airport are still living in illusions and after all that has happened still don't control passenger boarding properly, and thus aid the continuing rampage of terror.

I had to address the Moledet group about my book *Tzvishn Teichn un Vasern*. An unfamiliar woman approached me who apparently knew my father, may he rest in peace. She met him at Merson's slaughterhouse every Wednesday. She once asked him why does he sit and study in the breaks while slaughtering chickens. He answered: If I didn't study it would mean that the whole day passes by amid this refuse. In that way he was protecting his small corner. But how can one cleanse all the filth of the world?

JUNE 7, 1972

Today I visited the Rosenbergs. I do this from time to time. Unfortunately, they are terribly forlorn. Without a child, without family. They live solely with memories of their life among the Yiddish farmers out west. In the Congress milieu where he had worked from the early forties, he never managed to make close friends. He was always treated as a person of second rank. Merely an employee, on top of which he was found to be too deeply immersed in Yiddish. Now weeks can go by without a telephone call. They are both sick, she with a serious heart ailment. The solitude strikes you as soon as you walk in. They literally clung to me and begged me to come more often. No one remembers them any more. There was a time when they were in the very heart of community life. He was the most important statistician of Canadian Jewish life. It seems that it is necessary to form a group whose purpose should be to visit such people and ease their loneliness a little.

JUNE 8, 1972

Funny how little we really know people even when we think that we do know them. I knew that Husid sees only faults in everybody and "naturally" there was no Yiddish poet that he liked and for whom he could have a genuine attachment. All of them owe him something; he owes them nothing. This has long been known, but to perceive the heights it could reach, we had to wait for a petty event. Bunim Heller came to visit. A poet who endured the seven fires of Hell in the Soviet Union and Poland. Now, he has lived for a long time in Israel. So Elberg invited a few people, and we drove there together. Husid spoke about the visitor in the most derogatory terms and claimed that he was only going to please the Elbergs. He did not intend to go to his lecture since that would be an excessive sign of respect; even though Heller would be speaking about the murdered Soviet writers in a kind of memorial for the thirtieth anniversary of their deaths. "Why are we making such a fuss about them," Husid said, "there have been greater poets than them." He owes them nothing. At the gathering, Wiseman mentioned that this Sunday, Ravitch would be receiving the Manger Prize in Israel. It would be nice if we were to send a telegram. They asked Husid whether they should sign his name as well. So he answered, "No! What is there to celebrate?!" Is this only envy?

JUNE 9, 1972

I was at Yechiel's to take back "My Tangled Dream," which I had given him to read. I knew that he could no longer respond to a literary account as an imaginative, artistic vision. It was interesting to hear his reaction. He spoke for almost an hour and it became clear that he has no interest in artistic expression or characterization. My presentation of the exterminating angel's conquest is common knowledge, and therefore I should do penance and take upon myself the yoke of the heavenly kingdom. That way I will be able to save my soul. The whole tragedy escapes him. Everything is predetermined, the world must be punished but will not be destroyed. Individuals who encircle themselves in faith are the sacred people who will survive.

The complete plan of salvation is ready. Only repentance is missing. To the question: If this is in accordance with the plan, where is our free will and why does it take this form? He responds, this will be understood only when we perform the commandment: We will enact then accept. Initially to enact; after that one realizes what acceptance means, what it is that we have accepted. He is so immersed in this that only he alone sees and knows the future and he is full of pity for those unfortunates who, being blind, cannot see it. With this, he pours out Biblical verses, commentaries, and chunks of the *Zohar*, which, in his understanding, take on a different interpretation and content. He constantly enlists our father as his authority. Still, you have the feeling that he wants you to know that his knowledge is superior to Father's and unquestionably far beyond mine.

But on reconsideration it is evidently beneficial that he has so enclosed himself and fortifies himself with the sense of superiority, having found his way and is no longer lost. In the solitude of his existence, in the suffocating atmosphere of his home I found him still in *tallis* and *tefillin*. A basket of recently laundered clothing that he had hung up to dry. The entire room strewn with religious volumes and piles of newspapers, overflowing ash trays with cigarette butts, and in the kitchen, groceries readied for Shabbos. If not for his boasting about having found the right path, who knows if he would be able to endure this. In this way, too, perhaps, his condition is a part of the overall plan.

During our discussion, he blurts out words that cut to the quick. "If you take on the yoke and want to save your soul, and you know how, then you disregard your own wife, your children, and those you consider close to you; you survive." When I delicately questioned him: "What is this all for?" He shuddered: "What for? For the Master of the Universe and His plan." When I said: "Why does He have such a plan that does not include everyone?" His answer was: "When you attain knowledge, this too will be revealed." After all this I really don't know how "content" he actually is.

JUNE 13, 1972

"Why should we make up tales," Gorky, I think, said, "when life itself tells the most interesting stories." Riding home from the doctor I meet a man on the bus who considers himself a follower of my father. Whenever he meets me he spouts holy writ; wants to show off but only reveals his ignorance. In order to spare his feelings I respond uncritically. While sitting with him, Yalofsky, the former *Gemorah* teacher at the Talmud Torah, boards the bus. When he leaves I say to Yalofsky that I would like to visit the place where he lives - The Aristocrat, a seniors' residence. Startled, he looks at me and says that as long as you have your own home there is no need to go there. It is the final home.

JUNE 23, 1972

Today school closed. It was the last day of Sorke's teaching career. She is deeply affected by this. Still, I feel that deep in her heart she is happy to retire, in good health, and with the knowledge that she could continue teaching and does not have to because of financial need.

JUNE 28, 1972

Last night I learned that Cherniak had died. Saw him here in Montreal just a few weeks ago. It had truly looked like his last voyage. He was already terribly ill on his way back home. I still see the look on his face as he stood leaning on his cane in the doorway of the room. All the time we spent with him in the hotel he cried continuously, grieving for Fanya without whom he could not, nor did not, wish to live. He simply awaits that day and hopes that it will not be long in coming. At the same time, he was still preoccupied with, and expressed biting opinions as usual, on a number of cultural issues with which he had become acquainted while he was in New York at the YIVO conference. He was almost the last of his generation, outshone most of them, yet identified with them whether from near or from far. He was always a rebel, but still bore responsibility for the social order. His love for Fanya was extraordinary, not to be measured by our time alone. A pity on our great loss. I had expected to hear the news almost every day, since I knew that he didn't feel well and was rejecting any help. Still the news oppressed my heart, taking my breath away, and I felt a physical reaction to a deeper, inner shock. I felt very close to him, despite the fact that very often we had differences of opinion. All aspects of their home-life are dear to my heart. There is such an emptiness surrounding us now – encompassing me – that there is no one left to reach out to. Speaking to his son, Shoel, he told me that after he had made all the funeral arrangements he found a note of his father's expressing his desire that I should be at the funeral to speak a few words. But I was in such a state that neither Sorke nor the family would permit me to make such a journey. This now lies on my conscience, torturing me, and preventing me from writing a remembrance of him. The right words don't come and I can't recover from the assault – one of whose symptoms is a sense of vagueness that disrupts concentration. The best remedy is to rest at home and stay away from company. But this evening I must go to a reception for Sorke organized by the Peretz Shule teachers at the Fishman house. This reception is also hard on Sorke at this time because it engendered bad blood since it conflicted with an evening welcoming back the Ravitchs from their trip to Israel where he had received the Manger Prize. (Incidentally, the reason for the hurried convening of a welcoming reception when many of us will be unable to attend is the fact that the Yiddish Committee knows that in the fall the Jewish Public Library will be holding a large public celebration, so they want to be the first. A sort of petty-politics and cultural wars.) Sorke feels happy that the teachers with whom she has worked wish to say goodbye at a special evening. It gives her a good feeling.

JUNE 30, 1972

The evening for Sorke was very successful. Warm and friendly and mixed with nostalgia from everyone, which was expressed through the singing that Botwinik led, and in the words of some teachers, especially in Raizel's heartwarming recollections as a pupil and now a teacher. And, of course, in Sorke's remarks. At last Friday's farewell luncheon when Nachum spoke about Sorke, Ella Wasserman stood up and interrupted him and related her feelings as a former pupil about Sorke as a teacher. I wanted very much to say something as well, but was so upset by the news about Cherniak and the attack I suffered subsequently that I simply couldn't open my mouth. Today when I feel better I think that if I had spoken I would have maintained that at the present time when anyone who can speak out throws overheated phrases and barbs at teachers and assesses the teachers as outmoded and almost obsolete, it is an obligation to say a good word to a teacher who is retiring. Especially to one like Sorke, who was close to being an ideal teacher, with her devotion and her constant concern for the educational aspects of a teacher's role. She belongs to a generation of teachers who did not have formal training but who were teachers by instinct. She was part of a group of teachers whom we nurtured and educated, managing to create a bridge from the original founders. And from the beginning did things that are now looked on as novelties. Alone, she carried everything, the straw and the mortar, and suffered all the pains of the Yiddish school system. As the principal's wife, she never tried to distinguish herself from other teachers, while for the pupils she served both as an older sister and a mother. Her esthetic appearance was exemplary as were her classroom preparations. It is a pity that she is leaving the school, but one must step aside from an era whose time has passed. May the best of that era be remembered fondly.

JULY 25, 1972

Yesterday, I learned that Yishaiah Rabinovitch has also passed away. He had been afflicted with incurable illness for many years. Still it came suddenly, like thunder. Especially as he had been dead a week without our knowing. I was planning to phone and remind him about his promise to visit us next month. I still haven't recovered from the shock of Cherniak's death, so this hit me even more, leaving me in a state of bewilderment. He was younger than us, and our friendship goes back to the Winnipeg days. He was a deep thinker and bitter with self-knowledge, fully aware that he was not valued highly. Even the bit of recognition handed out to him by Israel's President Shazar last year didn't please him, knowing how many begrudged him this and murmured behind his back. He really deserved to have a place of honour among the critics of Hebrew literature. But they hardly understood his work and couldn't cope with his bitterness. On the phone his wife Soreh related to me his remarks before his death: "I hardly have any friends who appreciate me. There is nothing more for me to do here." What a final destination he had reached. In Toronto there were no Yiddishists who would deliver the eulogy; Professor Portnoy eulogized him in Hebrew. Estranged from everyone in his lifetime, he remained solitary in death.

Last week spend a day and a half in the country at Chanaleh's. Enjoyed myself greatly, but felt a bit like a stranger as well. Lately, I feel more strongly the screen that exists between us; they are more distant from my world than I had thought. As if we observe each other through a crack. Then we went to a motel where the unfamiliarity of the place oppressed me, despite the fact that we were together with some close friends and the region was magnificent. I thought that being in the country, I would, as in the past, hasten to my writing table. But I still find myself in a kind of trance that restrains me from beginning something new. I barely managed to revise three of my Bible stories. Very difficult to work on pieces from the past. Too many changes are to be avoided but I feel compelled to make some. It is more of a mechanical, rational application than one of true creativity. And the constant apprehension about what was happening at home with Gittel didn't allow me to be free of worries and concentrate on my writing. It looks like I am much more exhausted, mentally and physically, than I am ready to admit.

AUGUST 6, 1972

I was in Winnipeg barely three days. The flight was very nice. It takes about three hours from here to there. The few remaining souls who still remember me stayed very close and gave me a gracious welcome. Yet it was sad and bitter for me. The evening was conducted on a very high level. I believe that I was able to extol that generation and the Cherniaks in a manner that they deserved. A large audience attended. Most of them gave me the impression of being people who looked like cut-down trees, and whose stumps gave off a sheen of decay in a bright evening. Of the very aged, no one remains except Fyvel Simkin, a simple, extraordinary man of the people. The others are either deaf or blind, afflicted with illnesses that keep them housebound or institutionalized. I tried my best to see them all, and also wandered around the cemetery where the entire generation is laid to rest with handsome tombstones adorned with flowers. All is quiet about them. Rarely does anyone find their way to them.

The town is still in the same condition, half village, half city. The second generation advanced on every front: politically, assuming prominent positions in the provincial and municipal governments. All of my former students have prospered financially and professionally, assuming leadership roles in the city and the province. Two of them are ministers, but marked by their provincialism and marginality. In their approach to Jewish issues they are definitely remote, despite their claim that their parents were ghetto Jews. Their parents, however, looked out of the ghetto toward a broader world. They see only their city, their province, and are not rooted anywhere, neither in Jewish life nor public life in general, where they merely play at politics. I couldn't help but have this feeling during visits to their offices at the ministries, where they sit on high-backed chairs, at desks stacked with piles of memoranda. But you only have to look into their eyes or exchange a few words with their deputies to recognize that they are only strangers there, temporary. They have very little connection to the lives of their fathers and mothers, and therefore have no feeling for the proverbial, "I sit among my people." It was pathetic to see how excited they were after my remarks about that generation that had created a home in this new, strange place.

It was very hard for me to travel to the Shloshim and to be there. Still I am pleased that I managed it. I felt that I had to repay an outstanding debt. The darkest moment was at the Kellers' house. Everything was the same as it was forty years ago. Ethel is nearly blind and deaf, all wrinkled and hardly able to move. She sat on the same chair as she had years ago, above which hung the portrait of Velvel Keller with his half-mocking smile, as if he were about to chew on his silver cigar-holder and ask, "So do you still think it is all worthwhile?"

AUGUST 20, 1972

Yesterday I met with Husid after his return from Israel. He returned overflowing, laden with impressions, unfortunately most were sombre. The tumult of Israeli life gives rise to the dreadful comparison with the destruction of the Second Temple: divisions in the national consensus; unprovoked hatred; moral wrongdoing among individuals as well as the government's treatment of minorities; and a tough struggle for the moral face and soul of the society being created. The Yiddish writers are alienated and they fight among themselves about petty or significant matters. It doesn't look like a single people, but rather a tribal quarrel with traditions from the varied worlds and centuries. The Hebrew writers, too, feel isolated, and are without firm ground to stand on. The most radical orthodoxy carries on a bitter war about who is a Jew in accordance with *Halachah*, which has its resonance here with rabbis accusing each other of atheism and the destruction of Judaism. A number of *Agudas Yisroel* rabbis, supported by their American colleagues, called for a general fast to protest the edicts of the state, which many of them declare publicly is an "evil government." And this on the occasion of the 25th anniversary of the founding of the State. The culture war, which we feared and wished to avoid, has, it seems, broken out. How little inclined we are to learn from our own history.

AUGUST 22, 1972

Today we accompanied to his eternal rest the truly great Anglo-Jewish Canadian poet, A.M. Klein. Actually he had not been among the living for the past fifteen years since he suffered a nervous breakdown and never recovered. The real cause is not truly known. The only thing that was said at that time was that he was overwhelmed emotionally and mentally by the fact that he couldn't complete his profound interpretation of James Joyce, whom he esteemed greatly. There is probably more to it than that. What we knew of him revealed that he was quite inclined toward mysticism, and some of his visions were clearly enunciated in his writings and speeches. And he was deeply moved by the events of the war and the catastrophe that befell the Jews. His addresses upon his return from visiting Europe and Africa, and his descriptions of Jewish life there, were highly poetic and a cry from the heart. In his *The Second Scroll* you could sense the great lyricism and hallucinatory images with which he identified. A tragic occurrence and a heavy loss because he could not project all this into his art and thus remain unscathed.

At his funeral you could see almost all those who are still survivors of the tumultuous years of the '40s and '50s. From socialists to the orthodox, assimilationists, Yiddish writers and cultural activists. And perhaps a few from the English community too. An odd symbol of the sad funeral was the fact that the single eulogy was delivered by a strictly orthodox rabbi, Rabbi Hirschprung, who was his neighbour. Unfortunately, he tried to speak about poetry and naturally he spoke in Yiddish. The distorted mirror of our existence here: Yiddish writers and activists are, as a rule, eulogized in English, while an English poet was eulogized in Yiddish, and moreover, in a traditional manner of the most archaic mode.

AUGUST 24, 1972

Last night there was a meeting of the committee to publish my book – or books – at the Rosenfeld's home. Nearly everyone was there, more than thirty people, among whom were almost all the local writers and poets, including Ravitch and Rochl. There was a pleasant atmosphere. After Motty's introduction and my description of materials that are ready for the press, Yisroel spoke in his usual heated and critical manner regarding my excessive modesty, and that my role as writer should take precedence over that of being a teacher. At the same time he delivered a very fine analysis of the Bible stories, which will be the first volume to be published. They distributed cards for prospective contributors toward the fund of $10,000 that they seek to raise. For myself it is a kind of collective effort, which gives much pleasure because without my knowledge family and friends got together to publish my books. On the other hand, I feel ill at ease having to depend on the good-heartedness and friendship of others.

Throughout the evening I felt joyful and sad at the same time. I recalled my father's commentary long ago, when he found out how Sholem publishes his books; and then when he himself had to do the same thing in order to publish his books: "The wisdom of the pitiful lies in his living with humiliation; the wisdom of the lowly resides in his knowing how to accommodate humiliation." Deep inside me there is a gnawing feeling that a touch of beggary and shame is associated with this. Dvora and Hershel had the opportunity to demonstrate their wholehearted support and announced that they would contribute a thousand dollars, which is most generous. After this, two others indicated that they would give $500 and $250 respectively. It appears that friends will respond generously. I read a chapter of the Bible stories – Abraham banishes Hagar – which made a strong impression. Ravitch was very enthusiastic by its scope and the language. As is my custom, I couldn't sleep the whole night after this.

SEPTEMBER 5, 1972

A black day for Israel and the world. The terrorist attack on the Israelis at the Munich Olympics – the place designated for terror – kept the world in suspense all day. The whole world is helpless in the face of several desperadoes who are the very antithesis of the concept of human brotherhood. The few hours in the evening when we thought that the captured Israelis had been saved turned into the nightmare of the late evening announcement that all had perished in the shootout at the airport where they had been brought, ostensibly to be flown to Tunisia. What happened there we will probably never know. Do tragedies require explanation? To what purpose? Now Israel mourns her victims. The official world had a memorial service and announced that the Games must continue. The Games will be cancelled for only one day and that's all. Precisely on this day I handed my Bible stories to the printers. Neither my hand nor my spirits inclined me to remain a writer and to "derive satisfaction," so to speak, from the representation of human experiences. Everything appears to be senseless. Understandably, sensitive souls cannot maintain control and go on living with the "normal."

For the tiny bit of land that we tore out of the desert and for the bit of joy that enables us to call a patch of sky our own home, we are paying with so many sacrifices and how many more will we be paying for? And at the same time we fear that this bit of earth actually produces so many thorns and is a far cry from the ideal dream of a heavenly Jerusalem. "Woe is me for my desires, and woe is me for my creations."

OCTOBER 9, 1972

Gittel's condition becomes more and more grave. She, poor soul, knows only intermittently what is happening to her or where she is. The most difficult for us is living with a thought that we can't articulate to each other. There are moments when the idea surfaces: What is the point of this suffering? Why didn't she have the good fortune to leave in full consciousness? It seems as if we pray for her death. Is this the bitter consequence of old age, that the closest family must experience the bitter taste of death and bear the guilt-feeling of having assisted, in thought, to the passing of one whom you have loved and were bound to all your life? Transforming love into a burden, almost into hatred, which you perceive as a self-destructive poison. It is too frightening to follow this thought to a conclusion.

Yisroel had harboured the glowing hope that by accepting the position at Bialik High School he would be helping the cause of Yiddish. The reality however is that children will be children and have no special reason for studying Yiddish. And today's children have no respect at all for their elders or teachers. The middle-class homes from which they come have raised them without any sense of value. They haven't the slightest respect for things or people, and it often looks as if they feel and know nothing about the meaning of value. Everything is a game, an entertainment, or a stunt.

The echo of the conflict between left and right, secular and religious, which rebounds from Israel horrifies us. I'm always reminded of a priest's question to me as we stood in Nazareth before an old church: "You were twice given the chance to be the keepers of Israel, which you lost. Will you be able to hold onto it this third time?" He asked this with a quivering, numbed voice. The culture wars and the mean-spirited attitude of the Israelis toward the Russian immigration puts everything under a terrible question-mark. I am left speechless whenever I meet with Zionist friends and hear how they speak about these matters with regret but without feeling the deep tragedy and danger. I am overtaken with dread reading Israeli poets and novelists where one senses a helplessness and a fear over what is happening. But their work can't heal the oozing wound. And how they can still occupy themselves with literary theory and petty politics is beyond understanding. This makes it difficult for me to initiate anything; I make a start but can't continue, a fog in front and behind me. From the dreams alone I ought to write several nightmarish tales, but who needs this? Who would want to think about and understand this?

NOVEMBER 24, 1972

It was a bitter time when the school board refused to grant Sorke her pension. Two years ago it had been decided that on retirement every teacher who had worked more than twenty-five years was entitled to a pension. She had worked for thirty-three years. Their explanation is that in giving me a pension they had included her. After much clarification and pressure on several school activists, they came out with a resolution to give her a lump sum in compensation. In order to smoothe things over they want to revoke the earlier decision on the quiet so that none of the veteran teachers would automatically receive a pension and that each case would be dealt with individually: one would receive a pension, another just a lump sum, and yet another would get nothing. Simple robbery. Everything depends on who has better support among the board members. In principle I feel that we cannot accept this. Because of this rumours are circulating that the Zipper family is out to rob the school, which has no funds. Some of them, friends of long standing, so to speak, intercede on our behalf, but only halfheartedly. On one hand, they attempt to dispense verbal honours at every occasion, but on the other hand they can't elevate themselves above the earthbound concerns to consider that after so many years of work teachers are entitled to an honourable pension and not to charity. Leon Teitlebaum is prepared to do favours but not to negotiate on the basis of a morally just principle. So too Leibl Roskies says that he doesn't know all the facts. As for the rest, there is nothing to be said. The intelligentsia, including the principal, are on my side, at least that is what they say, but they rationalize the issue as a residue of the old dispute between the Peretz Shule and the Folk Shule and hence stand aside. This could develop into an open conflict that could force me to distance myself from the schools, which are no longer close to me any more. I feel estranged and remote from the spirit and style of today. It is really impossible to recognize the school as it once was. The dilemma is: I don't want to damage the cause but without an open conflict nothing will be resolved. I can't allow an obvious case of injustice and discrimination to be considered just. This takes up time and confounds my thoughts.

Still, with hidden reserves of energy I nevertheless managed in the last few weeks to do the final corrections for the book *In Di Getzelten fun Avrom*, which is now going to press. And I contacted an artist to get some illustrations. Also completed a lengthy essay on I.J. Schwartz commemorating the first anniversary of his death, and an essay on Rochl Korn to mark the publication of her new book of poetry. It troubles me that the essential writing that I would like to do still eludes me.

Last week I heard a magnificent group of Greek singers under the direction of the renowned Theodorakis. It was more than a marvelous concert. The Greek audience empathized with the singers' depiction through song and word of Greece's epic tale in recent decades. This made for a thrilling experience and almost a kind of mythic ceremony. I experienced something like this back in 1936–37 at a concert for the Spanish Civil War fighters where the audience and the artists were at certain moments like a flow of lava. Many of the musical phrases and words strongly recalled Jewish experiences and the horror of predestined afflictions.

These experiences made it painful for me to sit through an evening commemorating the murdered Yiddish writers who perished under Stalin, may his name be effaced. The main speaker, Elie Weisel, who is such a sensitive artist, at certain points got caught up in the web of political critique of the writers to the point where he castigated them more than honouring them. The whole tragedy of that generation and that era, which contains all the signs of the *Shabsai Tzvi* epoch, was overlooked and disregarded. I felt as if I had been slapped. However the audience enjoyed it immensely – so much for the audience.

DECEMBER 7, 1972

Last Sunday was the official opening of Bialik High School. There was a decent audience but not as large as befits the occasion. None of the local writers or well-known educators – they weren't invited. Very few of the present-day teachers. Very few of the former supporters of the school are still with us. There were a few and along with them I felt like a guest at a stranger's wedding. Everything was carried out in English, not one Yiddish or Hebrew poster. The decorations prepared by the teachers and the activists announced their identification with the latest in "progressive education." Entirely lacking in Jewish flavour. The only Yiddish speech was my own; Wilchesky, who by the way spoke very well, and Wiseman, who poured out his heart relating some reminiscences, spoke both English and Yiddish. I tried to set out the main points of the educational philosophy shared by Wiseman and myself. Underlined our approach, which proclaimed dignity to all things human and Jewish. They heard us out attentively. Even stood to honour us. But I felt like a guest at a stranger's celebration, as if I had been speaking to deaf ears. We were speaking of another school that had once existed.

How extraordinary are the ways of our history. Every day there appears in the newspaper an announcement about the children or grandchildren of the elite of the former Yiddish writers from the Soviet Union who are arriving in Israel. Amongst them are Markish's wife and son and Michoels' children. Almost the entire artistic constellation of the second generation have already migrated from there. How they will adjust to life there, God only knows. Meanwhile we say a blessing for everyone of them.

DECEMBER 19, 1972

Last night the executive took up the letter that Sorke had sent them, defending her right to a teacher's pension after thirty-three years of teaching. The atmosphere was heated and painful. Their complete dishonesty became evident in their manoeuvre to try to revoke the previously accepted principle and thereby avoid giving her what she was entitled to. That revocation would mean that she would be included in the terms of my pension. It would seem that the principle of pension for the older teachers was meant only for those who have no other source of income. And they will negotiate each case individually, with the decision left up to the committee. The only ones who defended the principle of obligatory pensions were Motty and myself. The others contended that too much money was being allotted to a single family, and retold stories about the bargaining sessions at the time of my retirement. Others wanted to refer the issue to a commission, but this was defeated by the administration. The president, along with a few others, spoke like autocratic figures dispensing favours and were chagrined when, after all they had done, found that we rejected their offer and desired to establish a principle that would apply to everyone. It appeared to me to be like the old powerful and well-to-do figures in Tishevitz. They were entitled to live in luxury, but the rabbi and the ritual slaughterer were not. They were not deserving of more than bread and water. At the meeting my ears kept ringing with these words: My forty-six years and Sorke's thirty-three years of labour at the school hang in the balance. The arrogance of the establishment lay in the fact that they were insulted by her refusal of a one-time gift and dared to oppose their decision by demanding a pension no matter how large or small it might be. As if their majesty had been insulted. On the other side were the ordinary mean-spirited begrudgers who hid under the mantle of protecting school funds. As it looks now, they outweigh us. Another illusion burst. After listening to my case they asked me to leave so that they could speak more freely. I had the feeling that the time had come to leave outright, just as I had left their autocratic fathers and grandfathers in Tishevitz.

Later they asked Motty to leave as well. It would appear that they don't feel able to speak their minds in his presence. See how far things have come. I didn't sleep all night and can't shake off its effects till now. Motty just called to say that Sheskin, the secretary, had called him with the information that they were unable to reach a decision and had sent the issue back to the officers committee once again. This means that after all something of a breakthrough has occurred, because earlier the chairman had maintained that he would not take up the matter at the committee again.

This afternoon the *Apollo* astronauts returned from the moon.

JANUARY 21, 1973

Back two days already from Miami. It went by like a dream. The first time that we summered in the winter. It is incredible that in a matter of a three-hour flight you are actually in the brightness and warmth by a shiny mirror-like sea that shimmers, beckons, and caresses. It is another world there. Your eye is accosted by masses of elderly people wherever you go or stroll. Age is not so burdensome there as it is here. Made many notes about the local characteristics, which I hope to work on later. The few weeks there were really one big celebration. Old friends came to see us and we made new ones, including *landsleit* and relatives whom we didn't know lived there. Everyone encircled us with warmth so we had very little time to rest. But we refreshed ourselves and with every good day we thanked the children in our hearts for persuading us to take the trip and for the financial aid and taking care of Mother. My two lectures there left a good impression. Met a wonderful family of Hebrew teachers and learned a new *niggun* from them – a marvellous one. She, Esther Perach, is a former pupil of Yitzchak Lamdan, so even Hebraists attended. The first lecture was on the writings of Menachem Boraisha, "In the Context of His Generation" – the title they gave it - was a revelation for them. At the Rochl Korn evening a large audience was present. A true in-gathering of the exiles from the entire country. Who is not to be found here. I began to be embarrassed by the compliments that I was given and the manner in which Wohl introduced me to the audience. It was troubling that the organizers are rather sloppy and do everything perfunctorily. The lecture hall had poor acoustics and a microphone that didn't work. And somehow they are ashamed to say that they still believe in something. Still, the private gatherings in some of their homes were very successful. All are retired and live on pension. But judging by the condominiums in which they live, it looks like the Hebrew teachers had looked after themselves, so now they can afford to live there in the winter in their own homes and to summer around New York or Boston, in their own homes too. May they take pleasure in this.

JANUARY 28, 1973

Last night we spent an evening at the Kupferszmidts with the guest Esther Markish. Today I heard her speak at the mass meeting at the Queen Elizabeth Hotel. Looking at her and listening to her, it is actually difficult to grasp that we are really looking at a person of flesh and bones. She is truly the symbol of an immense mystery that is being enacted before our eyes and it is barely possible to explain how a people which had conscientiously silenced itself to any Jewish sound had all at once become vocal. Now they are the Zionists, the most nationalistic, and risk everything in their struggle against the evil empire, and are paying the full price. And she too has no explanation. A unique fruit has grown on the tree in that desert created by fifty years of "revolution."

JANUARY 30, 1973

The mass meeting for Esther Markish was very well attended. Lermer introduced her to the audience in Yiddish most aptly. The chairman spoke in English and French. She spoke Yiddish with difficulty and French fluently. The questions from the audience were most relevant. She conducted herself very well, but the mystery of the new reawakening remains inexplicable. It looks like one of those events in Jewish history that keeps repeating itself, and where the accepted norms of explanation no longer apply. Tuesday morning she visited the students at the Bialik High School, but the sense of exultation that could have made this a profound experience for the children was missing.

FEBRUARY 7, 1973

Was at the printer's yesterday to return the proofs. Every time that I submitted the final corrected galleys of the book I felt in a holiday mood. Somehow, this time I feel that it is not a new accomplishment that would be both a summation as well as a continuation, a kind of underscoring of the sum total of my work. But now I know that I am still somewhere in the middle. The most important book of my life has yet to be written and the time, according to the calendar, may turn out to be all too short. One should make haste, but something still prevents me from sitting down each day and writing. There are so many beginnings and middles that I don't know which to take on first, and become entangled in side issues. I am not yet exclusively a writer, that which I always wished to be, but never reached that goal.

FEBRUARY 8, 1973

Today I had a lengthy discussion with Yechiel. That is, I just asked one question and he expounded on this for over an hour. His reply was interspersed with interpretations and reinterpretations of the Rambam and Ramban, Rebbeh, and Or haChaim. He cited prooftexts from the *Zohar*, from father's religious texts, and constantly spiced it with Chasidic tales and sayings heard from father – of blessed memory – and others. My question had been a simple one about Rebbeh's aphorism: "There are those who achieve success in one hour; and there are those who achieve success in several years." Why does it say, "Rebbeh wept and said." So Yechiel delved into the concept of the "World to come" and who is deserving of it. It turns out that only special individuals are elected, along with those who advance themselves toward divine spirituality, and then come those who can reach their level through true repentance and good deeds. The simple masses are swept along by these individuals. The weeping of the Rebbeh is due to the fact that one must labour strenuously yet everything might be lost in one hour. "There are those who lose the world-to-come in one hour." And this was followed by a dissertation on questions of holiness and faith among the saintly, who, by following them, even a simple Jew can attain grace. And in this way women too gain a higher level of merit through their husbands. He constructed a complete world picture that hung by a hair. And the hair is fortified with faith. And in Montreal too there are Jews who are worthy or have attained the divine spirit, and they can, in a critical hour, perform redemptive deeds. If it wasn't for the differences of opinion that spoil everything, we would be much closer to our goal.

You can't interrupt or refute him. First, because he doesn't allow this, because it flows from him like "the spring that grows mightier as it flows," and spreads over into several branches. Second, it is not worthwhile refuting him because as he pours out his heart you feel that he must speak out and empty himself after so many days and nights of loneliness and self-isolation. And most importantly he is sustained by his keen thinking and his steadfast grip on faith. He can accommodate the rationalistic with the Chasidic approach, and can smooth over the Baal Shem Tov's way of putting exclusive faith in the simple person with Ibn Ezra's conception that denies the simple person a share in the world-to-come.

After hearing him out, he went back to the sink to wash the pot that he had been scouring when I had entered. It seemed to me that he had somehow eased his mood. "The essential thing is to win over at least one Jew and bring him to divine service. We can't rely on the masses whose faith has been spoiled. Every individual who has faith bears the entire yoke himself." It was something of an oblique gesture that the whole discussion was bent on returning me to righteousness. Praise be the believer! In one of his stories he told of the Husatiner Rebbe, of whom it was said that he was a sealed urn, containing glowing coals of holiness. That was the reason that his face flamed whenever he prayed or presided over his table. After his exposition, Yechiel's face was quite fiery.

FEBRUARY 25, 1973

Yesterday morning the 23rd of Adar aleph, about 8:30 in the morning, Gittel breathed her last breath with a gasp, "Oy" that remained fixed in the unknown. She had just swallowed her last spoon of porridge. Asked to be taken to the bathroom. Walked unsteadily. As soon as we sat her down, she began, as usual, to call: Sorke, Yankel. But something of a heightened anxiety was evident in her cracked voice, "Take me," she barely whispered and kept her eyes closed. Hurriedly, we grasped her. Almost had to carry her to the bed. Lying her down, Sorke, as usual, encouraged her to help raise herself by placing one foot on the mattress so she could be positioned better and to make her comfortable on her cushions. However, I immediately sensed that she was not responding. I looked at her face and shuddered at her glassy stare and said: Don't you see what is happening? Sorke began to call out to her, rubbing her face with alcohol as she had done several times previously in the last few weeks when she did revive. This time she did not respond. Bubbles appeared on her tongue – and gone. The anguished face of the past weeks became more and more calm, and something of a yellow tint began to veil her face. Called the police, an ambulance arrived with a doctor who certified her death. Almost an entire morning was occupied with filling out the necessary papers by the house physician until she was taken to Paperman's. The peacefulness on her face was quite indescribable. Like salvation. It would appear that the transition to death is simply an arrival somewhere in the unrevealed. Only the road leading there is so difficult.

All day relatives came to the house. Even those who for years had never ventured into the house of groans. That evening Sorke cried all night. I too often woke up with a start, imagining that we heard her calling: Sorke, Yankel, Layah. Suddenly the house feels empty, her cries and moans of the past few months hover in all the corners. I still tremble as if I hear it now.

FEBRUARY 28, 1973

The funeral took place yesterday. Rabbi Denberg and Leib Tencer gave the eulogies. Tencer spoke intimately and with warmth and truly gave a picture as she was. And the Rabbi as well, in his way, with great reverence and tact. I thought that I would do it myself, but yesterday during the day I felt that I would break down. Why should one display one's grief in public. Certainly they are all family and friends, nevertheless still distant. "And Aharon was silent" – Holy Writ says.

MARCH 5, 1973

Today arose from *shiva*. All week people came, including those who previously never once came to see her. It was a burden to us, still it is difficult to sit all alone. The noise of people and even allowing oneself to indulge in conversations intended to lighten the mood also have a place in the arrangements of the living. The heartache does not go away. Even when one forgets for a while you feel a twinge in the heart: She is there under a heap of earth and snow, and here it is like a celebration – one dies alone. A shuddering thought even runs through your mind: "It will be the same at your passing." And you accept it. What choice do you have? Especially hard when the crowd leaves and you are left alone. Her groans and shouts from that concealed place resound in our ears. She was with us for fifty-three years. We began as three, became five, and were three once again. Difficult to adjust to being only two. The emptiness torments me terribly and I can't concentrate on anything, neither reading nor writing. It troubles me as well that many times in the last few years I found it difficult to be tied to the house, to this place, because of her. And a hint of a wish to be free from this would run through my mind. It makes me shiver yet: gained my freedom at her expense. Is this a type of just retribution? It is frightening to draw this thought to its conclusion.

APRIL 1, 1973

At the YIVO evening I met the poet Rogel who has suddenly crossed over to writing in English, which is not a bad thing if he thinks that he can do it. The trouble with this is that he wanted to give the impression that he is renouncing Yiddish because he wants to be more influential in English, and Yiddish no longer gives him that possibility. His slim volume in English is mediocre, but the professors who value literature only for its utility have embraced him. It seems that he is beginning to feel uncomfortable about this. So he tried to engage me in a discussion: Why is he being regarded so negatively? So I had to tell him what had created this bad impression. He denies that he had said that he no longer feels himself to be a Yiddish poet – the press misconstrued things. It is to his credit that he wants to set the record straight. The fact that after so many years of estrangement and not attending our gatherings, he now has the desire to come and make an appearance and wants to justify himself is reason enough not to reject him.

Last week I received the English journal "Prism International," which published my short story "The True Image" in Sacvan Bercovitch's translation. It is a good feeling to know that somewhere complete strangers will be reading you. But it is unpleasant to hear from those very close expressing their happiness: "Now the younger audience" – others say, the world "will read you too, and know about you." The implication is that ours is still not a world. So be it.

What is occurring among the Hebrew poets or writers is really inconceivable. All the fashions arrive there belatedly, but they do arrive. So too the fashion of defending arch-reactionaries, fascists, and blatant anti-Semites, with the excuse that "their social errors" should not obscure their accomplishments for "world literature and art." The most obvious recent example was Ezra Pound. The writer Avidan, in the literary supplement of *Davaar*, almost turns him into the greatest innovator and the most exalted in world poetry. And that he is a martyr who, by whatever means, should be recompensed. For his treasonable deeds during the Second World War he actually deserves a medal for non-conformity. All his anti-Semitic outbursts are also part of his piercing the blisters of society. Added to this, you can also find anti-Semitic sentiments in Avidan's work and the works of his generation of Hebrew writers. In his response to Moshe Dor, another Hebrew poet and journalist, who had attacked him for this, he disclosed that not too long ago it was customary for many of the young Hebrew poets to refer to Jews in the Slavic as "*Zhidlak*" and other such terms. So why get excited over this?

APRIL 11, 1973

Last Sunday, for the first time I think, I spoke at the memorial for the martyrs of the *Shoah*. The Warsaw *landsmanshaft* organized it very well. The truth is that in attending these public memorials year after year, I have said to myself many times that there is no need to go. It always left me with a bitter aftertaste. All the arrangements are more of a theatrical than an authentic experience. This time I was in doubt about accepting. But knowing the people, I assumed that they were in earnest. There was a large audience and most of them were victims themselves. So the atmosphere was totally different from previous public meetings. The ceremony was impressive. Rabbi Hirschprung on this occasion found a few appropriate words to say and the children of Igenfeld and Augenfeld recited several fitting poems by Katzenelson wonderfully. It left the impression that they understood what they were reading. My few words too left a strong impression. I developed the concept of *Kiddush HaShem* and how the martyrs – both those who were passive or active – were part of that eternal concept. I felt that I had touched an important and sensitive chord in the audience who were not accustomed to dealing in such a manner with this subject.

MAY 7, 1973

Yom HaAtzma'ut – Israel Independence Day. I couldn't convince myself not to attend the celebrations organized to mark Israel's twenty-fifth anniversary. The arrangements emphasized the hoopla around it more than the true emotion of the experience. There was one with group dancing and a torch parade to which I really would have liked to go. But it is too hard to drag myself down with a bus. My strength begins to fail me. So I went to the children's celebration at the school because someone offered me a ride. It was more of a heartache than a holiday. Here too there was only tumult, entertainment that could have been suitable for any occasion, not particularly for an Israeli celebration. All was in disarray, more than a thousand children were milling about, running around, and could hardly get near the game booths. It made no impression on anyone unless the trip there could be considered an experience. If each school had had a separate celebration it certainly would have left a deeper impression. Somehow, wherever one turns, no one seems to be concerned with educational experiences. Seeing the new era wiping away everything we had striven to accomplish, the heart is enveloped by sadness. As opposed to this, the reception at the consulate was quite festive. There was a holiday mood with a large crowd from all strata and persuasions. Although here too it was obvious that those who were invited from the Jewish crowd were those with deep pockets. Very few of the intelligentsia and activists from peoples' organizations.

From there we went to the meeting of the J.I. Segal Fund jury committee. The juries submitted the names of the prizewinners. For educational achievement the prize went to Rabbi L. Kramer of the *Lubovitch Yeshiva* – a fine gesture and a well-earned appreciation for his founding of the *yeshiva*. I remember when he arrived here, one of the first harbingers from amidst the terrible war, empty-handed. We donated our old school benches when they opened the *yeshiva* in a private house. Today they have an impressive building with a vibrant educational institution. For English, the jury could not reach a unanimous decision because of an odd reason. The book that they were considering for its literary worth was found, by the jury, to be deficient in Jewish content. According to the statutes the submissions should contain Jewish content, but what that means is not specified. Because of this their decision left an aftertaste. For Yiddish literature, the jury (of which I was a member) selected Rochl Korn for her book *Oif der Sharf fun a Reggeh*, and Chava Rosenfarb for her trilogy *Der Boim fun Lebn*, a most significant book of prose that comprises the years 1939 to 1943. For achievement in theatre, a special award for Chayele Gruber, also well deserved.

MAY 14, 1973

It has been an awful week. Rochl Korn refused to accept the award and wishes that her name not be associated in any way with the J.I. Segal Fund. Lermer and I met with her to discuss the matter. She still feels hurt because five years ago, according to her, she was insulted when she was not awarded the prize for her book, which coincided with her seventieth birthday. It appears that the gossip-mongers had then convinced her that some of the jury members had particularly wanted to give Husid the prize and therefore they rejected her book since it had recently received the Bookland Committee Award. The whole episode was fabricated and made vicious by loose tongues. For her, however, it is a fact and she feels so strongly about it that she had sworn never to have anything to do with the Fund. As much as we tried to convince her, nothing helped. She feels, as she puts it, as if it were scar tissue that she cannot rid herself of. Her decision leaves a double sense of bitterness: for the slap in the face to all of us; and her personal sense of injustice that cannot rise above this foolish obsession. Especially since it is now her seventy-fifth birthday, which should be marked as she deserves. But now it will be quite difficult.

JULY 15, 1973

It would seem that with the removal of specific responsibilities both the will to do something and the belief that it is necessary and worthwhile become atrophied. The most bitter feeling arises because personal belief in one's life-work has somehow floated away into the unknown. So there is no longer the satisfaction of accomplishment. Even attending a meeting where you undoubtedly know that you have to speak out against certain wrongs perpetrated against teachers now seems worthless. And you can no longer risk things that do not affect you. You stop seeing people and their conduct objectively, and you stop trying to influence them. But like a mannequin, you have no faith that you can do anything for them, nor that they can do anything for you. A grotesque blind game.

JULY 30, 1973

Yesterday I attended a literary gathering that was the first of its kind I had attended since arriving in Canada. A group of young poets and writers who write in English, among them former students of mine, who had asked to meet with the local Yiddish writers. Nearly all of them came. It was a stirring experience to see young people deeply involved in writing, most of them in the contemporary style, individualistic and satirical. It took place at Chava Rosenfarb's house, which has an artistic ambience and where the bearded and amulet-wearing writers fitted in well. At the outset we felt constrained. But slowly we warmed to each other and became closer. It emerged that they are interested in what the Yiddish writers are doing and want to work together to translate into English as much as possible. And they seem to feel more at home in the Jewish milieu. Some of them are unambiguously Jewish according to their subject-matter and the stylistic treatment of their subject-matter. They want to be identified as Jewish creative writers. This gave Ravitch the opportunity to repeat the saying of Baal Machshoves, "One literature in two languages," which he extended to "One literature in three languages." Elberg, who has recently assumed the position of spokesman, accepted positively the experiment of working together.

He had doubts whether we could get down to a concrete project at once. I too spoke in the same vein but requested of them that they clarify their aims including their desire to become Jewish writers and to work in this milieu not merely as Canadian writers. Naturally, no concrete decisions were arrived at. Everyone was pleased with having met, especially after they had read their poetry, and in one case, prose. It seems that they have a number of quite talented people amongst them. In the discussion that followed the readings, the poems were lightly criticized because of their experimental qualities, the prose writer was criticized a little more harshly. But it is evident that we can anticipate much more from them, and, with time, improved quality. We should keep an eye on the poets Schneider, Sarna, and the writer Boyarsky. All three come from Yiddish-speaking homes. Sarna's parents were Yiddish teachers; Schneider is the son of a rabbi and his mother-tongue is Hebrew; and Boyarsky is the son of an honest working-man, a survivor of the war. He seems to be religious, wore a *yarmulke* during the meeting. At least from these three, one can see that their background is almost the same as the local Yiddish writers. We will have to maintain close relations with them.

SEPTEMBER 19, 1973

The entire foundation of Jewish education rests on sand. A financial crisis is looming and a philosophical crisis eats from within. Despite all the plans for cultural activities of the Jewish Public Library and others, financial need stares out of every corner because of the leaders who are at the helm, and the nature of their outlook. The *Keneder Odler* is struggling and will finally have to close. Our Yiddish-speaking circle is worn out, and those who have the money are still bound to the old concept of philanthropy and their whole outlook is misanthropic.

At one time, difficulties never weakened me. On the contrary, they strengthened my resolve in overcoming them. Or I simply disregarded them and persisted in my work. Now they disable me and I only want to lie down in seclusion. I know that I must not capitulate, that I must fight it. Whether I can overcome it remains highly doubtful. I accepted to teach a course in *Mishnah* and *Aggadah* twice a week to the grade 9 of Bialik High School. When I teach, the old spark and flame are reignited. But then the indifference returns and raises the question: What for?

Last Sunday we unveiled Gittel's tombstone. The final tribute, as we call it. I said a few words about her and, later, people said that I had given her a *tikkun* – restored her to a spiritual wholeness. It was not easy for me, almost broke down in tears. But I felt that I had to do it. However, the emptiness in the house remains and the pain is as raw as it ever was.

YOM KIPPUR EVE, 5734

A fall evening, dreary outside with a light rain, exactly fitting my mood. The last few days seem to me just like those of the final days of the 1930s when Jewish refugees knocked at every door while the arrogant world turned a deaf ear and shamelessly refused to admit them. In Evian, before the entire world, they outdid each other with excuses about why they could not open one small door for Jews. Now the only open transit door via Austria was sealed, ironically by a Jewish voice. How tragic must have been the discussion of Golda Meir with the premier of Austria – a Jew. How devilishly symbolic. The world protests a little, but who can listen to the world when it has isolated Israel and constantly condemns her at every opportunity, not even batting an eyelash. And this same world surrenders to the Arab terrorists in pious hypocrisy. Don't they know that precisely as in the past, not only Israel will be drenched in blood. They will all pay for building up this monster. Meanwhile, it is horribly sad. How alone we still are in this kind of world.

Religious Jews will say: In the face of evil, the saintly man is gathered to his ancestors. Now Aaron Zeitlin too is no longer with us. Almost the last of a towering generation, he had participated in both our literatures and was immersed in the depths of the Jewish ethos, just as he was at home in the classics of world literature and learning. Just days before the grand celebration in honour of his seventy-fifth birthday his heart stopped and it was over. Now he knows whether there is a life in the hereafter – a world of truth. Our cultural pillars are becoming sparser and an emptiness hovers in all corners.

OCTOBER 8, 1973

It is now the third day that Israel is once more drenched in blood and we here can only shudder with them and stumble about as in a nightmare. Yom Kippur morning, Syria and Egypt attacked and it would appear that Israel was not adequately prepared and suffered tremendous losses. At this point the true situation is not clear. All the Arab nations, with the exception of Jordan, are rushing aid to the Syrians and Egyptians. Meanwhile "the world" looks on, waiting to see what will emerge from this. And China and Russia are not even allowing the issue to be debated at the Security Council. Even though the Egyptians admit that they are the aggressors, still everyone angrily accuses Israel of being the attacker. In the early hours, it even seemed that the Egyptians were allowed to cross the Suez Canal, so they too could demonstrate their military prowess and erase the humiliation of their national defeat in 1967. Possibly this might lead to peace. Now it looks like the battle will be costly. What is at stake again is the very existence of Israel. Being over-confident these last few years is costing Israel a great deal of blood. Tonight a mass meeting is taking place at the Shaar Hashomayim Synagogue. Oddly, the event is being organized by the Combined Appeal and not by the Zionist Organization and the Congress, as if it were only a fund-raising issue.

OCTOBER 9, 1973

Today is already the fourth day of the war. All the Arab nations, except Jordan, are rushing aid to the Arab side. China and Russia play their game as expected, continuously postponing the meetings of the Security Council. News bulletins from the front are still very ambiguous, though everyone seems to acknowledge that Israel is slowly gaining the upper hand. One thing is now clear: It has cost enormous losses. Jews here are overwrought, banging at the government's door and conducting an emergency campaign. Many young people are clamouring to fly to Israel, and the consul does not advise the Israelis to fly home, even at their own expense, until they are summoned.

When I got to school in the morning, where I give a course in *Mishnah* and *Aggadah*, there was a hurried meeting of the teachers and principal. The tension could be noted on the faces of everyone and in their words. The children are restless and want to do something. There were proposals that letters be written to the UN, the Canadian government, to soldiers in Israel, and especially to the wounded. I suggested that they bring a gift from their own savings so that they can feel that they are giving something of themselves, and that this should be decided by the students' council.

In the classroom the atmosphere was restrained and somewhat depressed. One teacher asked the other teachers not to show their feelings to the children, but encourage them through explanations. When I came into the class, that same teacher had already told them about the letter-writing and most of them had eagerly begun. I tried to engage them in a discussion that even in the greatest crisis one should not lose control so that one might continue to act. We have to protect our human qualities and not succumb to hatred. The tragic event, which costs so much blood on both sides, must always be kept in mind. The tradition says: If your enemies fall, do not rejoice. One student jumped up, "Does this apply to the enemy too? They started it!" When I responded, "The enemy as well," he simply didn't want to accept it. This cut into my heart. How our world has poisoned the souls of our very young.

OCTOBER 10, 1973
FIFTH DAY OF ISRAEL'S STRUGGLE FOR SURVIVAL

By today it appears that there will not be a quick end to the war. Amongst themselves the great powers are also dragging things out. Russia, which had suffered from the Damascus bombing – her embassy was hit – came out openly against Israel and walked out of the Security Council meeting. Nearly all the Arab nations are now participating directly in the war. Whether Israel can endure a longer war is a big question.

Last night there were gatherings in all the thirty-three synagogues; this was in addition to the previous two mass assemblies held earlier in public halls. The mood is tense. Everyone feels the seriousness of the situation. I don't know what the response to the Appeal was, but it looked as if everyone contributed. There were only two speeches, earnest and to the point, and the cantor chanted the *El Moleh Rachamim*. There was a large audience, many young people, but the hall wasn't packed. It brought to mind my first such meeting where we came together in true fear. It was in Tishevitz following the Lemberg pogrom. Doubtless, the fearful shuddering was more intense, and the helplessness more evident. We, the youth, immediately after the meeting, took to organizing self-defence, without consulting the adults. Here, no other option is available except for contributing sums of money. And the response of the audience really was encouraging. I met people there that I hadn't seen at Jewish affairs for the longest time. Among them former pupils whom I hadn't seen for years. Still you could feel a sense of helplessness, even from the speakers.

OCTOBER 16, 1973

Today the fragmentary news from the front looks better. Israel is close to Damascus and has crossed the Suez in several places. Probably to destroy the fortifications there and surround the enemy on that side. It certainly is a real bloodbath there, still we have to accept this as good news. The war between David and Goliath must be won by such astonishing actions. At the meeting of the plenum of the "United Nations" – what a scandalous name – the so-called "neutral" nations, amongst them many that Israel had helped with advice and resources in the last few years, voted unanimously – seventy newly created opinionated nations and seekers of justice – that Israel is the aggressor and must be punished. Odd how our ancient sources speak of the nation of Israel as a sheep among seventy wolves. America has finally publicly announced that she is now sending arms to Israel. One friend amongst all the wolves. Albion England refused to send arms. She is as kosher as a pig's foot in her neutrality; she trains Iraqi officers and technicians. The losses, it seems, are extraordinarily high. What the heart thinks should not always be expressed: That the Israelis were misled by their own bravado and did nothing until it was too late. But what purpose would be served now if the guilty ones were found out?

LAST EVENING OF SUCCOS, 5734

With each day that the war drags on, the heavier is my mood. The hatred against Israel, orchestrated by Russia "the ur-father of all abominations," grows more potent on all sides. Especially after Russia's use of oil as a whip. It is actually being said that behind the scenes they are seeking ways to stop the war, but to Israel's disadvantage. In America this has actually evoked a widespread opposition. She is sending aid to Israel and publicly declares that she cannot be dependent on others in her foreign policy. But there too there is no shortage of enemies. However the churches have aligned themselves with Israel this time. Meanwhile people are dying and the tragedy is that even the achievement of victory will not mean peace. A heavy stone lies on my spirits and oppresses me. As Fein writes, "What do they want of us?" Witnessing the many trials we have suffered all these years – and we can place them on the scales of history – we come to the realization that they simply do not want us to exist. This brings on the deepest depression. Being awake is no help; even worse is nightmarish sleep. Before my eyes rush images of the trampled bodies of our children, and a deep-set guilt eats away at me: Why are we here, while they there are being set aflame for the fourth time. It is cruel to be in the line of fire, but even more cruel to always be an observer in the distant Diaspora.

OCTOBER 24, 1973

Yesterday, Teitlebaum, Kage, Lermer, Sarah Rosenfeld, and myself met to deal with *Keneder Odler's* request for a subsidy – which was refused. As a businessman, Teitlebaum considers the request from the viewpoint – which he expresses every year – that this is a business that has no customers. Our arguments, based on the cultural value of a Yiddish newspaper that the Jewish community must assume responsibility for, were partially successful and he promised to arrange a meeting with the officers of the AJCS. He maintains however, that the *Keneder Odler* Committee must carry out its own campaign to which the AJCS will contribute their share. They cannot take on the entire responsibility. At the same time he informed us that the Emergency Campaign for Israel will net over $20 million, excluding bonds. For fire and blood money can be found – and it is good that this is so. But for a cultural issue, which makes everything worthwhile, not even pennies are available.

OCTOBER 26, 1973

Letters are beginning to arrive from Israel. An agonizing shudder resonates from them, along with a fatalistic acceptance of their destiny that this is the way it has to be: Every few years you have to take your life in your hands and fight for your existence. They are confident of their victory yet know that this is not the final struggle. The last few days see us caught up in a raging whirlpool, one step away from a world war. Russia speaks openly about direct intervention and about sending troops ostensibly to observe the cease-fire, which has only partially taken effect. It looks like Egypt is about to collapse and Russia will not allow this. America responds by putting its army on the alert. In the Security Council resolutions are passed and they continue to talk. Aside from America, no one has a good word for Israel. All the "saints" of the world demand righteousness from wounded Israel, which won't allow itself to be destroyed.

NOVEMBER 30, 1973

Only single individuals, here and there, dare to say a good word for Israel. The majority is silent or is openly ready for a new *Tisha b'Av*. In antiquity, the destruction was interpreted and justified – by us and the world outside – to the "sins" of Israel. And it is just the same today. The only sinner in this righteous world is Israel. Even the devil no longer laughs.

Despite all this, from time to time one must summon up one's strength and speak publicly, even to find words of encouragement. One ought not permit oneself to add to the helpless despair. I was in Toronto and spoke about Boraisha's approach and contribution to Yiddish literature. The audience swallowed every word. In my own heart, however, privately the worm of doubt gnaws away. But am I not, once again, fashioning an illusion, based on a philosophy of faith and purposeful meaning – because without it would be impossible to endure one miserable day.

DECEMBER 16, 1973

Received a letter from the poet Shimon Halkin. Just a few lines in which he writes that his family is all right, but many close friends suffered losses. "Everything that I thought about this people has unfortunately come to pass. There is no single people of Israel, particularly those in the Diaspora, who desire to live in their countries," he concludes. Look how extreme opinions have become. Shimshon Meltzer, on the other hand, writes a long letter. His sons are at the front, and he is happy that they were on leave for a few hours and left again, and is actually full of hope that somehow things will be stabilized. The bitter disappointment will lead to a clearer national reckoning. Both of them dangle in the air and it feels as if the fear for the existence of the State stands before everyone's eyes. What can we say after that? I feel that I must be there as soon as possible and together with them experience these terrible hours.

JANUARY 1, 1974

The new year arrived in semi-darkness in most parts of the world, accompanied by an overwhelming dread of total darkness. And in Israel it arrived at a time of quaking desperation in the face of their own destiny. They negotiate and tremble at each rejection or compromise. Both actions bear the risk of being only a rung in the step-by-step path to Israel's downfall, God forbid. The most bizzare theories are advanced regarding actual possibilites. It makes your skin crawl. And the elections in Israel indicated the striking confusion in "the nation that dwells in Zion" – as the flowery phrase goes. On the one hand they voted for Likud, with its slogan "Not One Step Further." And on the other hand, the Maarach remained the largest party which can form a government able to compromise. The populace punished them by reducing their seats because of previous mistakes, but mandated them to continue governing. No other alternative existed and some compromise is required, even though this is only a temporary respite from war. The heads of state travel back and forth to Washington, while their counterparts travel to Moscow to the bosses of the world. And who knows what concoctions they are cooking up there.

JANUARY 6, 1974

I went to visit Ravitch, a broken vessel, poor man. You can barely understand a word he says. He is afraid to stand up and take a step. When he finally stands up to walk, and if someone supports him, he starts to shuffle rapidly and then stops abruptly as if he had struck something. It is painful to watch and an awful pity on poor Rochl. He can no longer write and this tortures him. After that wonderful celebration, what a terrible week. And we persist in asking for an old age. The sadness of the adage, "Do not forsake me in my old age," dogged me all the time I was there and I can't free myself from it.

FEBRUARY 2, 1974

The town is in a turmoil with Rozansky's arrival. This is his annual visit, which deals with the Yiddish classics he is publishing. His dynamism and his deeds restrain one from making any comments that would hurt him. Despite everything, he does a great deal. He is always received with respect. This visit has a specific purpose: one of these volumes will be – as he refers to it – Canadiana. In his view it should be a book that reflects on Canadian Jewish life through literature. Many of us maintain that it should represent the work of Canadian Yiddish writers, not exclusively devoted to Canadian content. So we came together at the Ravitchs' and argued at length about this. Some, like Husid, who in general looks at everything negatively, is dismissive of every subject whatsoever in the name of esthetics. He was trampled on without mercy. My view was that it shouldn't be called Canadiana because, on the whole, there is simply not a specific Canadian-Jewish subject matter here. And that the volume should present the works of Yiddish writers. The Canadian content, which some writers deal with – for example like Sholem – will certainly be acceptable. In principle, the essays should definitely be Canadian, while poetry and fiction should meet the aesthetic standard. In the end this was the understanding we reached. However, Rozansky demanded the materials in the next few days, and because of his energy and insistence, I am afraid that the project will be half-baked. He severely insulted the writers who had no Canadian motifs, and resorted to the old-fashioned slogans that they do not serve society, etc., etc. So an aftertaste remained.

FEBRUARY 8, 1974

At the board of directors' meeting an intense discussion took place on the proposal to close the afternoon schools. They lose too much money. The attitude of many board members is that education is a business that must pay for itself. We barely managed to shout down this view. The provincial government is pressuring the schools to convert to French, and if not, they will not be subsidized. And as there is no Jewish community funding, and English instruction cannot be pushed aside, this means that the change will affect Jewish studies. Here, too, there are many who are prepared to comply. And even though this means that the school loses its reason to exist, most have become accustomed to the mere rhetoric of education, and thus acquit themselves. This issue will still have to be thoroughly aired.

OCTOBER 15, 1974

Nearly three-quarters of a year has passed without being able to jot down my notes. In Israel I was able to note certain impressions and thoughts, here and there, but until now I still can't return to them. The tragic experiences there, and our three months of being part of the heroic struggle with its countless casualties, as well as the great despair and disbelief in the grand vision that pervades all social strata, left me literally mute and depressed.

The reality brought the song within me to an end. I still can't apply myself to anything. Everything that I do is performed like an automaton.

The prospect of a book on Israel is questionable. When we returned from Israel ten years ago, I was full of impressions and thoughts that resulted in a book. This time I keep seeing before my eyes the open graves of the soldiers whose bodies had not been recovered. Surrounding them is a brilliant sea of red and white flowers, between the chalk-white gravestones. And in my ears there still roars the acute question of a young priest in Nazareth, "You returned twice to this place without being able to hold on to this land. Will you be able to keep it this third time?" Never before has the bitter, despairing cry of pain by the prophet Amos been so clear to me: "Who will raise up Jacob, because he is so small."

Yesterday was a black day for Israel and the world at the assembly of the United Nations. A hundred and five nations decided to admit the Palestine Liberation Organization (read: terrorists who have sworn to destroy Israel) to the debates on the Middle East. Only four nations voted against, twenty-odd abstained, amongst them our own Canada. All the evil in the world is united. There is no doubt that the world will pay dearly for this. Yet what benefit will we have from this? If we were at least inwardly strong, then we could say: "Wait just a moment until the anger passes." But we are not only inwardly torn apart but literally shattered. Nevertheless life here takes its normal course. Neither the best in the world, nor ourselves, have the power to raise a thunderous outcry. The devil, with hideous laughter, strides on high again, and one by one the conduits of faith in mankind and the world are stopped up. A terrible edict hangs over us. In a time of misfortune, my father could console himself with the verse, "We have nothing to lean on but our Father in heaven." As for me, only darkness emerges from the place where "our Father" is ostensibly hiding.

MOTZEH SHABBOS; CLOSE OF THE SABBATH
PARSHAS LECH L'CHA
OCTOBER 26, 1974

Today was the second day of staying home because the doctor ordered a rest of two and a half weeks, no exertion and no participation in any work. He assumes that unknowingly I had a heart attack. In truth I feel no pain, only a kind of heaviness around the heart, fatigue, and an inability to concentrate. Somehow I can't believe this has happened and am unafraid. Though from Sorke's glances and the children's pretending to be unconcerned while still constantly inquiring about my health, I'm left with a strange feeling. Truth to tell, I have been expecting something like this for the past few months. Becoming fatigued easily, feeling discouraged, every bit of news left a bitter mood and an interior voice saying, "In any case, there is no point in undertaking new work." Had the feeling that I am just wasting time and not accomplishing the necessary tasks that need to be completed. This evening is the tribute for Rochl Korn that I had helped organize. I looked forward to this event, truly a real celebration. So I am left celebrating the joyous occasion on my own in silence.

It is unbelievable, and I don't want to believe, that last week's evening for Chayele Gruber was my final appearance as public speaker. Still, it seems to me that I am at peace and ready for the silence that begins to encircle me. I feel that I did what I could, to the extent that I was able.

DECEMBER 22, 1974

The last few weeks of rest and isolation have obviously had a positive physical effect, though from time to time there is some pressure around the heart, but it passes. Not being able to attend meetings nor participating in community affairs has a calming effect in the sense that you are freed from the responsibility of taking sides, but it also leaves the feeling of being an outsider. Very often the thought arises: What remains now is to count the numbered, precious days. You can't add more, and you need not begin anything since you will not be able to complete it anyway. This works on my will to write, which is nearly atrophied. In all this time I have only jotted down one piece on Israel. All other plans are piled up in a heap and I can't touch them.

Meanwhile, Chanukah has come and gone. The children and grandchildren were here. Lovely to be with them. Yet more and more I feel our spiritual estrangement. We can still manage to have a discussion, such as it is, but to share a deep experience, to join our voices in song, and to grasp the significance of this is rare. I have always had the feeling that an invisible wall stands between us. Most of the time I hum a *niggun* to myself that they don't hear. I am overcome by a feeling of pity when I watch the youngsters, the grandchildren, in their games and fights among themselves. Oh what an awful world they are growing up in, and what kind of spiritual support do they have to sustain them? Did I give them anything? Do they want to take anything?

DECEMBER 23, 1974

Yesterday I began reading Yehuda Elberg's novel *Oifn Shpitz fun a Mast*. The first chapters unfold at such a pace that the horror of those catastrophic times continually leaps out at you from all sides, particularly in the interior monologue that accompanies the realistic situations and images racing before your eyes. And all this raises a troublesome, vexing question in my mind: How terrible it is for the artist who alone must create and express human degradation patterned on actual realities, but still perceive it through his own vision. Is that an aspect of the tragic mode of creation? What a horrible dimension this adds to human existence and creativity. How can he face himself after having observed human beings so degraded? How can he even smile sometimes to himself, his wife, his child, and devote himself to the ordinary routines of the day?

MARCH 23, 1975

Came through some difficult months and was only able to write letters. Even the four weeks in Florida didn't lighten my mood, though from day to day I felt better there. The warm sun and glittering sea during the day, and the distant, unidentifiable hum under the moonlight by night, calms yet deepens the loneliness of people who come here at the end of days, already disabled with weakened limbs. They walk along the seashore to regain a bit of health and to grasp as much pleasure as they can before it is too late. It's pathetic to see how, early in the morning, the walking and cycling begins. Some hurrying and others stopping suddenly to perform exercises, violently wrenching their stiff limbs. And still others, deep in thought, pace themselves slowly just like the seagulls that form a line facing the sun in deep silence, as if they were gazing somewhere beyond the sun's flames and then take off with a shriek in search of food amidst the crowd of walkers who don't even pay attention to them.

The comments by readers and writers on the book *In Di Getzelten fun Avrom,* or in its Hebrew title, *B'Ohelei Avraham*, are exceptionally good. Articles have appeared both here and in Israel. And the sale of the book, especially of the Hebrew version in Israel, is surprising. But still, it doesn't lift my creative spirits. I am always tired and my head is heavy. Sometimes I make the attempt, but the desire immediately dissipates. And when the day ends, there is a feeling of emptiness.

The nights are even worse, full of nightmares. In my sleep I sense that time is running out and I can't grasp it. I am enclosed by a tightening ring, a nightmarish presence, which I can't recall on awakening but the inexplicable heaviness weighs on me. I tried to describe this to the doctor, but he says that I must free myself from this through activity, the cause is not physical. But how does one liberate oneself? I try to immerse myself in ancient sacred texts, searching for meaning in our ancestors. But I seldom find anything. He hopes that with the coming of spring the external conditions – the grey skies, the sharp winds – will disappear and things will begin to blossom everywhere including myself. Then once more I will regain the desire to create. May it be so. I try again to force myself to sit at my desk, first writing down notes for myself to be used later – if there is a later – for something significant. Maybe this will help.

[APRIL 7 OR 8, 1975. JEWISH GENERAL HOSPITAL]

All the doors are closing. People pass by no longer seeing you. Was it all only an illusion? Even so, it was still a good life. Farewell. Don't try to convince yourself otherwise. I am very, very, tired dearest ones.

WEDNESDAY

What can I tell you that you do not know yourselves. Take care of mother and the children. And if you can, publish the books. I know that I am dead tired of this bitter world. There was a great flaw in creation, especially in humankind. Don't mourn too long. Everything is one enormous illusion. I am terribly tired.

APRIL, 1975

During the ten days that I spent in the hospital I had three dreams in which I was summoned. The first time, the mist was so thick with faces and all sorts of visions that I could not recognize them nor could they recognize me. I only heard: "How much longer will you remain there, you have been gone for such a long time." This hurt me and I responded, "This is none of your concern, have I taken anything away from you? And if I had remained and been destroyed with the whole family, would that have made it easier for you? This way, I was able to rescue a lot of people." So the fog lifted and generations of townsfolk and children jostled each other as my mother's smiling face appeared through the fog, drawing close to my face nodding approval, " Of course, you're perfectly right."

"Mister Zipper I have to draw blood. It is time to get up."

The second time, I knew that it was midnight and a crowd of familiar people – whose names I could not remember – were walking about the Tishevitzer lanes, shoving against me and exclaiming in astonishment, "Look at this, he has returned. Why don't we inform the authorities? Hasn't he been free long enough?" Another voice replies, "I don't know his name." "And if you did know his name, you low-life, would you betray him after fifty years? Don't you know what he accomplished by escaping from here? Just look around and see how many flower pots and get-well cards fill the room. He established an entire community there. See how their faces glow in his presence. I'm telling you to shut your mouth and cease maligning him." The clear image of my father hovers over all the shadows, which are transformed into silhouette-like figures. And a pale light brightens the grey dawn.

"Mister Zipper, swallow this pill," says the dark skinned nurse, her smile showing off her dimples.

The third time there is an outcry and tumult from well-cared-for children being harassed by emaciated demons who are shouting, "Hasn't the time come yet? When will it come?" And the smiling children reply, "What do you know about time? What remains to be done with time?" At this point the smiling face of Avreml Gonshor appears, saying, "Do you remember how you placed me on your shoulders and introduced me to the children? You said, in a voice that sang, 'He comes from far, far, away.' Don't look at them, come with me now, I want to ask you what I should do with my child." "It isn't time yet, it isn't time yet," chanted the children, "not yet time."

MAY 7, 1975

I looked forward to spring and hoped that the warmer weather would ease my condition. However, on Monday, April 7th, suddenly I had another heart attack. The doctor still considers it a mild attack. I was in the hospital for three weeks. The first days I was in a trance, more asleep than awake. Then things improved. Now it is almost two weeks since I have been home. Still very tired and most of all I don't feel like doing anything; everything seems superfluous and unnecessary. I no longer believe that things ought to be done. Nevertheless, for the last two days, I have been trying to answer letters. The reaction of friends, both near and far, encourages me slightly, but the nights are filled with nightmares. I awake more fatigued than ever. Above all, there is the fear that I can no longer do anything. I know that this is an emotional reaction, but I still can't free myself from the feeling that the chapter of my active life draws to a close, and what I had wished to accomplish – writing the book about my Canadian experience – is now beyond my reach. I sense that something heavy lurks behind my back.

Among the notes and papers written in the hospital there are some small pages evidently written in the first days when I was still in intensive care. [See above entry for April 7, 1975.] And the longer sheets were written in the second week. Looks like the feeling of dying was part of the attack. Fragments of this feeling are with me to this day. I try to overcome this. Will I be successful? The feeling that I had expressed there still keeps recurring: "All the gates are closing. People pass by no longer seeing you."

MAY 12, 1975

The days are lovely and warm. The tree in the garden has blossomed. Sitting outdoors these days, I noticed that the first buds to open were those facing the northwest. The sun shines on them nearly a whole day. Only the cherry tree hasn't bloomed. Stands like a spinster amongst blooming, adorned mothers. It grieves me to see them like this. Have had several visitors who bring the breath of the outside world and ongoing life. While they are here I feel well. But when they leave, I am saddened. And looking through the window I feel detached, having lost contact with the world. Some visitors leave me with the sense that everyone looks upon me in this way. But yet I know that I must help myself. I try to draw thoughts together, and take examples from others who overcame this condition. Plans for new creative projects come to mind, but I still can't undertake them.

JUNE 1, 1975

Today at lunchtime was the first time I went among people, and moreover, attended the wedding of a pupil whom I had taught eighteen years earlier. I remember that time as if it were today. A woman with a little girl of five or six years old comes into my office when we were still located on Duluth. The mother had a beseeching expression, and the child with a blank look as if she understood nothing, but with an odd stubbornness in her eyes and sharply etched mouth. "I actually have a Yiddish school not far from our house," she tells me, "and I have already been to all the Yiddish schools, but no one wants to admit my child," she says, breaking into tears. "They advise me to send her to an institution. She is nearly six years old, and still can't speak properly, and doesn't have the comprehension of other children her age. How can I send her away, this mute tongue? They told me that you attend to such children and that your teachers are prepared to help them." During the mother's tale, the little girl concentrated totally on her mother's lips and sort of stretched and stood on her tip-toes as if to show her full height and suddenly stammered, "Malca isn't dumb, not dumb." This tore at my heart and her keen gaze scalded me. I learned that she had already been in public school for a few days and had been sent home since she was taller than the children of her age, and was unable to participate with them. The children laughed at her and the teachers lost patience. In addition, the psychologists diagnosed her as someone who could not be considered as teachable. But noting her determined expression and her outcry, it seemed to me that this child had character and wanted to overcome her difficulties. So I said to the mother that I would very much like to help her but would have to examine the doctor's report, and especially speak to the teachers of kindergarten, which was the grade where they would be able to give her attention and let her do what she was capable of. And that the parents had to promise to cooperate with the teachers and me in the case of any difficulties. I will call her tomorrow with my decision.

"We are simple people and we will do everything you tell us," the woman said as she stood up and took Malca's hand, asking her to thank me. Malca, however, clung to the desk, refused to leave and stammered angrily (she had presumed that I had refused to accept her): "Malca's dumb, Mr Zipper doesn't want me either." The manner of her speech cut at my heart and I felt as if she had thrown nettles at my face. "He is like everyone else," she barely stammered in her hoarse voice. Putting her arms around her mother's dress, she dragged her to the door as if she wanted to escape from here as quickly as possible. This scene moved me so deeply that I ran after her and immediately decided. "Come Malca, I will show you the kindergarten where you will be coming tomorrow morning to be with all the little children." She let me lead her and standing in the room murmured once more, "Malca not dumb? Not dumb." My hand is still warm from the handclasp of gratitude she gave me then.

It wasn't easy to convince the teachers and especially the children to consider her as one of their own, and as one who had special privileges to do as she pleased. But we overcame this. Her will and her determination to achieve was indescribable. She had to repeat kindergarten and until grade two she repeated each class in order to achieve the minimum standard. This was accomplished with the help of Motty, who was the school's psychologist, and the efforts of the teachers and children, who grew accustomed to her. And above all, because of her strong will and our exempting her from examinations and reducing her workload. Due to these arrangements, she was able to complete all seven grades. After that, I was able to convince the principal of Outremont High School to admit her and allow her to progress in the school in a similar fashion with a special program. After finishing high school she was ready to undertake clerical work. At first she got a job in her father's store, where she became accustomed to keeping things in order and even to attending the cash register. Now she works effectively in an office where she does technical jobs. There she met a young man. So how could I not attend such a wedding? It was very moving to see the betrothed couple. And beside him Malca stood two-heads taller, virtually a lovely, blooming rose. She had conquered her dullness. She led him by the hand. What will become of such a couple, who knows? My heart trembles. Still, in all this time she was guided toward becoming a worthy person and her face shone with happiness. "I will never forget you and Motty as well," she whispered over and over again. Naturally, her parents cooperated all the time and remain grateful to this day. It became their custom to bring a bottle of whiskey as a present every Chanukah.

JUNE 4, 1975

Last evening I went out among people for the first time since my heart attack to see the play that Dora Wasserman and her group had prepared, *A Bintel Brief*, Avraham Shulman's dramatization of the letters to the editor of the *Forwarts* at the beginning of the century. One can only marvel at what one person with great love for the theatre and stubborn persistence can accomplish. Of all the attempts at creating a theatre group, she was successful in taking Canadian Jewish young men and women and training them to portray Jewish life that they had never seen but had only heard about in our schools or from their parents. A large number of them were former pupils of ours. They act with such enthusiasm and emotion that it extends to the audience. She has been working with the group for nearly two decades and is always attracting new actors. What determination can achieve! The national and cultural value of her theatre for the local Jewish audience cannot be overestimated. They have been performing for more than two weeks and the spectators come twice or three times to refresh themselves with the familiar melodies and the group's enthusiasm. I certainly came home tired, but it was worth it.

JUNE 9, 1975

Yesterday was at the J.I. Segal Awards evening, now in its seventh year. The prizewinners, except for the artists, are all well known: Y. Elberg, Shainzohn, and Adele Wiseman, a former student from Winnipeg. A very fine evening, though the program was a bit too long. Barrels of flowery language that threaten to make you gag. Only the artist, Jan Menses, said a few appropriate, tasteful words. I was somewhat annoyed that here too there is a tendency to forget the original founders. Both on the invitation and at the evening, the accomplishments of the Rosenfelds – who had established the fund and took the initiative to attract other contributors – was minimized. Today's activists think that in this way they do themselves a favour. For myself, it was an emotional experience to see so many familiar friends and family for the first time after my heart attack. They gave me strength and at the same time wore me out with their warm blessings and happy exclamations at seeing one another once again. Today I am really very tired, but it was worthwhile attending that celebration.

AUGUST 7, 1975

This week there were two memorial dates: The outbreak of World War I, when on the second day, Tishevitz began counting her casualties and recited the prayer justifying divine judgment to the very end of the war. In the same days of *Elul*, in the days of Hitler, may his name be erased, the entire town was destroyed, and now lives on only in our literary works and in the memorial book. Then, too, the *shofar* was blown in the houses of study and in the synagogue and the sound hovered somewhere in the emptiness.

OCTOBER 6, 1975

Already a week since the High Holidays have passed. And the month of our wedding anniversaries have gone by. Fifty years of our wedding, twenty years of Ode and Motty's, eighteen years of Chana and Mark's, as well as their son Jonathan's Bar Mitzvah. The anniversaries will be celebrated this month with the children on a trip to the mountains of Vermont. The Bar Mitzvah celebration was wonderful. There were a number of out-of-town guests. It gave me the feeling of happiness that I have lived to see this, as well as a feeling of anxious hope for the Bar Mitzvah boy, who has reached the first step. He is delighted with his presents and those that will follow. The weddings, however, especially ours, is for us a glimpse into the past from which we draw strength. Especially when we compare ourselves to others, we were truly blessed, even in the most trying of times. Certainly it is a joyful event, but given my mood of the last few months, I still can't focus my senses to experience the complete pleasure. There is a red thread constantly before my eyes saying: "You see, I am becoming shorter and shorter so don't lose a moment." But that in itself paralyzes one's will to undertake anything or make long-range plans. So I waste time and occupy myself with petty matters that are in essence not creative and not what I desire. A strange discouragement holds me in its spell. Could it mean that the wellspring of creation has dried up? There are so many explanations for this. Sometimes physical weakness, but mainly spiritual emptiness accompanied by the feeling: What for, why, and for whom?

Yesterday I visited Melech Ravitch in the hospital, where he is recovering from a prostate operation. It turned out to be a rather fine day. When we entered he was dozing, breathing heavily through his open mouth in which could be seen several black, gnarled, stumps of worn-down teeth. His nose, turned upward, trembled as did his rigid knees under the sheets. When he awoke, for a moment he stared at us as if without recognition, but when Rochl told him, "The Zippers are here," he broke into a smile and mumbled, "Of course," and stretched out his hand to us and began to relate something that we barely understood. But Rochl clarified his words by explaining to us that for the past few days, after she leaves, a student sits in the room supervising the patients because nurses are on a partial strike, which results in insufficient care. It appears that Ravitch thinks that the student wants to harm him so hides from him in bed. When the student approaches him to change his position, he becomes even more frightened. It seems that his pills bring on a semi-hallucinatory state, and the view he sees from the sixth floor can also induce images of fantasy. All the roofs of the buildings on both sides are constructed in the gothic style with cornices and vaults that appear to lie in shadows even during the day when struck by the distant light, recalling the medieval towns of Europe. At night they look like an enchanted castle. So he often feels as in a trap, and images emerge that he had once seen during his early experiences and travels. When Rochl and Sorke left the room for a few moments, he winked at me to bend over toward him and in broken sentences began to relate a two-part story. "Rochl doesn't understand, but you will understand. He looks like a man from the mountains with a double mask at the back of his head, and an angry expression on his face, and is constantly asking, "What are you doing here, why don't you go home." Then he wears a sailor's cap and stands on a ship. He prevents me from entering and laughingly says, "Do you have a ticket to travel? You are better off going home." At this point he smiled. "This has been occurring for several days." When Rochl returned she gave him something to drink, despite his objections, but she convinced him and after several swallows, he calmed down and made an effort to say something, but it was difficult to grasp what he wanted. His mouth straightened but didn't open.

OCTOBER 9, 1975

According to the Jewish calendar I turned seventy-five last Tuesday on the second day of *Cheshvan*; on the general calendar it comes out tomorrow, the tenth of October. Today in the evening, the children along with Rivke and Berl and their children are coming to celebrate, as it were. Next weekend we will be going out to Vermont to mark our fiftieth wedding anniversay, and on that occasion will include all the other significant dates: the wedding, the birthday, and the fiftieth year in Canada. Chaim Weinshel and Fradle and Barry Freidenreich will also be there. A big to-do. I have mixed feelings, it is a joy and a sadness. After all, it celebrates a closure and not a beginning with a long vista. I still would like to do so much, especially creative work, where the philosophical saying, "It is not up to you to complete the work," does not apply. Incomplete creative works are an interrupted chord that destroy artistic wholeness. Obviously, this affects your mood, hindering you at the outset from even beginning a major work. This troubles me continuously.

OCTOBER 22, 1975

Last weekend the children took us to Bolton Valley Lodge in Vermont to mark all the anniversaries and my birthday. Chaim Weinshel, a close friend from the twenties in Ustilla, came from Milwaukee. Having a witness to my early beginnings made this a special event. It was in Ustilla that my community work actually began. This was impossible in Tishevitz. For the son of a ritual slaughterer it was sufficiently audacious to risk sneaking into the community meeting place. But in Ustilla, despite being illegal too, I could act without restraint. And the HaDor Hatzair encircled me with warmth and considered me as one of their teachers and leaders. Fradle and Barry Freidenreich, friends of ours and our children were here too, a family connection that goes back to Fradle's parents, Chaim Pomerantz, may he rest in peace. He was a fine Yiddish teacher and cultural activist, who was cut down in his 50s. And his wife, Pessie Pomerantz Honigbaum, may her years be extended, is a fine poet.

OCTOBER 23, 1975

The resolution of the "humanitarian" commision of the United Nations to consider Zionism as identical with racism naturally stinks of oil. However, what it indicates unequivocally is that the world does not remember and is ready for a horrible descent. They think that only the designated victim will suffer, and afterwords they will bemoan the victim's fate. But this time it won't work that way. If the world, and the so-called free world, will not restrain the uncontrolled so-called third world, which, no matter what justifiable grievances they have, doesn't mean that Israel or the Jews are responsible, and if they won't understand this once and for all, then Samson's cry, "Let me die with the Philistines," will have to be repeated. Meanwhile Israel is isolated, only America is an open friend, but also with reservations. And the other twenty nations who voted against the resolution this time only did it because of America. The skin crawls to think that only thirty years after the Nazi era the majority of the world's nations speak the language of Nazism, and the devil licks his chops, laughter in his eyes. Strange how symbolic this is. Seventy nations – actually seventy states – had voted against Zionism. Factually, this means voting against Israel and the people of Israel.

OCTOBER 31, 1975

After a delay of more than a year, the school leaders once again began to organize a celebration in honour of the sixtieth anniversary of the schools. They want to combine it with an evening to honour Wiseman and myself. They don't know, or they pretend ignorance, of the fact that in regard to us, we are not at all in the mood for this now, and not only due to poor health.

When I proposed such a celebration three years ago, I had in mind a festive occasion that would, in writing and speeches, reflect the values of the school and not just a time to honour individuals. At that time they didn't take this into consideration, played politics amongst themselves over issues that escaped me completely. We were both against the current game of dispensing honours, which would have engendered, I fear, much aggravation and very little pleasure, but the few older *chaverim* in the leadership simply beseeched us to have it since the mood of the activists is such that it threatens the whole structure of the school. Therefore they are hoping that this event will break the mood. If we refuse this would depress the activists further. So we subjugated our own feelings. Maybe it will have a positive effect after all. This won't be the first time that we do something against our will but had to so that peace would prevail.

NOVEMBER 14, 1975

Yesterday it was still autumn and the dried fallen leaves rustled under our feet. The naked trees, disrobed of their summer finery, stretched their bare branches like fingers upward in all directions, as if listening intently to that which had to come. At night the first snow fell and the branches are laden and bowed, surrendering themselves to the hovering mass that swings them earthward. It looks as if they are saying: "We have to stay close to one another and accept fate as it comes." The few evergreens at my window are crowded branch to branch and only the northern side is a solid wall. "This is the way we will survive." Thus they give in to the wind and the wet snowfall. The south side is wide open like a gaping mouth trying to breathe freely, avoiding suffocation. The children, encumbered in their warm clothing, are gleefully rolling wet snowballs and building tunnels with snowmen beside them. Where will these tunnels lead to? Are they mysterious passages to the sunny world that has suddenly disappeared, or is it just an illusory refuge where one can hide for the moment and lull oneself with a dream of non-existent sanctuaries?

The honorary evening took place on the 13th. There was a gathering of almost 600 people, amongst them former school activists, pupils, and friends. People came from Toronto and New York. The atmosphere was splendid, full of warmth. Unfortunately, it lasted too long, so the guest speaker, *Chaver* Katzman, declined to speak, since he had been left to the end. That was an indication that we should have involved ourselves in the organization of the program. I can't forgive myself for not having realized this earlier so that I should have been satisfied with a few words and given him my allotted time. Truthfully, I wanted to unburden myself, but this was insignificant as compared to his refusal to speak, which led to his grief, my own, and the audience's in general.

JANUARY 4, 1976

The last week, the so-called holiday week, we say farewell to the old year and anticipate the new one. Strange how every year at this time events run through my mind as if they were hurrying to be included in the old year, while others hasten to be among the first events of the New Year. Most of these are catastrophies: Fires that consume human victims; storms and tornadoes; airplane crashes; and earthquakes. Every morning has its allotment. At the same time everyone is getting ready to celebrate publicly or in the privacy of their homes. It gives the impression that everyone wants to seize the day or to put their best foot forward. Really, as if it is an enactment of "Let's eat and drink for tomorrow we die." An unconscious agitation vanquishes everyone.

JANUARY 10, 1976

We are getting ready to go to Miami. Sorke is busy packing. I am affected by strange feelings. On the one hand, there is a strong desire to go. I still retain the good feeling left by spending a month there with Rivke and Berl. On the other hand, I constantly see before my eyes literally hundreds of aged and feeble people walking around on the seashore doing all kinds of exercises to strengthen their limbs, and when you catch their glance you sense a kind of hidden fear that anxiously says: "Will this be of any help? Can we really hide from all the diseases which hasten the inevitable?" Or an image flits by of a crowd of middle-aged and old people with lifeless eyes and crippled limbs, especially women, dressed up as for an exhibition, sitting in rows on the front balconies, looking across Collins Avenue as if waiting for someone. Am I running away to hide, too? I know that it will be easier to get about there, and most importantly, I will be able to go out and not have to sit indoors. Maybe there the desire to write and express myself will return; and I am actually preparing a large number of notes to be worked on. Possibly there they will unfold and take on skin and bones. Though I have the feeling that it will not happen that way. A kind of shadow shakes its head regretfully behind my back. Who knows what it means or if it means anything at all, and even if it signifies something – we're going. Whatever comes, we will certainly avoid the cold here.

APRIL 9, 1976

Yesterday will be a week since I returned from the hospital with a "heart regulator" on the left side of my heart. The pacemaker, as it is called, keeps the heart beating normally and helps it function properly. According to the doctor's words, "better than before." But the feeling that has pursued me all year since the first serious heart attack – which the doctor called a mild attack – that I am living on borrowed time and feel as if I perceive everything as from "the other side," as Rochl Korn refers to it, is now even stronger. And even if during waking hours the feeling is less acute, it comes at night with weird dreams that are muddled but of an entirely different nature than the usual ones.

Two days later, the pain felt like deeply driven spikes and as soon as I closed my eyes I began to wander amid places unknown and the feeling of being in two worlds did not subside, even after I returned home. I have accustomed myself to the idea that beneath the skin close to my left shoulder lies a battery that I have not seen with my own eyes, but I feel it, which should aid in breathing, regulating the heartbeat. On the walks that I have taken, I do feel that it helps my legs as well, reducing the usual pain.

APRIL 25, 1976

The evening was held in honour of the publication of *In Di Getzelten fun Avrom*, both in the Hebrew and Yiddish editions, which had been postponed three times because of my illness. It gave me a good feeling to see such a large audience – about four hundred people – and hear all the good wishes. And today the phone calls persist. Whether the attendance was really an earnest response or merely a desire for a Saturday night's entertainment, or that it was improper not to attend, nevertheless, it was a moving experience. The speakers – Shimshon Dunsky and Chaim Spilberg – spoke thoughtfully and respectfully, and Chana Gonshor read excerpts very well. The audience responded enthusiastically. My remarks consisted mainly of acknowledging those past and present, intimates and acquaintances, who to this day have a share in my career and my writings. The event encouraged me somewhat, although in an audience of this size there were only three prospects to purchase the book in Hebrew, and nineteen in Yiddish. This undermined my sense of confidence. In truth, it can be said about the Yiddish edition of the book that a large part of the audience had obtained it earlier. While the Hebraists are not known as book-buyers, especially by local writers.

MAY 28, 1976

Yesterday evening was the first graduation exercise of Bialik High School. As might be expected at such an occasion, there was a large audience of parents, teachers, and some activists, in a festive mood. Not to speak of the youngsters, who were overjoyed with their achievements. They have no conception of what awaits them in their future educational institutions, where no one will stand over them and show concern for each individual. They were all radiant and behaved impeccably. I remember a large number of the pupils since their arrival in nursery and kindergarten. Now, they are grown up, some are reserved and bashful, others arrogant and aggressive in all their motions and even in their speeches. But in the words of several speakers a note of dissatisfaction could be felt with the school's outlook, which fails to provide a clear direction or lasting beliefs they could cling to; unable to answer the doubts that arise with maturity. They think that a secular education can provide this, but to my mind only a doctrinaire approach can do so, and then only to a certain degree of success and for a limited time. Still it is very important to discuss these aforementioned issues in all seriousness. It looks as if the younger generation seems unable to make peace with ambiguity. The speeches by the teachers were short and more literary than practical as befits a valedictory. Aside from the principal, Mr Robinson, who is not Jewish, no one characterized our institution as being essentially Jewish. This was only referred to here and there in the florid cliches and in reference to Israel. Ironically, it was he who called on the graduates to participate in the Jewish community here, and to consider a stay in Israel for a year or two in order to get a taste of physical labour and construction. Until his remarks and the speeches of the students in four languages, a cold wind blew from the head table, a kind of resigned detachment.

Wiseman and I were given the honour of granting the diplomas to the graduates. How long has it been since we bestowed the honour on the original founders and wished them long life and the hope that they would attend a high school graduation. Now we are the veterans and knowing how little the students are taking away with them even after high school left me feeling sad. Still, looking at the shining faces of the youngsters and listening to their clear though questioning thoughts, I reconsidered: The school still represents something substantial and marvelous in our vulgarized and uncivilized world. May even this small amount of knowledge serve them well. Ten years from now, I imagine, they will produce a good number of doctors, lawyers, professors, scientists, and intellectuals, as well as businessmen and journalists, and possibly one or two writers and poets. And the world will remain as it always has been. Who can envy them or prejudge them in advance? We can't ask for anything more than continuity, so we should be pleased that at one time we had lent a hand to this effort, and today, were able to enhance their celebration.

JULY 5, 1976

All last week the Jewish world, and it would appear, the western world too, were overwrought and confounded by the capture of a French airplane with more than 250 passengers, travelling from Israel to Paris. The release of the terrorists and most of the passengers through the intervention of the Ugandan bandit, and leaving more that 100 Jews as hostages, emphatically underscored the Jews' designation as victims and the world's helplessness. It appeared that Israel would have to give in to the terror in order to save so many lives. Like a flash of lightning and a legendary miracle, the grim defencelessness was lit up by the extraordinary deed of the Israeli commandos, who snatched the hostages from the very mouth of the terrorists, by swooping down on the tarmac at Entebbe with three airplanes, and with few fatalities freed the prisoners. The whole world sighed with relief and stood in wonderment at the daring exploit. The African dictators, with the exception of Kenya, join the world "liberator" Russia, and the Arab nations, who grit their teeth and demand a trial by the United Nations to condemn Israel for aggression. Idi Amin is the Cossack who lost out. And it is probably better this way; Israel will be able to demonstrate as she has done many times before that her accusers are those helping the terrorists. The western countries will be forced to speak openly now acknowledging the country that represents the conscience of humanity. The mysterious ways of history demonstrate ironically that the People of the Book take up the sword to show how to combat the evil of the world.

JULY 15, 1976

It looks like there is still a tiny bit of undetected justice in this disembowelled world. The Security Council, after permitting pails of hatred to be poured over Israel and trying to portray Uganda as the defeated Cossack, the Africans withdrew the resolution to condemn Israel since they realized that they had insufficient support. This time England, France, and especially America spoke with determination and praised Israel's action. Herzog was right when he said that the fact that they didn't pass the resolution was praise for Israel.

JULY 17, 1976

Because of the political machinations around today's opening of the Olympic Games – and I must grant that it was beautifully prepared and impressive; if only it were true that the Games were a symbol of the brotherhood of man – they pushed aside the truly important achievement of human science and the desire to penetrate the secrets of creation, in the landing of a spacecraft on Mars. For nearly a year it flew almost 250 million miles from the earth and began to transmit photos and perform experiments. It takes your breath away. The common imagination simply can not grasp how the robots are controlled from the earth by computers that react to the light-impulses, and they can even regulate and correct the robots' incorrect turns and moves. Actually, the whole world should be holding its breath and observing this achievement with pride and astonishment. Instead, they sit before the TV and stare in wonderment at the athletes. In truth the gymnastics are works of art, evidence of what man can achieve with his body; but on the whole, it is a show of strength, exhibiting the instinct to dominate and to deliver blows. The construction of the stadium and the security arrangements for the athletes, which make certain areas of the city look as if under siege, have cost over a billion dollars, and that is besides the expenses of each participating country.

JULY 25, 1976

Went to see the Canadian exhibition mounted for the Olympic Games at the Bonaventure Convention Centre. The range of Canadian riches and artistic creativity captivates the eye – from the primitive to the zenith of modern artistry. All the provinces are represented with their individual characteristics. It's a pity that this is taking place when the schools are closed, they should be taking advantage of this for educational purposes. It can also strengthen the national identity at a time when provocative nationalism is exploiting the language issue to divide the country. It was a wonderful idea to bring some young and older men and women from the far north of Canada. Eskimos and Indians from various tribes, and several white people, who, in sound and movement, portrayed their forms of recreation and ways of life. Their unique forms of art in stone, bone, and a combination of stone and wood, are part of the exhibition. Listening to them and seeing how primitive their mode of expression still is, and how their music emerges from the deep, lonely, cry of nature's elemental forces, we realize how far we have progressed from the primeval forest.

JULY 29, 1976

Went to visit Ravitch in the hospital. It was painful to see the disintegration of such a man before your eyes. You stand helpless, unable to do anything. He won't let the sheet cover him and lies uncovered, yellowed skin and bones, restless, open-mouthed, thin pointed nose, and only Rochl, who by now looks shrunken, can understand what he is saying. Continuously folding and pushing the sheet away from himself in a heap. "I have been imprisoned," he says angrily, and refuses to eat anything. Suddenly he calls out to Rochl, "Write a letter to the authors and tell them to form a committee to save Yiddish literature. There is still much to do." His eyes stare into a unknown world located beyond us. "Ride over to Sholem Asch's," he exclaims, suddenly awakening from slumber. At one point, it seems as if he recognizes me. "Tell Zipper, too, he will be able to advise you." Then the doctors come in along with his son Yossel, who has arrived from Israel. He caresses his head and weeps. Ravitch is preoccupied with his own agitation, and speaks to no one. Yet to the nurse who takes his pulse and blood pressure he responds "yes" or "no." When I tell him that he ought to eat and drink so he can get stronger and better, he glances away and mumbles, "That makes no difference, what is important is literature," and reverts to his restlessness. The doctors leave, saying that nothing can be done for him. I simply don't know what is happening to him nor the cause of his agitation.

AUGUST 23, 1976

Last night, at the end of Shabbos, the 22nd of August, Ravitch, may he rest in peace, was freed from his travails and terrible suffering. The funeral is scheduled for tomorrow at noon, the 24th of August. His solemn and noble outcry has been sealed off in a deaf world and his exalted dream remains suspended in reverie. It was known that the end was near. At our final visit of a few days ago it was terrible to watch his clutching Rochl's hand in his right hand, while his left hand twisted the blanket back and forth, continually pushing it as if to conceal a deep chasm. In his skeletal appearance he barely opened his eyes for a moment, nor closed his open mouth. Even though we knew, the news of his passing that came on Sunday morning truly made a hole in my heart, and upset me so that I still can't calm down. Sunday afternoon several people met with Rochl at her house. The majority of close friends are now in Jerusalem attending the Yiddish conference. After reading his will, the turmoil became even more acute. Especially due to his unambiguous statement that even though he believes in the immortality of the soul and only the body perishes, and he believes with complete faith that he can hear us as we now read his will, that his body should be cremated, and that his ashes should not be stored in a single place but should be scattered over the graves of Spinoza and Peretz. If this is unfeasible, then Rochl and the family should decide where to keep it. He would not mind if the traditional prayer of mourning were recited and a chapter of Psalms, as well as a number of his poems, were read. Some of us felt that a writer of such stature does not belong to himself alone, and I tried to give a theoretical basis to this conception by saying the respect for the dead requires that we accompany him into eternity in accordance with the generations-old custom of our people. Therefore we have the right to say, as the ancient sages held: "Those who forego the honour due to someone, forego their own honour," and in this way free the family from his written request to be cremated which wouldn't be acceptable by the general public as the proper homage due him. Many would consider cremation as an open sacrilege to the accepted tradition.

After extended deliberations and consulting with his son in Israel – and he too sought advice from several Israeli writers – the family decided to obey the will. And since he had requested a simple funeral, they interpreted this to mean that only the necessary measures should be carried out. A brief eulogy by Shloime Wiseman, a reading of his son's message, and a reading of two poems that he had designated. His Rochl insisted that she wanted to read them. Incidentally, Rochl's attitude toward him is somewhat pathological and pathetic. It is not only love, but a kind of religious reverence and submission to his will that borders on a compulsion to obey. "I feel that I must find the inner strength to do this for him," she said when I asked her whether she would be able to do this. In any event we asked Nachum Wilchesky to read the poems in case she was overcome. There will also be a reading of Psalm 15 and the mourning prayer, *El Moleh Rachamim*, read by myself. Under these circumstances, of course, it is not possible to invite a *chazan* who might be placed in an embarrassing position, and undoubtedly elicit unpleasant remarks from the zealots, of whom there is no shortage. It is the first time that I am participating in this way to give honour to the deceased. It would seem that one has to be tested in this too.

AUGUST 25, 1976

Yesterday was Ravitch's funeral. A large crowd attended. An honour guard stood at the coffin. In the private room upstairs we saw him at peace in the casket. All the distortions of his face, evident in the last few years and especially in the final weeks in the hospital, were wiped away. Beyond restlessness, beyond turmoil, just peace. It was a bit shocking to have photographs taken at this juncture, another stage of his passionate life. But Rochl desired this because in his will he had mentioned that if possible a plaster mask be made, his final condition vanquished by the mask.

Wiseman delivered the eulogy in a restrained and sensitive way, in succinct terms presented a picture of his life and deeds on earth. But I felt that what was missing was the grief of passing, and the personal pain. Maybe it is not possible to express this. But there was enough simplicity in his words that the unadorned remarks were most effective. Rochl herself read the few passages that Yossel had dictated to her over the telephone and then read the two poems, *There is No Death* and *Tropisher Koshmar in Singapore,* a beautiful poem, I consider it to be one of his best where his philosophy is rendered through story and image rather than direct statement. I very much wanted to recite Psalm 15 with my father's *niggun* if only because when I used to meet Ravitch he would ask me to sing a *niggun*. But I was held back by the feeling that I always have when I hear a *chazan* chanting verses of Psalms at a funeral and reciting the *Moleh* prayer with a *niggun* and showing off his voice, I feel that the *niggun* and the voice detract from the sense of respect due the deceased. So standing before the audience I decided that in reciting the words as simply as possible and without dramatic inflections would be more moving and authentic. I was deeply affected and I sensed the same emotion in the audience. Later, a number of people echoed this same sentiment.

SEPTEMBER 21, 1976

Last evening we returned from Providence, Rhode Island, where we had travelled with the children, to Joel's Bar Mitzvah. I had doubts about being able to travel back and forth on one weekend, a trip of eight hours by car each way. We decided to go; after all it is Leibl's first born. I still remember well the doubts Leibl had about giving Joel a Jewish education and sending him to our school. And when he decided to send him, he himself drew closer to Jewish life. When he moved to Providence and gained prominence in his field and in recent years became internationally renowned, he became more openly Jewish, and became an active member of the conservative synagogue, while his children became more closely bound to that form of *Yiddishkeit*. So we had to go and celebrate. Everything went well. It was a kind of family reunion on both sides.

END OF ROSH HASHANAH, 5737

One blow follows another. Leo Roskies is no longer with us. Suddenly he had to undergo a kidney operation to extract a kidney stone, which they had been waiting for a year to pass by itself. The operation was successful but his weak heart could not bear the strain. Just some days ago I saw him at the memorial for Ravitch, and now it is all over. He was a close friend and an extraordinarily gentle person, with a warm heart and open hand for every national cause, especially for Yiddish and Jewish education. Our circle becomes more and more impoverished. The generation disappears before our eyes, and there is no one to replace it. Of late, we look into each other's eyes in mute silence, but the message is clear enough: Who follows him, whose turn will be next? He was among the immigrants who came just after World War II, and his home immediately became the meeting place. Innumerable plans and programs were realized in that house. He assumed a leading community role and imbued his children with a deep attachment to continuity. Both his daughter, Ruth, and son, David, will contribute significantly to Jewish creative life in diverse fields. Now, he too is only a memory. For how long?

THE INTERMEDIATE DAYS OF SUCCOS, 5737

Just had several stressful but festive days. The Eismans were visiting, bringing with them the fragrance of their kibbutz. Their warm and humane manner of socializing quickly won over the members of our circle. The evening for them at the Farband House was attended by a large audience. His poetry is not easily understood by the general reader, but his own modesty and sincerity made him attractive. Even the writers were pleased with his reception. Sold a good number of his books and he also received an honorarium for the reading. The visit exhausted Sorke. It look like there comes a time when even pleasure and real happiness with close friends becomes onerous and tiring.

OCTOBER 25, 1976

Before we had a chance to rest up from the visitors from Israel, Fein arrived for a few days on his way home from Toronto, where he had given a lecture. He is always a welcome guest, with whom it is possible to have a serious discussion. But his constant nervousness arouses your own agitation. He finds it difficult to accept his loneliness in Boston. He recovered a bit here, in part from our hospitality and from several friends who invited him to their homes. We spent a wonderful evening at the Elbergs. There, one is immersed in Jewish history and surrounded by Judaic artifacts of diverse materials. It is a miniature museum of Jewish artifacts. Fein happened to be here too for Grosbard's evening, which had a large attendance. His eyes were literally filled with tears: "This can only be seen in Montreal." He simply couldn't believe his eyes. He was even astonished by the number of telephone calls that we receive from all kinds of people. "What a large circle of friends you have here! You have no idea how fortunate you are. My telephone hardly rings, except for my children." And he, in turn, has no one to call. Is this the fault of the city, or his own fault? It is very hard for him to select friends. His constant self-deprecation plays an important role in this. And especially now, after Chaya's death, he is really lost and can't find a place for himself.

NOVEMBER 12, 1976

The bond is severed. Yesterday we rose from *shiva* for Henneh, may she rest in peace. The youngest of the sisters is the first to depart from us. No use in asking questions. The pain is such that no comforting words can bring solace. She took with her all the wonderful talents that, due to her miserable fate, remained almost entirely unfulfilled. She carried all her dreams within, stored away for the future, until it was too late. Her turn to religion in recent years, and her cynicism about mankind, were significant factors in all this. In the final week she withdrew into the past of Tishevitz, and clung to her memories of father and mother's home, and what she had done for them in the last years of her life when she, in order to care for them, completely renounced her own life and career. Aaron, poor soul, hovered over her, exerted himself beyond his ability to ease her pain and give her encouragement. It is a sad sight to see his solitude now. Her leave-taking, before her time, has opened the abyss of the eternal death-sentence and stands palpably before her brothers and her only sister Shifreh, long may she live. We must persevere as much as we can, and support one another. Hasten to do what can be done. "O woe to her beauty which has passed from this world."

NOVEMBER 16, 1976

Yesterday will surely be counted as historic in the history of Quebec and Canada. In the provincial elections, the separatist party won by a huge majority. It was both a surprise and yet expected at the same time. The last Liberal government had lost the confidence of almost all sectors, due to its arrogant manner and corruption. This played into the hands of the separatists who campaigned under the slogan that they are for open and honest government and for separation in the distant future. Everyone was alarmed. The Jewish "leadership" greatly disturbed our community with the frightening threat that a victory of the separatists would mean the ruin of the Jewish community. It will now be difficult to even communicate with the new powers. The public threat that some of them made to leave the province was really foolish and harmful. Woe to us, saddled with such community leadership and those who speak in our name! Undoubtedly there will be several years of uncertainty and probably economic decline. But I don't think that we have reached the stage where we have to start packing up and leaving the province. Though nations usually act with their emotions and national pride in such instances, it is inconceivable that Quebec would actually separate from Canada.

DECEMBER 22, 1976. CHANUKAH, 5737

The cold and the wind are strong so we must sit in the house as in a cage. This adds to my restlessness and upsets my composure. A feeling of finding oneself constrained; hard to follow a thought to its conclusion.

Today I had a visit from a former student from the elementary school, who, after our discussion, still remained, I think, unmoved. He continued to recite his credo, his deep conviction that by becoming a "liberated Jew through belief in Jesus" he has cleansed himself of all sins, and lives in communication with God. When I tried to explain what the authentic belief in God means and what level one must attain to commune with God, he puts forward hackneyed Biblical passages. No sense at all of logical thinking. Historical events do not affect him. He is "liberated" and feels content with this. The commune in which he lives gives him support, and the New Testament is the final word in revelations. His contribution to the group consists in composing music for religious songs. He calls it Jewish music to the

God of Israel. No more, no less! How did he become entangled in this net? He feels that he has a grip on things, but where it leads he has no inkling. It prompts him to become more informed about essential Judaism, but he needs to probe more deeply. Meanwhile he is influenced by his new comrade-teachers, whose aura, it seems, gives him contentment. He says that he can discuss these matters more easily with pious *Chasidic* youth than with non-believers. They, the orthodox, are also fundamentalists. In his case I might have an explanation for the confusion of issues and his grasping at the Jesus cult. His home was atheistic and devoid of any folk symbols and experiences. He was constantly competing with his older brother who was better looking and more capable than he was, and who was leaning toward a career as musician or artist. He was a stutterer as well, and after completing high school he left home and began wandering across the continent. He wrote lyrics set to music that seems to have appealed to other such wandering souls like himself in San Francisco and Berkeley. His emptiness sought fulfillment and desired to demonstrate to his mother and father that he could stand on his own two feet. He says that he has a feeling of love for Yiddish and the Jewish melodies of his school days, but these are insufficient to fill his emotional world with belief.

INTERMEDIATE DAYS OF PESACH, 5737

Already two weeks since we returned from Miami after spending ten weeks there. Still haven't been outside for a walk except when the children pick me up with the car. I caught a cold soon after my return and can't get rid of it. In Miami it was possible to go out even on the cool and windy days. On sunny days I was able to walk for rather long stretches, and avoided taking the buses. I felt very well down there, and often completely forgot that I am a partial invalid who must constantly take care of himself. Because of that my mood too was elated and my consciousness almost free from worry. Here, everything is once again gloomy and oppressive. The desire to get involved, to make plans, is feeble and everything is done after much vacillation. In each case I am conscious of the numerals signifying my age, both as a reminder and as a warning. In addition to this there is the serious political situation in the province. The separatist government is ruled by nationalist emotions and also accompanied by the desire to instruct the minorities to know their place. And the principles of human rights are cast aside with the rationalization that they have to save their language and culture. Economically, this means ousting the English minority and consequently the majority of Jews too who are associated with the English cultural sphere, and taking their place. The dream of Canada as a land of two founding nations where other minorities can also develop freely is now even stoned and spat upon. Young people seriously consider leaving the province, seeing no future for themselves here. The Jewish schools are in great danger.

In order to obtain the government subsidies as in the last number of years, they demand so many hours of French that English subjects are relegated to very few hours, while Jewish subjects are left with almost nothing. Whether the Jewish community is ready to give up the subsidies and finance the schools by itself is a big question, and even if they were ready to do so, it is questionable whether the provincial Education Department would permit enough time to pursue a Jewish education that would be worthy of its name. Most importantly, Yiddish is affected. The mother-city, Montreal, will under these conditions diminish and all our efforts will, I'm afraid, become just a memory, a page in the chronicle of generations that were once here.

THURSDAY, APRIL 14, 1977. 26 *NISSAN*, 5737

After not attending school meetings for a year, yesterday I went to an executive meeting of the school. They are confronting major decisions brought on by the new language regulations of the separatist government. I am anxious to know of these matters, and, as well, I should be present. Sometimes a single voice can help clarify an issue. It has not yet reached the point of decision-making, yet according to the demands of the Department of Education the school would become almost totally French. Only three hours per week for English, and for the Jewish subjects no time is left. Otherwise, they say, the subsidies will not be granted. Naturally, the mood is depressing, because over a million dollars a year is at stake. Still we definitely cannot capitulate. The question, however, is whether the community is ready to assume the responsibility for the upkeep of the schools, and whether the increase of tuition will lead to a reduction in enrollment. As might be anticipated, there is the danger that the community will grow smaller, and especially the affluent classes. Next Monday there will be a meeting with the Minister of Education to find a compromise. Meanwhile they have cancelled the decision to construct a new building, which is needed. In the most optimistic reading, hard times are upon us. Put in flowery terms, the time for a true reckoning and the test of our principles has arrived. In my few words I tried to emphasize that our schools have a mission, both for the Jewish studies that aim to bring the Jewish child into Jewish life, and for the general studies, to connect them, through English, with the cultural life on this continent, and to adjust to the life of this province through French. A middle road must be found for this.

APRIL 27, 1977

Some days ago, Rabbi Hechtman of the *Vaad ha'Ir* asked me to come to his office by taxi, which he would pay for. He has something of urgency to show me and wishes to hear my reaction to it. And since I too wanted to talk to him about the *Keneder Odler* and about Gallay's pension, I immediately accepted and drove over. I surmised that it probably had to deal with his work, over many years, for Russian Jews. He sends parcels to individuals and prayer books, Pentateuchs, Hebrew calendars, prayer-shawls, and phylacteries to the Moscow community. It seems that he has contacts with the authorities there, via the Russian consulate in Montreal. He often travels to Russia and does his work without publicity. Only from time to time does a small notice appear when a shipment has been made. He never participates in the public demonstrations against the Soviet decrees. Like a great majority of orthodox Jewry, he maintains that he can be more useful for the observant Jews there through quiet negotiations. It is a wonder that despite the favours that he extracts from them, the Russians don't demand in return that he speak out favourably about their regime. To date no such statement has been noted.

After he had described how he finds open doors there, and "how he manages to get certain things done, with God's help," and that one can "talk to them rationally," he played a tape for me of his conversation with the president of the Moscow synagogue held several days ago. First of all, he thanked him for sending the Pentateuchs, Passover Haggodos, and phylacteries; they are still waiting for the prayer-shawls. Second, he thanks him for promising to visit during the jubilee celebrations for the president. At the same time he informs him that in the near future he will receive an invitation from "the highest level of authority, the minister himself," whose name he does not mention, that Hechtman should be a delegate to the Peace Conference being convened in Moscow in June, which will include all of "our orthodox groups."

I candidly told him that if he is "invited" he must make clear that he cannot bring greetings in the name of any institution, nor approve any resolutions. It appears that they want to exploit him for this purpose. He told me that he agrees with me and that he will consult the Lubavitcher Rebbe about this. He must be very careful not to lose the opportunity to continue the role he has performed till now.

MAY 10, 1977

The situation in the province becomes more difficult and oppressive. With the new language law it has become obvious that the minorities will have a tough time adjusting, and who knows how much of an adjustment will be necessary in order to live in this province. The new law, if it passes, will take away a significant number of human rights that we here have accepted as universal and unchangeable. They already conduct themselves as if they are politically separated from Canada. The young and professionals, and to a certain extent the business-people, already feel like strangers here, and the "For Sale" signs in front of houses on every street signify that the population is preparing to leave the province. Others are just transferring their savings to other provinces or to the States.

MAY 19, 1977

That which we had anticipated in fear has come to pass. A most difficult period is opening in Israel due to the "earthquake" – as they refer to the Israeli elections. The squandered legacy of Israel is trampled, and in the eyes of the world, Israel will appear to be the obstacle to "peace." Internally, it is a step backwards in all respects, with even greater civil strife. The voters there did what our local voters had done last November. They punished a corrupt leadership that had lost its convictions and their own direction, so they brought to the fore a party that will mislead even more, and threaten free choice. The collapse of an established social structure, with a record of achievements, endangers the entire edifice. Is it only the leadership that is at fault?

MAY 30, 1977

Dayan's defection to the Likkud and becoming foreign minister is a disgrace in and of itself, and a sign of the deep moral degradation and political horse-trading in Israel. It will not strengthen Likkud but will further fragment the remaining defeated party. There has never been such a painfully keen illustration of the prophet's outcry: "Who will raise up Yaacov, since he is so weak?!" No matter how you rationalize it, it is difficult to understand how in a few short years, they have dissipated their great legacy.

AUGUST 24, 1977

Today Shifra and the children rose from *shiva*. Every closure to a conventional custom leaves a profound effect. The moment when the mourners are told to rise and put on their shoes is a new breach in the bond with the deceased, a distancing that renews the pain yet drives him further away from us. That "other world " rises like a hidden barrier. Drinking a *l'chaim* with the worshippers also symbolizes this partition. Usually on these occasions, the custom is to recite the refrain: "*l'chaim*, may the soul be called to the Torah reading." Aside from Yechiel, long may he live, and Shmerl, the others who were present are very far from belief in this. Still, they conduct themselves just as their fathers and grandfathers had done. Shifra is so deeply immersed in these rituals, that in making her *l'chaim*, she behaved and spoke in the same way as our mother, may she rest in peace. Her words were something like this: "Sholem is not alone. His mother and father, your grandfather and grandmother, are with him, and our mother and father are with him. He is not alone. His memory stays with us and we will always hold him dear." Strangely pathetic, coming from her. No matter how far we have spiritually distanced ourselves from our parents, it seems that in times of deeply emotional experiences, we sense ourselves to be connected again and express ourselves and act precisely as they had. I noted the same thing when one of us led the prayer from the lectern. The melody, the intonation, even the body movements, are our father's, one of our uncles, or just a person close to us from that world where we grew up.

SEPTEMBER 20, 1977
DURING THE DAYS OF AWE, 5738

The balance sheet of Jewry, in the world situation, is a bitter one. They pressure Israel from all sides. Even the best of friends want "peace" at Israel's expense. The anti-Semitic cohorts have risen again all over the world. Once again it is hard to look one another in the eyes. In every Jewish community the heart flutters in anxiety. For those who are believers, clinging to the Messianic prophecies is a source of support. The doubters and sceptics don't even have this, so they confound themselves with words that can never become a prayer and with a deluded faith that does not give any support.

And in our family, the reckoning is distressing. The year 5737 tore away our sister Henneh and our brother-in-law Sholem, leaving raw pain in everybody. It is truly macabre. Henneh, who left nothing behind her except sorrow, when writing her poetry called herself "Avi-Goel" – father of her imagined redeemer – without reference to a mother. Sholem, the great lover of Yiddish culture and dreamer of future tomorrows, passed away while mourning the Russian Yiddish poets and dreamers of that future, which had murdered them only yesterday and today.

Of those of us who are still here, everyone has been scarred and, like a pomegranate, filled with the seeds of our own sorrow. Yechiel clutches the belief in a supreme being who is Lord of the Universe and who is following a plan that ultimately will lead to a redemption somewhere. One only has to glance at his bearded face to recognize the aura of fear he emits. He lives like a hermit and maintains his feeble body with next to nothing, and the slightest breeze can knock him over. He fortifies himself with his extraordinary mastery of the thousand-year-old labyrinth of Jewish thought in which he seeks and often seems to think that he has attained knowledge of the ultimate truth. As for me, all roads are darkened, and in my whole being feel that at this point I will no longer find the ultimate truth. I only see and experience life as a blind game. The nights are filled with nightmares, which miraculously are dispersed by the light of day, when one can occupy oneself with petty things on behalf of others, the family, and one's social world that seem to be worthwhile. For myself, I go to sleep and awake with the feeling of a deep, hidden intimation as H. Rosenblatt says in his poem: "The spinner spins until the thread is spent." I feel that the thread is becoming more and more fragile and shorter. Meanwhile the pacemaker beats away and helps my weakened heart. I think I do all I can so that my "assistant" – as I call it – should be able to carry out its task perfectly. But there is no need to delude oneself.

NOVEMBER 18, 1977

The most significant event in the struggle of the State of Israel and the Arab nations took place this week. Unexpectedly, Sadat from Egypt expressed his desire to come to Jerusalem to present his case. Israel, without hesitation, extended a formal invitation, and tomorrow evening he will arrive in Jerusalem and Sunday afternoon he will address the Knesset. This is such a sudden shift that, even if nothing comes of it, it is of historic importance. According to today's news, the entire Arab world has labelled him a traitor for breaching the united Arab front. But it is hard to conceive that such an astute politician as he would risk his entire career, and possibly even his head, if he did not feel that he could accomplish something. Could he possibly have had a Pharaoh's dream? Because realistically, it does not look as if this will bear fruit. One shouldn't delude oneself, but whatever the result, it is a start of something very important. Maybe it might be said of this event: What reason cannot accomplish, time will. How very interesting are the links in the chain of history. And how ironic that it is Begin who has the historic privilege to be in power during this event.

NOVEMBER 21, 1977

The whole world, literally, was in a state of tension on Saturday and Sunday due to the historic gesture of Sadat's flight to Jerusalem to address the Knesset. It can be said that all eyes and hearts were directed toward Israel. Truly unforgettable was the scene of his arrival and his speech to the Knesset in Arabic. The most important aspect of his speech was his courage to state that Egypt wants Israel as a neighbour and that "we do not want war any more." But beyond that he reiterated the same conditions held earlier. Menachem Begin, who, it would seem, was born under a brilliant, lucky star, responded enthusiastically on the desire for peace and the recognition of Israel's most powerful neighbour, but one didn't feel that he was ready to deal with the harsh terms. At the interviews they really were delighted with each other. But the question remains whether this historic opportunity will have the good fortune to be acted upon.

DECEMBER 1, 1977

Yesterday I attended a gathering in honour of Esther Markish, who was here as the guest of the Committee of 35, younger people who carry out demonstrations for the dissidents of Soviet Russia. I introduced her in Yiddish, honouring her and the memory of her great husband, and the Yiddish writers of the Soviet Union who were killed only because they were Jewish, although a number of them were not able to protect their Jewish identity with honour. She makes a better impression this time than she did on her visit several years ago when she was here. She exuded a cold and unwelcoming quality then. It appears that Israel as well as her travels to Jewish communities have had a positive effect on her. She spoke in English and a bit of Yiddish.

DECEMBER 2, 1977

Spent all day with Esther Markish. We were invited to come to the school where she was to speak to the pupils of Bialik High School. It was a moving experience to be among the four hundred young people in the auditorium. The encounter began with a telephone conversation to Moscow with the activist scientist Victor Brailovsky. She spoke to him in Russian and to the children in English and told him that this was a Chanukah celebration. A group of children lit the first candle, sang the blessings and the Chanukah songs, which he could hear. Then some children lit the other Chanukah candles symbolically in the name of well-known activists who were imprisoned. It was a very exalted moment and tremendously moving. In the hall one felt an electric quiver, which was carried beyond the narrow confines of the mute four walls. Later, she spoke a few words in Yiddish, and as she was instructed, repeated these in English.

DECEMBER 6, 1977

Yesterday and today I organized the first file of the letters received in the '20s until the mid-'30s. Almost 99 per cent of the people are no longer of this world. Their intimate words, desires, grievances, and loneliness speak from the grave. I had the sense of visiting the parental graves, and often felt like the sage Choni the Circle-Maker, who stumbles around a desiccated tree.

MAY 8, 1978

Have not noted anything for several months, not for want of subjects but simply because sometimes one is overcome by an aversion to even speak to oneself. You don't even want to reveal to yourself that everything that has happened to the present appears to you as a wilted leaf that, from the beginning, grew on a tree with roots in the sand. Now the winds of time have come uncovering the roots and I can only observe how the whole meagre edifice of a lifetime becomes scattered, and soon no vestige will remain. In that mood I left for Miami for three months. I got involved with that circle for a while, which in the main is a society of former activists. Though some of them still convince themselves that they are building and participate in projects that have meaning. While there, I received an invitation from the Concert Society to accept, along with Wiseman, the prize for artistic merit that they award annually to those who warrant it, according to them. At first, I thought I would not accept, since the present-day administrators have squaundered the essential direction of the school to the point where one can hardly recognize that at one time it had a unique approach. What good is their honour to me? They have not read my books and, in any case, don't know if they have value. But on rethinking, it still means that these people are interested in holding on to our past, at least externally. Despite all, the ceremony was dignified. I even felt that the younger generation that conducted the event were sincere in their warm remarks. The audience responded graciously but in my heart there throbbed the sense of emptiness. I think Bialik said this in a poem: "Woe is me, for I have become a coin rattling in your empty jug."

TISHA b'AV, 5738. AUGUST 13, 1978

Some days ago I was at the *Shule*. I could no longer recognize the rooms, the corridors. They had made such renovations to adapt the building to the needs of Bialik High School that it was impossible to discern any more the earlier layout in which there was so much of myself. The few pictures of Zuker, Sarah Caiserman, and Miller look down as strangers from their corner. And the same for the picture of Peretz. The materials that were transferred to the rented house on Chester, packed and stored away, have no place in the new locale. Who knows what will become of them? When I had to look up something in this archive my fingers were burning, and my heart beat rapidly from the myriad memories that emanated from the papers in the locked cabinets. Will someone ever come in contact with them? I had to interrupt my search and left the place with a heavy heart. The high school has swallowed the elementary school. While the elementary school was still here – even though its curriculum was already far removed from what it had been – it occupied the original place. Now that they have divided the classes into two other buildings, the site too has been erased. Only the name, the L. Zuker Building, is a gravestone for the past. We had warned them that with this arrangement they are undermining the future of the high school. But they only see the present and paid no heed. And with that the onset of the school's liquidation was sealed.

OCTOBER 8, 1978. *TISHREI* 7, 5739

The last few days saw a great fuss over the Nobel Prize Award for Literature to Yitzchak Bashevis – Isaac Bashevis Singer. It is a significant event not only for him but especially for the literature in Yiddish. For the Yiddish snobs it is a slap in the face, and for Yiddish literature it is an exultation. In her humiliation and grief, it is a joyous summons to the world stage. Whether Bashevis should have been the one to represent it is another matter. The only thing to be said is to appropriate the old adage: "Many roads lead to God." How things happen remains, above all, a true mystery. For instance, the Jewish labour movement and its parties built Israel and aspired to realize peace with its neighbours as equals. On the other hand, the Herutniks, who were in the opposition, did not permit them to take even one step in that direction. Despite all, history played its tricks and ironically Begin turned out to be the emissary who brought peace closer. Yiddish literature in its flowering awaited the world's recognition, but only now in its withered stage does she receive it, and by way of an artist of whom it is doubtful whether he expresses the true essence of Yiddish. In terms of artistic form possibly so, but in spirit and conception he is far from deserving. He seeks only to entertain and intrigue the reader. But such, however, is fate; so we must say, "This too is for the best."

OCTOBER 13, 1978

Last night attended the annual meeting of the schools. The hall was nearly filled with young people. All were parents of the elementary school and Bialik High School. Among them were only four or five elders from the earlier days. In leadership, none of them is present. Only a few former pupils recognized me and came to convey best wishes for the New Year, and at the same time expressed their dissatisfaction with the fact that their children come home from school without a Yiddish song on their lips nor with the emotional experience of a holiday celebration, which in their day captivated them and which they remember to this day. Why, they ask, has this been forsaken? Without this, all that remains are some memorized rules – "skills" – as they say in a foreign language, but not an education that touches the soul. How could they know that I myself feel like the lost Choni the Circle-Maker who awoke after a sleep of seventy years to find the world changed beyond recognition.

NOVEMBER 5, 1978. *CHESHVAN* 5, 5739

Last Thursday was my seventy-eighth birthday. The children insisted that we have supper together in a restaurant. They also invited Rivke and Berl. All in all I was very happy about this, but sitting with them and the grandchildren, the thought never left me about my father's response – may he rest in peace – when I asked him the age of the Husatiner Rebbe: "A Rebbe's age is never counted." It would seem that one doesn't want to acknowledge that as one reckons the years there are fewer of them to count.

Next morning, Friday, was the day when I usually visit Yechiel and have a talk with him. It is always of interest and he is in great need to have someone to talk to. I rarely interrupt him or argue with him. I think that he knows that his way of life – leading a hermit's life – isolated from the world, is not to my own liking. And that a great deal of his belief system in the worshipping of God, and observing everything only in the perspective of our ancestors, is far removed from me.

MIAMI BEACH, JANUARY 8, 1979

Nearly a week here and I am beginning to regain my health. My walking is easier and the fatigue dissipates bit by bit. I am still somewhat gloomy; although the relatives and friends, who have been here for a month or two, glow with happiness and carefree spirits. They are constantly organizing get-togethers and parties, as if those were the sole reason for being here. The second day we were here coincided with the reception to celebrate Bashevis's Nobel Prize award. I was reluctant to go for several reasons, but I reconsidered and decided that when Jews celebrate and wish to express their joy openly and in great numbers, one should be there and not absent oneself. So nearly 1,500 Jews filled the Shalom Synagogue. They gave him a standing ovation, though the sense of celebration was lacking. The speakers failed to establish a proper tone and even the Rabbi, speaking in English, could do no more than utter worn-out cliches. After that Bashevis rose and, without even greeting the audience, began to read a story about a thief, a sensualist, disguised as a Rabbi, a rogue. The story, in his usual manner, was packed with pornography and *dybbuks*. The audience's disappointment was immediately felt when, as soon as he had concluded, they stood up without even attempting the expected applause. It was humiliating and heart-breaking to witness.

JANUARY 28, 1979

Yesterday I received the official confirmation from the Multicultural Department of the Federal Government that they have allotted a grant of $3,900 for my book *Fun Nechtn un Heint* along with a few compliments. This is the first time that I have received such a government grant. It gives me a double pleasure, first because they are acknowledging a book in the Yiddish language as integral to Canada; as well the personal recognition. It will cover more than 50 per cent of the cost of publication. It is literally my first book that will result in royalties to the author.

By the way, I have sold about thirty copies not counting several given as gifts. Interestingly, I am complimented on those stories that convey strong emotion. Those in which one has to ponder my evaluation of the era receive few comments. It looks as if this subject fails to touch them.

MARCH 7, 1979

Today Carter flies to Cairo and then to Jerusalem with new proposals for peace. According to what is being said, Israel has already accepted the American proposals but Egypt has yet to consider them. It is a great move by Carter, but it doesn't seem to lead to a real peace. All three sides need peace, and probably desire it too, but the fear of peace is greater than the benefits of peace, both in Israel and Egypt. Although a failure would prove to be more detrimental for all three parties. Carter's gesture will probably go down in history as a grand diplomatic move that risks his own political career and the whole credibility of the U.S. in this chaotic world. Israel, on the other hand, risks its own future. If not for the distrust they have for each other an agreement might be a possibility. And all around, the devil, in different disguises, rages and rubs his hands together in pleasure.

The evening in memory of Pessie Hirshfeld-Pomerantz-Honigbaum was very dignified. Over one hundred people attended. It seems that even her closest friends here and in Chicago, where she had lived for many years, knew very little about her poetry. The ordinary reader only knows of those writers who are trumpeted in the marketplace, and hence had no appreciation of her personality and creative works. My insight into her poetry was a surprise and an enriching experience – as some of them related to me. Fradle flew in from New York and this added a great deal of significance to the evening and respect for the deceased.

MARCH 11, 1979

According to the news from Israel, it seems that Carter accomplished little for peace, but from his address in the Knesset it was clear that he emphasized Israel's intransigence on the part of the leaders, rather than the constant manoeuvering of Sadat. If his whole trip had had the aim of demonstrating that the guilt lies with Israel – then he certainly has shown that. Many had this suspicion much earlier. Does that mean that the proverb, "The Angel of Death slays, and gets his ways," is everywhere maintained. Who knows what more we can expect from an insulted and disappointed politician?

The Purim festivities this year are hardly joyous. The Hamans still have the royal seal in their grasp and Ahasuerus still sleeps the whole night through.

PURIM, 5739

When *Adar* arrives you have to increase your joyfulness. According to this, this Purim should be a joyous one. Finally a breakthrough in the peace negotiations. Carter receives much praise for his grand moves and for gaining the agreement from both sides. The details are not spelled out, but it certainly does not feel like a real celebration. The fear of peace looms large since the major party, the Palestinians, are throwing stones and bombs, which have already resulted in victims. So we smile and voice our satisfaction, but without joy.

ADAR 27, 5739. MARCH 26, 1979

My heart trembled along with the hands that signed the so-called peace treaty between Israel and Egypt. If the belief existed that this actually was the beginning of peace, after so many victims and horrors, then surely our hearts would overflow with happiness. But that belief is not here. The doubt grows bigger, especially after the beautiful chosen words that in a hidden way intimated that this was not what we had craved for so long. So I sat by the television but wasn't stirred when the three principals clasped hands in symbolic unity. As it was written: "They rejoice with trembling." It is undoubtedly an historic event and only time will tell if it is a new beginning or merely a bedazzling outburst between darkness and light.

AV 3, 5739. JULY 27, 1979

It is probably a natural feeling as one approaches the age of "courage," on turning eighty, that even subconsciously I have the feeling that wherever the eye glances, especially when I open my eyes in the morning or find myself in a new place, something wordlessly says to me: Absorb this; it might be that you are taking your farewell from all of this. It is a feeling that doesn't comprise a sense of angst or simple regret, merely the statement of fact. Together with this there emerges a clear demand: "Write about us. Don't let us disappear." Simultaneously, there appear before my eyes people whom I have known, experiences that, at the time, were engraved in my memory. They too silently signal: "What are you waiting for? Don't let us be forgotten." So I snatch a sheet of paper in order to jot down an impression, but it quickly swims out of reach. I can no longer find the appropriate form. The letters don't arrange themselves into words and the images float about in an abstract vacuum. Is this a mysterious premonition or simply an atavistic sensation of some kind? "The heart does not reveal its secrets in words."

CHESHVAN 19, 5740. NOVEMBER 9, 1979

Recent events chase each other at such a pace that it is impossible to catch one's breath. The atmosphere in the world thickens and strangely the great powers are helpless because of their fear to use their weapons that might lead to a greater catastrophe. The minor demons dance about committing every evil, knowing that their oil chokes everyone's conscience, and their rationalizations are based on past historical grievances, justifying the annihilation of an entire people in Cambodia. Meanwhile the promulgators of a hypocritical justice at the UN speak with half-twisted mouths. There is no one to laugh at the irony of the so-called "United" Nations.

Some meagre "comfort" can be found in the poet's prophecy: "He raises up the nations and destroys them," or "He who dwells in heaven mocks; he laughs at them." Meanwhile, however, Satan, with his thousands of evil eyes, is gasping with laughter. Crazed students occupy the American embassy in Iran, and the religious barbarian, Ayatolla, stands in the way of any negotiations, and the American giant has to plead with the PLO to act as mediator. Could it be that all these machinations, all things considered, are directed toward the heart of Israel?

Strange that most commentators do not emphasize the fact that any scoundrel can now do whatever he desires, and many will even justify their actions unable to perceive the tragi-comedy of this. They constantly point out that nothing can be done because Iran might – God forbid – cease to deliver oil and instead sell it surreptitiously for double the price. Always the commercial calculation. Little wonder that the Devil reigns and even wraps himself in a prayer-shawl of blue, and chokes with laughter.

1980–1982

AV 28, 5740. AUGUST 10, 1980

Nearly a year without making any entries. The year 5740 – which signifies destruction – has earned its name. It actually became very difficult to chase after all the physical and spiritual afflictions and give them expression on paper to be remembered. My mood is too dismal to give voice to "the secret weeping of my soul." I distracted myself by becoming involved in the preparation of Ch. L. Fuch's *Hundert Yohr Yiddishe un Hebraishe Literatur in Canada*, which will be published in the near future; and the trilingual anthology, which the Yiddish Committee has decided to publish. Amidst this I began to write a new piece, an expanded story of my fifty-five years in Canada. It is written in a complex form, moving back and forth in time, and portraying life in little Montvin, a kind of synonym for "the Jewish street" as it was called in the radical circles of those years. In this way I want to describe the inner life of the hero, Boruch Hoffman, and the surroundings that were swarming with remarkable types, both positive and negative. They were the ones who established the local Yiddish community life. Whether I will manage to complete this during my eighties – the years of strength – only hidden destiny knows.

2 *CHESHVAN*, 5741. OCTOBER 12, 1980

Today is the first day of my "years of courage." I feel an inner turbulence that is indescribable. The road I have travelled is hidden somewhere in the recesses of my memory, sunk in the world of the forgotten. What lies ahead is concealed by veils of hope and yearning, the wish to extract from that forgotten world its essence, which must be represented according to its era so that the passing of time into history (according to the Malbim's interpretation – may he rest in peace) becomes the eternity of Jewish creativity.

Some time ago *chaverim* and friends proposed to mark my birthday with a public celebration with all the paraphernalia that accompanies these things. The children suggested a get-together for everybody, all the family and friends. I didn't accept either. All my life I took care not to make a big fuss over myself; I detested the very idea. And now I cannot change myself. The day belongs to me, to Sorke whose part in the making of myself is incomparable, and the dear children and grandchildren – may they be healthy and strong; and in the distant world of the departed, to be united through memory with my mother and father and second mother – my mother-in-law – may they all rest in peace.

I embrace them all with love, including my only sister and my brothers, may they grow old in good spirits. Both those who acknowledged the date and those who didn't. In our family we never made any fuss over birthdays, only for deeds and accomplishments.

JULY 1, 1981. 29 *SIVAN*, 5741

Couldn't note down anything for many months. Suffered from heart failure in Miami. Regained my health after a lengthy period of rest when suddenly a new disaster knocked at the door and took away Yechiel, whom I had always looked up to. He was an extremist in all things, as a heretic in his younger days and orthodox in his older years. He was always feeble and constantly had to be rescued from the claws of the angel of death. For the last two decades he led a miserable life, still each of our meetings was an uplifting experience because he no longer existed in the mundane world. Daily existence was filled with hardships. To save himself from despair he lived solely with his books and instructing other Jews: clinging to the belief that everything is according to a plan by a higher authority.

Woe is me that I cannot even attend the funeral. The doctor forbade it. I am all alone in the house. Everyone is at the funeral. Shmerl entrusted the funeral rites to the ultra-orthodox. Yechiel's earlier life will most probably not be mentioned. And his role in educating a generation of Jewish teachers will also probably be recognized only in passing. That is what he wanted. I will miss him not only as a brother but as one to whom you could bring your perplexities. And even when the response was not in accordance with my outlook, it gives one the assurance to know that there is such a response armoured with the faith of generations. If I could only weep without restraint. My senses are frozen.

SEPTEMBER 5, 1982. *ELUL* 17, 5742

The last two years were occupied with helping Fuchs publish his lexicon on Hebrew-Yiddish writers in Canada. The first of its kind to be published here. Aside from the errors that resulted from his customary haste, it is a significant contribution to the literary creativity of Canadian Jewish writers.

Together with Chaim Spilberg, prepared a Canadian Jewish anthology in

Yiddish, English, and French. A collection and overview of almost everything that had been written in the last hundred years, especially in Yiddish. The reason that some writers were omitted was due to the fact that we could not find contributors willing or able to write about them. It appeared on time to coincide with the third World Yiddish Congress. The first reviews are beginning to arrive.

Gathered all my essays, both literary and social, and submitted them for publication. Received a grant for this from Multiculturalism Canada. The local writers are blessed by the government's recognition, at long last, of the cultural worth of minority writing for the country as a whole and offers financial support for their future development.

If one recalls that only forty years ago the government sought ways to prevent immigration, and established legislation to achieve that purpose. In particular, they discriminated against the nations of eastern and southern Europe – not to speak of Asia and Africa. And at the bottom of the ladder, the Jews were shut out completely, with the exception of special permits granting particular privileges. By contrast one can see the kind of changes for the better that have occurred in this country. Still it is strange that the government can be extremely liberal while there still exists enough racism and discrimination amongst all classes.

I also began to write a new novel called *In Land fun di Lachadikeh Vasern* [In the Land of Laughing Waters]. So far I have completed six or seven chapters. If my health permits it and my memory functions, it will be a broad and deep examination of the nearly sixty years of our living here. I got here at the end of 1925. It is clearly based on autobiographical material but it is not composed as a memoir.

In general, if one can put it this way, the end does not frighten me so much. I have accomplished the greater part of what I had set out to do. Of course, I am just in the middle of the novel and would like to see grandchildren settled, so would welcome more years; but a clear intimation about the future is evident. We should be content with our condition and not be perturbed by changes in my breathing.

Unexpectedly, after a year of discussion, I'm notified that I have been awarded the Manger Prize for Yiddish literature in the Diaspora. Our major prize in terms of status and scope. The president of Israel grants the award, and well-known writers are the jurists. It aroused tremendous joy among the friends here and in Israel. So much so that a headline writer salivated: The city rejoices, Zipper awarded the Manger Prize! And my brother Yisroel was alarmed by the fact that since the jury had mentioned my contributions as a teacher, it might be construed as an award in education, as witness the number of parents who congratulated me in public notices.

For myself, either case is not surprising, since a large part of what I managed to accomplish covers both fields. Just as some people question whether it is only for Yiddish or, in part, for Hebrew as well. I read it simply as it is written: "And his banner of love was over me." As long as it is Jewish creativity, with heart and soul.

So we were in Israel for four weeks with Ode and Motty. Without them we could not have undertaken this journey. For this they deserve our eternal thanks. We arrived in Israel just as the Lebanese War – "Peace in Galilee" – broke out. Strange how the bloodiest war, with the greatest number of casualties on both sides, is called "Peace in Galilee."

We settled in very comfortably by the sea in Natanya, and because of my weakness we invited all our friends to visit us. Saw almost everyone, and in some cases even visited others in their homes. Motty took us about in a rented car. Driving on the roads we passed many half-constructed buildings because the workers had abandoned them due to being called up for military service. The scattered building materials seemed to lie about, ashamed and hoarsely crying out, as if chasing our car: "Look at this. It pierces the heart. We could still continue with much more building, but we must abandon them to chaos." Only in a few places, especially when passing a kibbutz, could you see about twenty school-age boys busying themselves with some construction or working at a bare garden. Every squeal of the tires on the asphalt tore at my weakened heart. I had the same feeling listening to a discussion about the war. Each one defends his point of view sharply, without gradations. And still you sense that there is even a sharper and more pointed argument, shared by both antagonists, that burrows underground and gets lost in the deep: "Maybe this conflict should have been avoided?"

Whenever you come into a home, someone sits by a telephone, waiting. No one knows where their children or grandchildren are and when they will phone. You walk about all day without hearing or seeing the war, but it was enough to raise your eyes, looking north to south and see the helicopters flying by the seashore, to be overcome by an unusual fear: "Who are they carrying, and where?" And when you close your eyes at night, you are wrapped in a net of nightmares and a tangle of mountain peaks that open on twisted bottomless caverns. Only charred spikes protrude, warning you: "Beware, this is the end of the world!" And during a free-fall you feel that you are leaning against something, which sends a shudder through your whole body.

You hear a voice that comes from above and below, from the front and the rear: "The time has come." The voice is firm but sad. Like my father's voice. Last year when I had my mild heart attack, then too I heard the same voice in those nightmarish nights, but saying: "The time has not yet come." And it calmed me that the end was not yet near. It was a passing ailment.

When the same illness recurred on my return from Israel, we suspected something, especially Sorke. Dr Weiner gave up on me and no longer looked for any new treatments to improve my condition. In addition, the misfortunes with Yechiel and Dunsky, may they rest in peace, so suddenly torn away, began to remind me that we are from the same generation, and the disaster with Grade and now Rochl Korn, may they rest in peace, has really driven me crazy and I hear the voice quite differently. Sorke says that in my sleep I cry out such bizarre outbursts as if I were chasing someone away. When Sorke wakes me up it seems that someone else is following closely at her side.

Epilogue

The Final Journey

Yaacov Zipper died of heart failure on 14 April 1983 at the Jewish General Hospital. He had suffered for years from a crippling heart condition that was painful and debilitating. Circulation blockages impeded his walking and increasingly curtailed his activities; his journal entries from the 1970s became sparse and fragmentary, reflecting his fragile state of health and diminishing energies.

Yet despite his serious infirmities the last years were marked by his participation in literary endeavours that boosted his sense of pride and reaffirmed his vocation as a writer. Early in February 1982, a letter arrived from Israel informing him that he had been awarded the Manger Prize for Yiddish literature. The prize carried the name of Itzik Manger, a leading modern Yiddish poet. It was the most prestigious international award for Yiddish literary creativity granted by the State of Israel under the auspices of its president. The letter from the award committee chairman stated: "It was decided unanimously to award the 1982 Manger Prize to you, a Yiddish writer in the Diaspora, in recognition of your meritorious accomplishments in Yiddish literature and language."

Zipper was thrilled by the news and savoured the honour bestowed upon him when a large number of congratulatory notices appeared in the *Keneder Odler* and other Yiddish periodicals offering best wishes from fellow writers and friends. Against the advice of his family he decided to travel to Israel to receive the prize. It was an onerous journey but one that he could not be dissuaded from taking, so accompanied by Sorke and his daughter Ode and son-in-law Motty he embarked on a momentous trip. There can be little doubt that Zipper was aware that this would be his last encounter with Israel. He was determined to make it his valediction, taking his farewell from as many old comrades as he could visit or invite to their rented apartment. Particularly emotional were his meetings with survivors of the early years in the Zionist youth movement in Poland, some of whom had been members of a kibbutz since settling in Palestine in the 1920s. Others included family members who had found refuge in Israel after World War II.

These encounters with people from his past gave Zipper the sense of closing a circle; he had known them at the onset of his career in Poland and here they were, now aged and grey, but still spirited and lively, near its close. What stirred him most was the feeling that he was witness to an unbroken chain of vigorous ideals that extended from their origins in Eastern Europe when he had embraced them to the present moment when, in his old age, these ideals continued to exude something of their compelling power. He returned home grateful that he had endured so rich an experience, but physically exhausted.

His health continued to deteriorate and for lengthy periods of time he was treated in hospitals both in Florida and Montreal. But all hope for recovery was abandoned and Zipper finally succumbed, surrounded by his family.

The funeral, held on April 17th, was attended by hundreds, including family, *chaverim* from the Movement, former students, their parents, and community leaders. In his will Zipper had left detailed instructions about the proceedings he favoured. There should be few speeches; instead he asked for readings from his novels and short stories, and these were duly read by Leib Tencer. The eulogy also was given by Leib Tencer, Zipper's respected colleague, who addressed the hushed crowd on the subject of Zipper's dual role as educator and author, the two contesting aspects of his creative imagination. These were the vocations that he had always sought to bridge and they endowed him with the vision of Jewish renewal that had always guided his path. Just as Zipper had given numerous eulogies at the funerals of his family members and *chaverim* who had been active in pursuit of Jewish cultural continuity, so Tencer now celebrated the deeds of Yaacov Zipper, extolling him as an exceptional community-builder and an inspiring educator to generations of students. And despite his busy life as public servant and educational administrator, Zipper managed to write a considerable number of novels, short fiction, biographical sketches, and literary criticism. On the basis of literary productivity alone, he had earned his place in the pantheon of twentieth-century Yiddish literature.

What remained incomplete at the time of his death was the book he had yearned to write for many years. It was to be the fictional account of his own generation, the story of the immigrant experience in Montreal, the record of where they had come from and the lives they had made for themselves in Canada. This subject had been pressing down on him for the longest time. The journals often gave vent to his troubled conscience for having neglected the representation of the immigrant saga, and he bemoaned the fact that other less important matters had deprived him of the time for concentrated writing. In fact, he had made a beginning and six chapters do exist in manuscript form. They trace the trajectory of a young man's transformation, describing the evolution of the self as it fashions a new life after its liberation from the bonds of traditional religious authority and the young man's escape from that archaic world by transplanting himself in the landscape of twentieth-century Montreal. For Zipper, that story – his story – was of major historical value as the record of a young man's moral education, a witness to the profound social, cultural, and political changes that had challenged the ethos of the immigrant world, dramatically altering the lives that were touched by their sweeping powers.

Regrettably, that incomplete book will always remain incomplete, the unfinished remnant of a long and passionately engaged life.

APPENDIX:
THE WRITINGS OF YAACOV ZIPPER

It was Yaacov Zipper's practice to write the Yiddish version of his works first, to be followed, often many years later, by the Hebrew.

Books in Yiddish and Hebrew
Geven iz a Mentsh, Montreal, 1940
Ish Hayah Ba'Aretz, Tel Aviv, 1955
[*There was a Man* – five stories based on the life of Yisroel Baal Shem Tov, the founder of Chasidism]

Oif Yener Zeit Bug, Montreal, 1946
Me'ever Lanahar Bug, Tel Aviv, 1957
[*On the Far Side of the Bug River,* a novel]

Tzvishn Teichn un Vasern, Montreal, 1961
Bein Naharot u'Nachalim, Tel Aviv, 1967
[*Amid Rivers and Waters,* a biographical novel]

Ch'bin Vider in Mein Chorever Heim Gekumen, Montreal, 1965
["I Have Returned Once More to My Destroyed Home", a Holocaust commemorative poem]

In Di Getzelten fun Avrom, Montreal, 1971
B'Ohelei Avraham, Tel Aviv, 1974
[*In the Tents of Abraham,* narratives on biblical themes]

Fun Nechtn un Heint, Montreal, 1978
[*From Yesterday and Today,* a collection of stories and a journal of a visit to Israel]

Areinblicken in Yiddishen Literarishen Schaffen, Montreal, 1983
[*Glimpses into Yiddish Literary Creativity*, a collection of literary profiles and essays]

BOOKS IN ENGLISH
The Far Side of the River: Selected Short Stories, edited and translated by Mervin Butovsky and Ode Garfinkle, Mosaic Press, Oakville, Ontario, 1985.

BOOKS EDITED
Jubilee Book of I.L. Peretz School, Winnipeg, 1934
Jubilee Book of the Jewish Peretz Schools, Montreal, 1938
The Leizer Zuker Book, Montreal, 1968
Pinkas Tishevitz, Tel Aviv, 1970
Canadian Jewish Anthology (edited with Chaim Spilberg), Montreal, 1983

LITERARY AWARDS
Zukunft Literary Prize for "Die Magefeh" [The Plague], 1942
J. Friedland Award for "Dos Emeseh Bild" [The True Image], 1961
J.I. Segal Award for Yiddish Literature, Montreal, 1974
Ganopolsky Prize, Paris, 1979
Manger Prize for Yiddish Literature, Israel, 1982
Jewish Book Award for Yiddish Literature, New York, 1983

Zipper also kept a journal during his first year in Canada. For a study of this journal, see "The Journals of Yaacov Zipper 1925–1926" by Ode Garfinkle and Mervin Butovsky in *An Everyday Miracle: Yiddish Culture in Montreal*, eds. Ira Robinson, Pierre Anctil, and Mervin Butovsky, Véhicule Press, Montreal, 1990.

Glossary

HEBREW AND YIDDISH TERMS

Adar – sixth month of Hebrew calendar
Aggadah – the non-legal contents of the Talmud, includes ethical and moral teaching, legends, and folklore
aleph-beis – the ABCs; elementary level of knowledge
aliyah – to ascend, usually refers to immigration to Israel
Amalek – biblical nomadic people identified as enemies of the Jews
Av – eleventh month of Hebrew calendar

Bar Mitzvah – confirmation of Jewish male at age thirteen
Boruch dayan ha'emes – "Blessed be the true judge," benediction generally recited on hearing the report of a death
bris – circumcision

chai – "life" in Hebrew numerical value of letters is eighteen, hence "twice chai" equals thirty-six, the number of years of Zipper's principalship
chalutz – Israeli pioneer
chalutziut – spirit of Israeli pioneering
Chanukah – holiday commemorating the Maccabean victory
Chasidim – pious believers, member of mystical revival movement that arose in the eighteenth century. Also Chasidism, Chasidic
chaver – comrade, friend, (pl. chaverim), Labour Zionist form of addressing fellow members
chazan – cantor
Cheder – school for elementary religious education
Cheshvan – second month of Hebrew calendar
chupa – wedding canopy
chutzpah – audacity, impertinence
dybbuk – disembodied spirit of dead person that seeks haven in the body of a living being

Elul – twelfth month of Hebrew calendar
El Moleh Rachamim – prayer for the repose of the souls of the dead
Eretz Yisroel – Land of Israel
Erev Shavuos – eve of the Festival of first fruits and the anniversary of the revelation on Mt Sinai

Gabbai – title for official of a synagogue
Gemorah – designation for the commentary on the *Mishnah*; the *Gemorah* and the *Mishnah* comprise the Talmud
golem – an automaton, usually in human form, created by magical incantations

Haftorah – portion from the Prophets read following the reading from the Torah
Haggodeh – the narration of the Exodus story
hakofos – processional circuits around the synagogue carrying Torah scrolls
Halachah – system of Jewish rabbinical law
Hallel – liturgical hymn of praise
Havdalah – prayer recited at the conclusion of Sabbaths and festivals to indicate the distinction between the sacred day that has ended and the weekday that is beginning
Hoshanah Rabbah – the seventh day of Succos

Kabbalah – the mystical and esoteric doctrine of Judaism
Kaddish – mourner's prayer
Ketubbah – marriage contract
Kiddush – ceremony inaugurating Sabbath and festival meals
Kiddush Hashem – Sanctification of the Name, i.e. of God, signifies martyrdom
Knesset – Parliament of the State of Israel

landsleit – countrymen, immigrants who share a common geographical place of origin
landsmanshaft – organization of immigrants who derive from the same region

Maariv – evening prayers
maggid – an itinerant preacher
maskilim – intellectuals who participated in the Enlightenment movement of the eighteenth and nineteenth centuries to modernize Jewish life
Mazel Tov – good luck, a congratulatory term

Midrash – term meaning "to inquire," "to investigate," designates a method of Biblical interpretation [Mincha – afternoon prayers]
Misnagdish – opposition to Chasidism, based on rational precepts
Mishnah – legal codification containing the core of the Oral Law, a component of the Talmud
moror – bitter herbs, component of the Passover seder

niggun – melody and song usually wordless, product of the Chasidic movement

Pesach – Passover
pilpul – dialectical reasoning applied to the study of oral law
Pinkas Tishevitz – memorial book commemorating the destruction of Zipper's boyhood town, Tishevitz, during the Holocaust
Purim – festival commemorating the rescue of Persian Jewry through the mediation of Queen Esther

Rosh Hashanah – Jewish New Year
Rosh Yeshiva – head of rabbinical college

sabras – term designating native-born Israelis
Seder (pl. Sedorim) – ritual Passover meal
Selichos – penitential prayer, liturgical poem requesting forgiveness
Sephardic – linguistic and cultural mode of Mediterranean and North African Jewry
Shechina – Divine presence, represents the principle of divine immanence
Shekalim – Torah reading from Exodus, pertaining to Second Temple tax
Shir HaShirim – *Song of Songs*
shiva – seven-day mourning period
Shloshim – thirtieth day of mourning
Shmini Atzeres – last day of the Festival of Succos
Shmona Esreh – eighteen benedictions, main section of all obligatory prayers
Shoah – Hebrew term for the Holocaust
shofar – a ram's horn sounded on ceremonial occasions in the synagogue
shtetl – village or town in Eastern Europe
shtreimel – fur-trimmed hat worn by Chasidim
shul – synagogue
Shulchan Aruch – standard code of Jewish law compiled by Joseph Karo, first published in 1565
shule – school
Siddur – prayer book, pl. *siddurim*

Simchas Torah – Rejoicing of the Law, holiday marking the annual completion of the synagogue reading of the Pentateuch
Succeh – a temporary booth in which Festival of Tabernacles is celebrated
Succos – Feast of Tabernacles; erev Succos, eve of holiday

tallis – prayer shawl
Tanach – the Hebrew Bible
tefillin – Phylacteries worn by Jewish males at weekday morning services
Tevye – fictional hero of Sholem Aleichem's novels
Tisha b'Av – Ninth of Av, fast day of mourning for the destruction of the Temple
Tohu v'Vohu – Chaos, nothingness, Genesis 1:2
Torah – Pentateuch, Five Books of Moses
Tu b'Shvat – fifteenth of the month of Shvat; an arbor-day festival

Vaad ha'Ir – Jewish community council

yarmulke – skull cap
Yeshiva – academy devoted to the study of the Talmud and rabbinic literature
Yiddishkeit – Jewishness, an ethical Jewish way of life informed by Yiddish culture
Yizkor – memorial service, conducted in synagogue on specific holy days
Yohrzeit – anniversary of the death of close relative
Yom Kippur – Day of Atonement, the most solemn occasion of the Jewish calendar

Zhidlak – anti-semitic Russian epithet for Jew
Zohar – classic work of medieval Jewish mysticism

ORGANIZATIONS, INSTITUTIONS, AND PLACE NAMES
Agudas Yisroel – World religious movement opposed to political Zionism, founded in 1912
Allied Jewish Community Services – (AJCS) central body for fund-raising and social services for Montreal Jewish community
Arbeiter Ring – Workmen's Circle, socialist fraternal and cultural society founded in 1900, dedicated to the promotion of secular Yiddish culture

Bar Ilan University – modern orthodox university in Israel, founded in 1955
Boiberik – Yiddish camp for adults and children sponsored by the Sholem Aleichem Folk Institute, emphasizing secular *Yiddishkeit*

GLOSSARY

Bund – The General Jewish Workers Union in Lithuania, Poland, and Russia, founded in Vilna, 1897

Canadian Jewish Congress – (the Congress, Dominion Council) Representive body of the Canadian Jewish community, founded in 1919
Combined Jewish Appeal – Local and national fund-raising agency for Jewish communal services and financial contributions to Israel
Congress for Yiddish Culture – association to promote secular Yiddish Culture, founded in 1948

Der Tog – The Day, U.S. Yiddish daily, founded in 1914
Di Goldene Kayt – The Golden Chain, Israel's leading Yiddish literary quarterly, edited by Avraham Sutzkever
Di Yunge – group of Yiddish writers whose work began to appear in New York about 1907

Emek – Valley, generally refers to Emek Jezreel

Farband – Fraternal and cultural branch of the Labour Zionist movement
Feldafing – Displaced Person's camp in post-World War II, exclusively for Jews, in the vicinity of Munich
Folksbiene – New York Yiddish theatre group, founded in 1915
Folk Shule (Jewish People's Schools) – Labour Zionist affiliate, comprised elementary day schools and elementary and secondary evening school, founded in 1914
Forwarts–Forward – U.S. Yiddish daily with the largest circulation, social democratic orientation, founded in 1897

Habimah – Israel's national theatre
Habonim – Labour Zionist youth movement
Ha Dor Hatzair – Labour Zionist youth movement
Hechalutz – Labour Zionist organization that trained youth for cooperative life in Israel
Hillel – foundation serving the religious and cultural needs of Jewish college and university students
Histadrut – The General Federation of Labour in Israel, founded in 1920

Ichud Olami – World Labour Zionist Movement, organizational framework combining the Israeli movement and its Diaspora supporters
Inzichists – Introspectivists, group of Yiddish poets who in the 1920s emphasized personal introspective expression

JCA – Jewish Colonization Association

Jewish Teacher's Seminary – teacher training for secular schools, founded in 1946 and sponsored by the Canadian Jewish Congress

J.I. Segal Awards – literary awards for works on a Jewish topic written in English, French, Hebrew, or Yiddish; also award for contributions to Jewish education

Keneder Odler – The Canadian Eagle, daily Montreal Yiddish newspaper published from 1907 to 1988, in later years published twice a week

Keren Hatarbut – organization for the promotion of Hebrew language and culture

Knights of Pythias – Jewish fraternal order

Labour Zionist Organization (Poalei Zion, the Movement) – social democratic movement that combined Zionism with socialism, founded in 1897

LECHI (Lochamei Herut Yisrael) – armed underground military organization opposing British rule in Palestine

Lubavitch – original Russian centre of Chabad Chasidism; followers are referred to as Lubavitcher

Manger Prize – Annual Israeli award for Yiddish literature

Masada – Herod's mountain fortress, last outpost of the Zealots, who committed suicide rather than capitulate to the Romans

Merkaz Hatorah – Montreal yeshiva founded in 1941

National Foundation for Jewish Culture – U.S. organization supporting and initiating Jewish cultural programs

Nationaleh Radicaleh Shule (National Radical School) – forerunner to the Jewish Peretz Schools

N'Turei Karta – ultra-orthodox group that does not recognize the State of Israel

PEN – International Association of Writers

Peretz Shule (Jewish Peretz Schools) – Labour Zionist affiliate, comprised elementary day school and elementary and secondary evening schools, founded in 1913 as Nationale Radicaleh Shule

Pioneer Women – women's affiliate of the Labour Zionist movement

Poalei Zion – *see* Labour Zionist Organization

Talmud Torah – religious schools for elementary education

Tishevitz – Polish town where Zipper was raised and educated

Unzer Camp – Labour Zionist adult summer camp in the Laurentians

Yavneh – Palestinian town where R. Johanan ben Zakkai organized an academy in which sages formulated the basis of normative Judaism

YIVO – Institute for Jewish Research, founded in Poland in 1925

Zukunft (*The Future*) – U.S. Yiddish monthly, founded in 1892, secularist and socialist in orientation

INDIVIDUALS MENTIONED IN THE TEXT

Abel, Jacob – family friend and supporter of the Peretz Schools. A printer by trade, he published some of Zipper's early works

Alboim, Issachar – cousin and friend, active in Labour Zionist activities

Asch, Sholem – Yiddish novelist and dramatist, widely translated into many languages

Baal – Machshoves – pseudonym of Israel Isadore Elyashev, influential Yiddish literary critic

Becker, Lavy – Canadian Jewish leader, Reconstructionist Rabbi, and executive member of the Canadian Jewish Congress

Begin, Menachem – prime minister of Israel, 1977–83

Belkin, Shaya – Yiddish activist, journalist, and historian of the Labour Zionist movement, Canadian director of the Jewish Colonization Association

Bender, Charles – Rabbi and educator, co-founder of the Adath Israel Congregation and the Hebrew Academy

Ben-Gurion, David – Israel's first prime minister, 1948–53 and 1955–63

Bercovitch, Sacvan – professor of American literature at Harvard University, translated "The True Image," a story by Zipper

Bergner, Yossel – Israeli artist, son of Melech Ravitch

Berman, Joseph – manufacturer, active supporter of Jewish cultural activities, particularly the Jewish People's Schools

Beutel, Ben – president of the United Talmud Torahs

Bialik, Nachman Chaim – leading modern Hebrew and Yiddish poet

Bickel, Shlomo – American Yiddish essayist and literary critic

Bloomfield, Bernard – business executive, national president of the Canadian Histadrut Campaign

Boraisha, Menachem – American Yiddish poet and essayist

Borochov, Ber – foremost theoretician of Labour Zionism

Botwinik, David – music teacher in the Jewish People's Schools and the Jewish Peretz Schools, devoted Yiddishist

Boyarsky, Abraham – Canadian novelist and professor of mathematics

Braverman, Yonah – teacher, director of the Jewish Teacher's Seminary

Bronfman, Allan – Canadian industrialist and philanthropist

Bronfman, Samuel – industrialist, president of the Canadian Jewish Congress from 1939 to 1962
Bronstein, Yecheskiel – American Yiddish poet and essayist

Caiserman, Sarah – patron of the Jewish People's Schools and the Jewish Peretz Schools, wife of H.M. Caiserman
Chaitman, Wolf – teacher at the Jewish People's Schools
Chanina bar Chama – early third-century Palestinian scholar
Cherniak, Alter – lawyer, active on behalf of the Jewish Peretz Schools in Winnipeg
Choni Ha-Me'aggel – the circle-drawer, miracle worker in the period of the Second Temple
Craimer, Harry – served on the board of directors of the Jewish Peretz Schools

Dickstein, Moishe – prominent Labour Zionist, activist for the Jewish People's Schools
Dunsky, Shimshon – scholar and teacher at the Jewish People's Schools, where he served as vice-principal for many years

Eisman, Tzvi – Israeli Yiddish poet
Elberg, Yehuda – Yiddish novelist, playright, and literary scholar
Engel, Issie – member, executive committee, and president of the Jewish Peretz Schools
Entin, Joel – Yiddish journalist and editor, activist in the Labour Zionist movement
Eshkol, Levi – prime minister of Israel, 1963–69

Fein, Isaac – American educator, professor of Jewish studies
Fishman, Yena – kindergarten teacher, Jewish Peretz Schools
Freedman, Dan – active supporter and president of the Jewish Peretz Schools
Fuchs, Chaim Leib – Yiddish writer, author of biographical dictionary of Hebrew and Yiddish writers in Canada

Garber, Michael – lawyer, community leader, president of the Zionist Organization of Canada
Gershonovitch, Gittel – Yiddish teacher at the Jewish Peretz Schools and librarian at the Jewish Public Library
Glatstein, Yaacov – major twentieth-century Yiddish poet
Godinsky, Saul – Canadian Jewish Congress activist, liaison officer to the Protestant School Board

Gog and Magog – Gog, of the land of Magog, an anti-Messianic figure, eschatological concept derived from Ezekiel, 38:2

Goldberg, B.Z. – American Yiddish journalist and managing editor of the daily, *Der Tog*.

Goldmann, Nahum – international statesman and Zionist leader

Goodkin, Phil – active worker for the Jewish Peretz Schools

Greenberg, Hayim – American Labour Zionist leader, essayist, and editor

Grosbard, Hertz – actor and concert-reader of Yiddish literature

Grossman, Yaacov – educator, essayist, and activist for Yiddish culture

Gruber, Chayele – actor and director of Yiddish theatre

Halkin, Shimon – Hebrew poet, novelist, and educator, lived in U.S. and Israel

Handlin, Dr Oscar – American historian, educator, author of works on American immigration

Hartman, David – Rabbi and philosopher, led Montreal congregation before settling in Israel

Harvey, Samuel – Labour Zionist, president of the Jewish People's Schools

Hayes, Saul – lawyer and community leader, executive director of the Canadian Jewish Congress for many years

Herschorn, Sheeah – Chief Rabbi, chaired the Rabbinical Council of Quebec and the Jewish Community Council of Montreal

Hess, Moses – German socialist and father of socialist Zionism

Hirschprung, Pinchas – Rabbi and Talmudic scholar, founder of the Beth Yaacov Girls School

Husid, Mordecai – Yiddish poet and teacher at the Jewish People's Schools

Kaczerginsky, Shmerl – Yiddish writer, chronicler of the Vilna Ghetto

Kage, Joseph – author and scholar of the history of Jewish immigration in Canada, longtime executive director of the Jewish Immigrant Aid Society

Kalles, Hertz – librarian and bookseller, served as exective director and later president of the Jewish Public Library

Kaminska, Ida – leading actor of the Yiddish theatre

Kaplan, Mordecai – American Rabbi, founder of the Reconstructionist movement

Katzenelson, Itzchak – Yiddish poet

Katzman, Yaacov – American Labour Zionist

Kaufman, Yehuda – scholar, founder of the Jewish People's Schools

Klein, A.M. (Abraham Moses) – major Canadian-Jewish poet and novelist

Korn, Rochl – major Yiddish poet
Kovner, Abba – resistance partisan in World War II, Israeli poet
Kronitz, Leon – educator and principal of Solomon Schecter School, executive director of the Zionist Organization of Canada

Lamdan, Yitzchak – Hebrew poet and editor, author of the epic poem, *Massadah*
Landis, Joseph C. – American professor of Yiddish and editor of the periodical *Yiddish*
Lehrer, Lippeh – American psychologist and teacher, active in secular Yiddish educational institutions
Leivick, H. – major modern Yiddish poet and dramatist
Lermer, Arthur – Canadian economist, active in Yiddish cultural affairs
Lestschinsky, Yaacov – pioneer in the sociology and demography of Jewish life
Loewy, Jacob – businessman, collector of rare Judaica, president of Federation of Jewish Community Services and United Israel Appeal

Magid, Melech – longtime principal of the United Talmud Torah Schools
Malbim, Meier Leib ben Yechiel Michael – nineteenth-century Rabbi, scholar, Bible commentator
Manechovsky, Moishe – writer and teacher in Yiddish secular schools
Manger, Itzik – renowned modern Yiddish poet
Markish, Esther – wife of the Soviet Jewish writer Peretz Markish
Maze, Ida – Yiddish poet, her Montreal home was a gathering place for Yiddish writers
Meltzer, Shimshon – teacher of Jewish studies in Canada and Israel
Mendelsohn, Mordecai I. – educator, founding principal of Adath Israel Hebrew Academy
Miller, H.A. – longtime president of the Jewish Peretz Schools
Morgenthaler, Henry – physician and activist for women's abortion rights
Moshiach ben Yoseph – Messianic warrior figure, considered predecessor to the Davidic messiah

Niger, Samuel – American Yiddish literary critic

Opatoshu, Yosef – Yiddish novelist and short-story writer

Parness, Avraham – active supporter of the Jewish People's Schools
Pat, Dr Emanuel – Yiddish journalist, cultural activist
Pat, Jacob – Jewish labour leader, teacher, and author
Peretz, Isaac Leib – Renowned author and poet, seminal figure in Yiddish literature

Pomerance, Sol – personal friend, aided in the design of several of Zipper's publications
Pomerantz, Chaim – American Yiddish teacher, active in Yiddish cultural and educational affairs
Pomerantz, Gershon – Yiddish poet and publisher
Pomerantz Freidenreich, Fradle – American educator, active in teacher-training institutions in the U.S. and Israel
Pomerantz Honigbaum, Pessie – American Yiddish poet

Rabinovitch, Yishaiah – Hebrew and Yiddish author, critic, and educator
Rabinovitch, Yisroel – editor of the *Keneder Odler*, musicologist, and essayist
Rambam, Moses ben Maimon (Maimonides) – medieval philosopher, physician, and codifier of Talmudic law
Ramban, Moses ben Nachman (Nachmanides) – medieval Spanish Talmudist, Kabbalist, and Biblical commentator
Ravitch, Melech – pseudonym of Zacharia Chune Bergner, Major Yiddish poet, who organized many literary and cultural institutions in Australia, Argentina, Mexico, and Canada
Ravitch, Rochl Eisenberg – librarian of the Jewish Public Library, wife of Melech Ravitch
Rogel, Joseph – Holocaust survivor and Yiddish poet
Rogzansky, Samuel – Argentine Yiddish publisher and editor
Rome, David – director of the Jewish Public Library, research-historian at the Canadian Jewish Congress Archives
Rosenberg, Louis – major demographer of the Canadian Jewish community, national research director of the Canadian Jewish Congress
Rosenfarb, Chava – Yiddish novelist, poet and literary essayist, Holocaust survivor
Rosenfeld, Dvora – Yiddish activist, founder of the I.J. Segal Literary Awards
Rosenfeld, Dr Hirsh – supporter of Yiddish cultural activities, founder of the I.J. Segal Literary Awards
Rosenfeld, Sarah – active supporter of Yiddish culture, organizer of the Montreal Mameh Loshn Group and Klez Kanada
Roskies, Leib – committed supporter of Yiddish culture
Rubin, Ruth Rivka – musicologist and Yiddish folksinger, compiler and editor of Jewish folk songs

Sack, Benjamin G. – Historian and journalist, author of *History of the Jews in Canada*
Sadan, Dov – Yiddish and Hebrew writer and scholar
Sarna, Lazar – lawyer, poet, and editor

Schwartz, I.J. – American Yiddish poet, translator, author of the epic poem *Kentucky*
Segal, J.I. – major Canadian-Yiddish poet, teacher, and literary editor of the *Keneder Odler*
Segal, Louis – American Labour Zionist leader
Selah, Benjamin – Israeli consul in Montreal
Selchen, Mark – journalist and editor of the Winnipeg Yiddish daily, *Dos Yiddishe Vort*
Shabsai Tzvi – pseudo-messiah of the seventheenth century
Shaffir, Moshe Mordecai – Canadian Yiddish poet and teacher
Shainblum, Yechiel – teacher, art teacher at the Jewish People's Schools
Shainzohn, Yosef Dov – author of Hebrew textbooks, vice-principal of Adath Israel High School
Shapiro, Judah J. – first secretary and executive officer of the National Foundation for Jewish Culture
Sharett, Moshe – Zionist leader, Israeli prime minister and statesman
Shazar, Zalman – Third president of the State of Israel
Shtrigler, Mordecai – modern Yiddish author and editor, chronicled the Holocaust
Singer, Isaac Bashevis – famous Yiddish novelist, Nobel Prize laureate
Soreh bas Tovim – author of Yiddish prayers for women, c. seventeenth century
Spilberg, Chaim – president of the Jewish Public Library, Yiddish literary critic, journalist, author of studies on Hindu religion and philosophy
Steinberg, Max – Canadian business executive
Steinberg, Sam – founder of major grocery chain, philanthropist
Steinman, Eliezer – Hebrew author, novelist, and essayist
Sussman, B. – secretary-treasurer of the Jewish Peretz Schools
Sutzkever, Avraham – major Yiddish Poet, editor of *Di Goldene Kayt*; Holocaust survivor
Switzman, Harry Hershel – graduate and supporter of the Jewish Peretz Schools

Teitlebaum, Leon – president of the Jewish People's Schools
Tencer, Leib – teacher, vice-principal, and later principal of the Jewish Peretz Schools. Taught Yiddish language courses at McGill University
Tolmatch, Chaim – Yiddish author, pioneer activist in educational and theatrical activities

Wasserman, Dora – actor and director, founder of the Yiddish Theatre in Montreal
Weinreich, Uriel – professor of Yiddish literature, compiler of Yiddish-English/English-Yiddish dictionary

White, Frank – Active in the Farband, Labour Zionist movement
Wilchesky, Nachum – teacher and principal of the Jewish People's and Jewish Peretz Schools, broadcaster of Hebrew and Yiddish radio program
Wiseman, Adele – Canadian novelist, essayist, and teacher
Wiseman, Shloime – educator and scholar, longtime principal of the Jewish People's Schools or Folk Shule
Wolofsky, Max – publisher of the *Keneder Odler*

Yellin, Shulamis – teacher and poet, author of memoirs
Yungman, Moishe – Israeli Yiddish poet

Zahler, M. – treasurer of the Jewish Peretz Schools
Zeitlin, Aaron – Hebrew and Yiddish writer
Zhitlovsky, Dr Chaim – philosopher of secular *Yiddishkeit*, influential writer
Zuker, Louis – pioneer of the Canadian Labour Zionist movement, a founder of the Jewish Peretz Schools
Zukerman, Boruch – American Labour Zionist leader
Zygelboim, Samuel Mordecai – Polish Bundist leader, committed suicide in London in 1943 in protest against the world's indifference to the Holocaust

INDEX

Numerals in italic refer to the Glossary

Abel, Jacob, 79, 110, 168, *351*
Agudas Yisroel, 256, 272, *348*
Alboim, Issachar, 68, *351*
Allied Jewish Community Services (AJSC), xviii, 129, 213, 216, 290, *348*
Arbeiter Ring (Workmen's Circle), 58, 113, 194, 239, *348*
Asch, Sholem, 154, 310, *351*

Baal Machshoves, 285, *351*
Bar Ilan University, 133, *348*
Becker, Lavy, 52, 66, 175, *351*
Begin, Menachem, 321, *351*
Belkin, Shaya, 198–9, *351*
Bender, Charles, 13, *351*
Ben Gurion, David, 18, 164, 227, *351*
Bercovitch, Sacvan, 282, *351*
Bergner, Yossel, 211, *351*
Berman, Joseph, 49, 68-9, *351*
Beutel, Ben, 52, 169, 173, 252, *351*
Bialik, Nachman Chaim, 68, 323, *351*
Bickel, Shlomo, 201–2, *351*
Bloomfield, Bernard, 143, *351*
Boiberik, 127, 200, *348*
Boraisha, Menachem, 278, 291, *351*
Borochov, Ber, 165, *351*
Botwinik, David, 243, 269, *351*

Boyarsky, Abraham, 286, *352*
Braverman, Yonah, 121, *352*
Bronfman, Allan, 121, *351*
Bronfman, Samuel, 43, 45, 47, 50, 60, *352*
Bronstein, Yecheskiel, 91, 185, *352*
Bund, 57, 64–5, 128, 240, *349*

Caiserman, Sarah, 70, 79–80, 106, 135, 323, *352*
Canadian Jewish Congress (Congress, Dominion Council), xviii, xxii, xxiii, 8–10, 13–24, 29, 37–8, 42–3, 45, 47, 51–2, 54–5, 59–61, 92, 100, 106–7, 119, 127–8, 133, 144, 160, 172–4, 187, 192, 198, 216, 240, 252, *349*
Chaitman, Wolf, 108, 249, *352*
Chanina bar Chama, 248, *352*
Cherniak, Alter, 136, 222, 268–70, *352*
Choni Ha-Me'aggel, 130, 141, 324, *352*
Combined Jewish Appeal (UJA, United Jewish Appeal), xxiii, 8, 41, 60, 129, *349*
Congress for Yiddish Culture, 45, 47, 49, 210, *349*
Craimer, Harry, 22, 40, 48–9, 52, 54, 60, 140, *352*

INDEX

Der Tog (The Day), 49, 51, 185, 238, 259, *349*
Di Goldene Kayt (The Golden Chain), 91, 119, *349*
Di Yunge, 249, *349*
Dickstein, Moishe, 11, 22, 24–5, 38–9, 46, 51, 57, 60, 70–1, *352*
Displaced Persons, 13, 37
Dunsky, Shimshon, 124, 165, 195, 254, 258, 264, 307, 335, *352*

Eisman, Tzvi, 313, *352*
Elberg, Yehuda, xxii, 91, 132, 150, 264, 266, 285, 295, 301, 314, *352*
Emek, 204, *351*
Engel, Issie, 140, 191, 212, 261, *352*
Entin, Joel, 7, *352*
Eshkol, Levi, 139, 164, 188, *352*

Farband, xxii, 2, 7, 10, 28, 46, 49, 51, 113, 132, 145, 313, *349*
Fein, Isaac, 136, 290, 314, *352*
Feldafing, 13, *351*
Fishman, Yena, 268, *352*
Folksbiene, 113, 115, *349*
Folk Shule (Jewish People's School), xvii, xxiii, 9–10, 17, 19, 20–2, 24, 26–7, 31–4, 37, 39, 41, 43, 57, 60–1, 68, 85, 106, 120, 144, 179, 195, 212, 215–17, 220, 223, 239, 243, 262, 275, *349*
Forwarts (Forward), 49, 51, 259, 300, *349*
Freedman, Dan, 74, *352*
Fuchs, Chaim Leib, 331–2, *352*

Garber, Michael, 15, 18–19, 22, 52–3, 172, *352*
Garfinkle, Motty, xlii, 67, 91, 95, 140, 243, 273, 277, 300, 334, 339
Garfinkle, Ode, xix, xlii, 67, 71, 73, 91, 95, 108, 243, 302, 334, 339
Gershonovitch, Gittel, 262, *352*
Glatstein, Yaacov, 193, 254, 258, *352*
Godinsky, Saul, 161, *352*
Gog and Magog, 149, *353*
Goldberg, B.Z., 66, *353*
Goldmann, Nahum, 44, *353*
Goodkin, Phil, 85, *353*
Greenberg, Hayim, 261, *353*
Grosbard, Hertz, 115, 314, *353*
Grossman, Yaacov, 58, *353*
Gruber, Chayele, 284, 295, *353*

Habimah, 113, 115, *349*
Habonim, 210, *349*
Halkin, Shimon, 291, *353*
Handlin, Dr Oscar, 98, *353*
Hartman, David, 228, *353*
Harvey, Samuel, 22–3, 38, 52, 59, 92, 99, *353*
Hayes, Saul, 8–9, 14–16, 18, 20, 22, 24, 27, 43–5, 47–52, 59, 61, 70, 119, 131–32, 141–2, 215, 233, 243, *353*
Hechalutz, xv, 20, 154, 204, *349*
Herschorn, Sheeah, 45, *353*
Hess, Moses, 234, *353*
Hillel, 204, *349*
Hirschprung, Pinchas, 272, 283, *353*
Histadrut, 15, 117, 145, 172, 175, *349*
Holocaust, xxii, 239, *349*. See also Shoah
Husid, Mordecai, xxii, 124, 183, 185, 196, 200, 266, 271, 284, 293, *353*

Ichud Olami, 133, *349*
Inzichists, 254, *349*

JCA, Jewish Colonization Association, 198, *349*
Jewish Teacher's Seminary, 8, 22, 24, 27, 32–3, 254, *350*
J.I. Segal Awards, xxi, 214, 237, 240, 264, 284, 301, *350*

Kaczerginsky, Shmerl, 76, *353*
Kage, Joseph, 290, *353*
Kalles, Hertz, 237, 251, *353*
Kaminska, Ida, 190, *353*
Kaplan, Mordecai, 242, *353*
Katzenelson, Itzhak, 283, *353*
Katzman, Yaacov, 213, 305, *353*
Kaufman, Yehuda, 227, *353*
Keneder Odler, xxi–xxii, 14–15, 33, 37, 43, 54, 102, 104, 108, 119, 140–1, 222, 230–1, 256, 259, 286, 290, 317, 339, *350*
Keren Hatarbut, 124, 170, *350*
Klein, Abraham Moses, 10, 272, *353*
Knights of Pythias, 56, *350*
Korn, Rochl, xxii, 45, 56, 110–11, 132, 135, 176, 273, 276, 278, 284, 292, 295, 302–3, 306, 310–12, 335, *354*
Kovner, Abba, 261, *354*
Krishtalka, Shifra, xix, xlii, 63, 319
Krishtalka, Sholem, xlii, 319
Kronitz, Leon, 21, 119, 154, *354*

Labour Zionist Organization (the Movement, Poalei Zion), xv, xvii, xviii, xx, xxi, xxiii, 6, 24, 113, 179, 222, *350*. See also the Movement, Poalei Zion
Lamdan, Yitzchak, 278, *354*
Landis, Joseph C., 193, *354*
LECHI, 166, *350*
Lehrer, Lippeh, 109, 127, *354*
Leivick, H., 47, 49, 101–2, 113, *354*
Lermer, Arthur, 58, 124, 135, 222, 255, 279, 284, 290, *354*
Lestschinsky, Yaacov, 226, *354*
Loewy, Jacob, 129, *354*
Lubavitch, 33–4, 209, 236, 252, *350*

Magid, Melech, 13, 38, 62, 111–12, 131, *354*
Malbim, Meier Leib ben Yechiel Michael, 331, *354*
Manechovsky, Moishe, 165, 200, *354*
Manger, Itzik, 339, *354*
Manger Prize, 243, 266, 268, 333, 339, *350*
Marder, Aaron, xlii, 314
Marder, Henneh, xix, xlii, 314, 320
Markish, Esther, 277–9, 322, *354*
Masada, 121, 152, *350*
Maze, Ida, xxi, 99, 100, *354*
Meltzer, Shimshon, 291, *354*
Mendelsohn, Mordecai I., 13, 43, *354*
Miller, H.A., 14–16, 18, 20–1, 24, 28, 40, 42, 48–9, 52–4, 87, 130, 323, *354*
Merkaz Hatorah, 34, *350*
Morgenthaler, Henry, 124, *354*
Movement, the, 7–8, 10–11, 21–2, 24–6, 29, 37–9, 43, 49, 51, 55, 57, 60–1, 118, 145–6, 154–5, 210, 250, 254, 340. See also Labour Zionist Organization, Poalei Zion

National Foundation for Jewish Culture, 45, *350*
Nationaleh Radicaleh Shule (National Radical School), *350*
Niger, Samuel, 47, 49, 68, *354*

Opatoshu, Yosef, 47, 49, 56, *354*

Parness, Avraham, 179, *354*
Pat, Dr Emanuel, 248, *354*
Pat, Jacob, 47, 49, *354*

Peretz, Isaac Leib, xvii, 57, 311, 323, *354*
Peretz Shule (Jewish Peretz School), xvii, xviii, xix, xxii, xxiii, 17, 19, 24–5, 33, 39, 47, 51, 60, 66, 69–71, 76, 86, 103, 139, 144, 211, 215, 220, 229, 244–5, 251, 262, 268, *350*
Pioneer Women, 7–8, 10, *350*
Pofelis, Berl, 251, 303, 306, 324
Pofelis, Gittel, 28, 32, 90, 185, 274, 280
Pofelis, Rivke, 251, 303, 306, 324
Pomerance, Sol, 80, 113, *355*
Pomerantz, Chaim, 45, 103, 303, *355*
Pomerantz, Gershon, 183, *355*
Pomerantz Freidenreich, Fradle, 103, 243, 303, 326, *355*
Pomerantz Honigbaum, Pessie, 304, 326, *355*

Rabinovitch, Yishaiah, 269, *355*
Rabinovitch, Yisroel, 10, 11, 15, 20, 25, 27, 33, 37, 39, 41, 43, 49–52, 95, 102, 105, 110, 114, *355*
Rambam, Moses ben Maimon (Maimonides), 151, 279, *355*
Ramban, Moses ben Nachman (Nachmanides), 279, *355*
Ravitch, Melech, xxii, 124, 159, 183–4, 198, 202, 211, 255–6, 266, 268, 273, 285, 292–3, 302, 310–13, *355*
Ravitch, Rochl Eisenberg, xxii, 196, 273, 292, 302–3, 310–12, *355*
refugees, 12, 29, 66, 287
Rogel, Yosef, 282, *355*
Rogzansky, Samuel, 122, 258, *355*
Rome, David, 118, *355*
Rosenberg, Louis, 198, 265, *355*
Rosenfarb, Chava, xxii, 124, 284–5, *355*
Rosenfeld, Dvora, 272, 301, *355*
Rosenfeld, Hirsh, 272, 301, *355*
Rosenfeld, Sarah, 290, *355*
Roskies, Leib, 275, 313, *355*
Rubin, Ruth, 110, *355*

Sarna, Lazar, 286, *355*
Schwartz, I.J., 137, 249, 258, 275, *356*
Segal, J.I., xxi, 40, 135, *355*
Segal, Louis, 7, 15, 44, 46–7, 62, 69, 118, *356*
Selah, Benjamin, 124, 147, *356*
Selchen, Mark, 46, *356*
Shabsai Tzvi, 276, *356*

Shaffir, Moshe, xxi, 44, *356*
Shainblum, Yechiel, 251, *356*
Shainzohn, Yosef Dov, 301, *356*
Shapiro, Chana, xix, xlii, 67, 71, 73, 81, 90, 95, 109, 122, 205, 270
Shapiro, Judah J., 44–5, 98, 254, *356*
Shapiro, Mark, xlii, 71, 81, 90, 205, 302
Sharett, Moshe, 68, *356*
Shazar, Zalman, 129, 142, 244, 270, *356*
Shoah, 139, 234, 263, 283. *See also* Holocaust
Shtern, Amalia, xlii
Shtern, Avrom, xiv, xix, xlii, 30, 62–4, 144, 169, 219, 273, 294, 325
Shtern, Gittel, xix, xlii, 63–4, 249, 319, 332
Shtern, Sholem, xlii, 85, 150, 293
Shtern, Sonia, xlii, 180, 196
Shtern, Soreh, xlii, 44, 47–8, 53, 92
Shtern, Yechiel, xix, xlii, 4, 25–6, 30, 32, 40, 63–4, 92, 149–50, 197, 232, 265–6, 179–80, 320, 332
Shtern, Yisroel, xix, xlii, 20, 45, 63, 273–4, 333
Shtrigler, Mordecai, 165
Singer, Isaac Bashevis, 103, 260, 324, *356*
Soreh bas Tovim, 87, 100, *356*
Spilberg, Chaim, 132, 307, 332, 344, *356*
Steinberg, Max, 103, *356*
Steinberg, Sam, 80, 102, *356*
Steinman, Eliezer, 137, *356*
Sussman, B., 222, 251, *356*
Sutzkever, Avraham, 76, 119, 183, 261, *356*
Switzman, Harry Hershel, 85, *356*

Talmud Torah, 6, 27, 34, 37, 51–2, 60, 140, 143–4, 159, 169, 182, 215, *350*
Teitlebaum, Leon, 275, 290, *356*
Tencer, Leib, 41, 54, 82, 91, 94, 105, 125, 219, 245, 248, 251, 281, 340, *356*
Tishevitz, xiv, 5, 33–4, 57, 67, 74, 88, 136–37, 157, 170, 189, 239, 256–7, 259, 277, 289, 297, 301, 303, 314, 344, *350*
Tolmatch, Chaim, 248, *356*

Unzer Camp, 51, 253, *350*

Wasserman, Dora, 197, 300, *356*
Weinreich, Uriel, ix, *356*
White, Frank, 44, *357*
Wilchesky, Nachum, 119, 218, 276, 312, *356*
Wiseman, Adele, 301, *357*
Wiseman, Shloime, xxiii, xxiv, 13, 19, 22–4, 38, 51, 59, 62, 68–9, 71, 120, 123–4, 130–2, 135, 142, 144–5, 195, 200, 213, 238, 243, 258–9, 262, 266, 276, 304, 308, 311–12, 323, *357*
Wolofsky, Max, 20, 105, *357*

Yavneh, 152, *351*
Yellin, Shulamis, 86, 124, 192, 264, *357*
YIVO, ix, 136, 262, 268, 282, *351*

Zahler, M., 15–16, 20–2, 24, 28, 31–2, 40, 42, 54, 72, *357*
Zeitlin, Aaron, 221, 287, *357*
Zhitlovsky, Dr Chaim, 136, 210, 227, *357*
Zipper, Sorke, xvii, xix, xlii, 39, 73, 78, 86–7, 96–7, 100, 108, 122, 158, 171, 178, 184–5, 248, 263, 268–9, 275, 277, 294, 302, 314, 332, 334–5
Zuker, Louis, 8–9, 11–12, 14–16, 18–22, 24, 26, 36, 38–40, 42, 45–8, 50–1, 54, 60–1, 66, 68–72, 79–80, 117–18, 126, 234, 323, *357*
Zukerman, Boruch, 226–7, 231, *357*
Zukunft (The Future), 176, 344, *351*
Zygelboim, Samuel Mordecai, 239–40, *357*